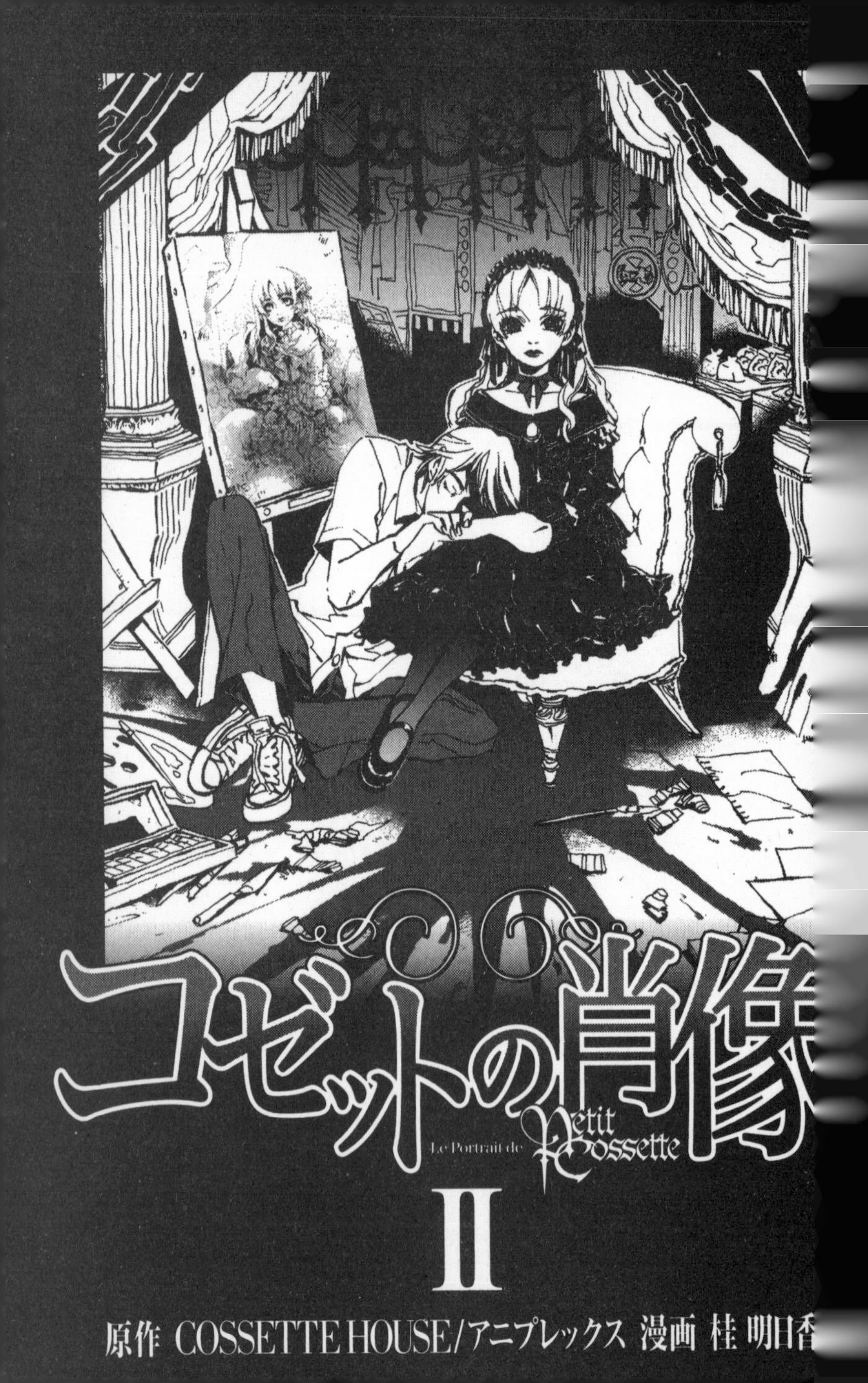

コゼットの肖像

Le Portrait de Petit Cossette

II

原作 COSSETTE HOUSE/アニプレックス 漫画 桂 明日香

Le Portrait de Petite Cossette Vol. 2
Written by Cossette House/Aniplex
Illustrated by Asuka Katsura

Translation - Aska Yoshizu
English Adaptation - Gina Ferenzi
Retouch and Lettering - ANDWORLD Design
Production Artist - Courteny Geter
Graphic Designer - James Lee

Editor - Tim Beedle
Digital Imaging Manager - Chris Buford
Pre-Production Supervisor - Erika Terriquez
Art Director - Anne Marie Horne
Production Manager - Elisabeth Brizzi
Managing Editor - Vy Nyugen
VP of Production - Ron Klamert
Editor-in-Chief - Rob Tokar
Publisher - Mike Kiley
President and C.O.O. - John Parker
C.E.O. and Chief Creative Officer - Stuart Levy

A 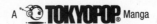 Manga

TOKYOPOP Inc.
5900 Wilshire Blvd. Suite 2000
Los Angeles, CA 90036

E-mail: info@TOKYOPOP.com
Come visit us online at www.TOKYOPOP.com

ISBN: 1-59816-531-3

First TOKYOPOP printing: November 2006
10 9 8 7 6 5 4 3 2 1
Printed in the USA

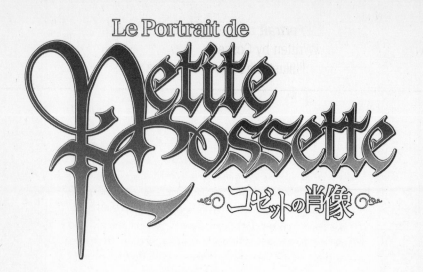

Le Portrait de Petite Cossette

コゼットの肖像

Vol. 2

Art By
Asuka Katsura

Story By
COSSETTE HOUSE / ANIPLEX

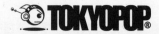

HAMBURG // LONDON // LOS ANGELES // TOKYO

The story so far...

Eiri Kurahashi is an art school student with a job at a local antique store and an unexplainable obsession with a portrait of a Victorian-era girl named Cossette. It's a portrait with a strange history—everyone who has owned it has been murdered in a bizarre fashion. However, it's when the new owner of the portrait nearly kills himself that Eiri decides to get involved. And that's when Cossette begins speaking to him...

No one else can hear or see her, and Eiri's not about to tell his friends that he's been talking to a ghost. But Cossette is a ghost with problems—a ghost in need of help. And she has no one to help her but Eiri. The problem is with Cossette's former possessions. Each one of them is cursed, and each one has been causing its owners to go insane. But how long can one deal with cursed objects and hysteria before descending into madness himself?

In an attempt to recover one of Cossette's possessions—a clock—Eiri finds himself fighting for his life against a police officer driven mad. In the process, the clock starts, throwing Eiri back in time and into a memory hidden deep inside Cossette's mind.

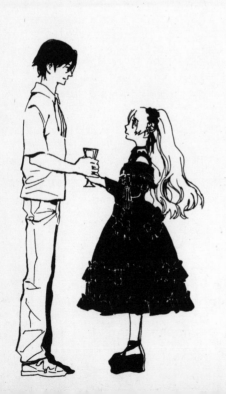

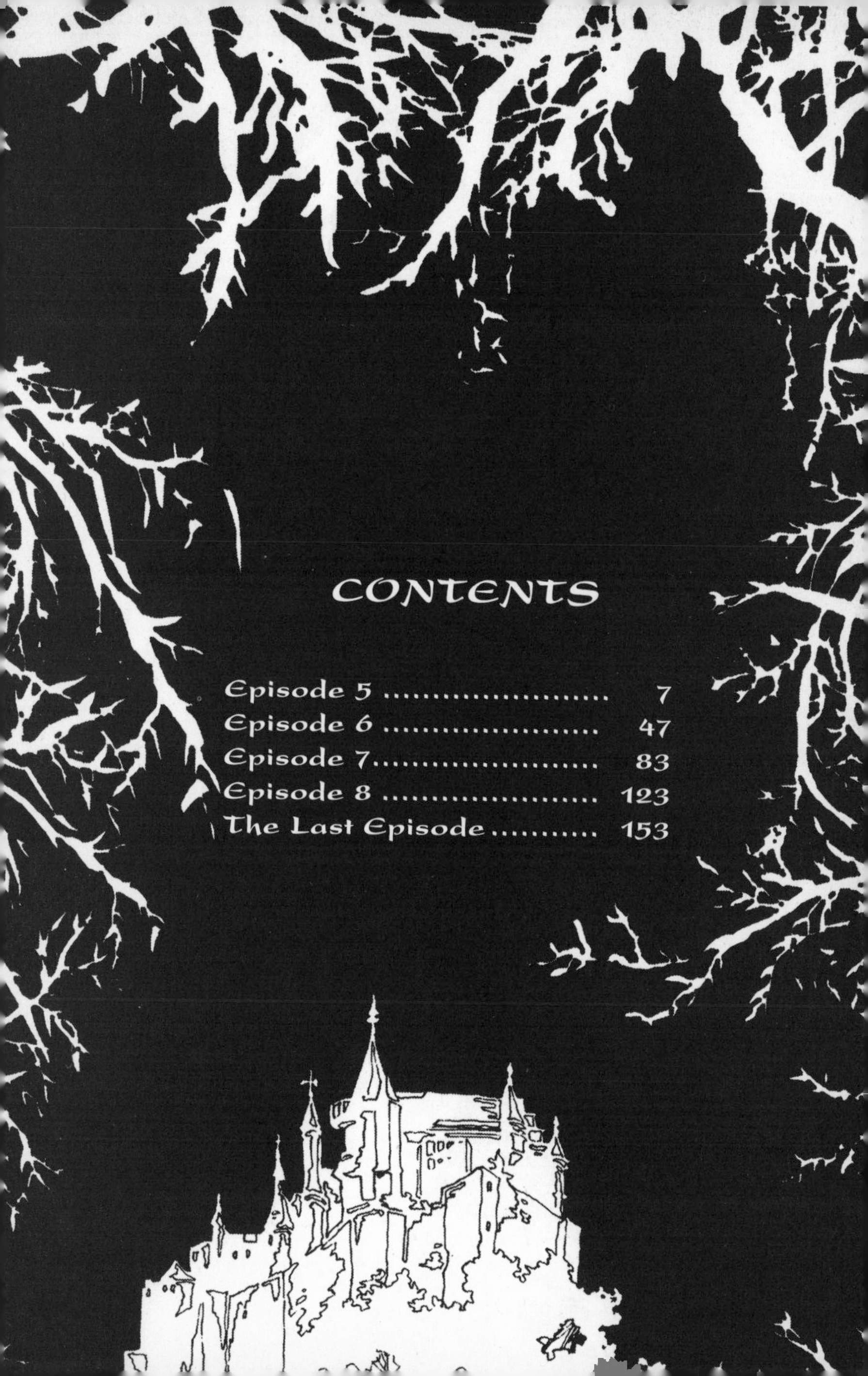

CONTENTS

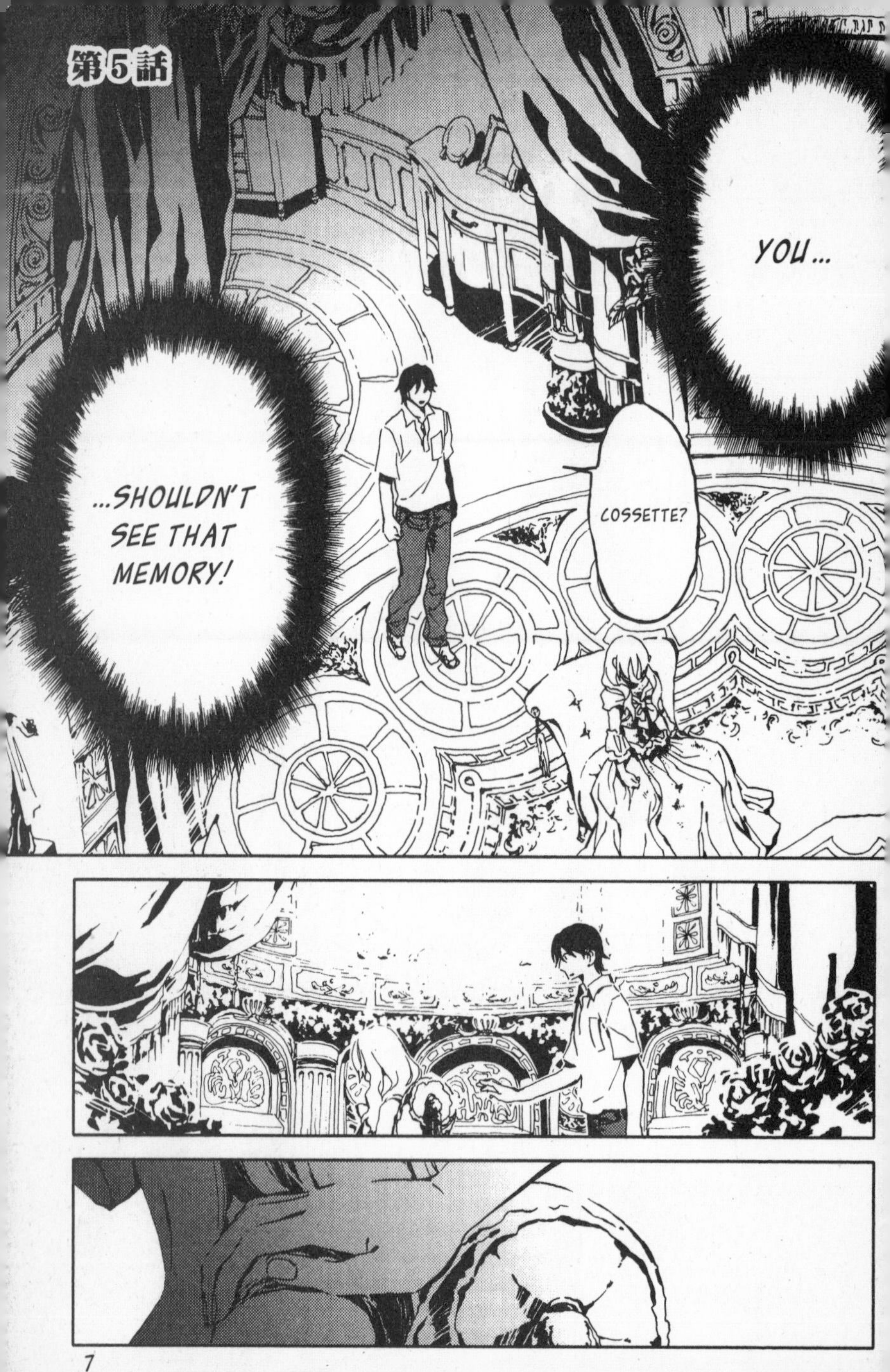
第5話
YOU...
COSSETTE?
...SHOULDN'T SEE THAT MEMORY!

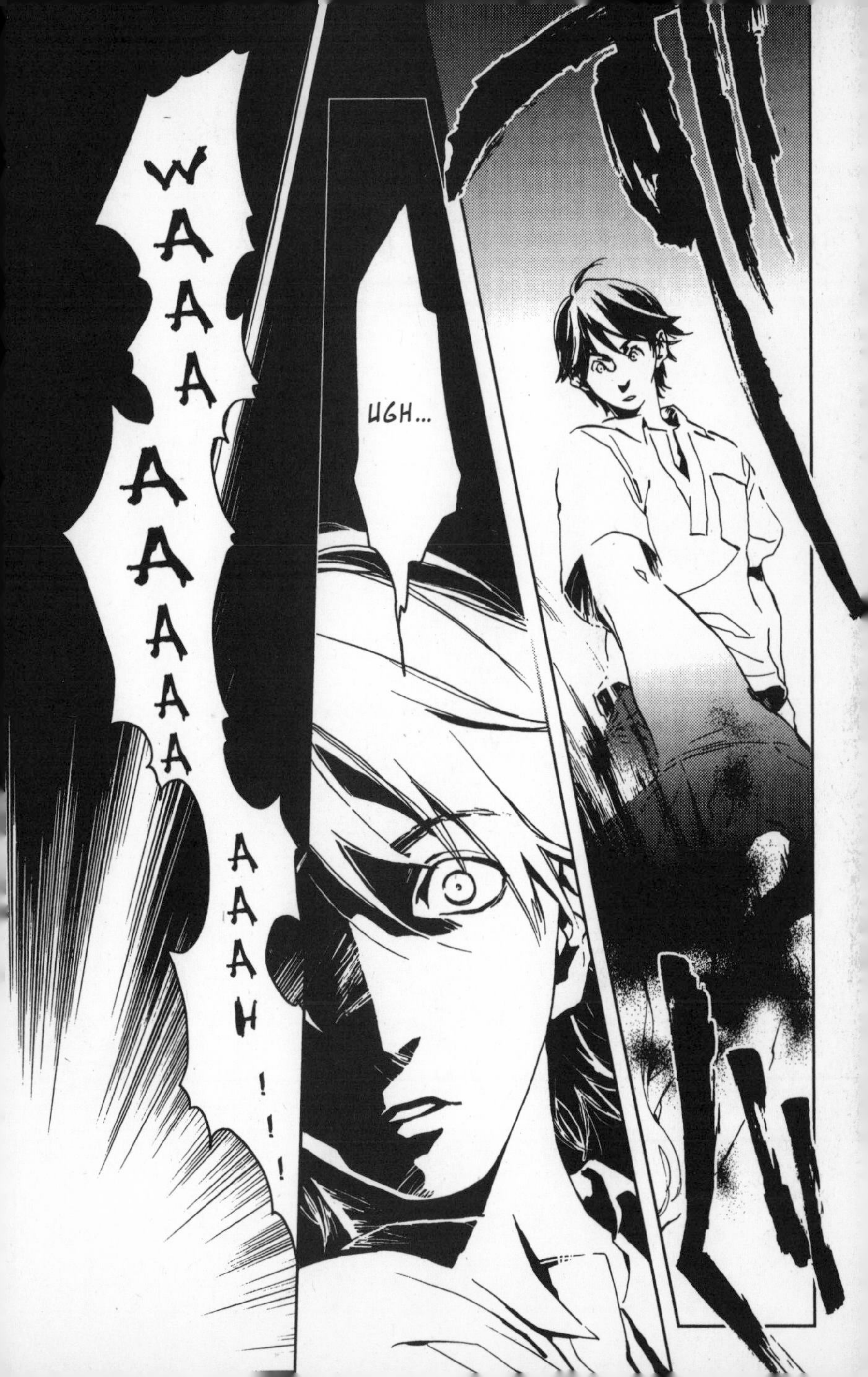
UGH...
WAAAAAAAAAAAH!!!

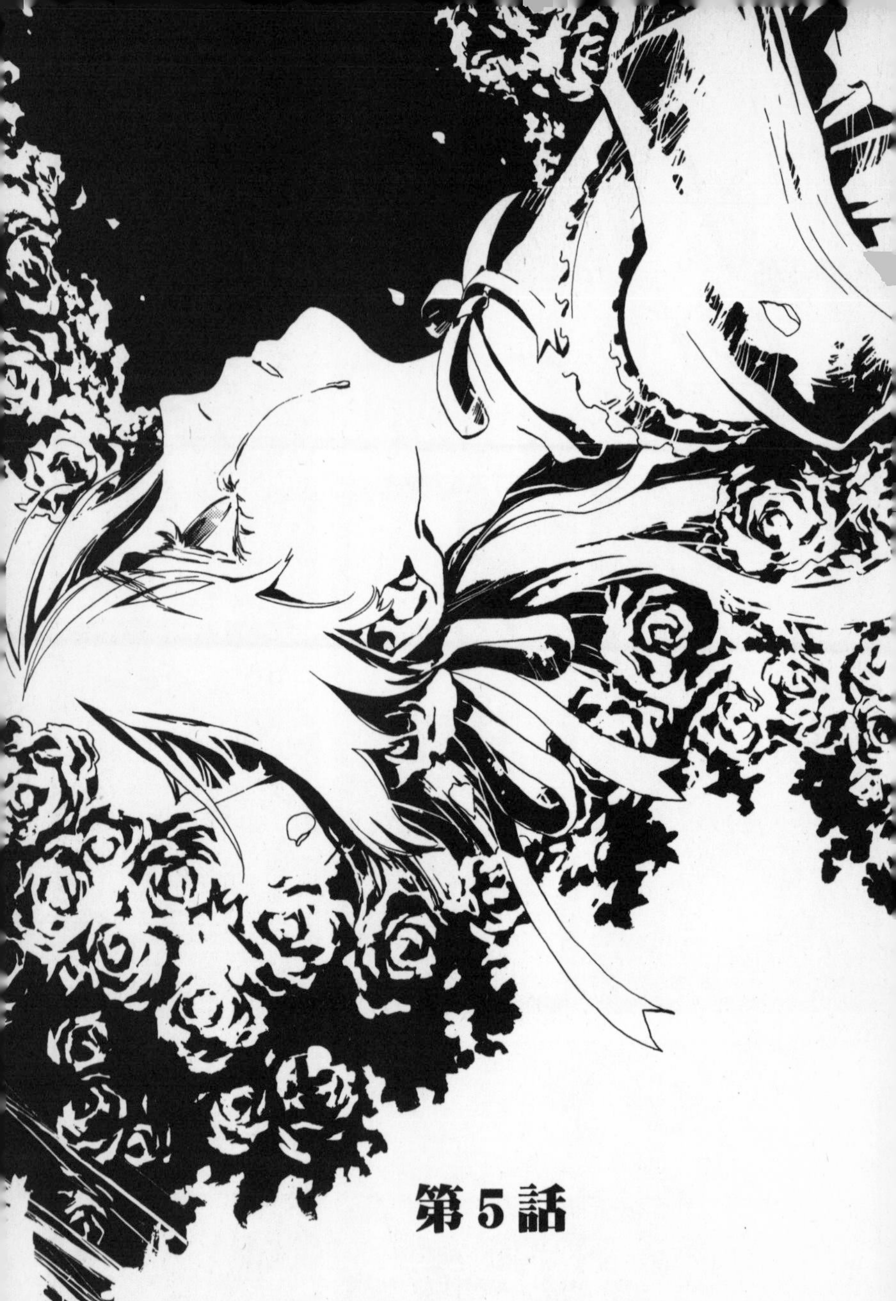

第5話

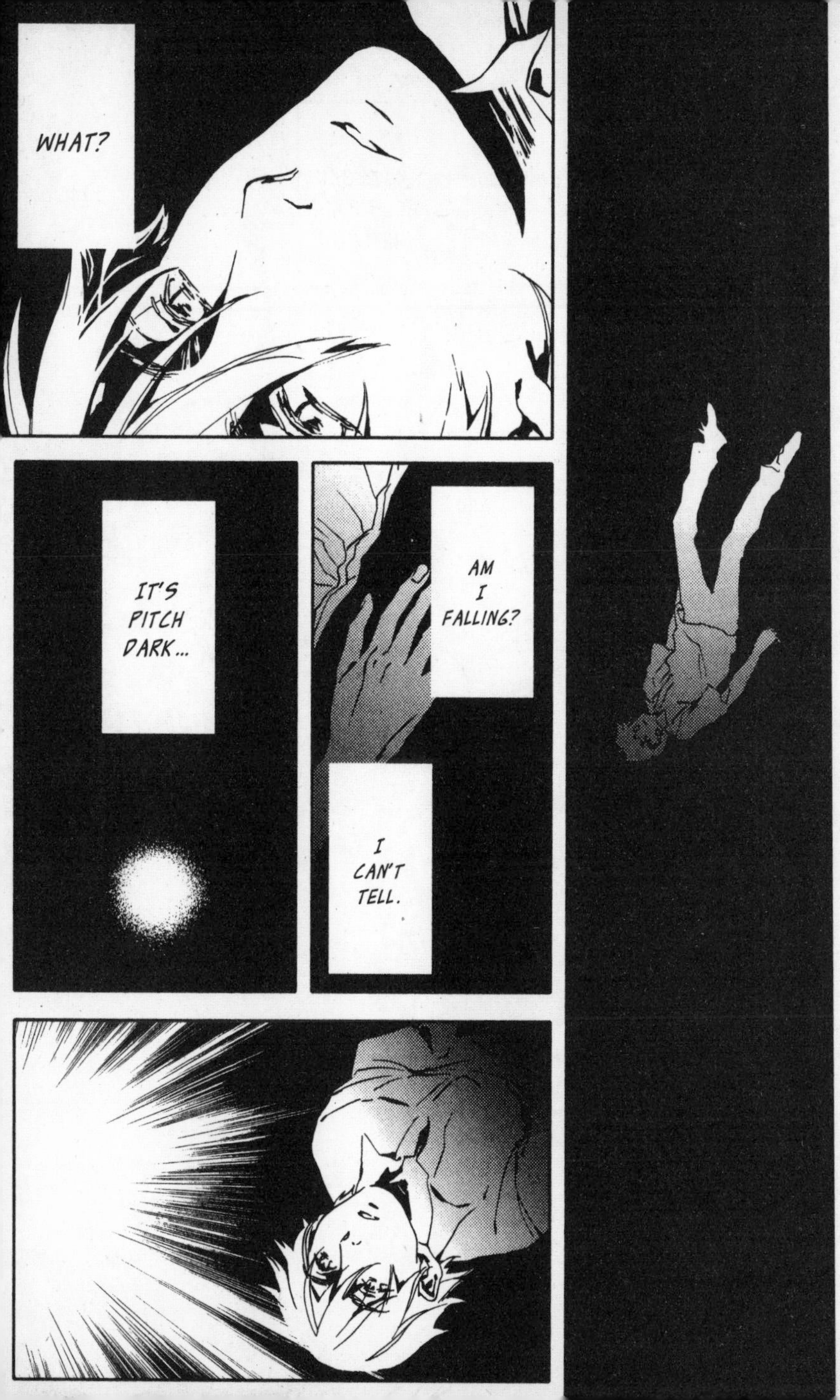
WHAT?
AM I FALLING?
I CAN'T TELL.
IT'S PITCH DARK...

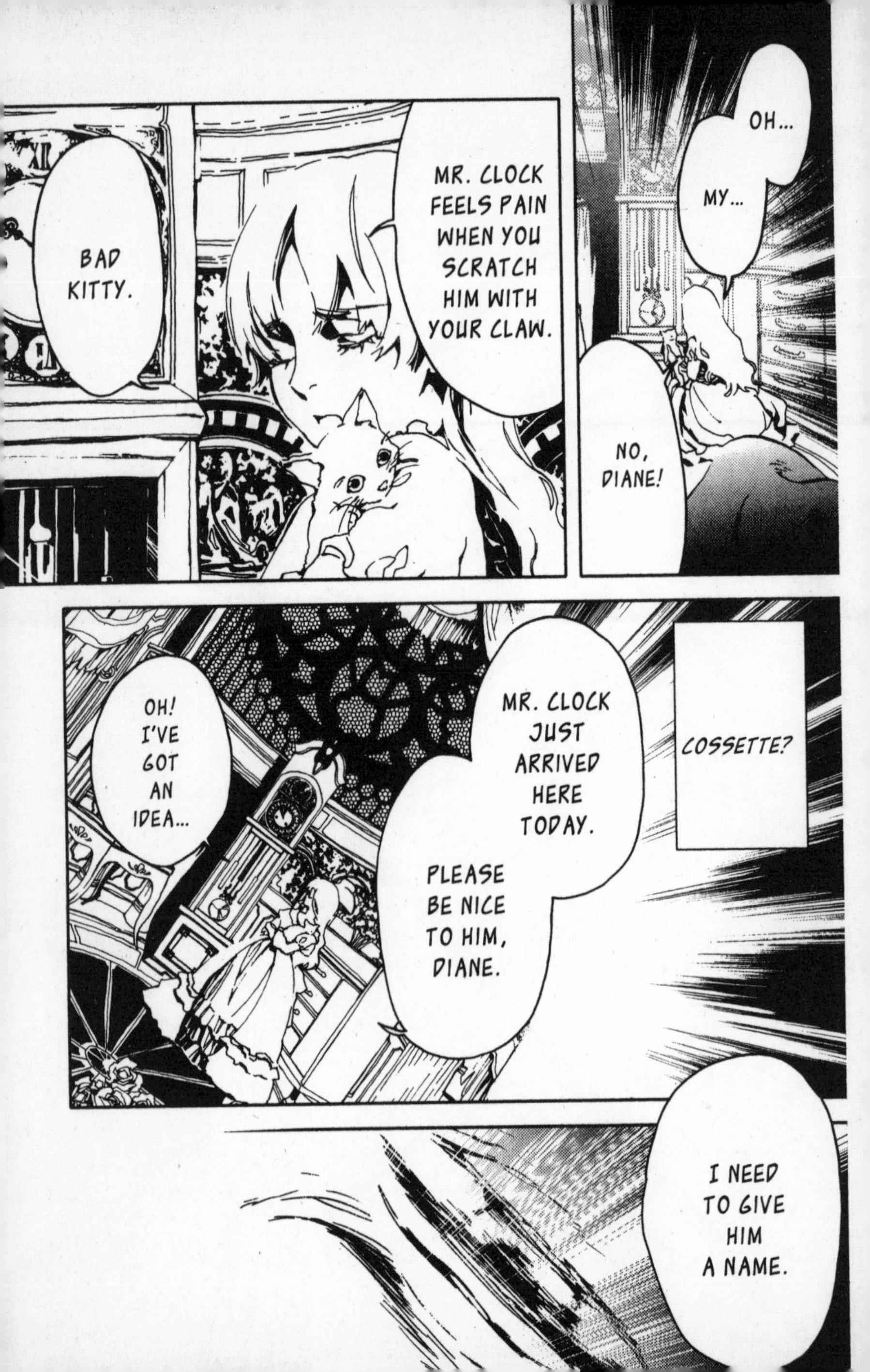

OH... MY...
NO, DIANE!
MR. CLOCK FEELS PAIN WHEN YOU SCRATCH HIM WITH YOUR CLAW.
BAD KITTY.
COSSETTE?
MR. CLOCK JUST ARRIVED HERE TODAY.
PLEASE BE NICE TO HIM, DIANE.
OH! I'VE GOT AN IDEA...
I NEED TO GIVE HIM A NAME.

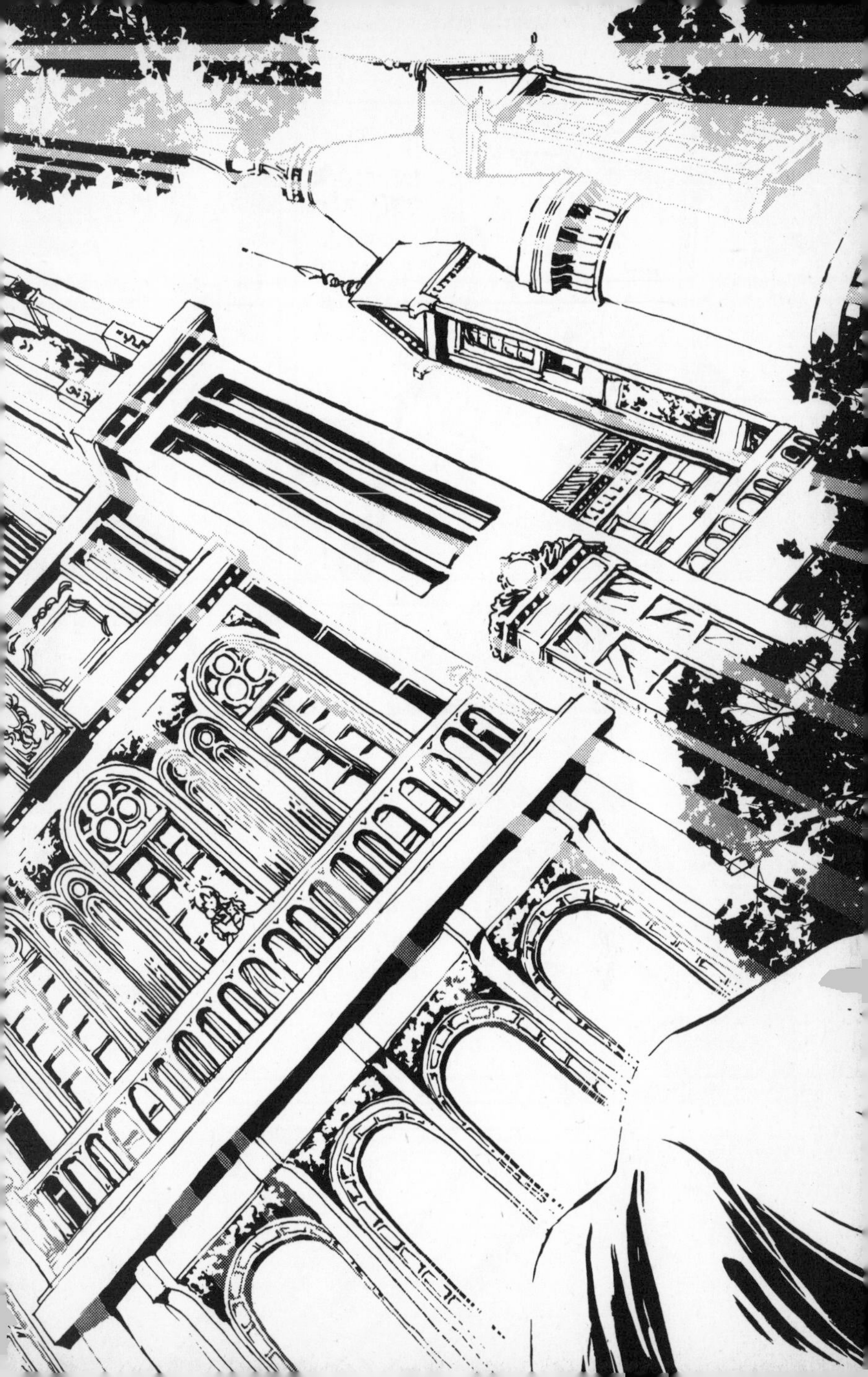

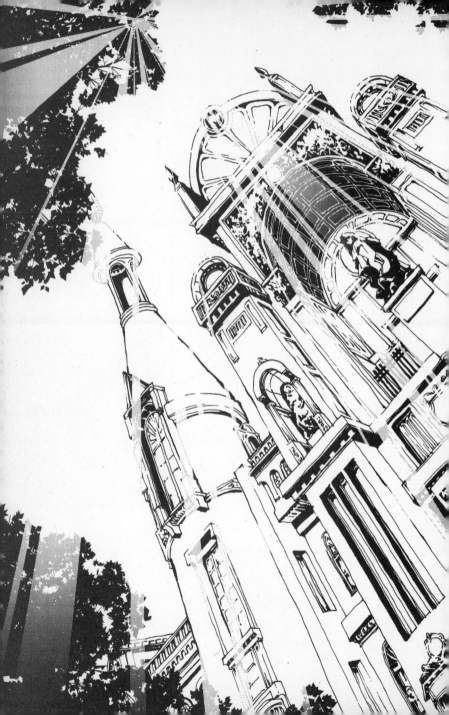

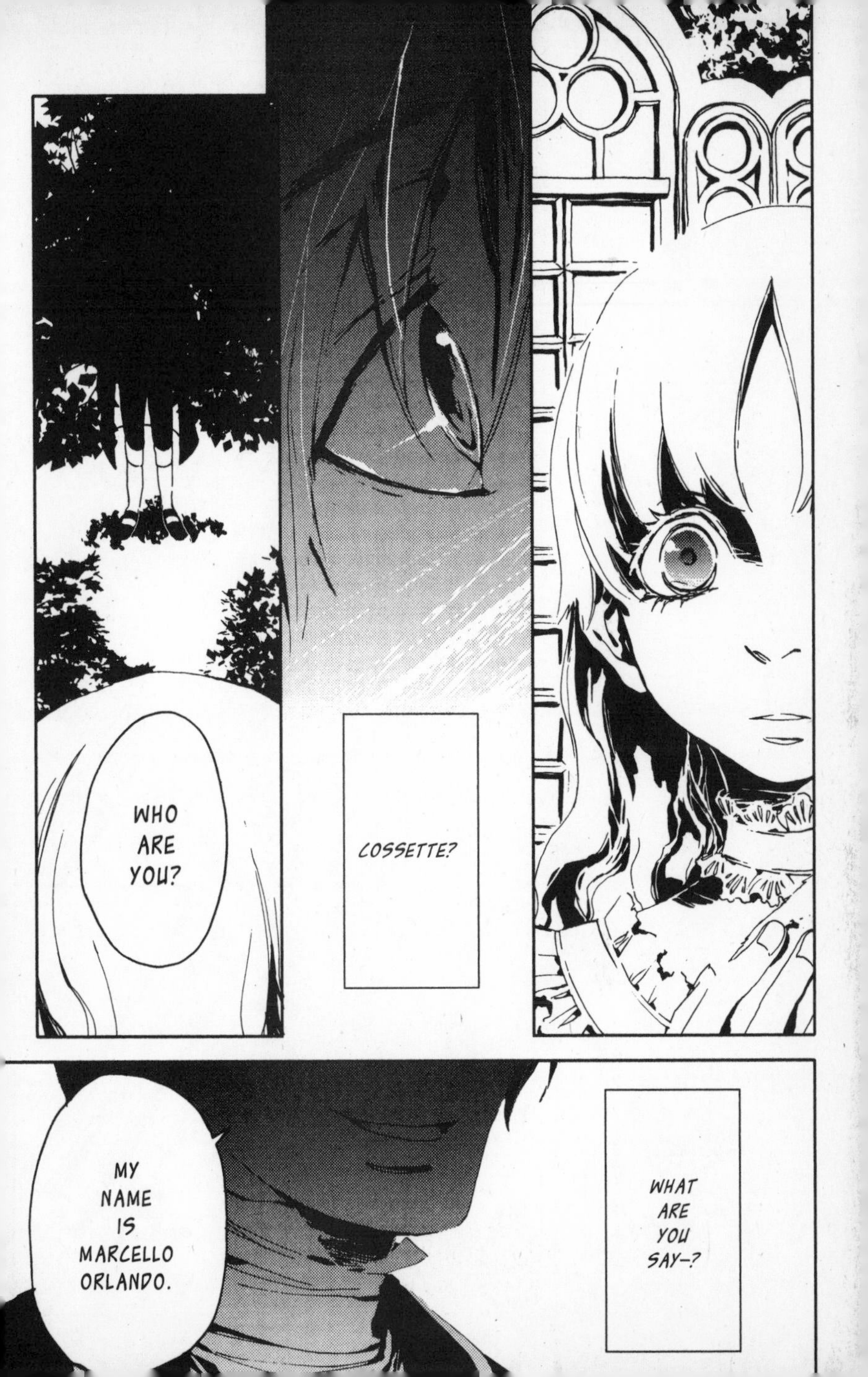
COSSETTE?
WHO ARE YOU?
WHAT ARE YOU SAY–?
MY NAME IS MARCELLO ORLANDO.

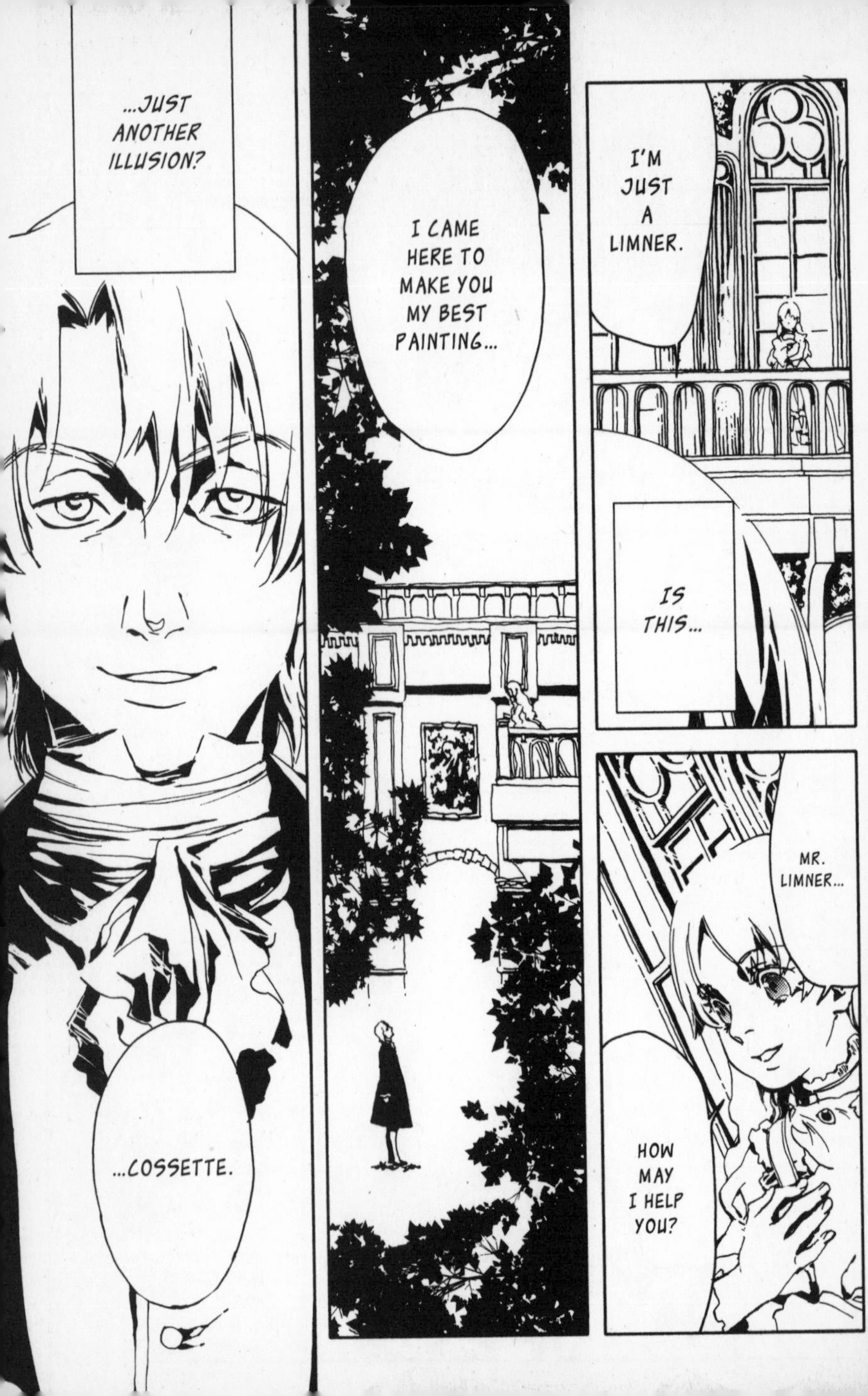
I'M JUST A LIMNER.
IS THIS...
MR. LIMNER...
HOW MAY I HELP YOU?
I CAME HERE TO MAKE YOU MY BEST PAINTING...
...JUST ANOTHER ILLUSION?
...COSSETTE.

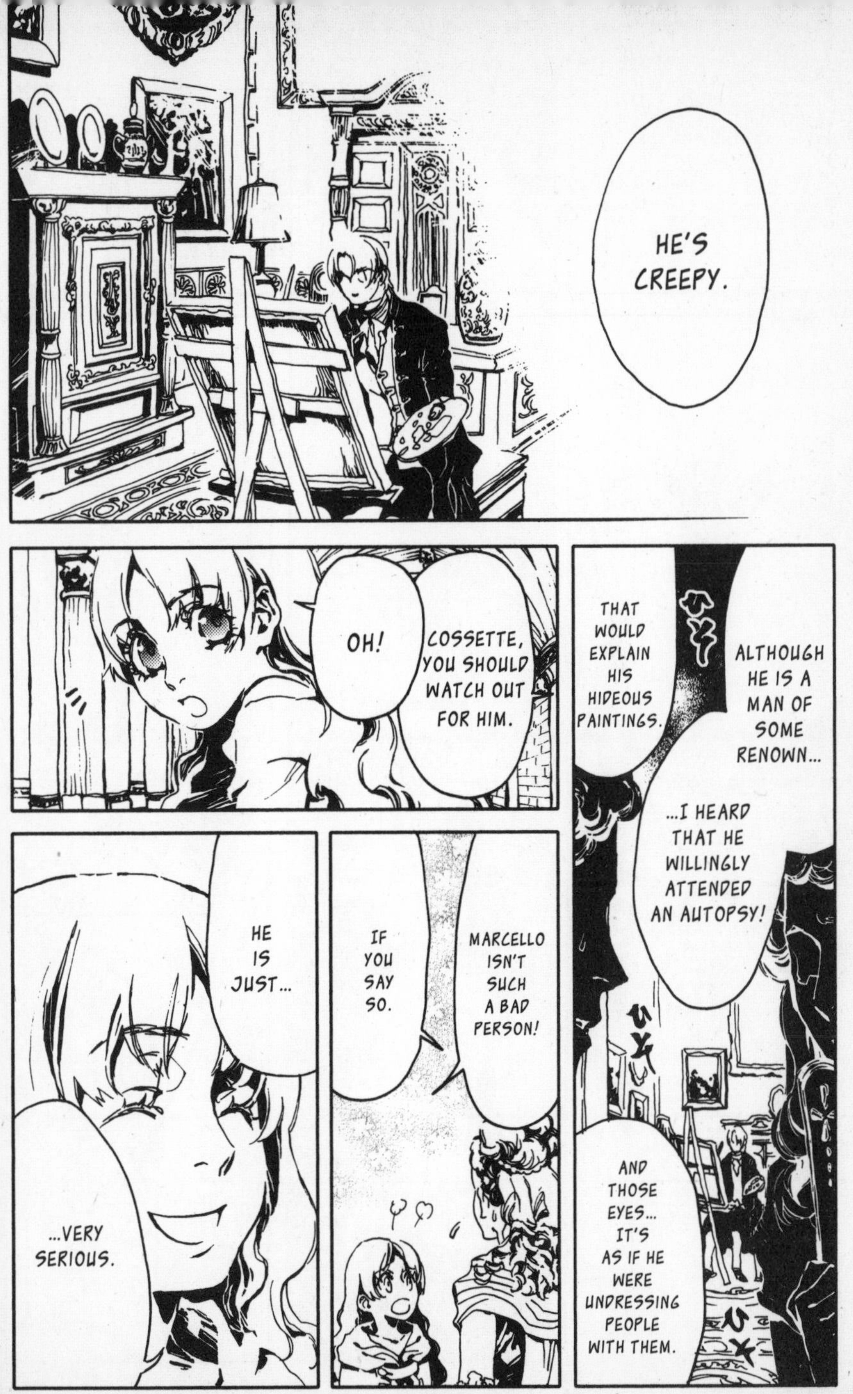
HE'S CREEPY.
ALTHOUGH HE IS A MAN OF SOME RENOWN...
...I HEARD THAT HE WILLINGLY ATTENDED AN AUTOPSY!
THAT WOULD EXPLAIN HIS HIDEOUS PAINTINGS.
AND THOSE EYES... IT'S AS IF HE WERE UNDRESSING PEOPLE WITH THEM.
COSSETTE, YOU SHOULD WATCH OUT FOR HIM.
OH!
MARCELLO ISN'T SUCH A BAD PERSON!
IF YOU SAY SO.
HE IS JUST...
...VERY SERIOUS.

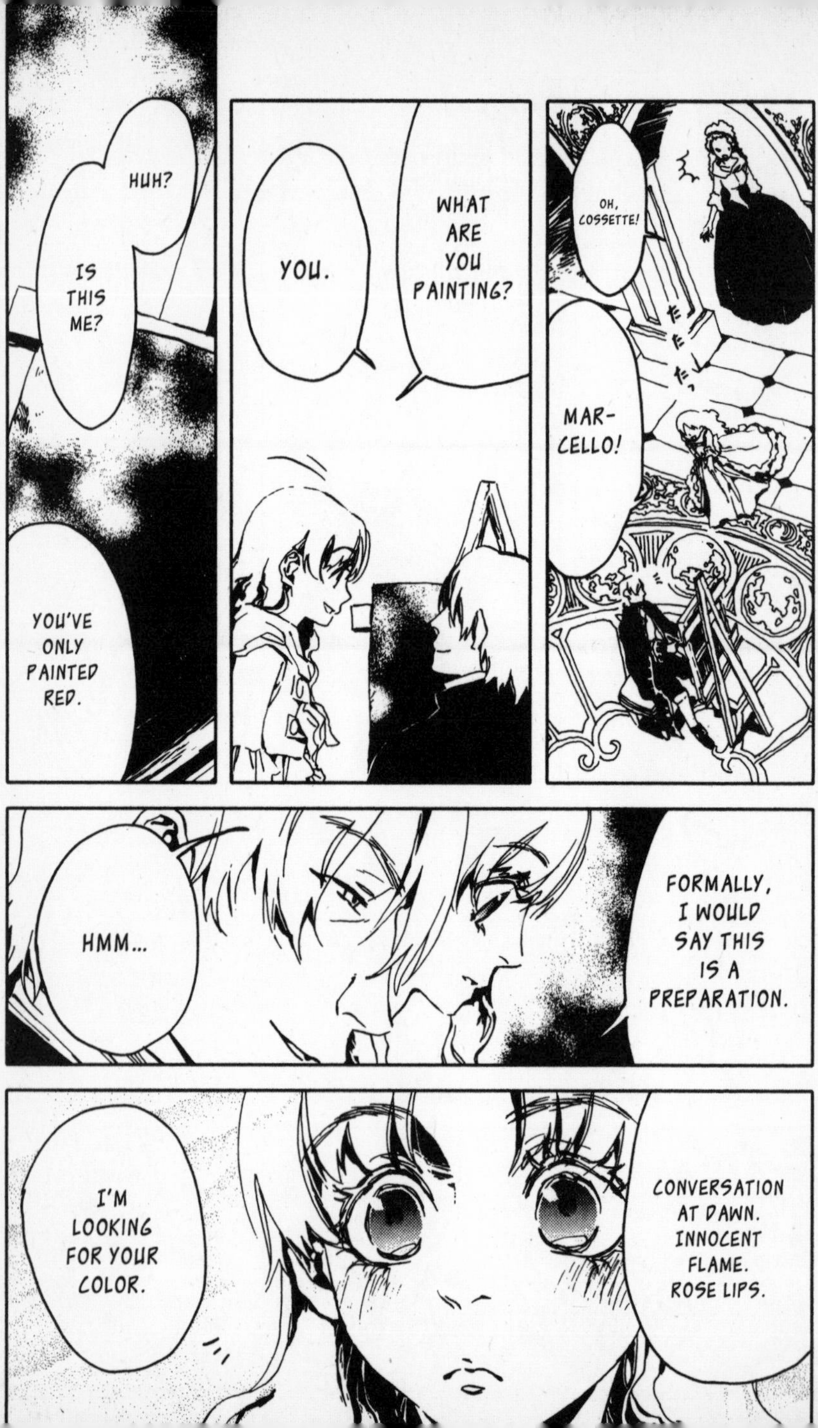
OH, COSSETTE!
たたた
MAR-CELLO!
WHAT ARE YOU PAINTING?
YOU.
HUH? IS THIS ME?
YOU'VE ONLY PAINTED RED.
FORMALLY, I WOULD SAY THIS IS A PREPARATION.
HMM...
CONVERSATION AT DAWN. INNOCENT FLAME. ROSE LIPS.
I'M LOOKING FOR YOUR COLOR.

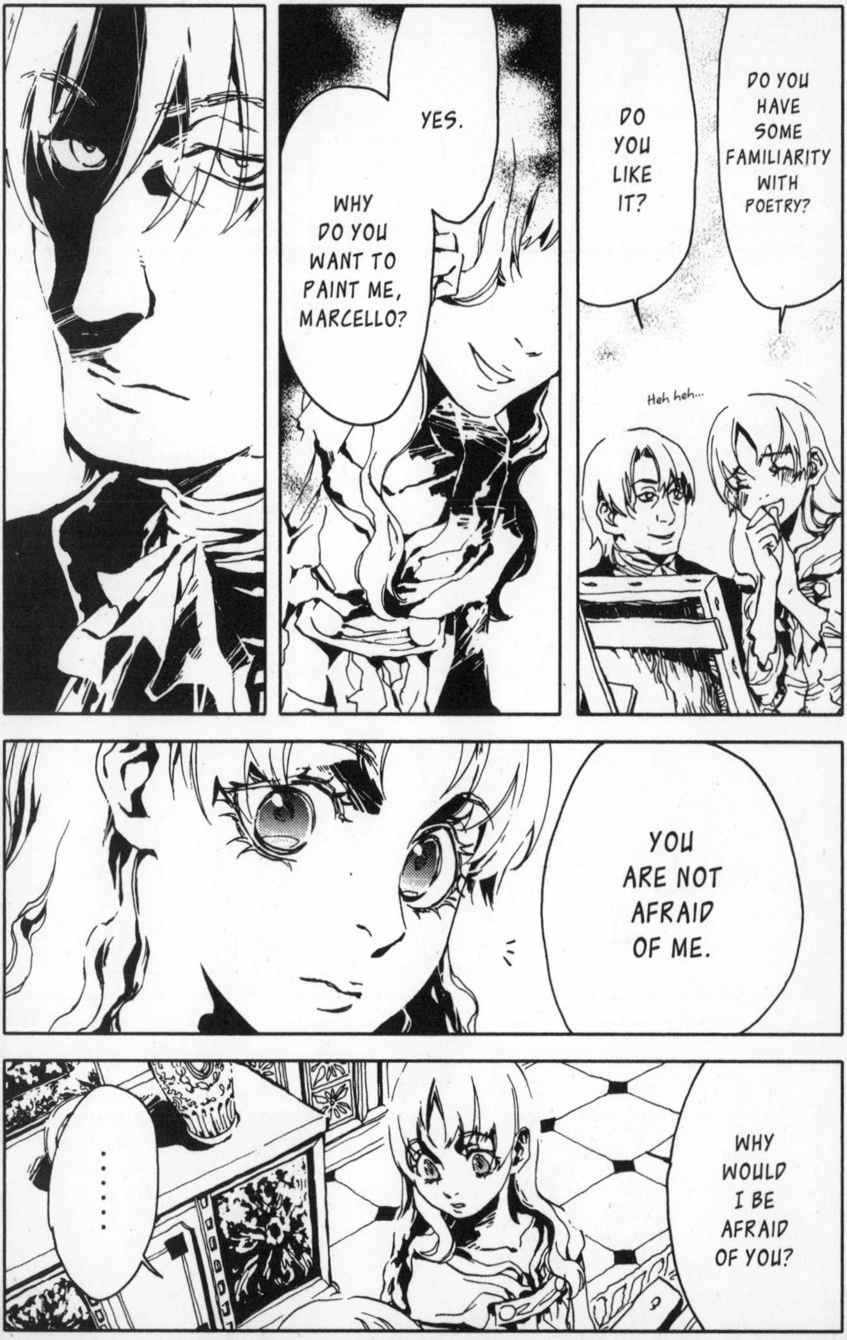
DO YOU HAVE SOME FAMILIARITY WITH POETRY?
DO YOU LIKE IT?
Heh heh...
YES.
WHY DO YOU WANT TO PAINT ME, MARCELLO?
YOU ARE NOT AFRAID OF ME.
WHY WOULD I BE AFRAID OF YOU?
......

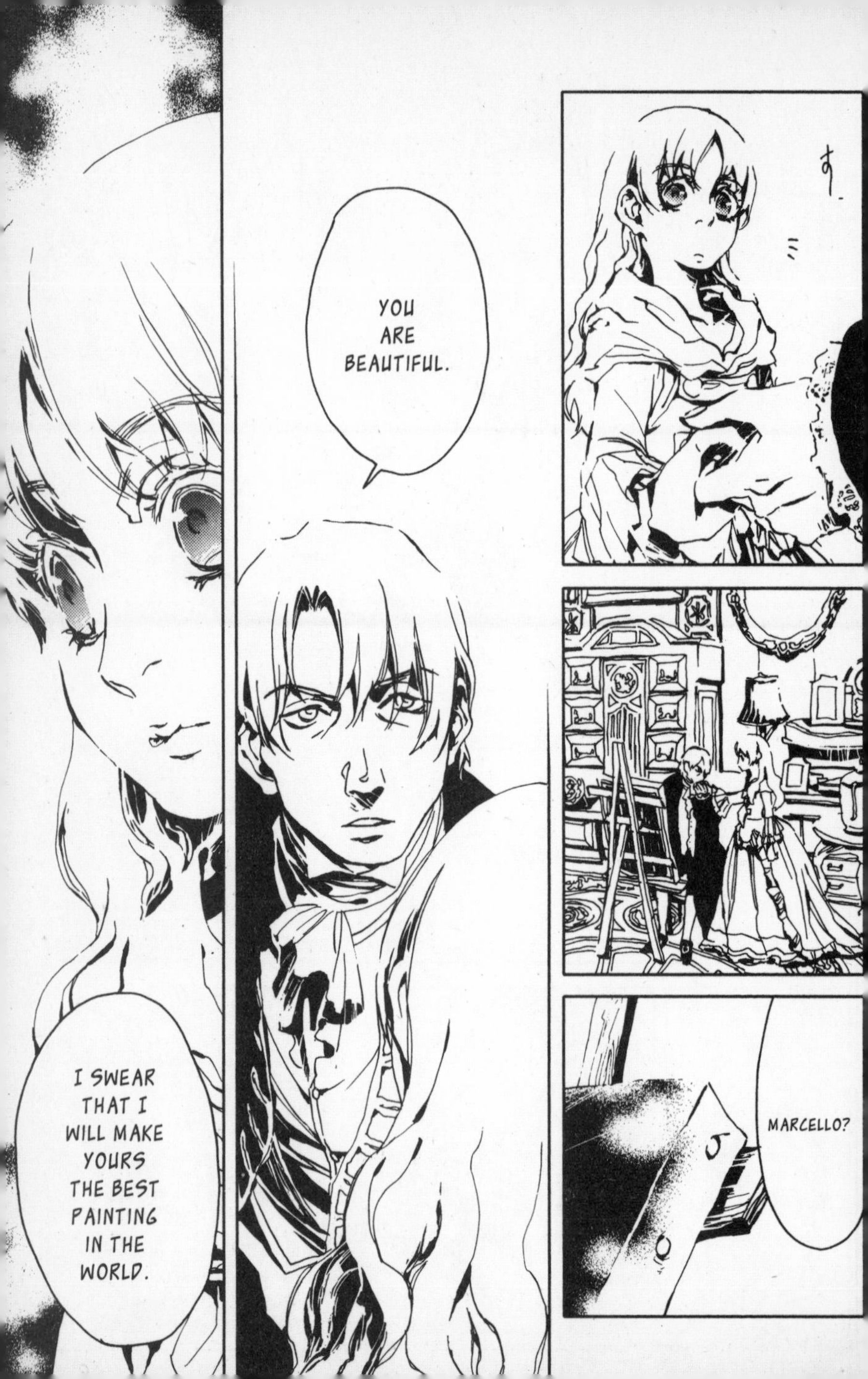
す
MARCELLO?
YOU ARE BEAUTIFUL.
I SWEAR THAT I WILL MAKE YOURS THE BEST PAINTING IN THE WORLD.

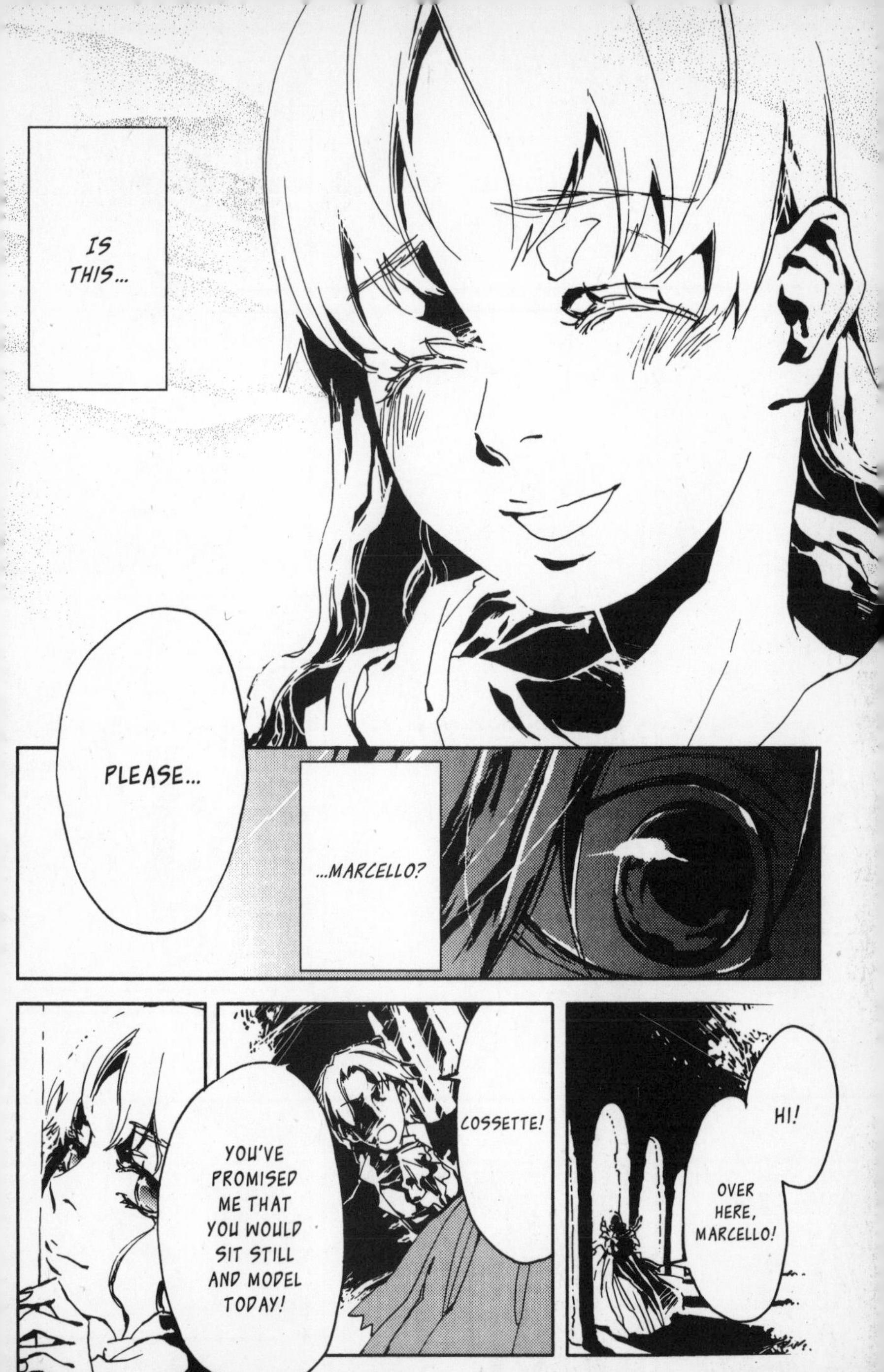
IS THIS...
PLEASE...
...MARCELLO?
HI!
OVER HERE, MARCELLO!
COSSETTE!
YOU'VE PROMISED ME THAT YOU WOULD SIT STILL AND MODEL TODAY!

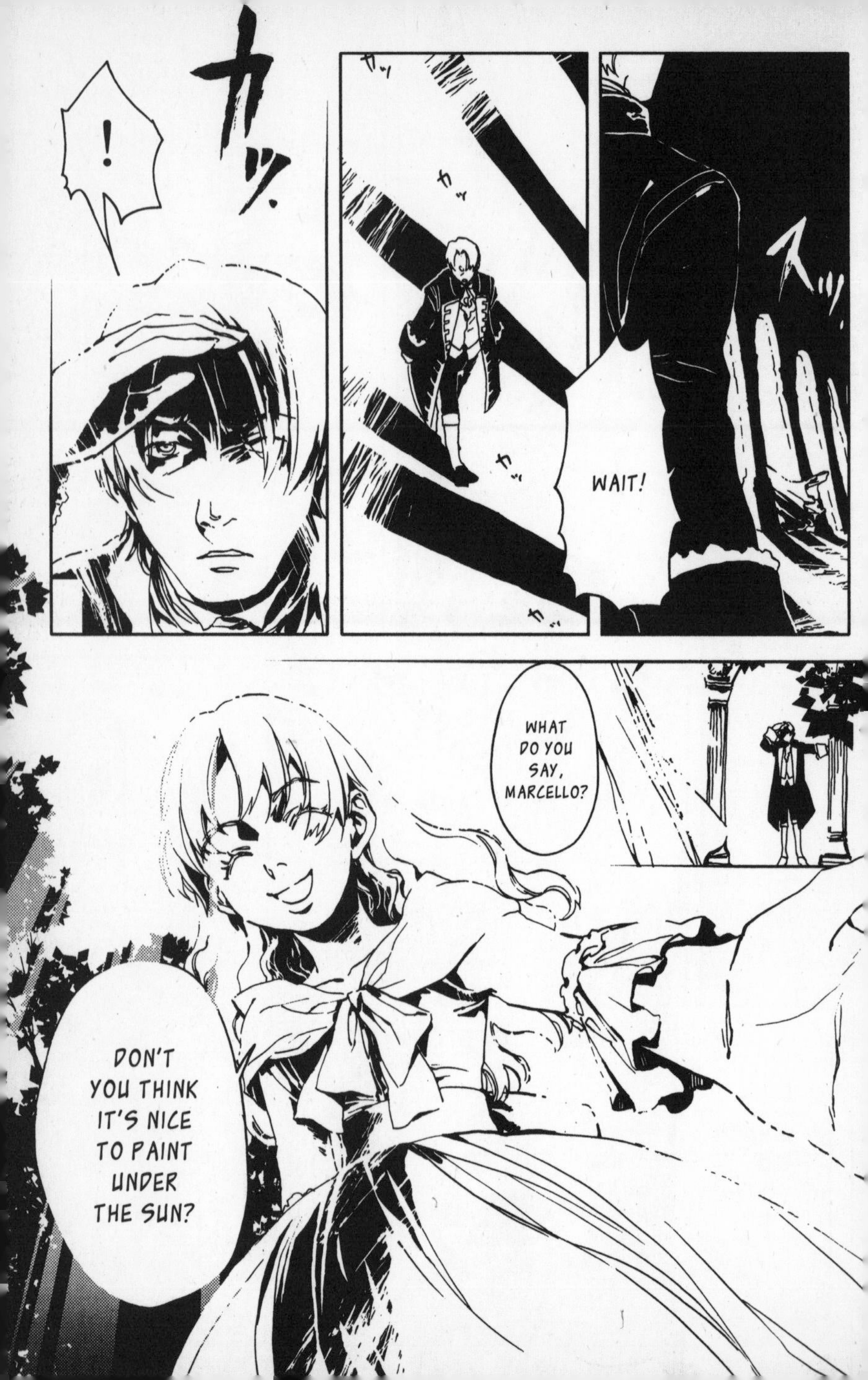
WAIT!
カッ
!
WHAT DO YOU SAY, MARCELLO?
DON'T YOU THINK IT'S NICE TO PAINT UNDER THE SUN?

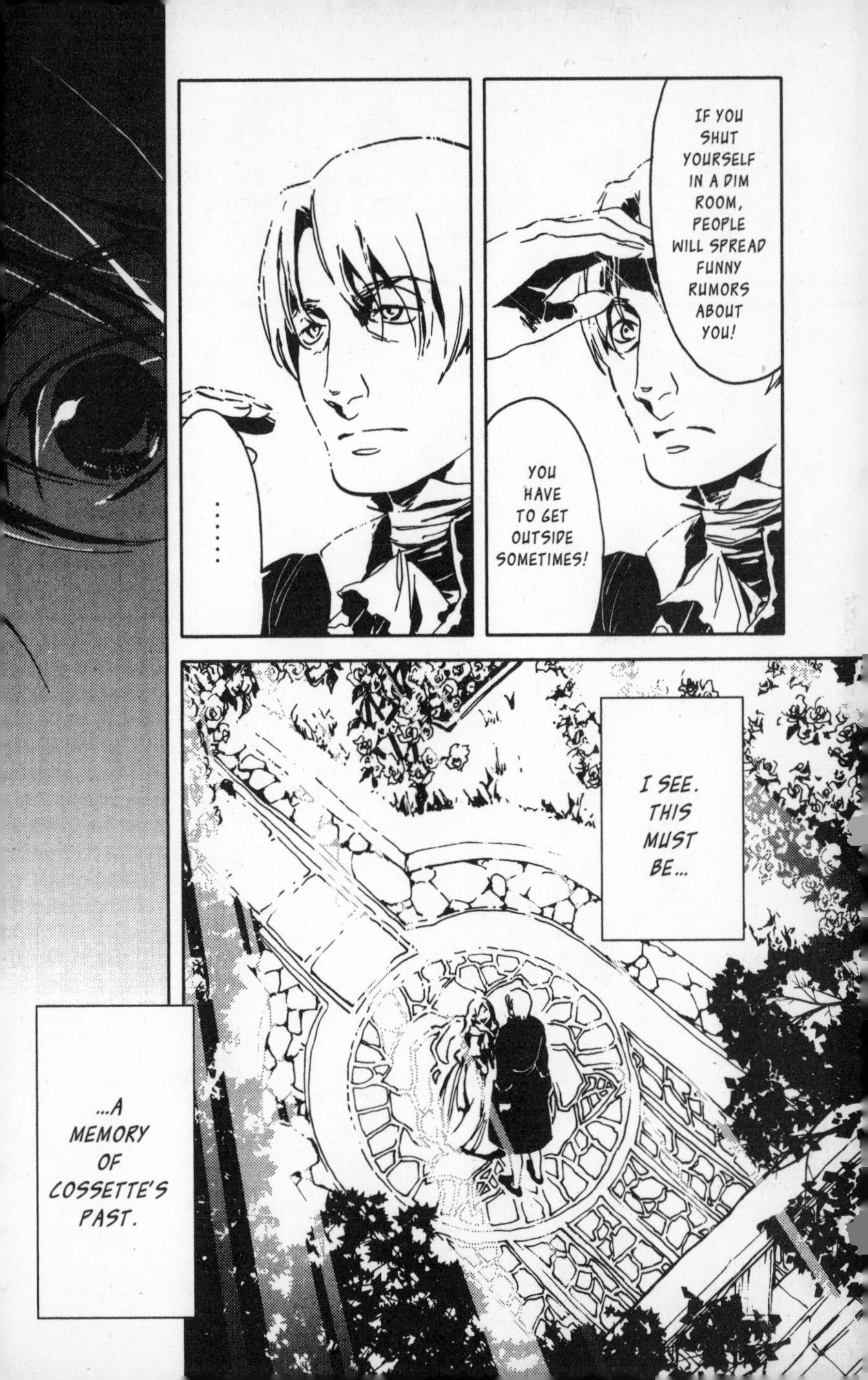
IF YOU SHUT YOURSELF IN A DIM ROOM, PEOPLE WILL SPREAD FUNNY RUMORS ABOUT YOU!
YOU HAVE TO GET OUTSIDE SOMETIMES!
......
I SEE. THIS MUST BE...
...A MEMORY OF COSSETTE'S PAST.

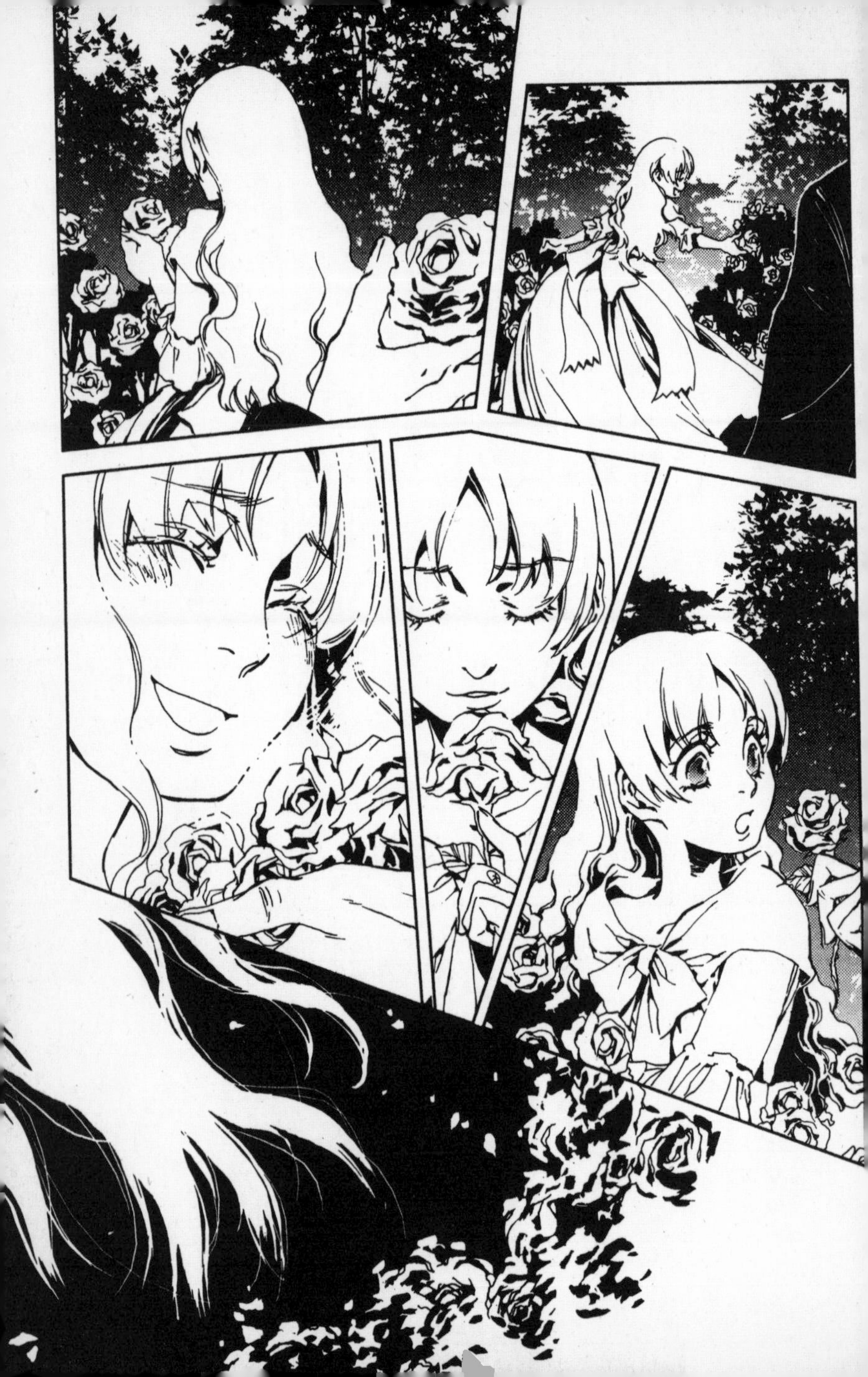

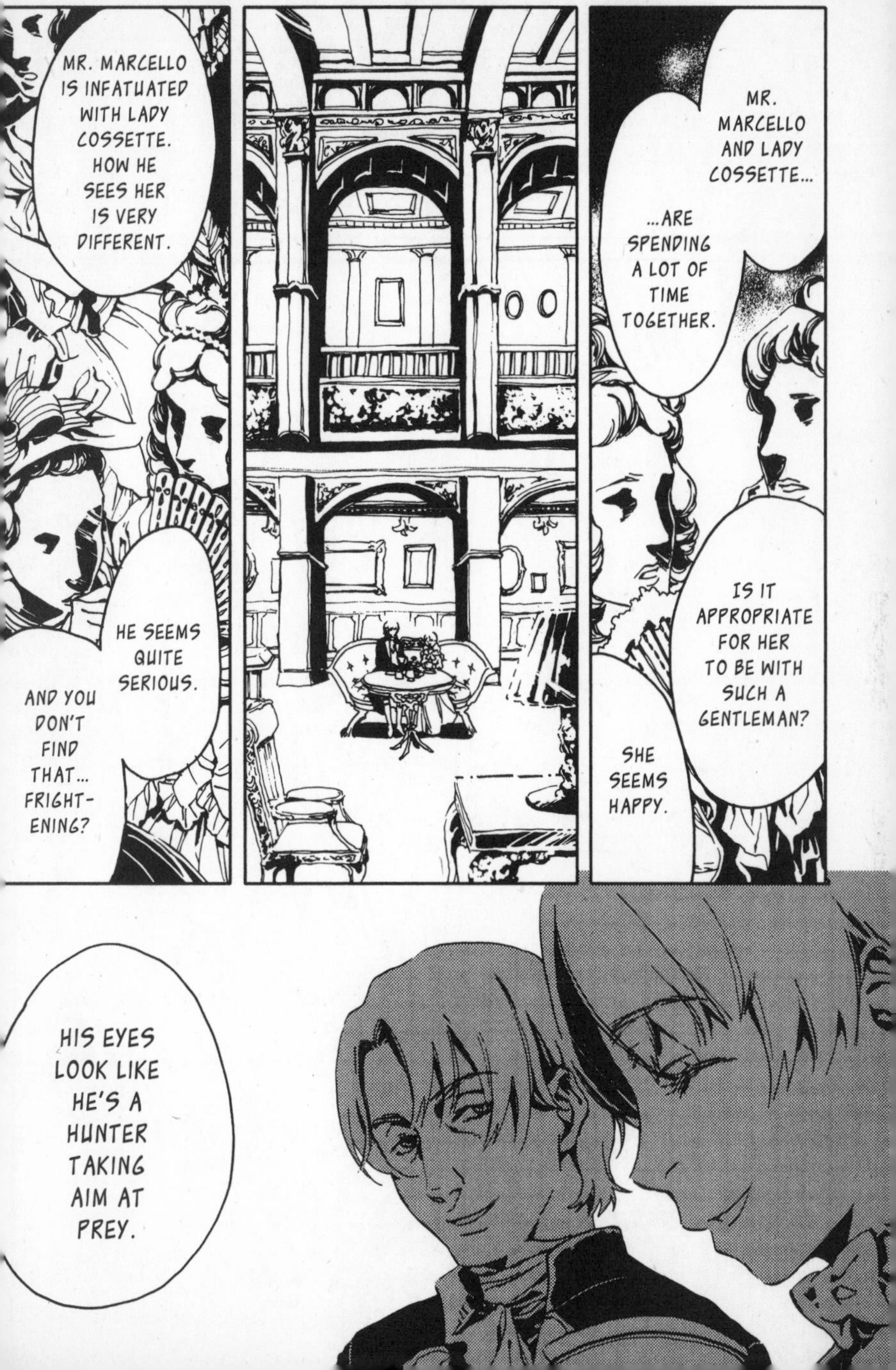
MR. MARCELLO AND LADY COSSETTE...
...ARE SPENDING A LOT OF TIME TOGETHER.
IS IT APPROPRIATE FOR HER TO BE WITH SUCH A GENTLEMAN?
SHE SEEMS HAPPY.
MR. MARCELLO IS INFATUATED WITH LADY COSSETTE. HOW HE SEES HER IS VERY DIFFERENT.
HE SEEMS QUITE SERIOUS.
AND YOU DON'T FIND THAT... FRIGHT-ENING?
HIS EYES LOOK LIKE HE'S A HUNTER TAKING AIM AT PREY.

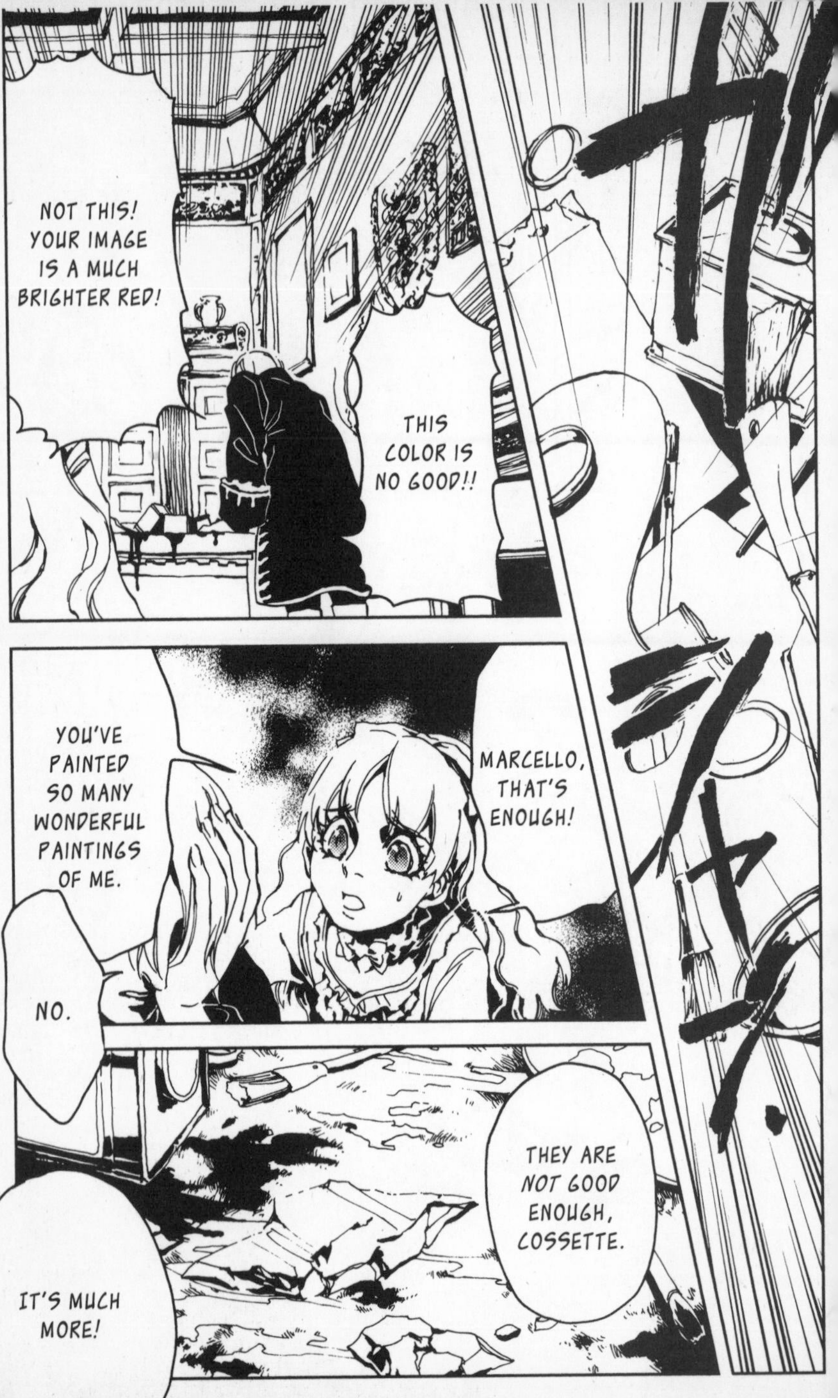
THIS COLOR IS NO GOOD!!
NOT THIS! YOUR IMAGE IS A MUCH BRIGHTER RED!
MARCELLO, THAT'S ENOUGH!
YOU'VE PAINTED SO MANY WONDERFUL PAINTINGS OF ME.
NO.
THEY ARE NOT GOOD ENOUGH, COSSETTE.
IT'S MUCH MORE!

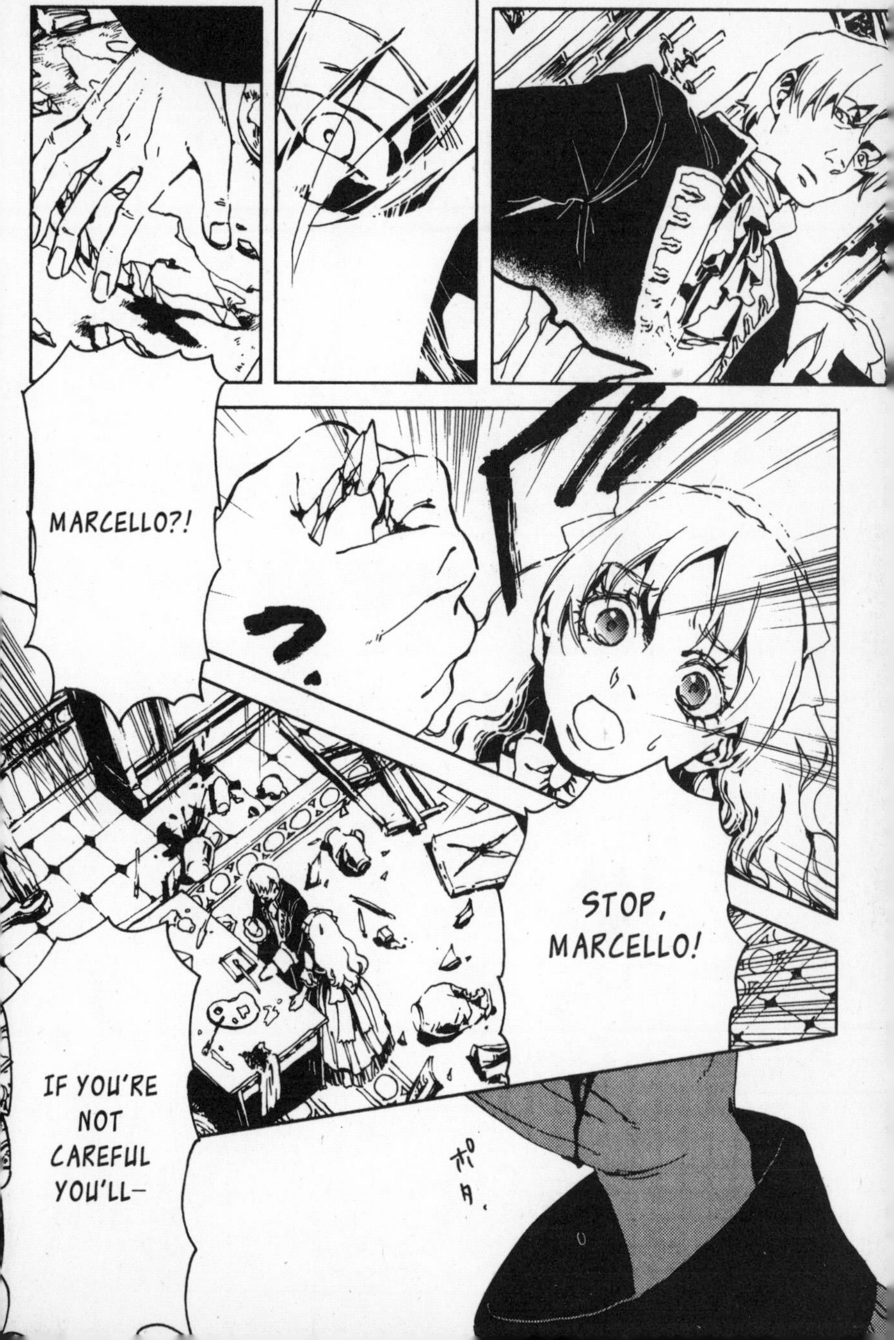
MARCELLO?!
STOP, MARCELLO!
IF YOU'RE NOT CAREFUL YOU'LL—
ポタ

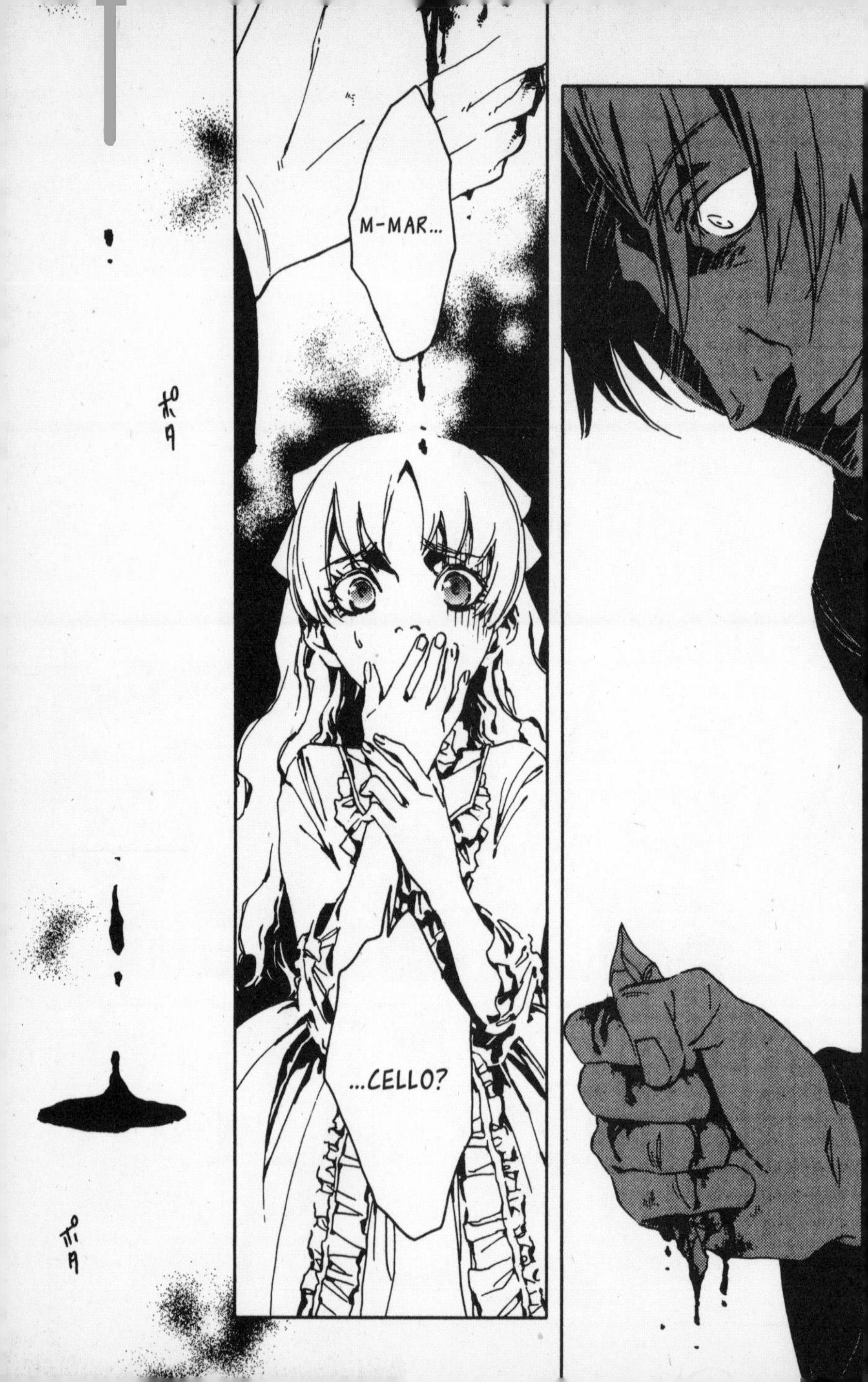
M-MAR...
...CELLO?
ポタ
ポタ

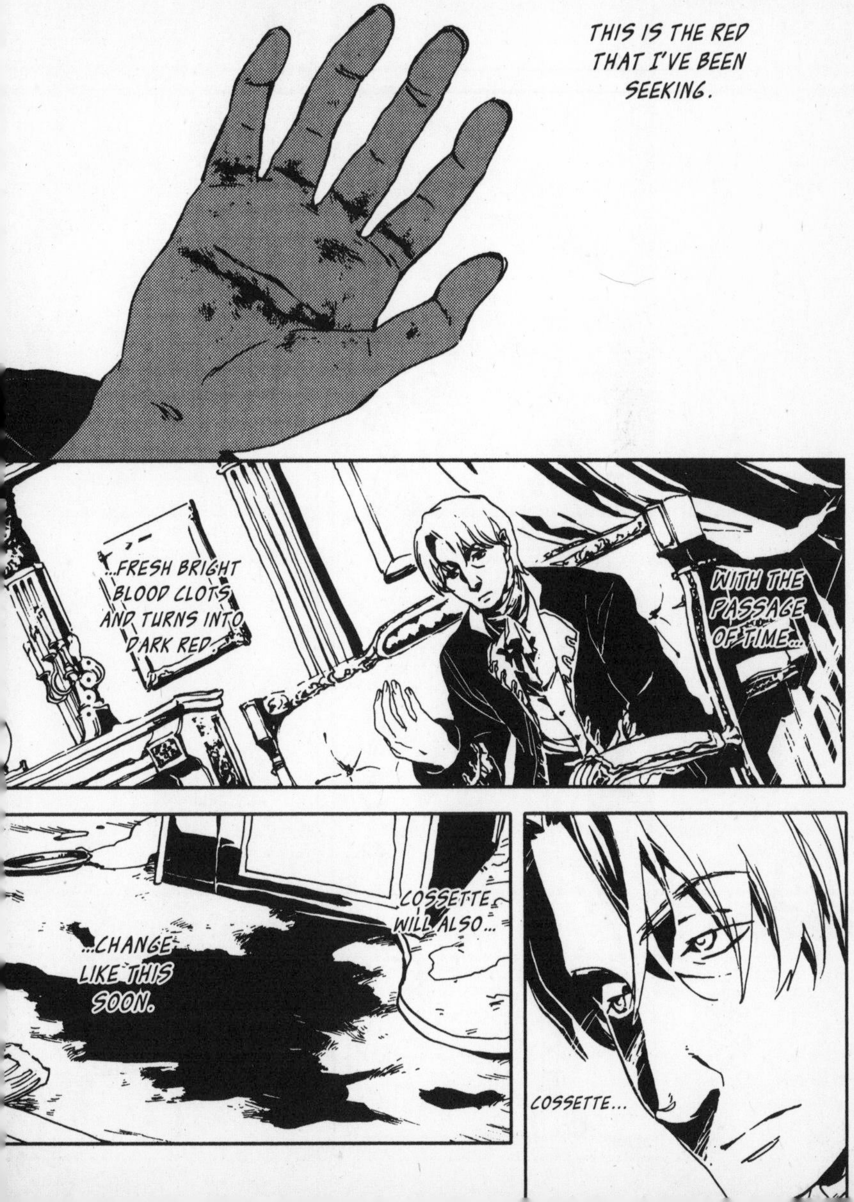
THIS IS THE RED THAT I'VE BEEN SEEKING.
WITH THE PASSAGE OF TIME...
...FRESH BRIGHT BLOOD CLOTS AND TURNS INTO DARK RED.
COSSETTE...
COSSETTE WILL ALSO...
...CHANGE LIKE THIS SOON.

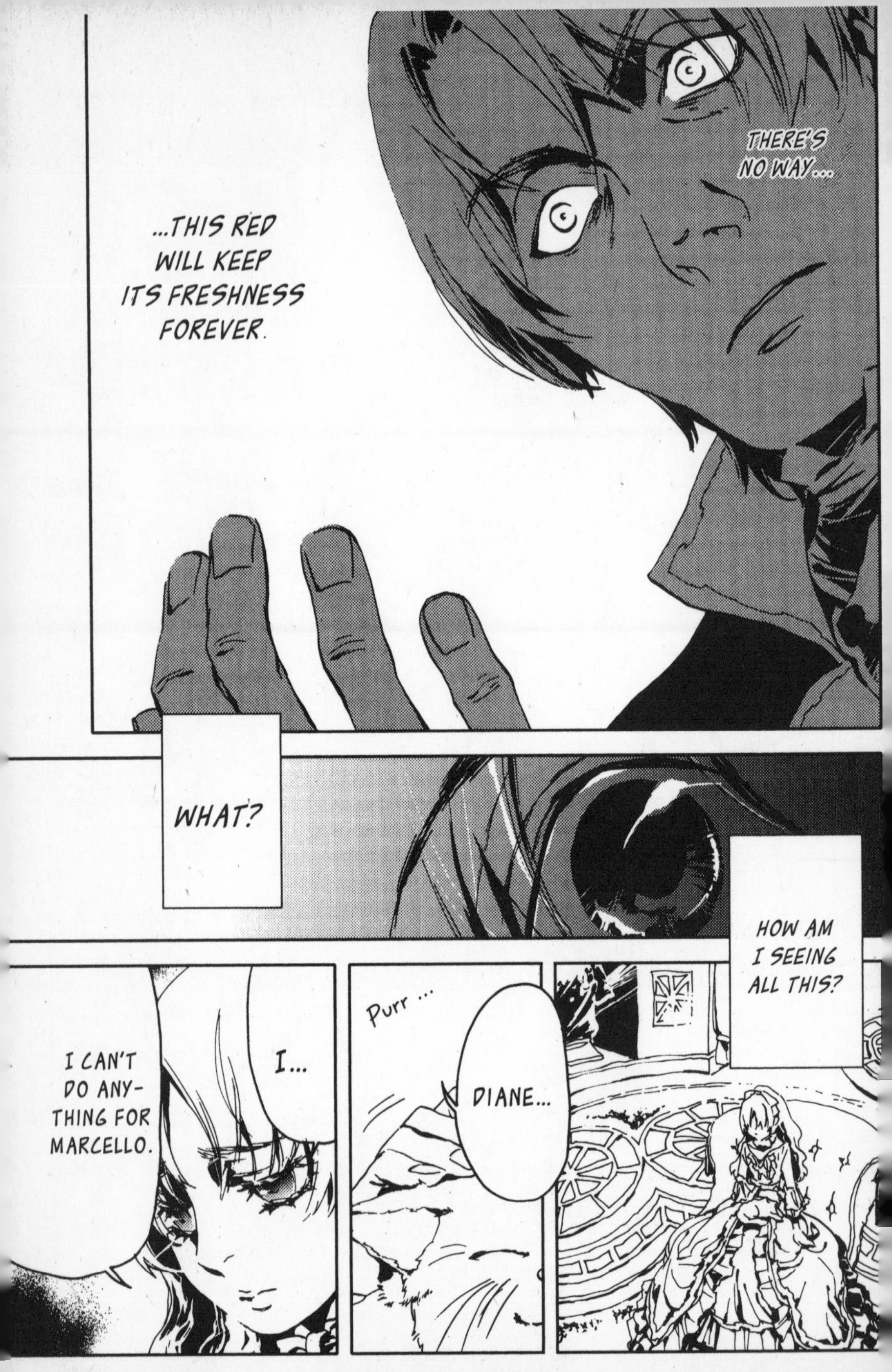

THERE'S NO WAY...
...THIS RED WILL KEEP ITS FRESHNESS FOREVER.
WHAT?
HOW AM I SEEING ALL THIS?
Purr ...
DIANE...
I...
I CAN'T DO ANY-THING FOR MARCELLO.

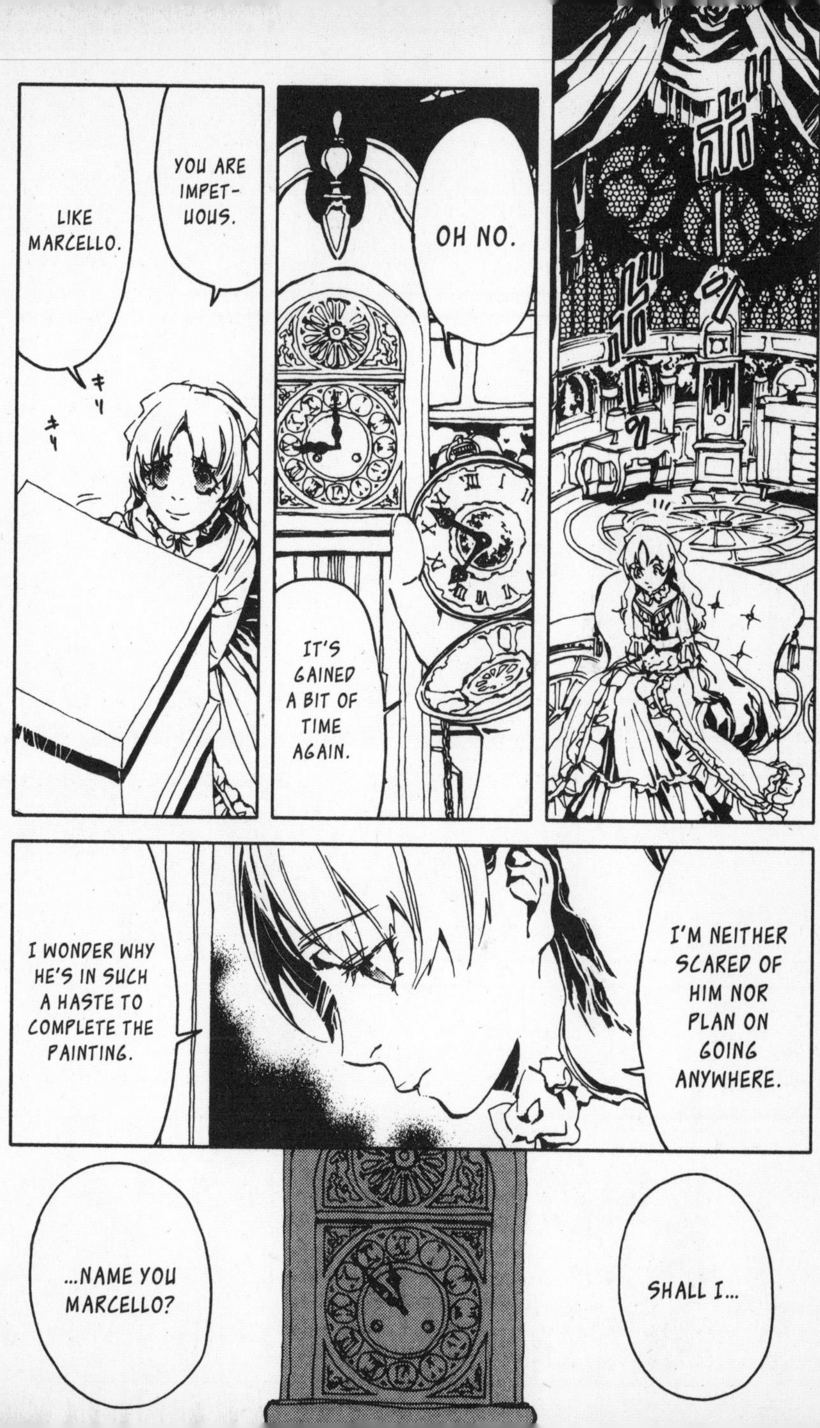
OH NO.
IT'S GAINED A BIT OF TIME AGAIN.
YOU ARE IMPETUOUS.
LIKE MARCELLO.
I'M NEITHER SCARED OF HIM NOR PLAN ON GOING ANYWHERE.
I WONDER WHY HE'S IN SUCH A HASTE TO COMPLETE THE PAINTING.
SHALL I...
...NAME YOU MARCELLO?

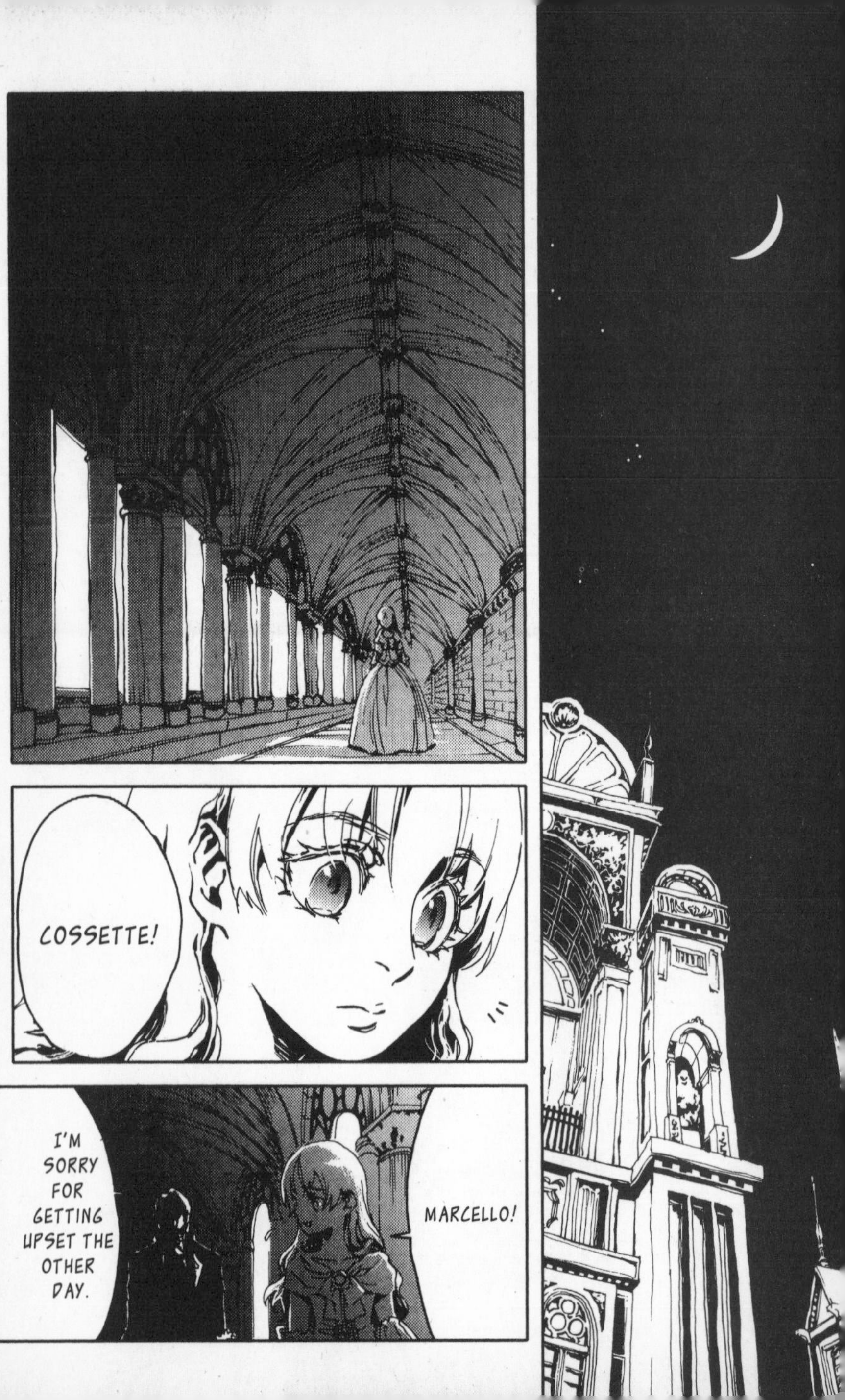
COSSETTE!
MARCELLO!
I'M SORRY FOR GETTING UPSET THE OTHER DAY.

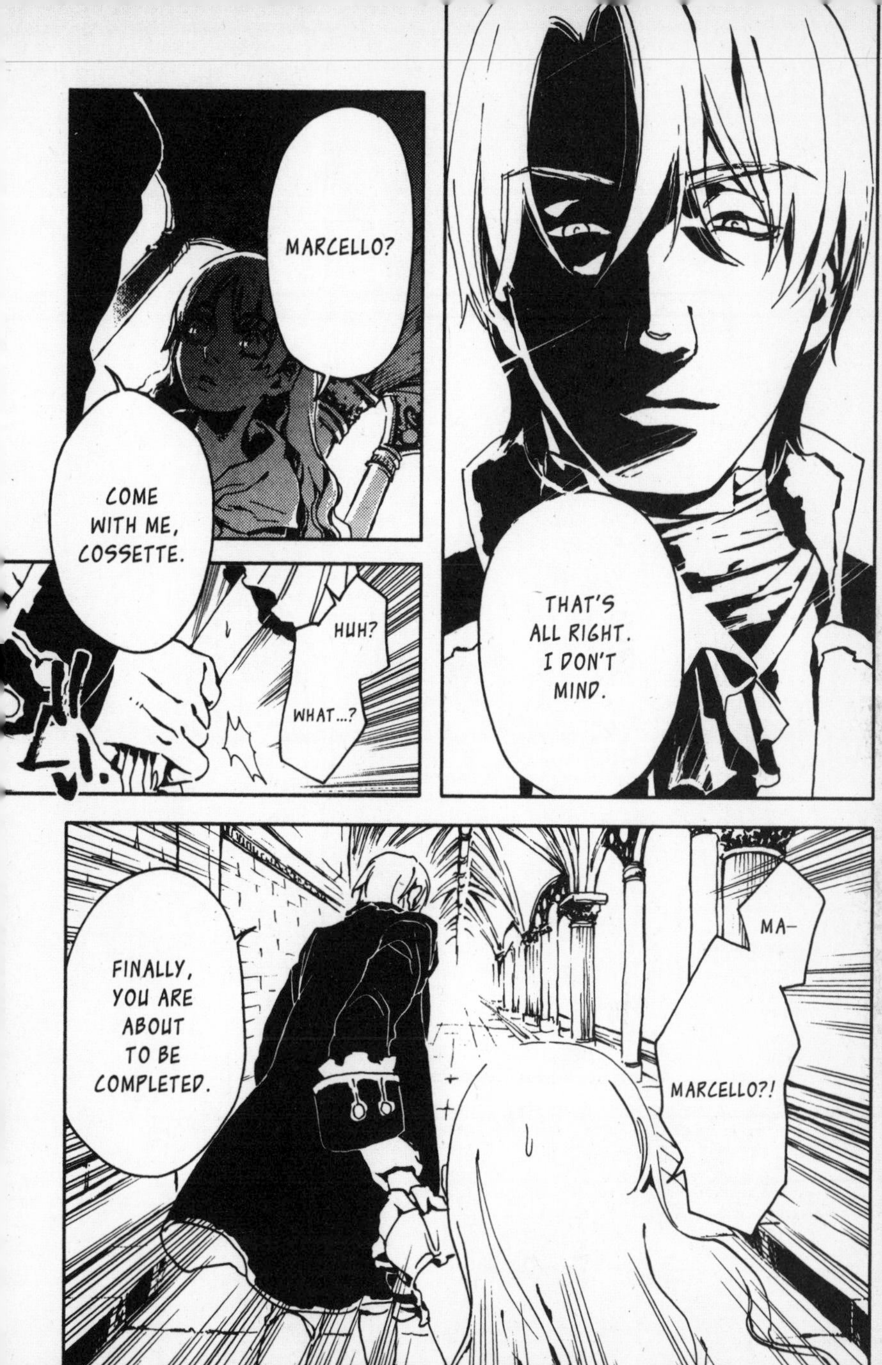
THAT'S ALL RIGHT. I DON'T MIND.
MARCELLO?
COME WITH ME, COSSETTE.
HUH?
WHAT...?
MA-
MARCELLO?!
FINALLY, YOU ARE ABOUT TO BE COMPLETED.

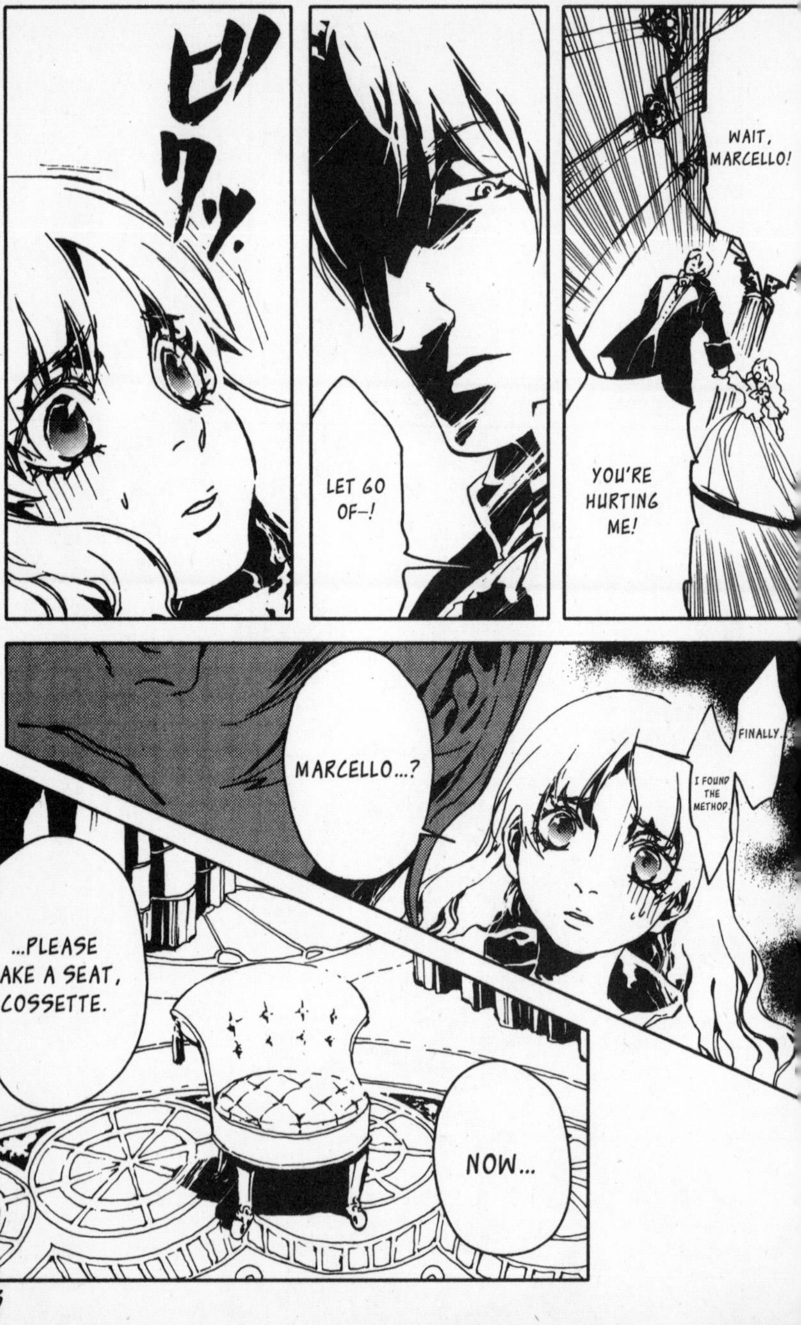
WAIT, MARCELLO!
YOU'RE HURTING ME!
LET GO OF—!
ビクッ!
FINALLY...
I FOUND THE METHOD.
MARCELLO...?
NOW...
...PLEASE TAKE A SEAT, COSSETTE.

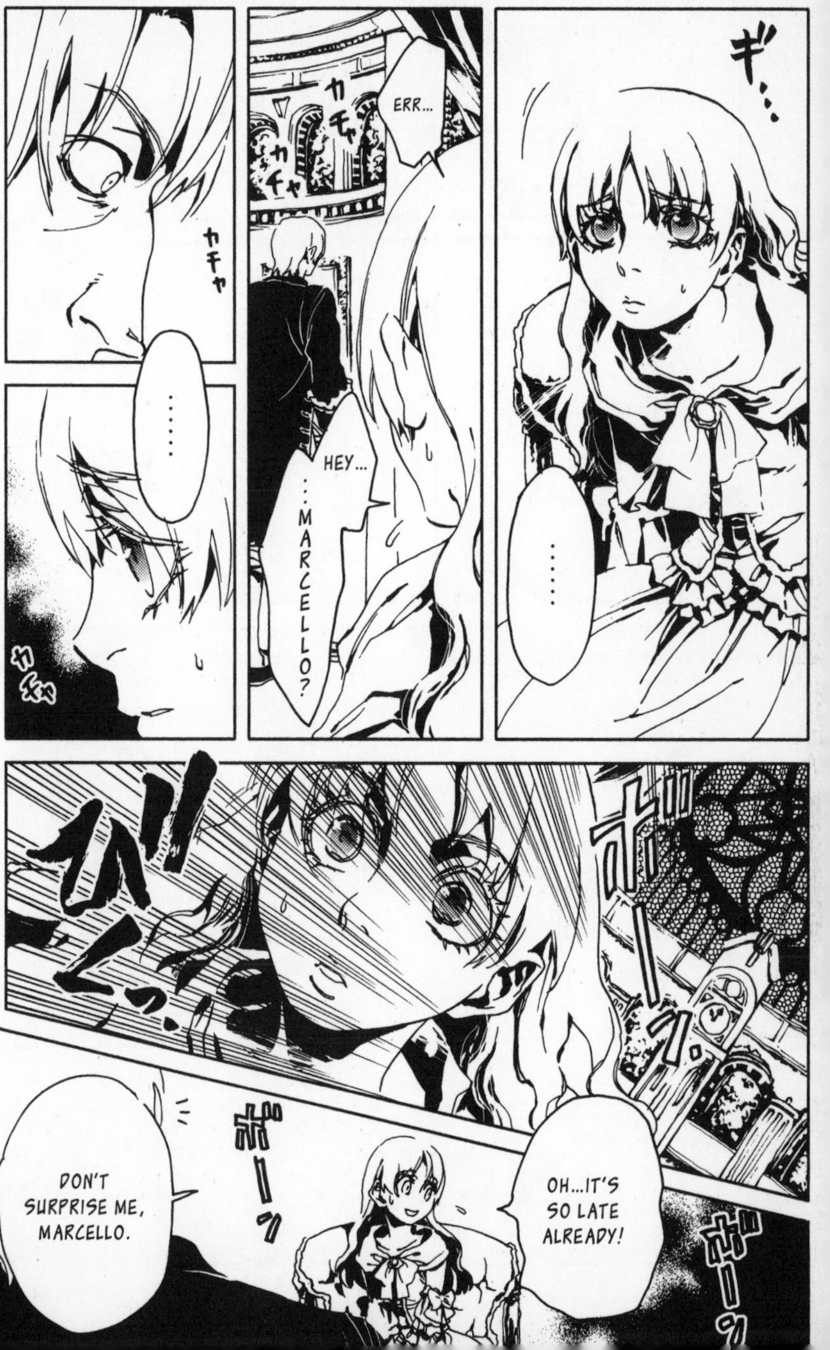
ギ…
……
ERR...
カチャ
カチャ
HEY...
...MARCELLO?
カチャ
……
ボーン。
ビクっ!!
OH...IT'S SO LATE ALREADY!
ボーッ
ボーッ
DON'T SURPRISE ME, MARCELLO.

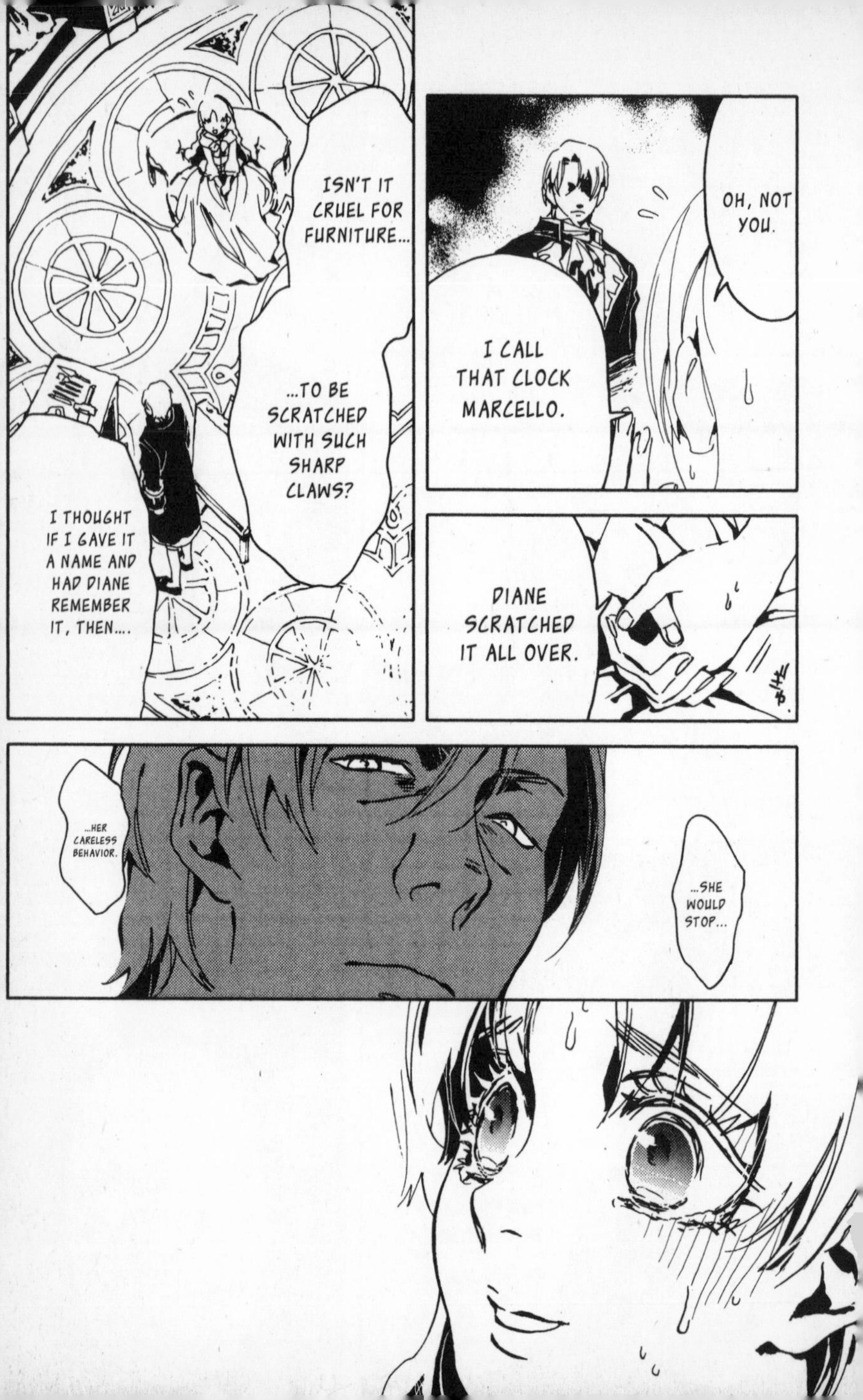
OH, NOT YOU.
I CALL THAT CLOCK MARCELLO.
DIANE SCRATCHED IT ALL OVER.
ISN'T IT CRUEL FOR FURNITURE...
...TO BE SCRATCHED WITH SUCH SHARP CLAWS?
I THOUGHT IF I GAVE IT A NAME AND HAD DIANE REMEMBER IT, THEN....
...SHE WOULD STOP...
...HER CARELESS BEHAVIOR.

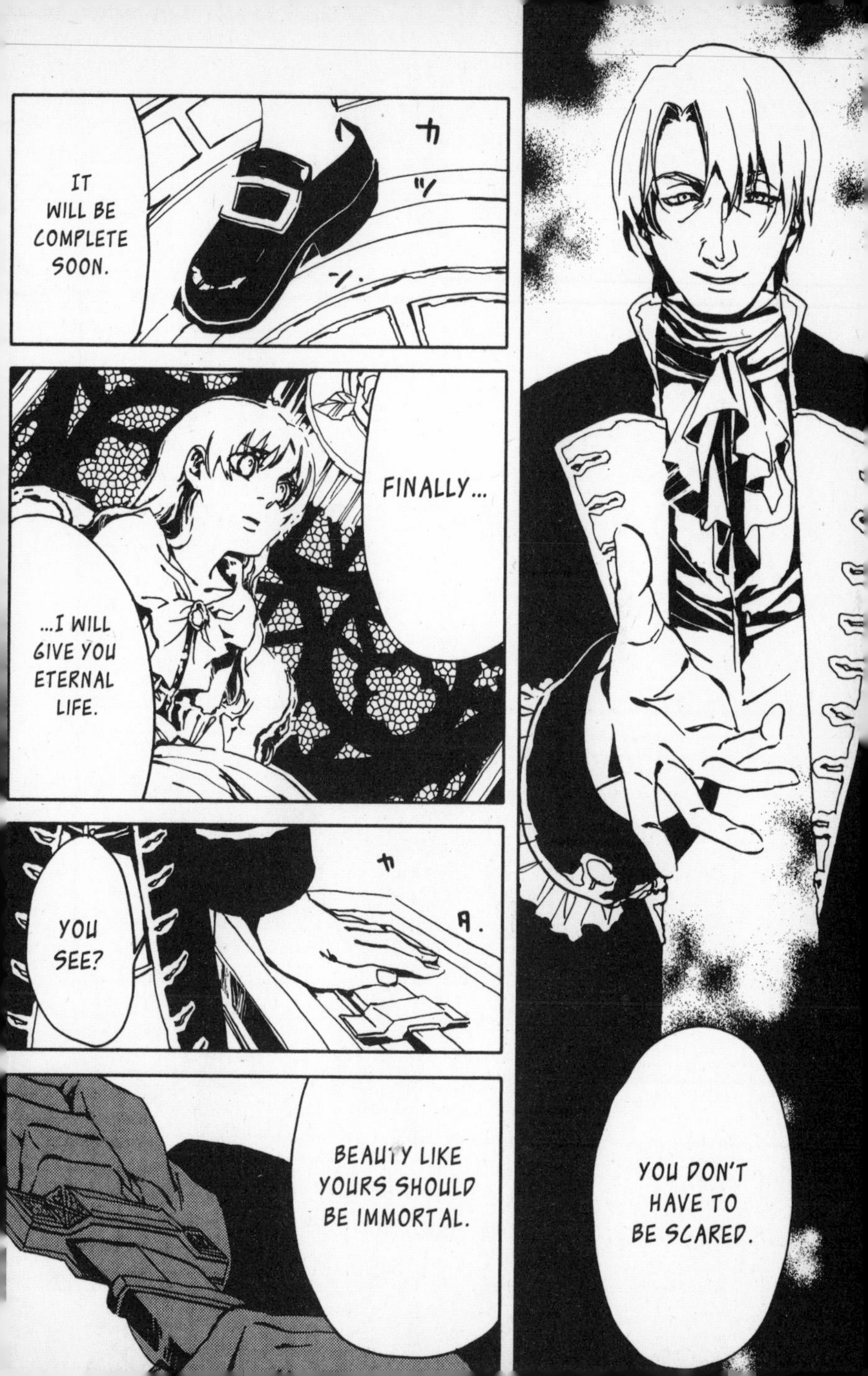
YOU DON'T HAVE TO BE SCARED.
IT WILL BE COMPLETE SOON.
カツ
FINALLY...
...I WILL GIVE YOU ETERNAL LIFE.
カタ
YOU SEE?
BEAUTY LIKE YOURS SHOULD BE IMMORTAL.

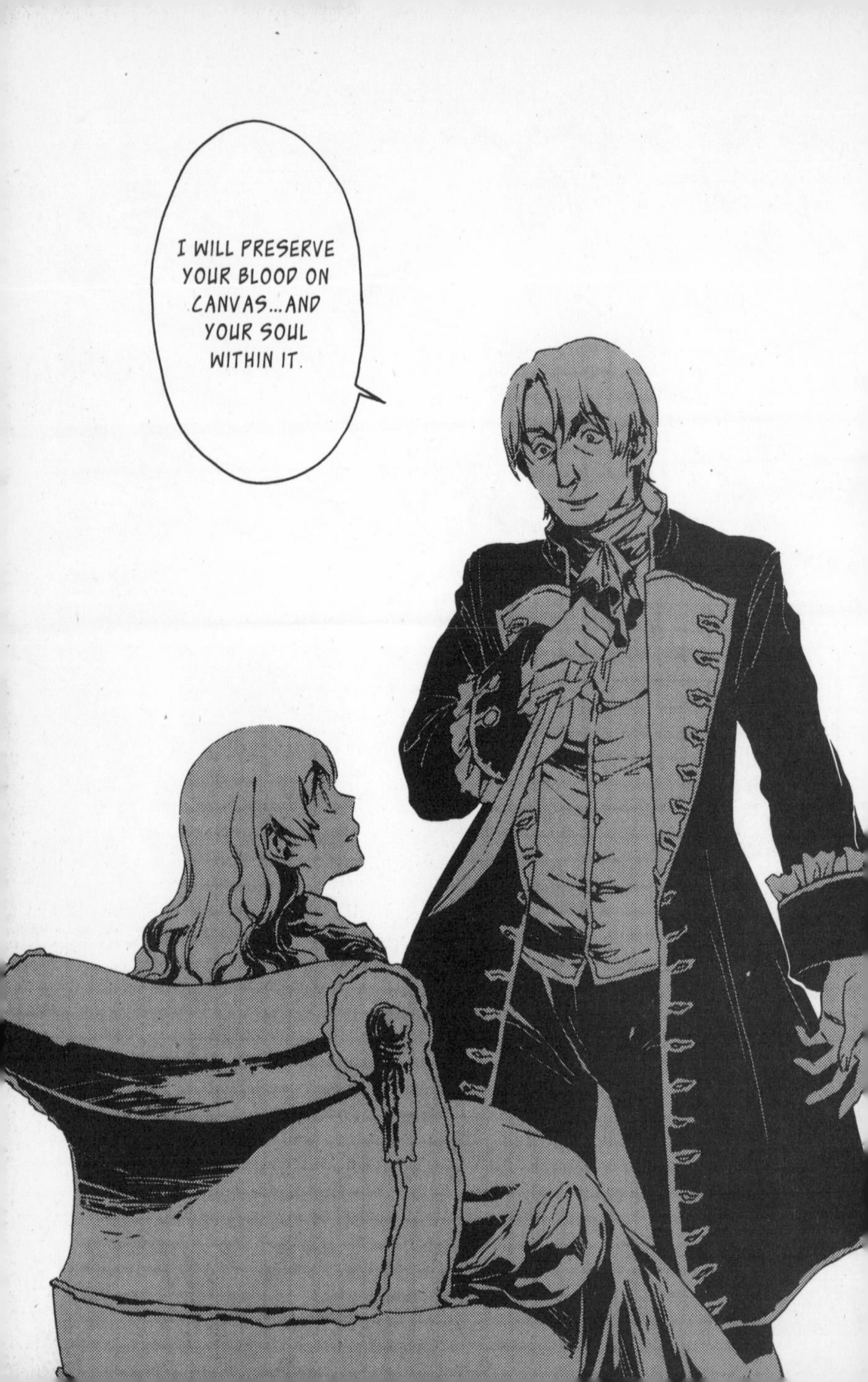
I WILL PRESERVE YOUR BLOOD ON CANVAS...AND YOUR SOUL WITHIN IT.

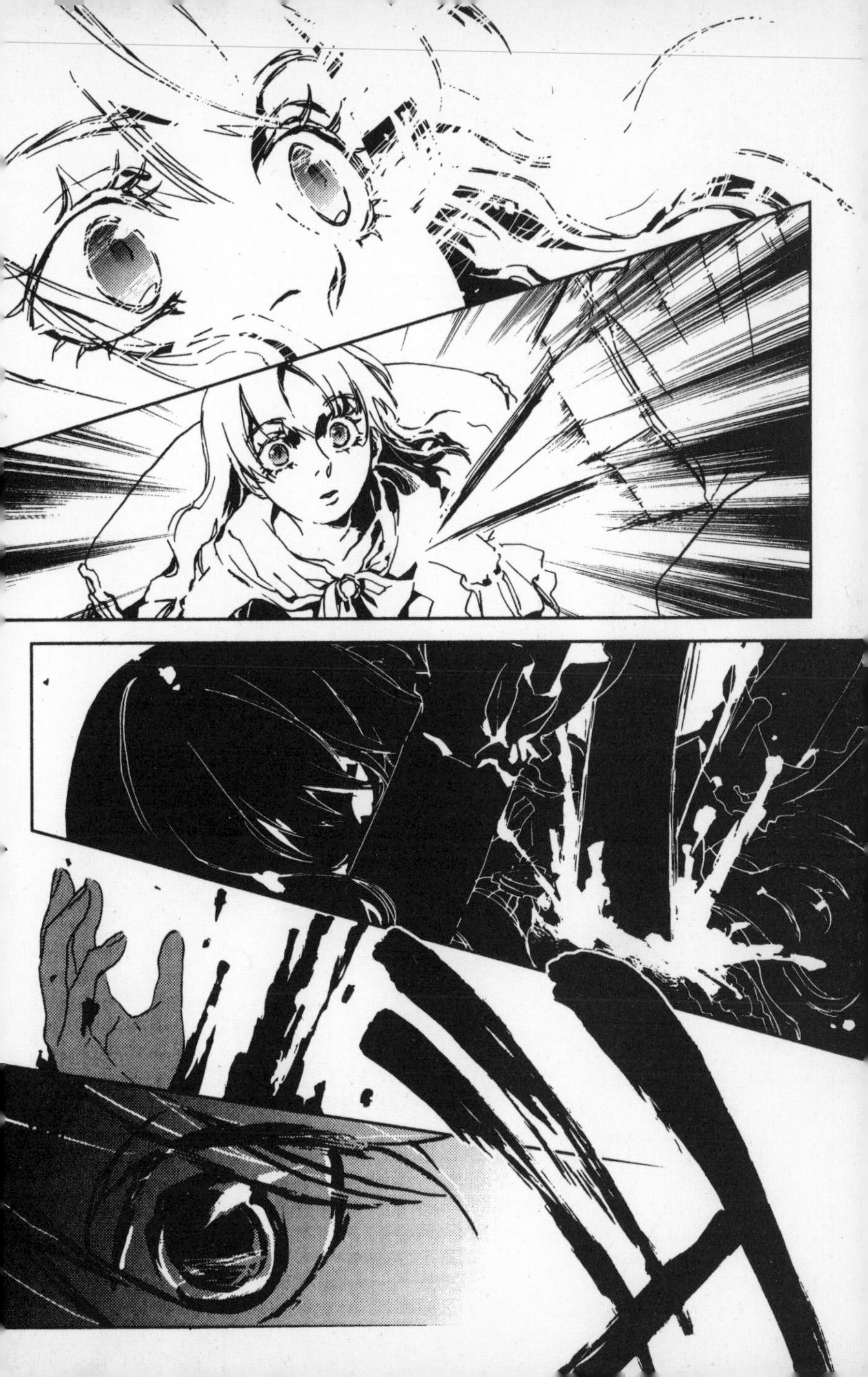

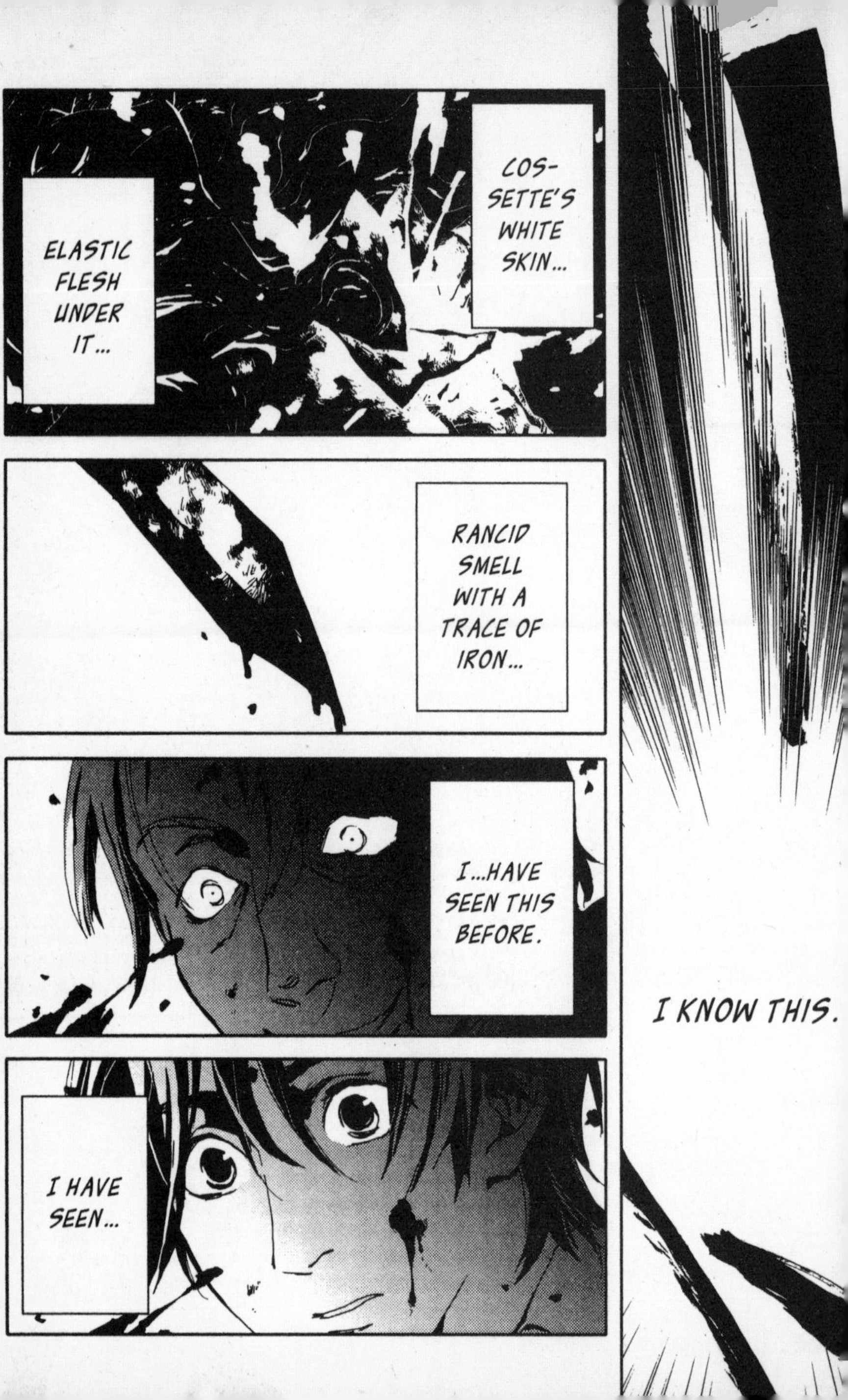
COS-
SETTE'S
WHITE
SKIN...
ELASTIC
FLESH
UNDER
IT...
RANCID
SMELL
WITH A
TRACE OF
IRON...
I...HAVE
SEEN THIS
BEFORE.
I HAVE
SEEN...
I KNOW THIS.

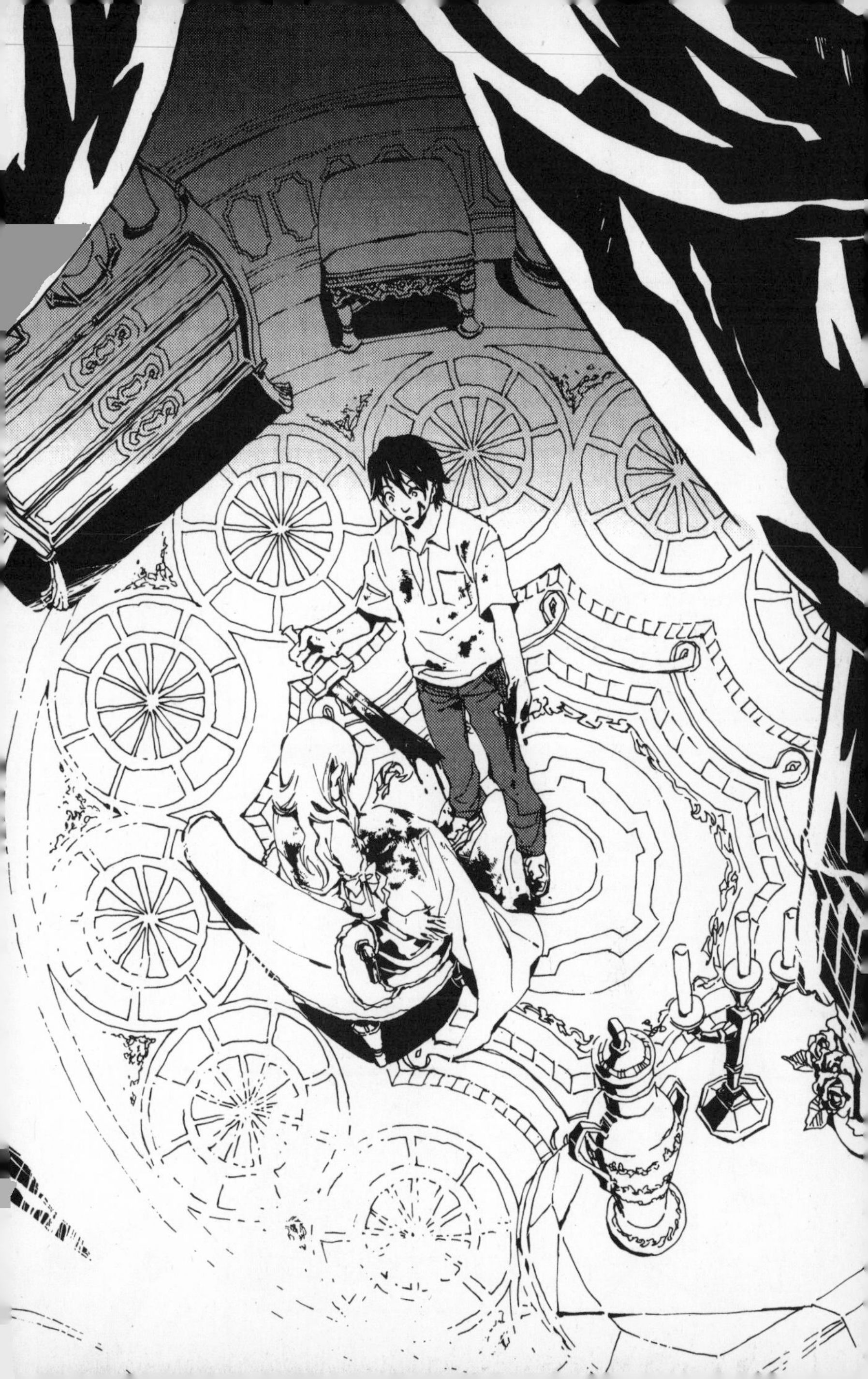

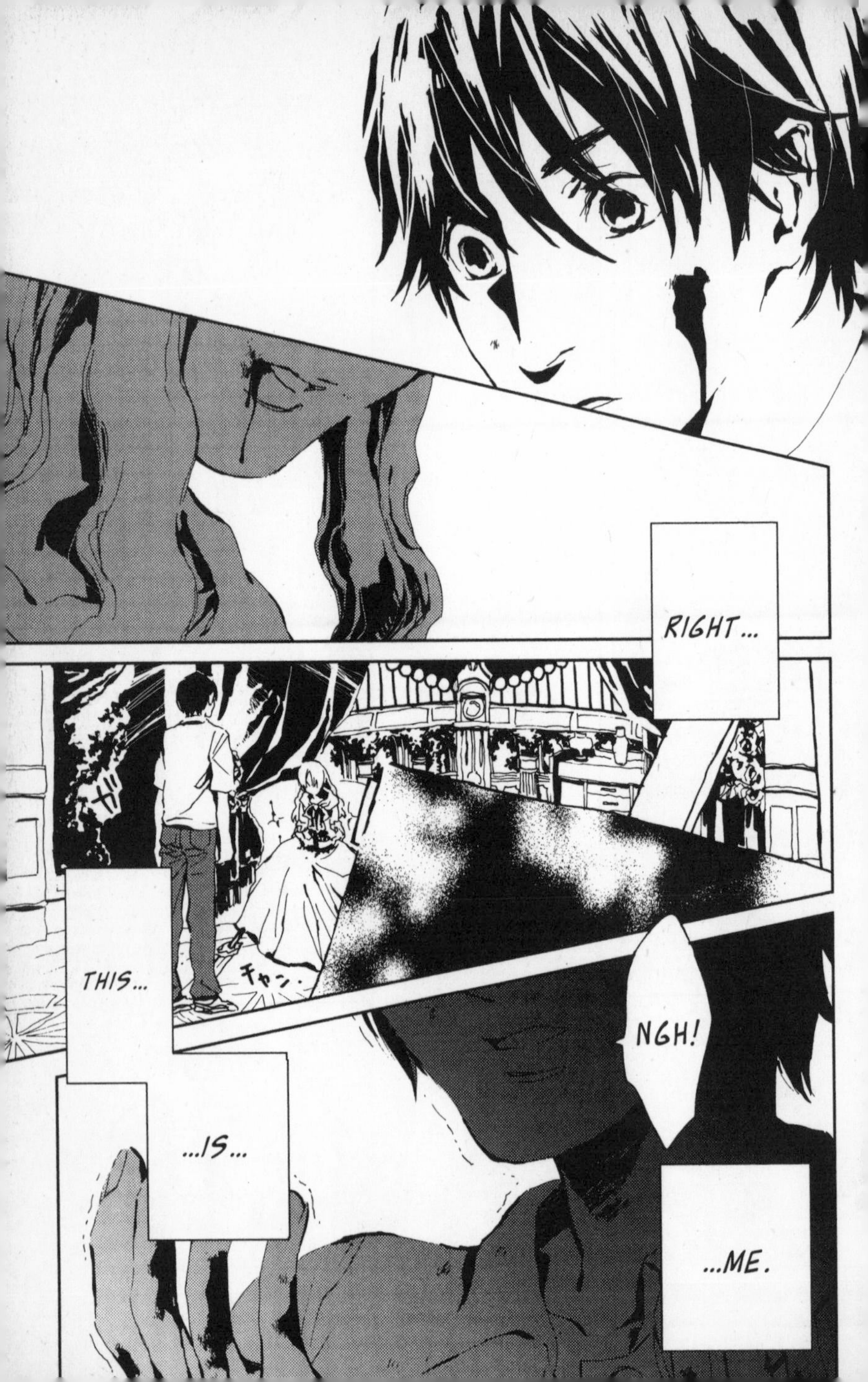
RIGHT...
チャン
THIS...
...IS...
NGH!
...ME.

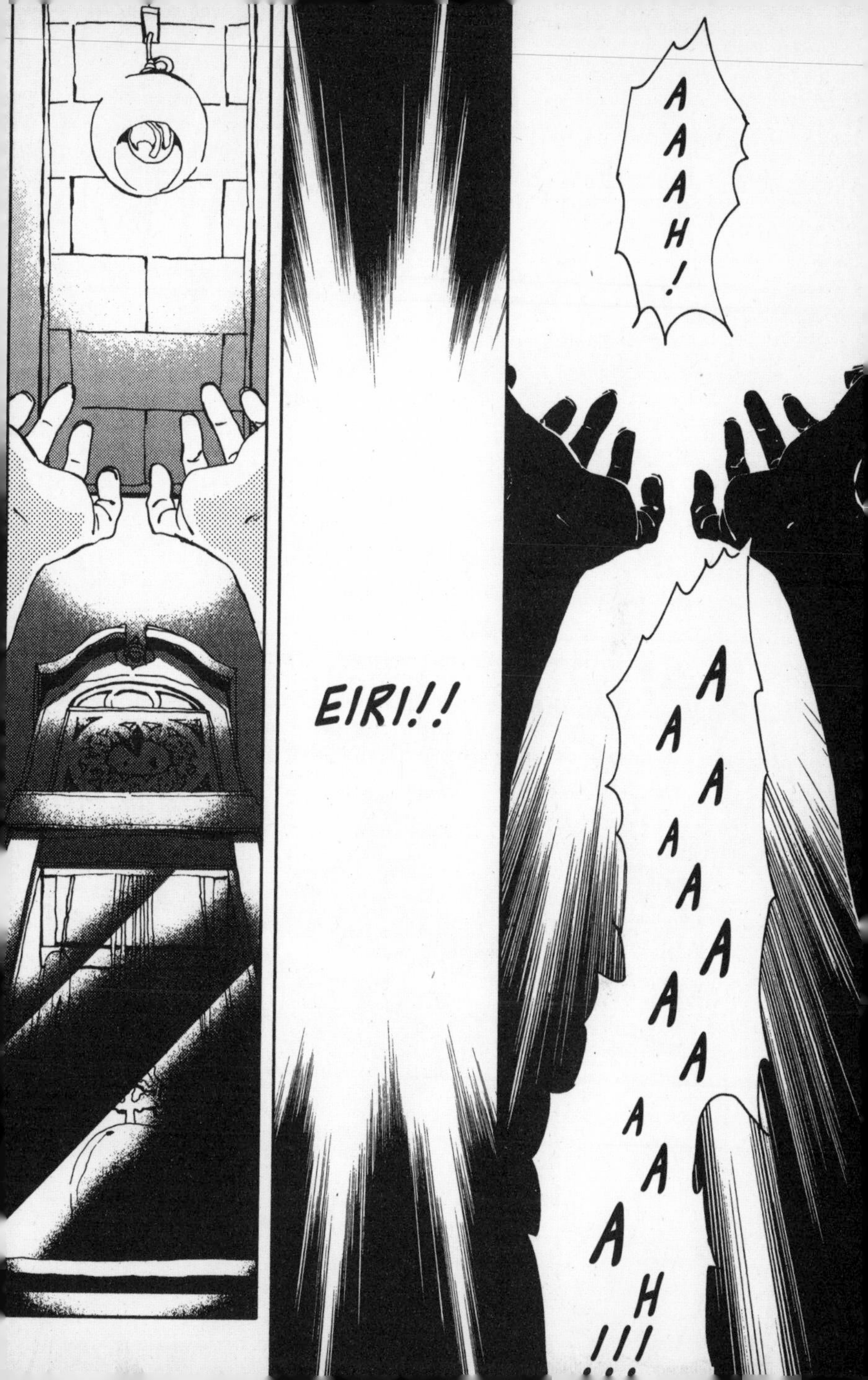
AAAAH!
AAAAAAAAAAAH!!!
EIRI!!

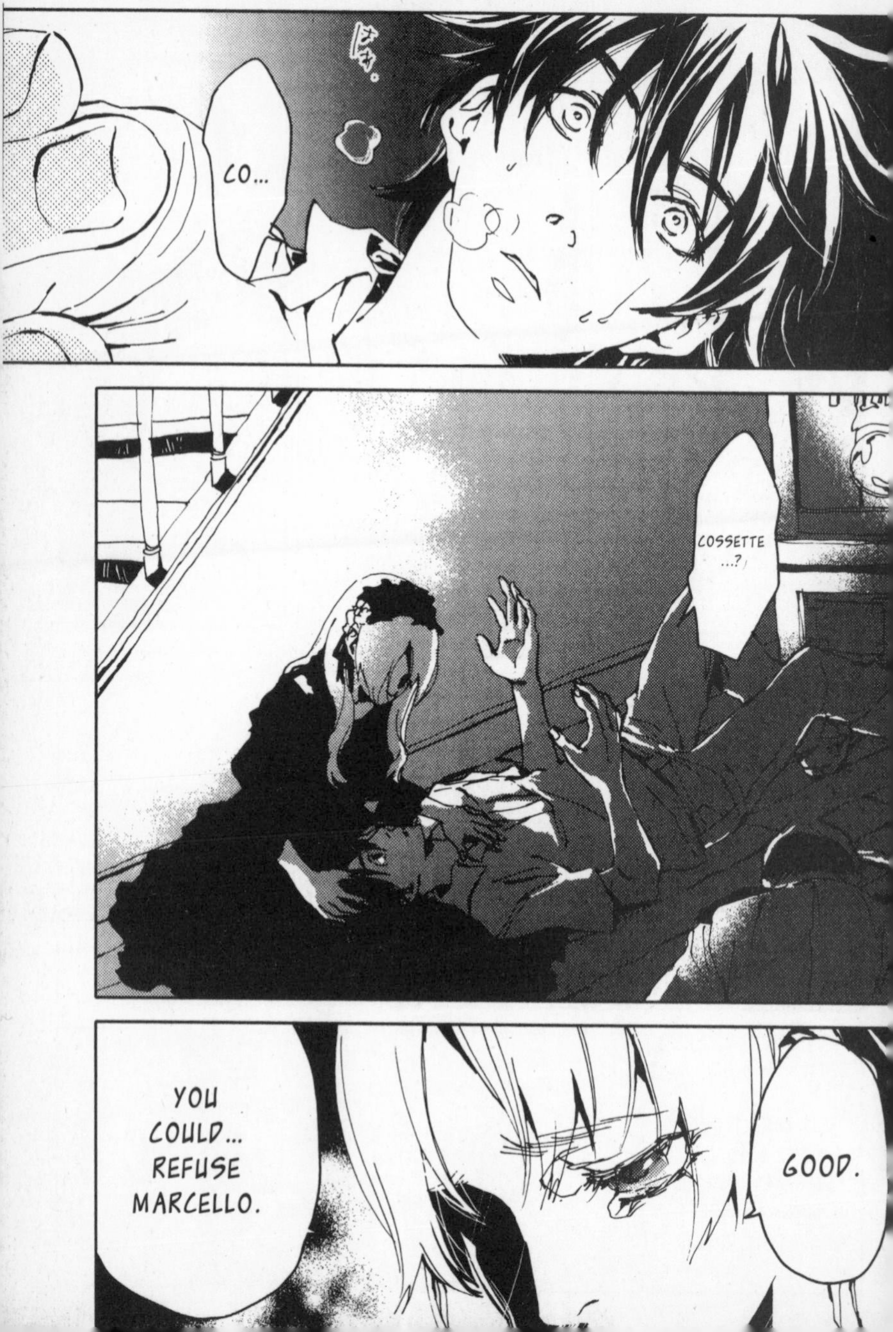
CO...
COSSETTE ...?
GOOD.
YOU COULD... REFUSE MARCELLO.

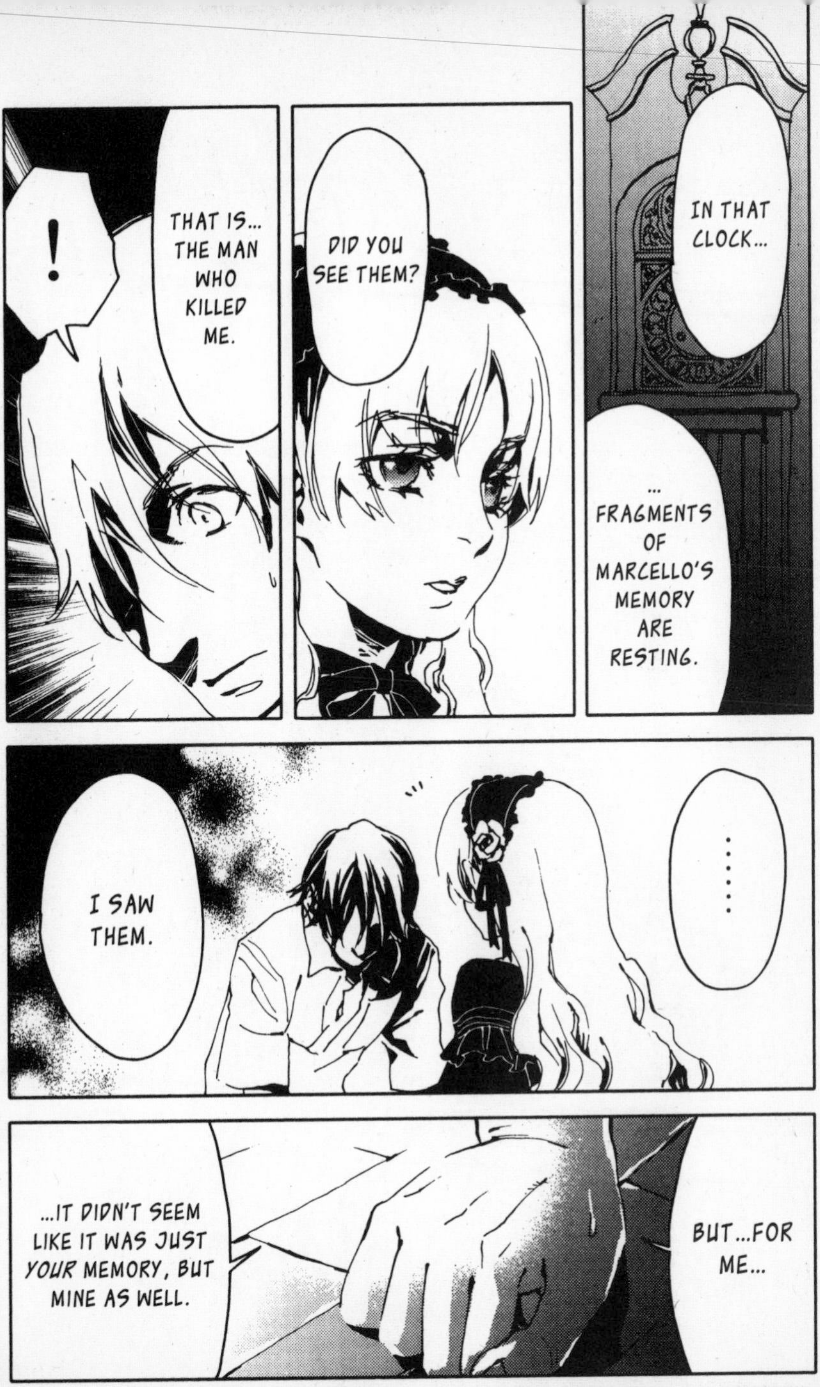
IN THAT CLOCK...
...FRAGMENTS OF MARCELLO'S MEMORY ARE RESTING.
DID YOU SEE THEM?
THAT IS... THE MAN WHO KILLED ME.
!
......
I SAW THEM.
BUT...FOR ME...
...IT DIDN'T SEEM LIKE IT WAS JUST *YOUR* MEMORY, BUT MINE AS WELL.

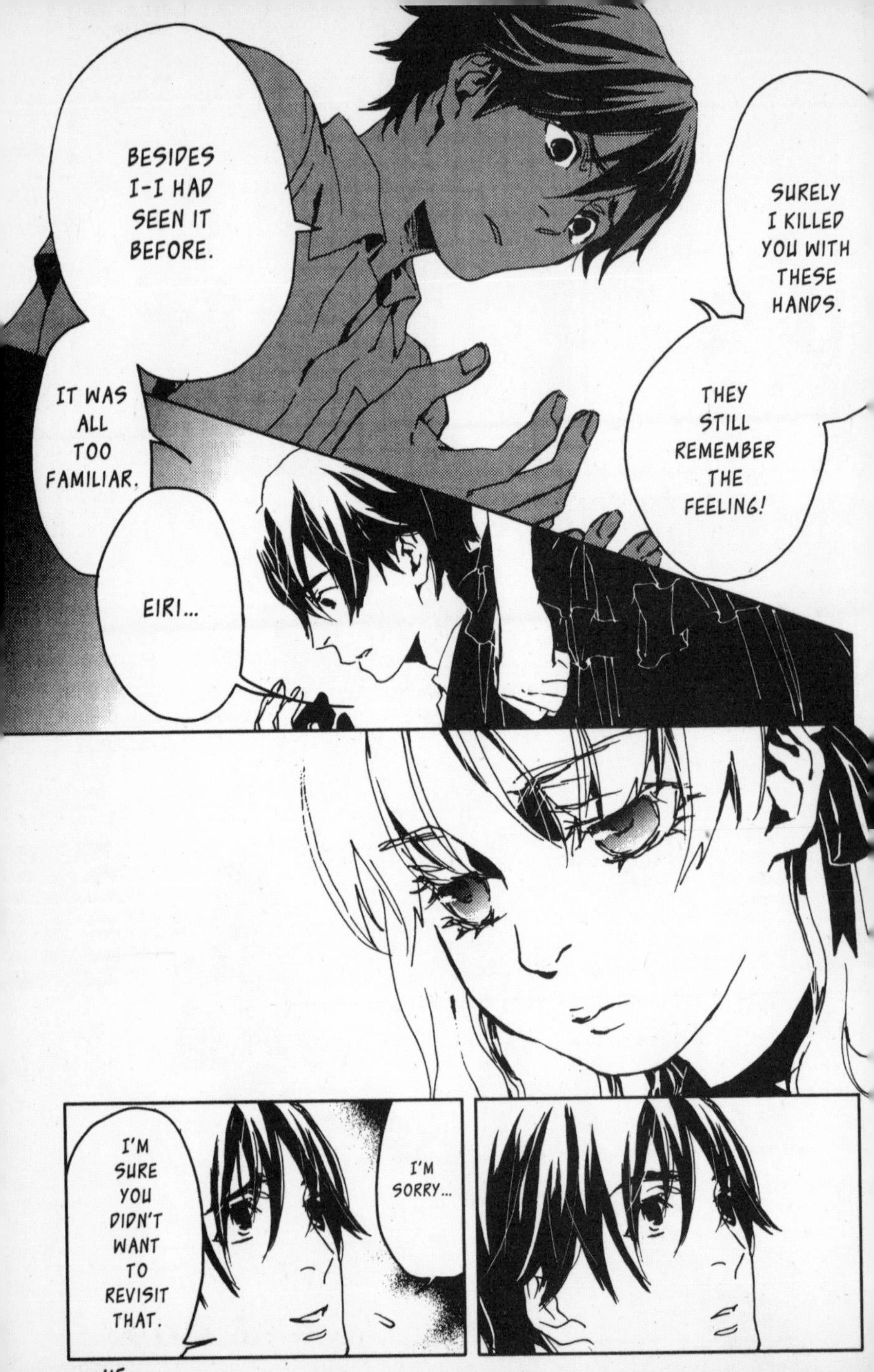
SURELY I KILLED YOU WITH THESE HANDS.
THEY STILL REMEMBER THE FEELING!
BESIDES I-I HAD SEEN IT BEFORE.
IT WAS ALL TOO FAMILIAR.
EIRI...
I'M SORRY...
I'M SURE YOU DIDN'T WANT TO REVISIT THAT.

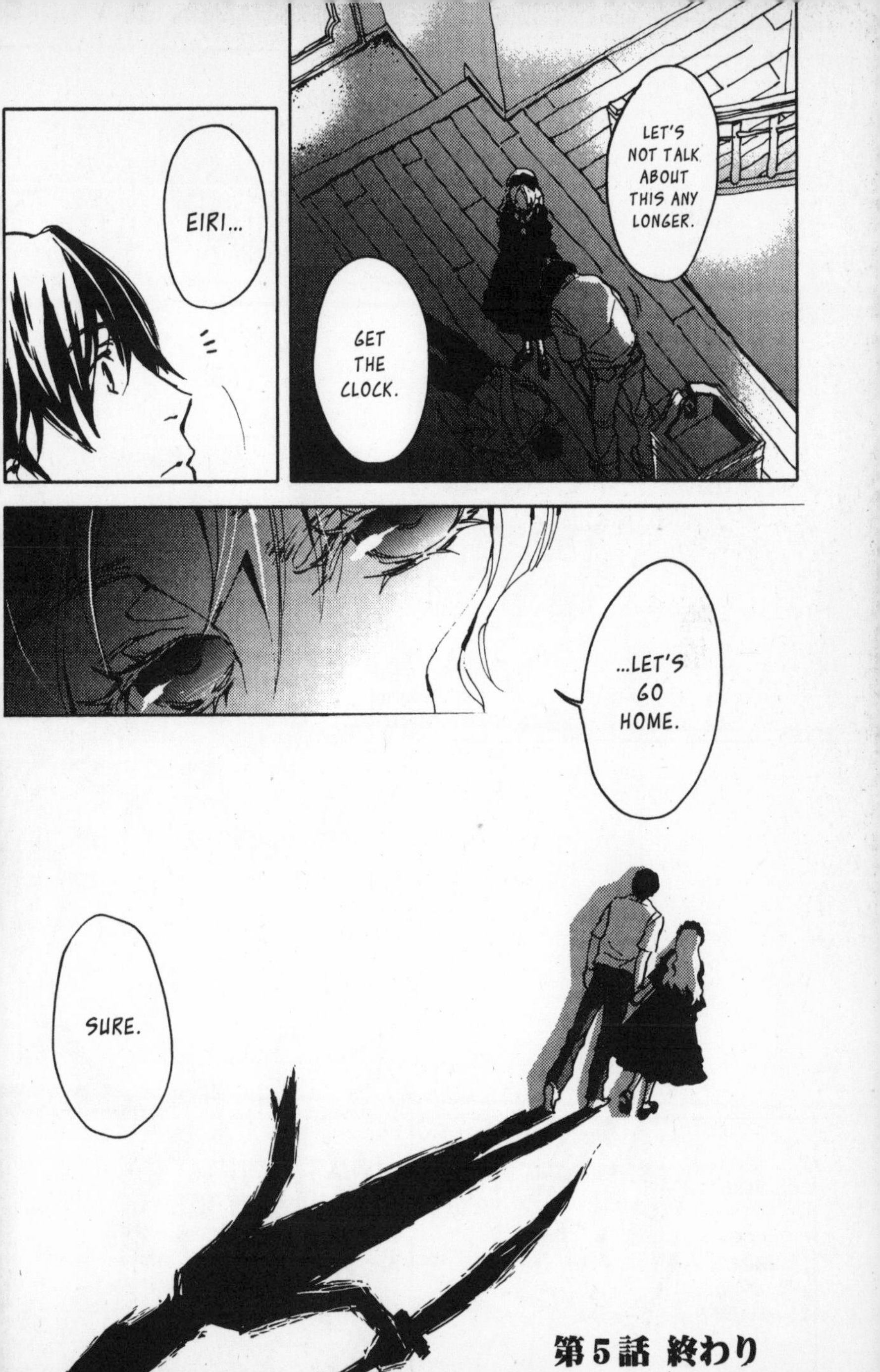
LET'S NOT TALK ABOUT THIS ANY LONGER.
GET THE CLOCK.
EIRI...
...LET'S GO HOME.
SURE.

第5話 終わり

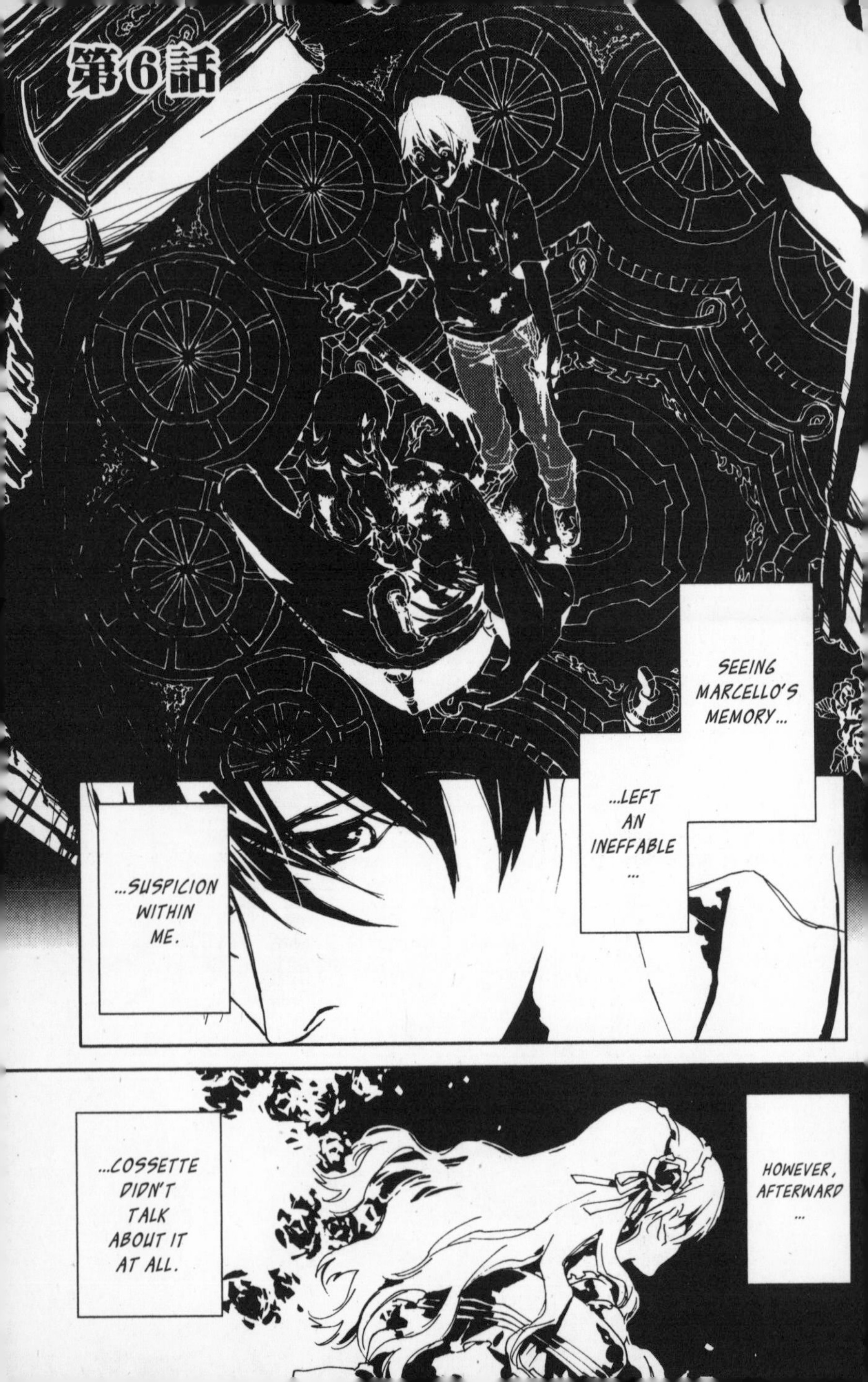
第6話
SEEING MARCELLO'S MEMORY...
...LEFT AN INEFFABLE ...
...SUSPICION WITHIN ME.
HOWEVER, AFTERWARD ...
...COSSETTE DIDN'T TALK ABOUT IT AT ALL.

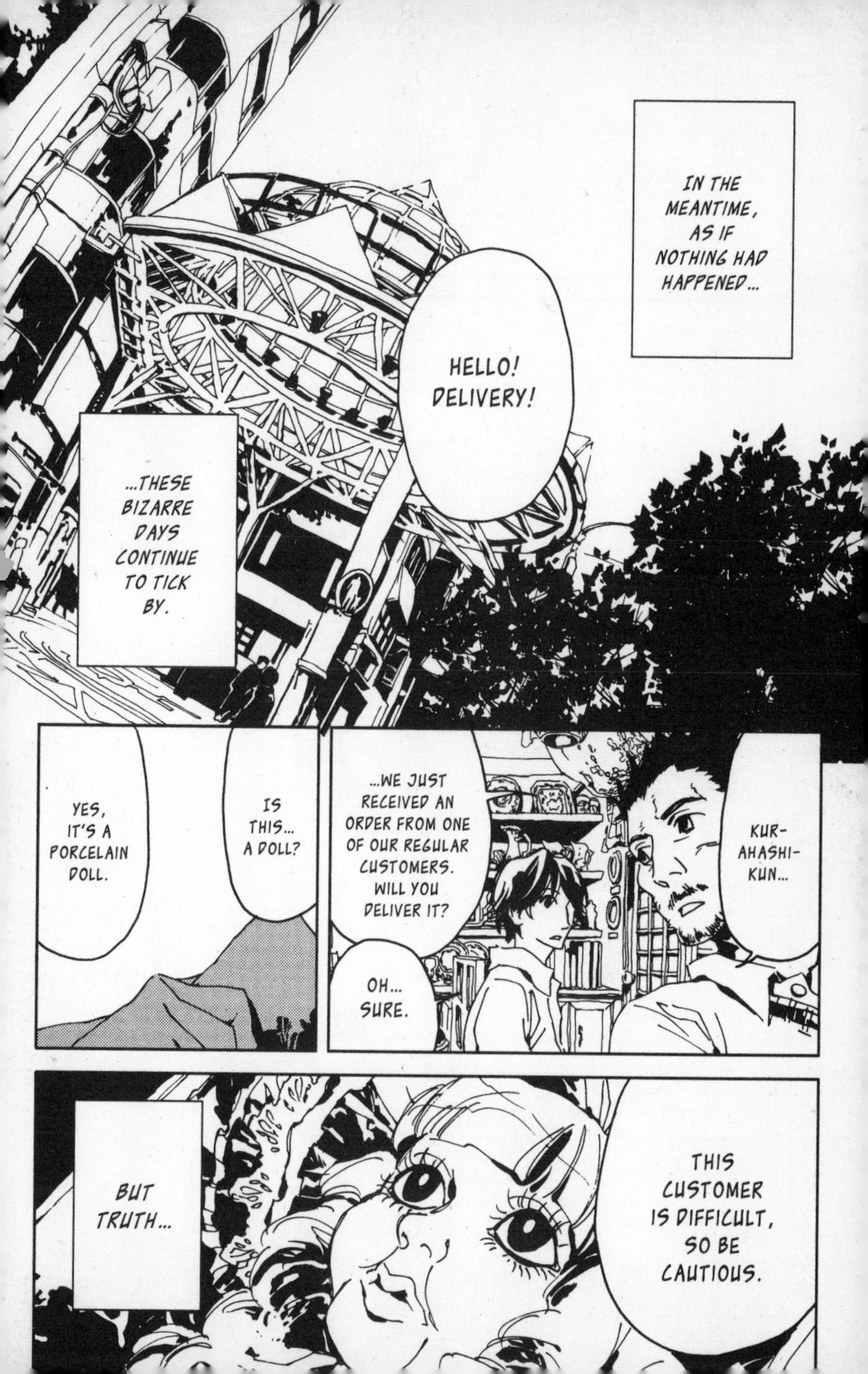
IN THE MEANTIME, AS IF NOTHING HAD HAPPENED...
HELLO! DELIVERY!
...THESE BIZARRE DAYS CONTINUE TO TICK BY.
KUR-AHASHI-KUN...
...WE JUST RECEIVED AN ORDER FROM ONE OF OUR REGULAR CUSTOMERS. WILL YOU DELIVER IT?
OH... SURE.
IS THIS... A DOLL?
YES, IT'S A PORCELAIN DOLL.
THIS CUSTOMER IS DIFFICULT, SO BE CAUTIOUS.
BUT TRUTH...

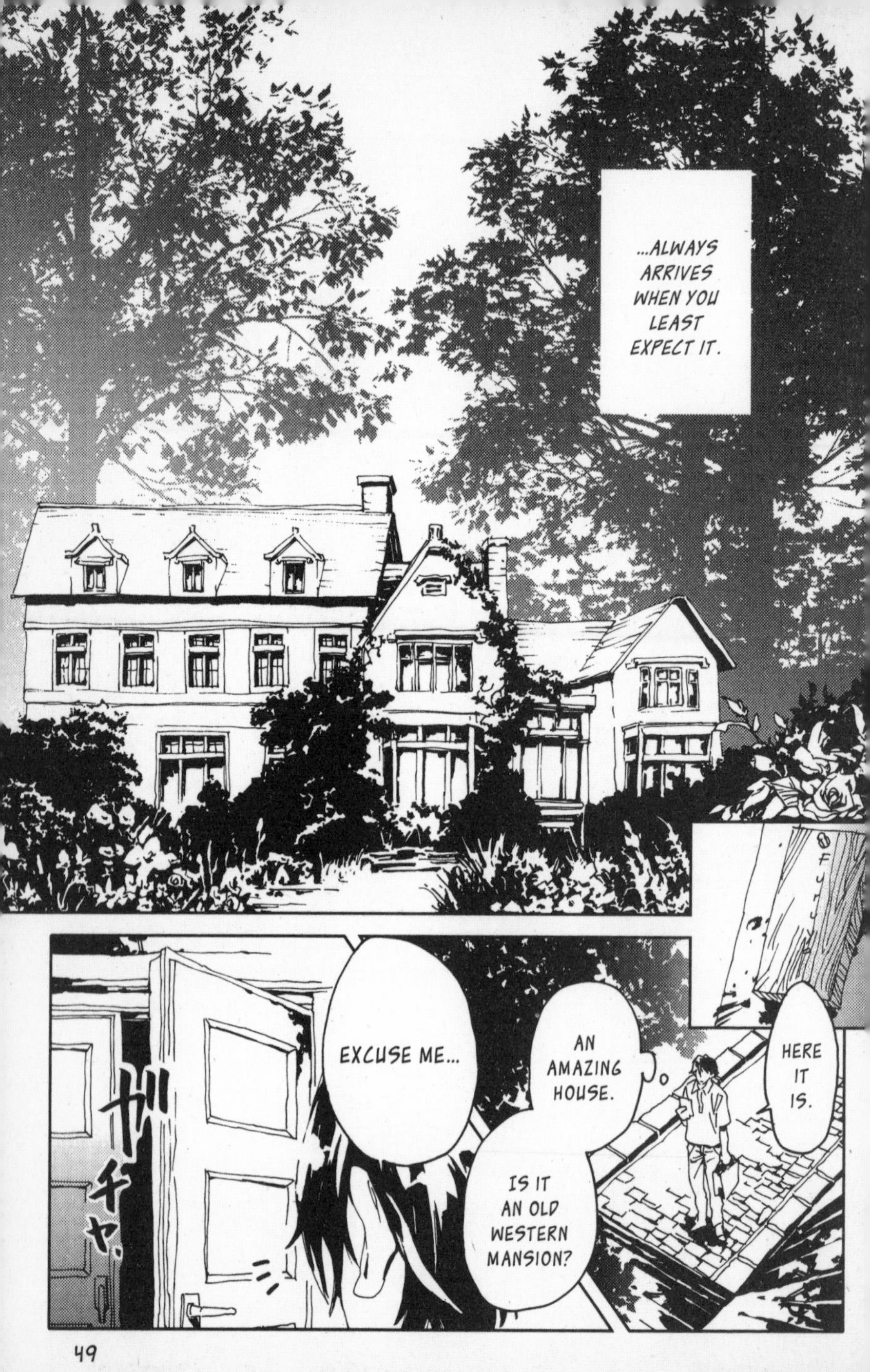
...ALWAYS ARRIVES WHEN YOU LEAST EXPECT IT.
HERE IT IS.
AN AMAZING HOUSE.
IS IT AN OLD WESTERN MANSION?
EXCUSE ME...
ガチャ

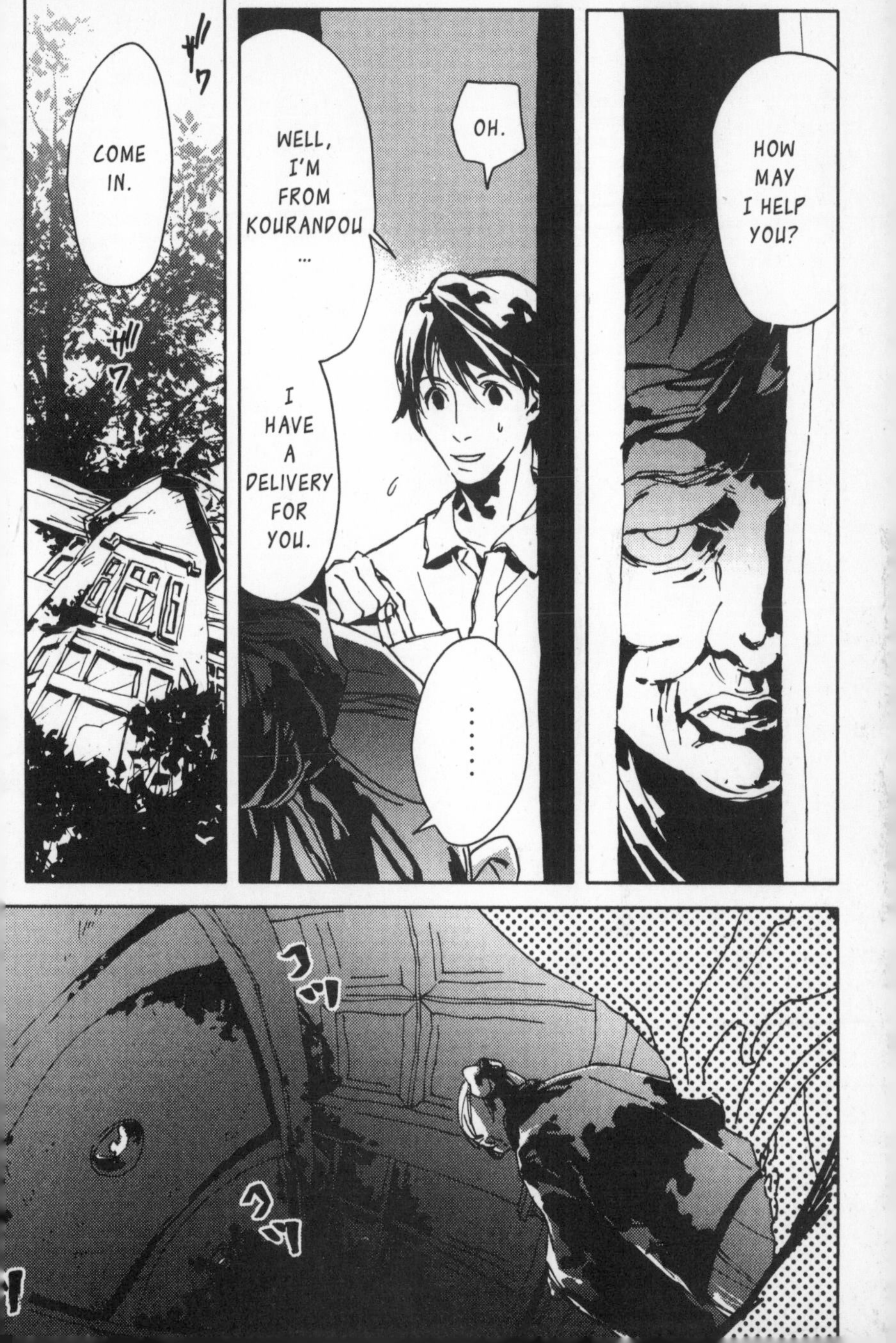
HOW MAY I HELP YOU?
OH.
WELL, I'M FROM KOURANDOU ...
I HAVE A DELIVERY FOR YOU.
......
COME IN.

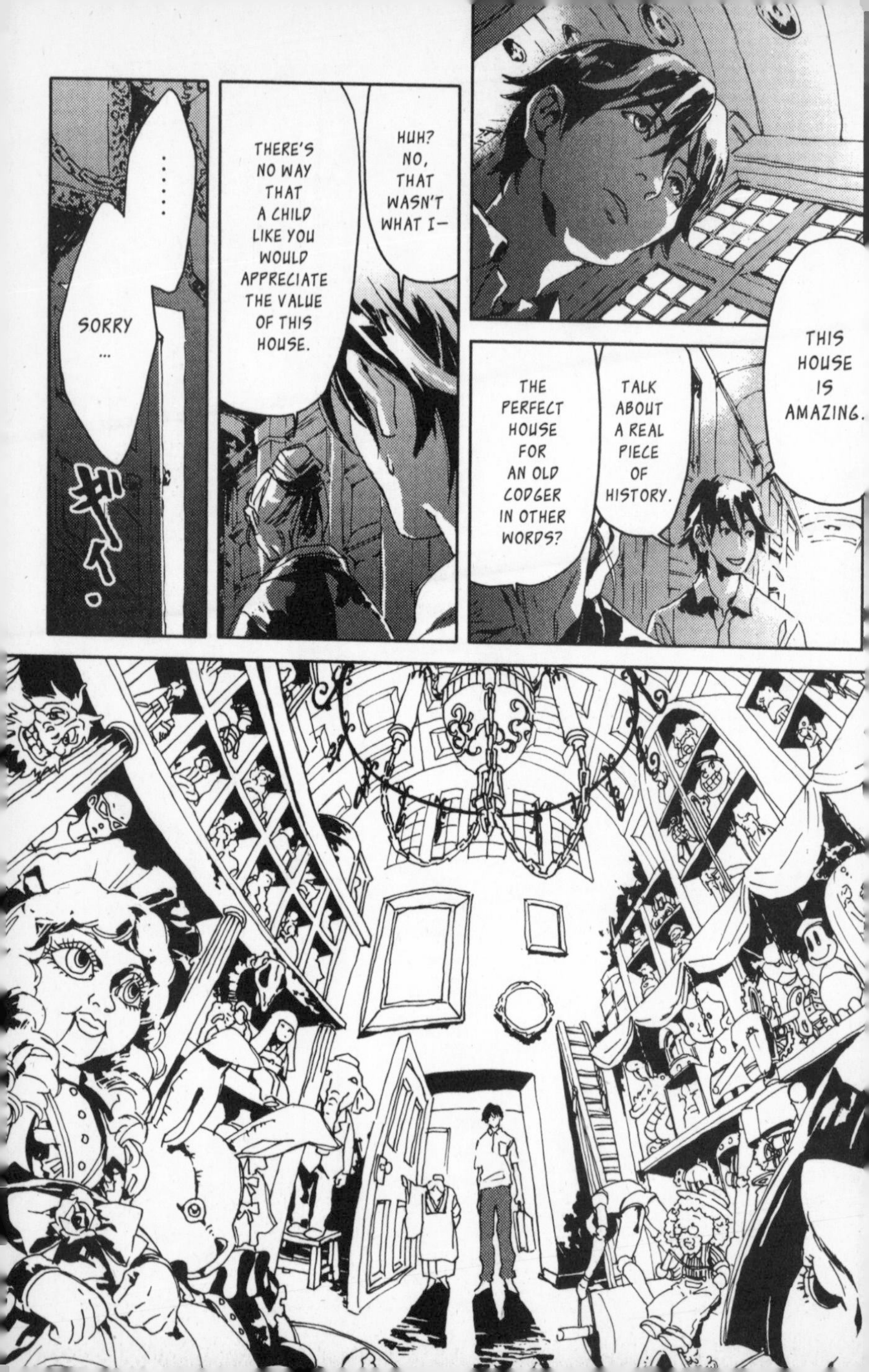
THIS HOUSE IS AMAZING.
TALK ABOUT A REAL PIECE OF HISTORY.
THE PERFECT HOUSE FOR AN OLD CODGER IN OTHER WORDS?
HUH? NO, THAT WASN'T WHAT I—
THERE'S NO WAY THAT A CHILD LIKE YOU WOULD APPRECIATE THE VALUE OF THIS HOUSE.
......
SORRY ...
ギィ

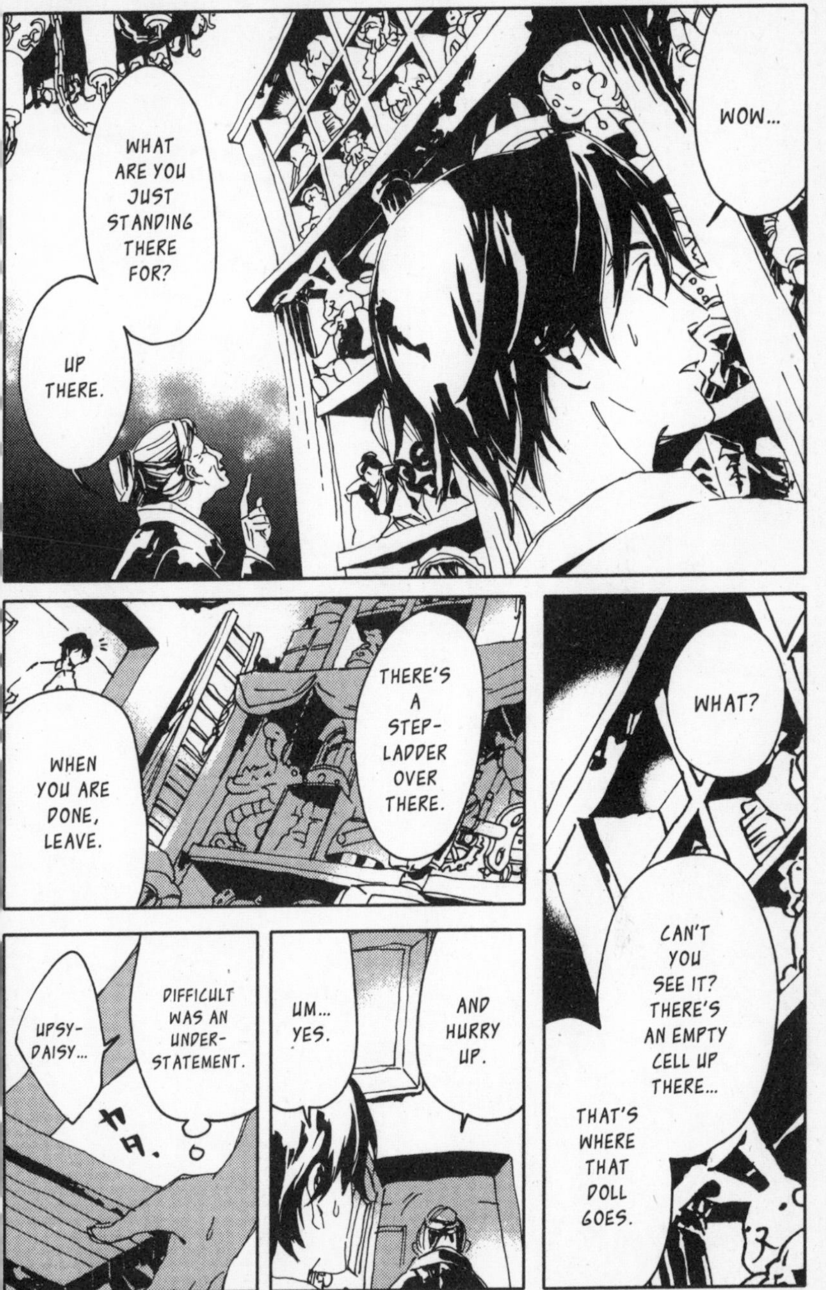
WOW...
WHAT ARE YOU JUST STANDING THERE FOR?
UP THERE.
WHAT?
CAN'T YOU SEE IT? THERE'S AN EMPTY CELL UP THERE...
THAT'S WHERE THAT DOLL GOES.
THERE'S A STEP-LADDER OVER THERE.
WHEN YOU ARE DONE, LEAVE.
AND HURRY UP.
UM... YES.
DIFFICULT WAS AN UNDER-STATEMENT.
UPSY-DAISY...

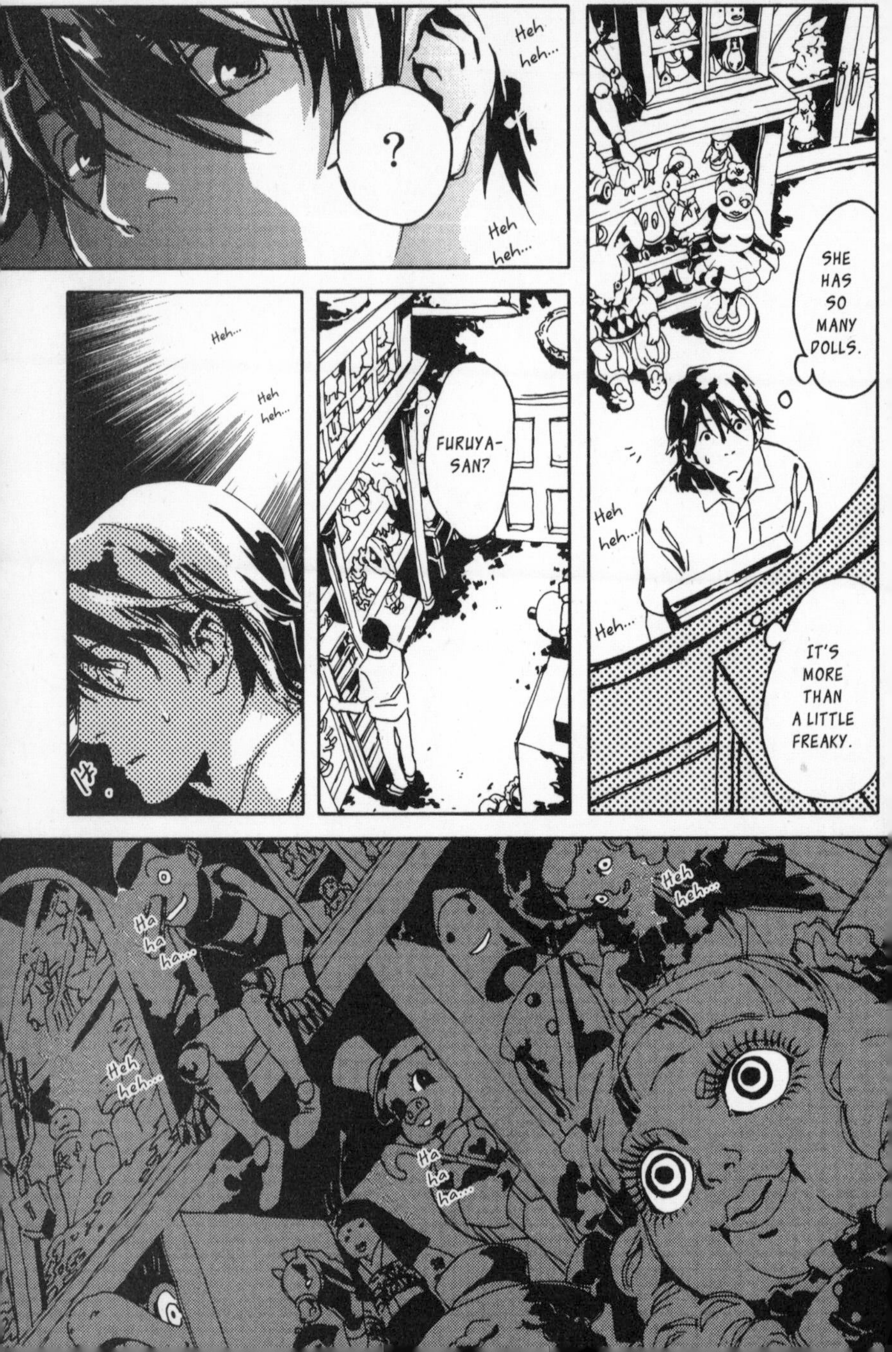
SHE HAS SO MANY DOLLS.
Heh heh...
Heh...
IT'S MORE THAN A LITTLE FREAKY.
Heh heh...
?
Heh heh...
FURUYA-SAN?
Heh...
Heh heh...
Heh heh...
Ha ha ha...
Ha ha ha...
Heh heh...

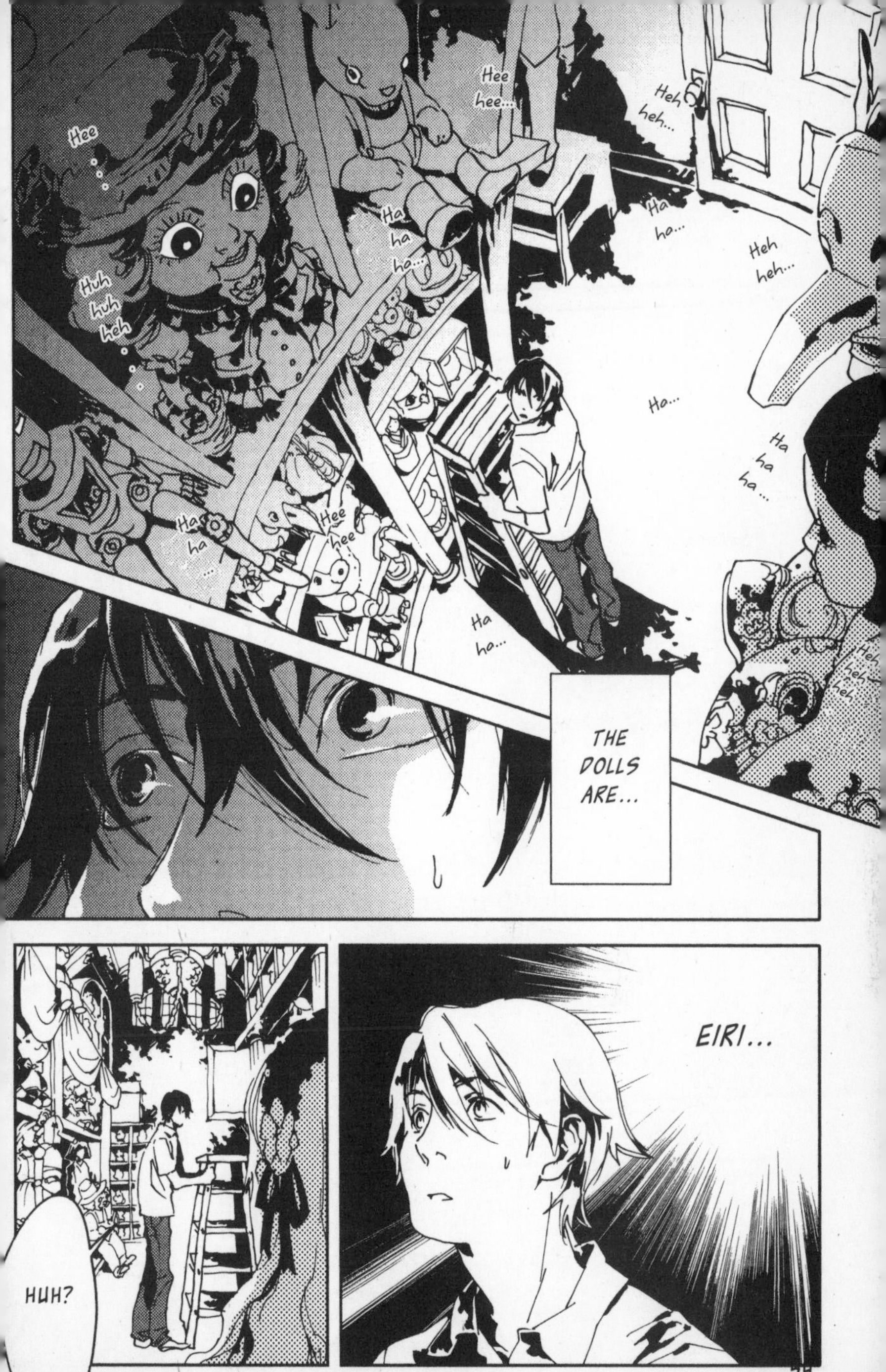
Heh heh...
Hee hee...
Ha ha...
Heh heh...
Ha...
Ha ha ha...
Heh heh heh
Ha ha...
Hee...
Ha ha ha...
Huh huh heh
Hee hee
Ha ha...
THE DOLLS ARE...
EIRI...
HUH?

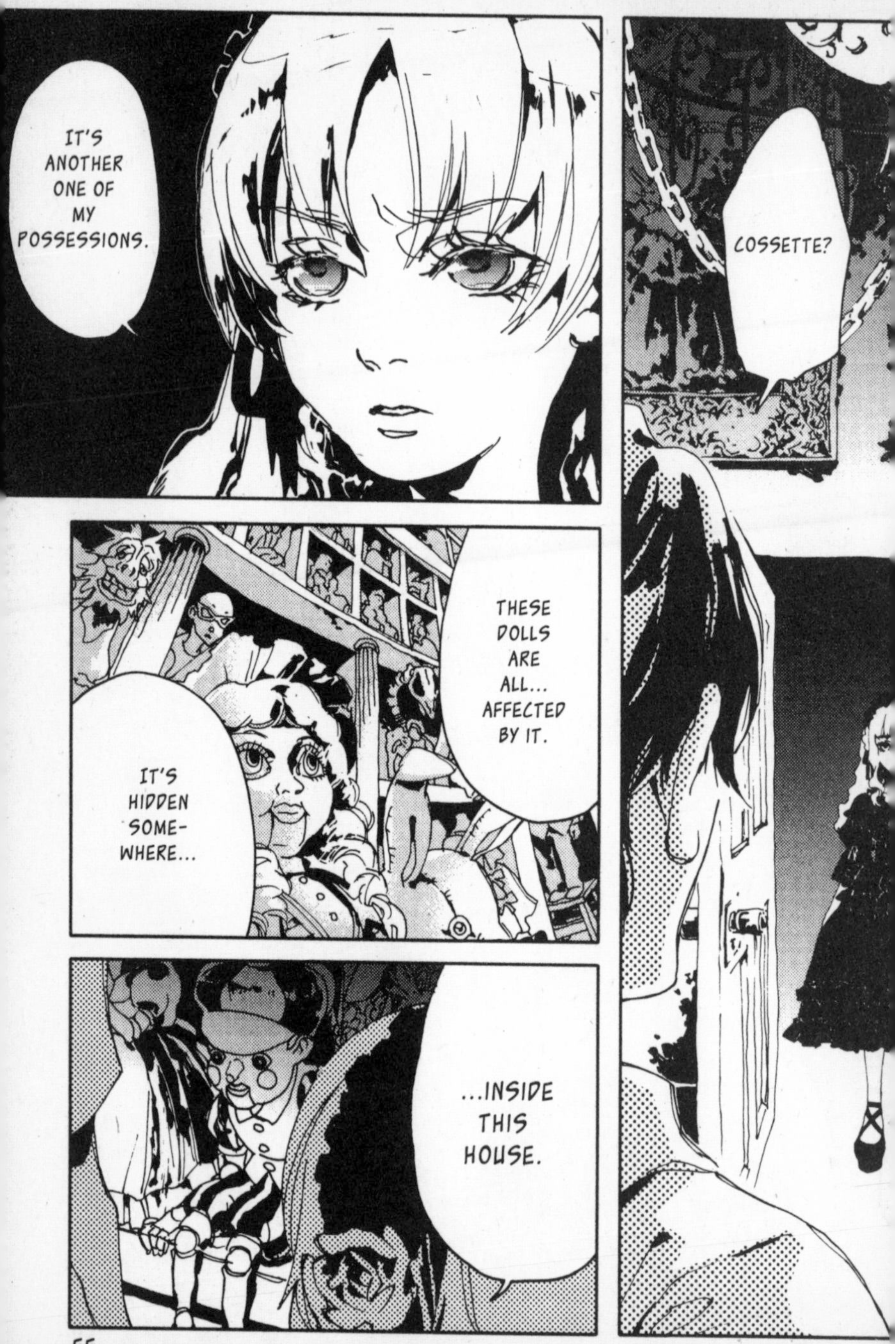
COSSETTE?
IT'S ANOTHER ONE OF MY POSSESSIONS.
THESE DOLLS ARE ALL... AFFECTED BY IT.
IT'S HIDDEN SOMEWHERE...
...INSIDE THIS HOUSE.

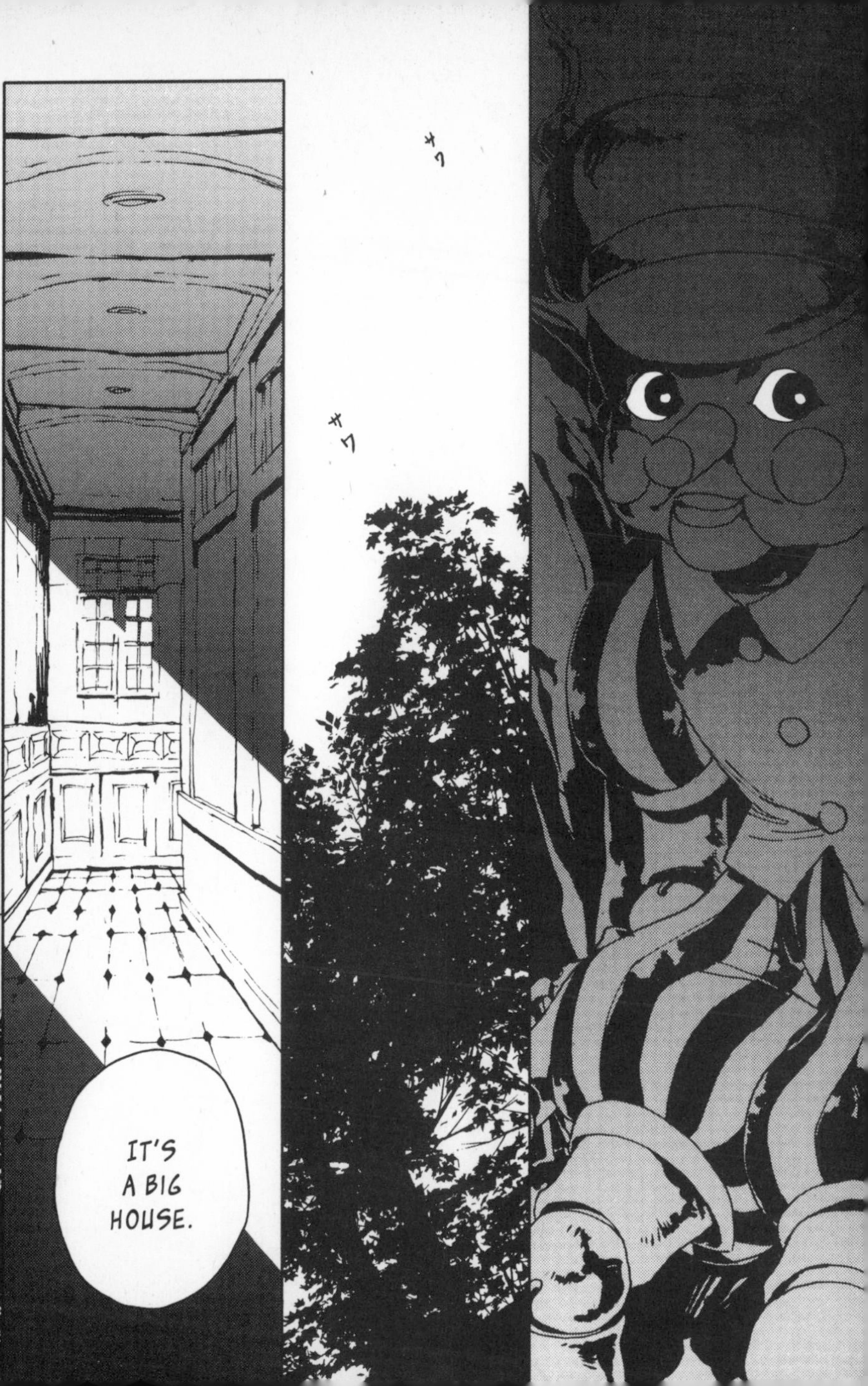
IT'S A BIG HOUSE.

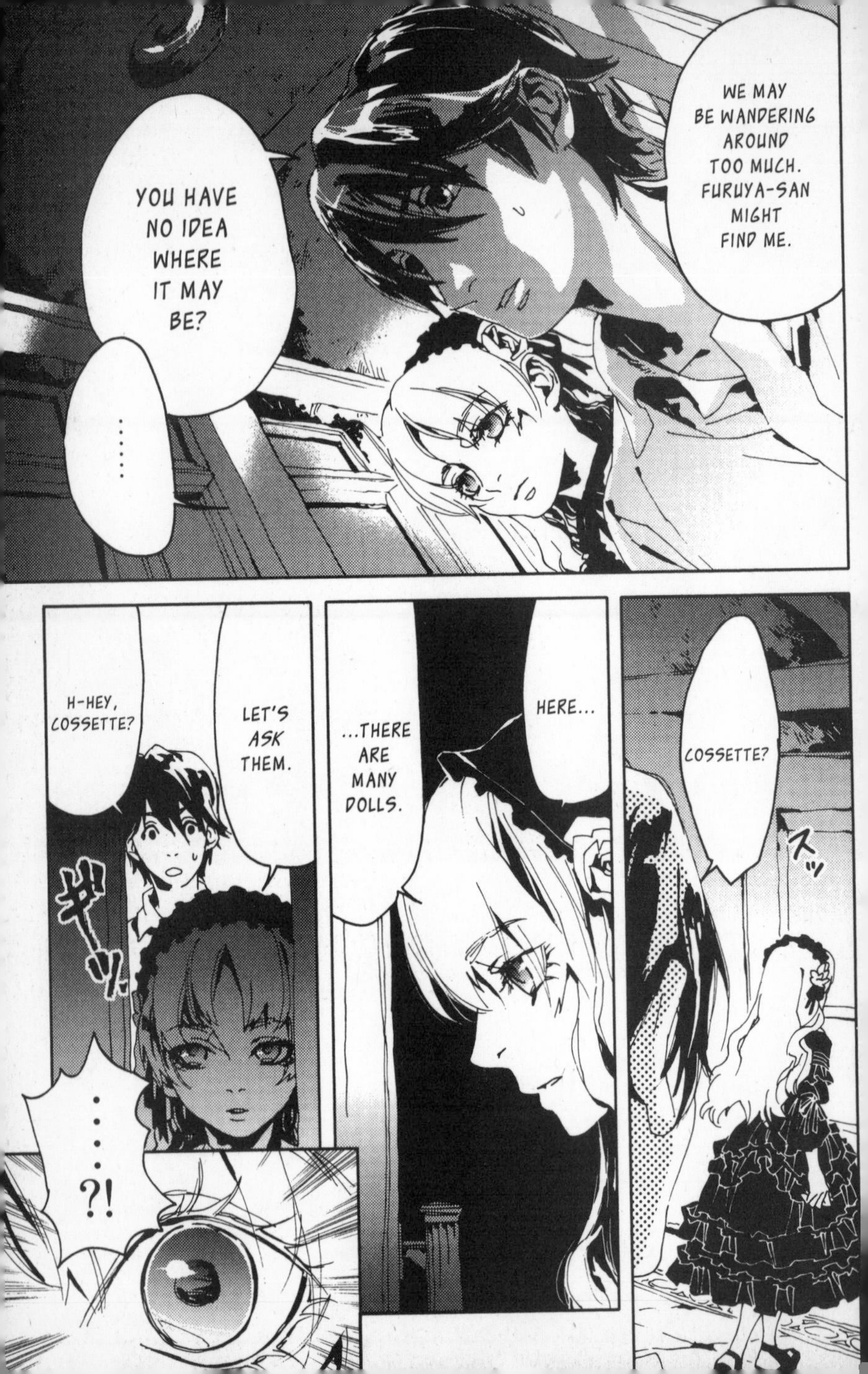
WE MAY BE WANDERING AROUND TOO MUCH. FURUYA-SAN MIGHT FIND ME.
YOU HAVE NO IDEA WHERE IT MAY BE?
......
COSSETTE?
スッ
HERE...
...THERE ARE MANY DOLLS.
LET'S ASK THEM.
H-HEY, COSSETTE?
......
?!

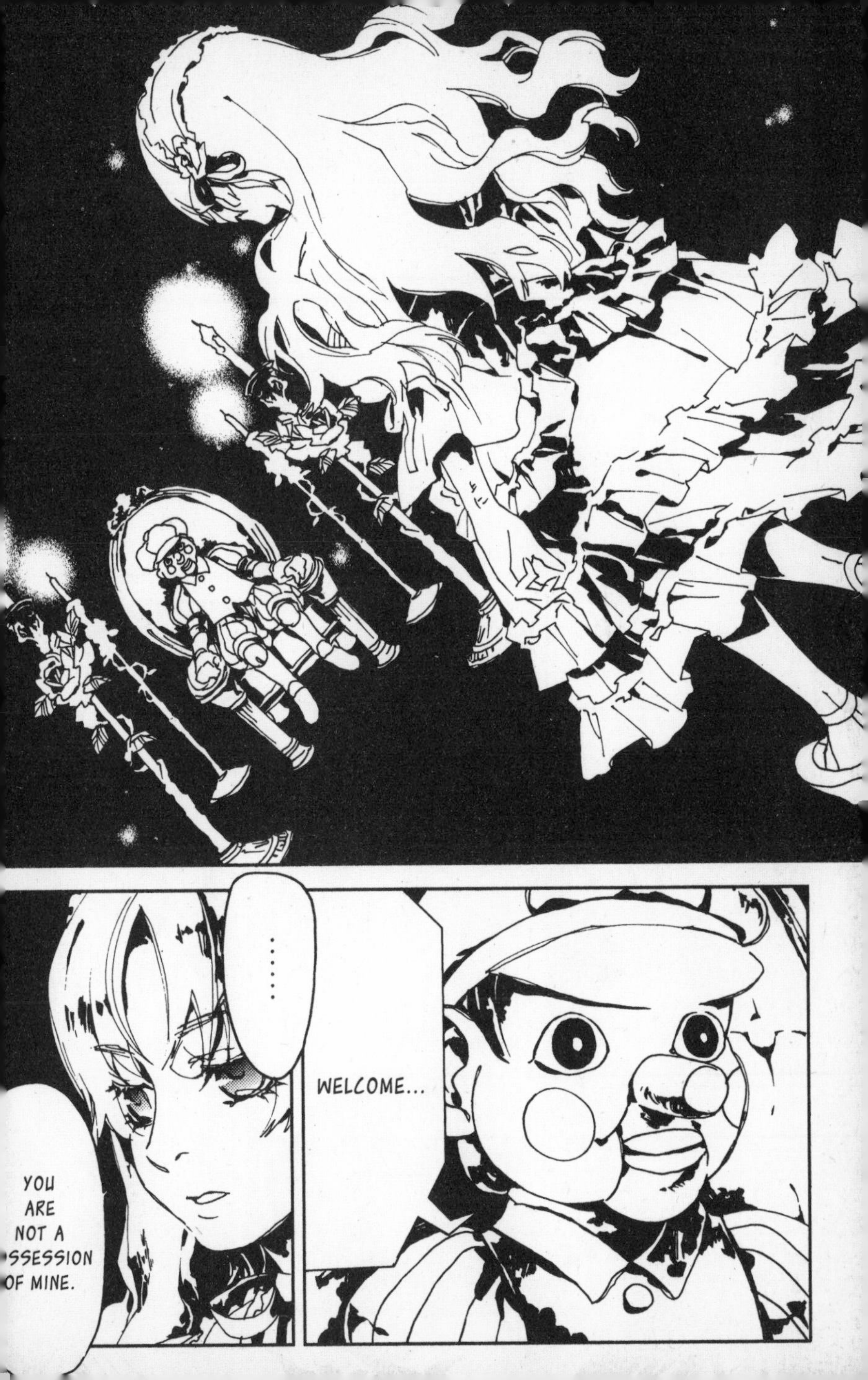
WELCOME...
......
YOU ARE NOT A SSESSION OF MINE.

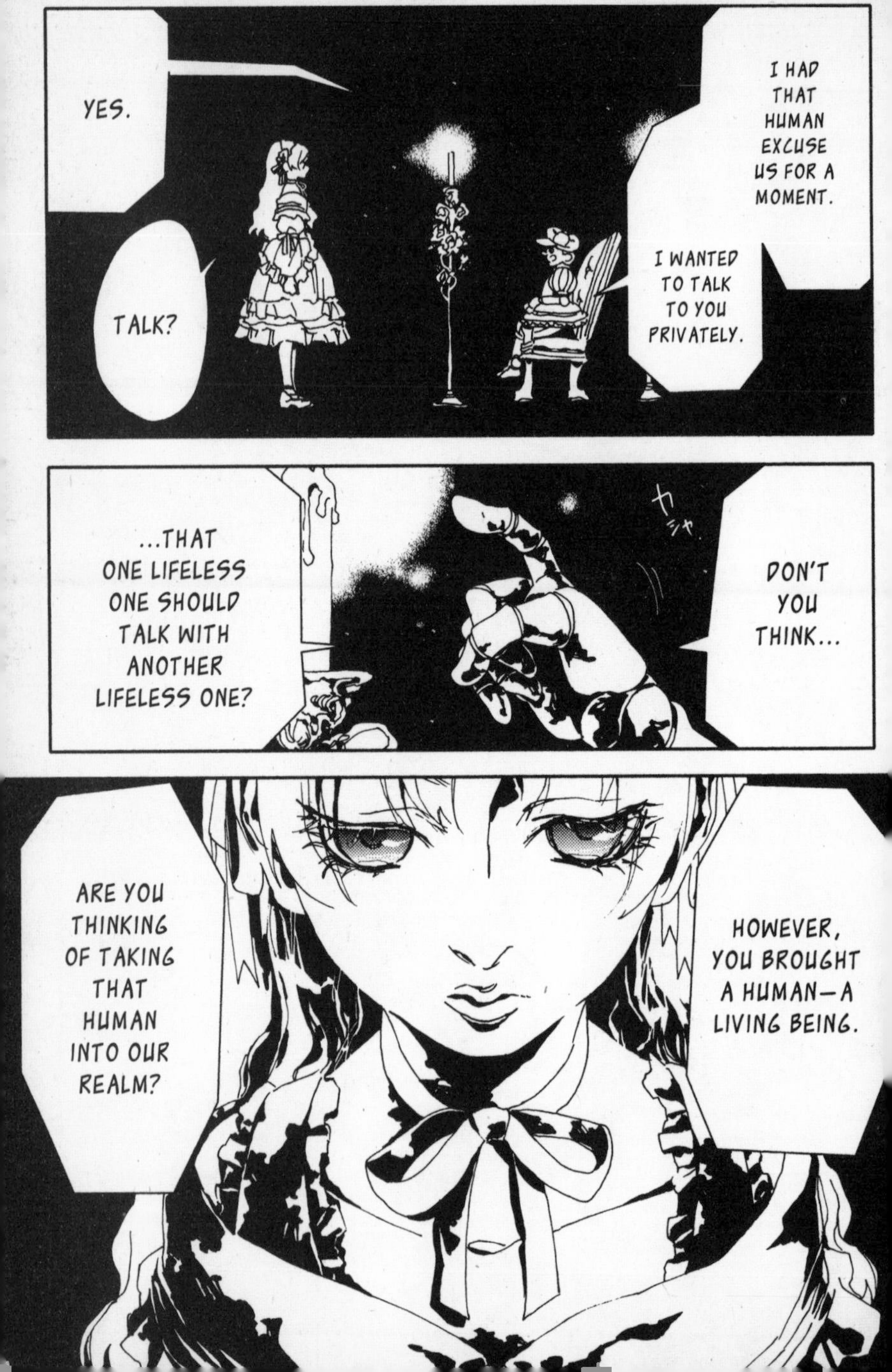
I HAD THAT HUMAN EXCUSE US FOR A MOMENT.
YES.
I WANTED TO TALK TO YOU PRIVATELY.
TALK?
カシャ
DON'T YOU THINK...
...THAT ONE LIFELESS ONE SHOULD TALK WITH ANOTHER LIFELESS ONE?
HOWEVER, YOU BROUGHT A HUMAN—A LIVING BEING.
ARE YOU THINKING OF TAKING THAT HUMAN INTO OUR REALM?

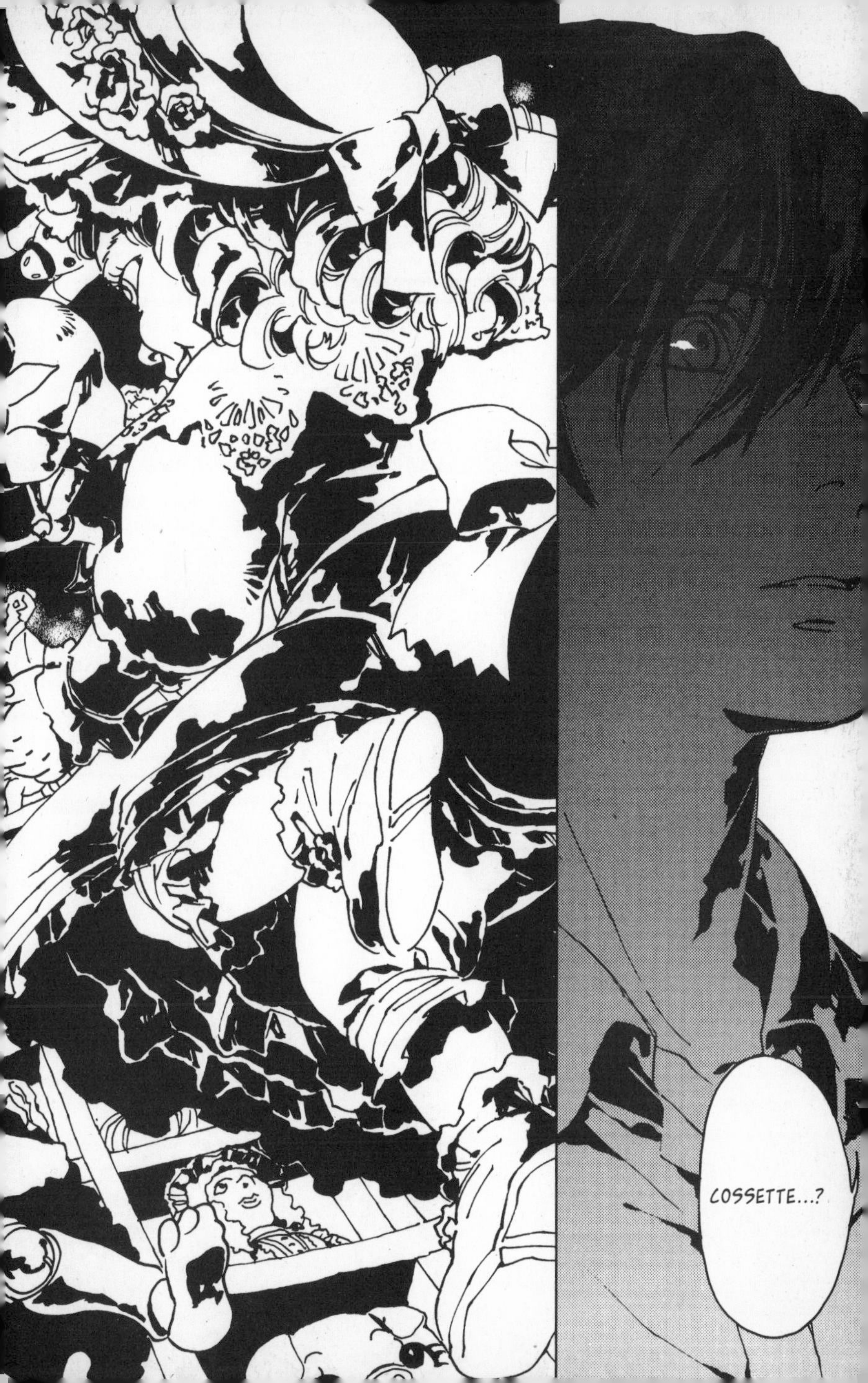
COSSETTE...?

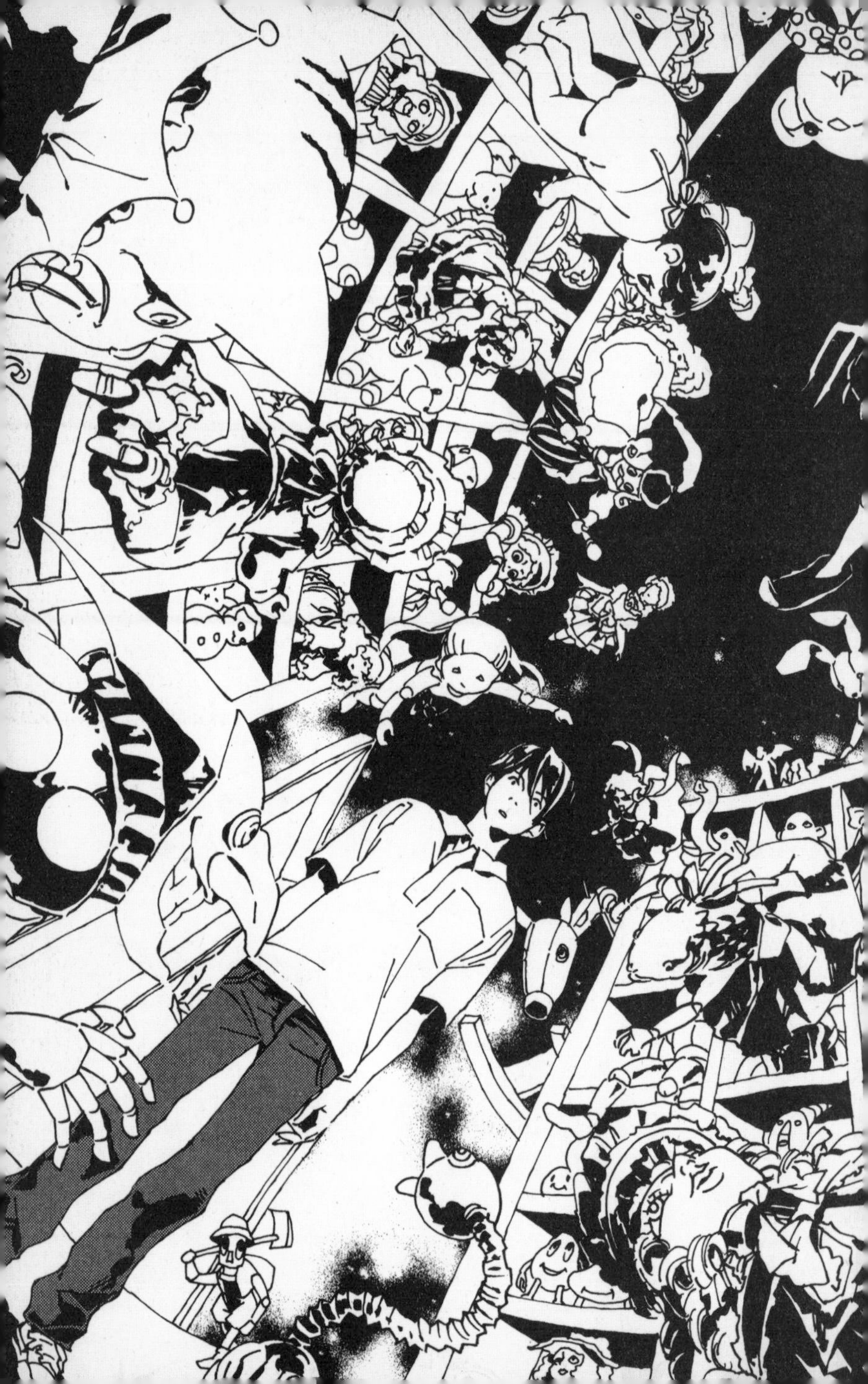

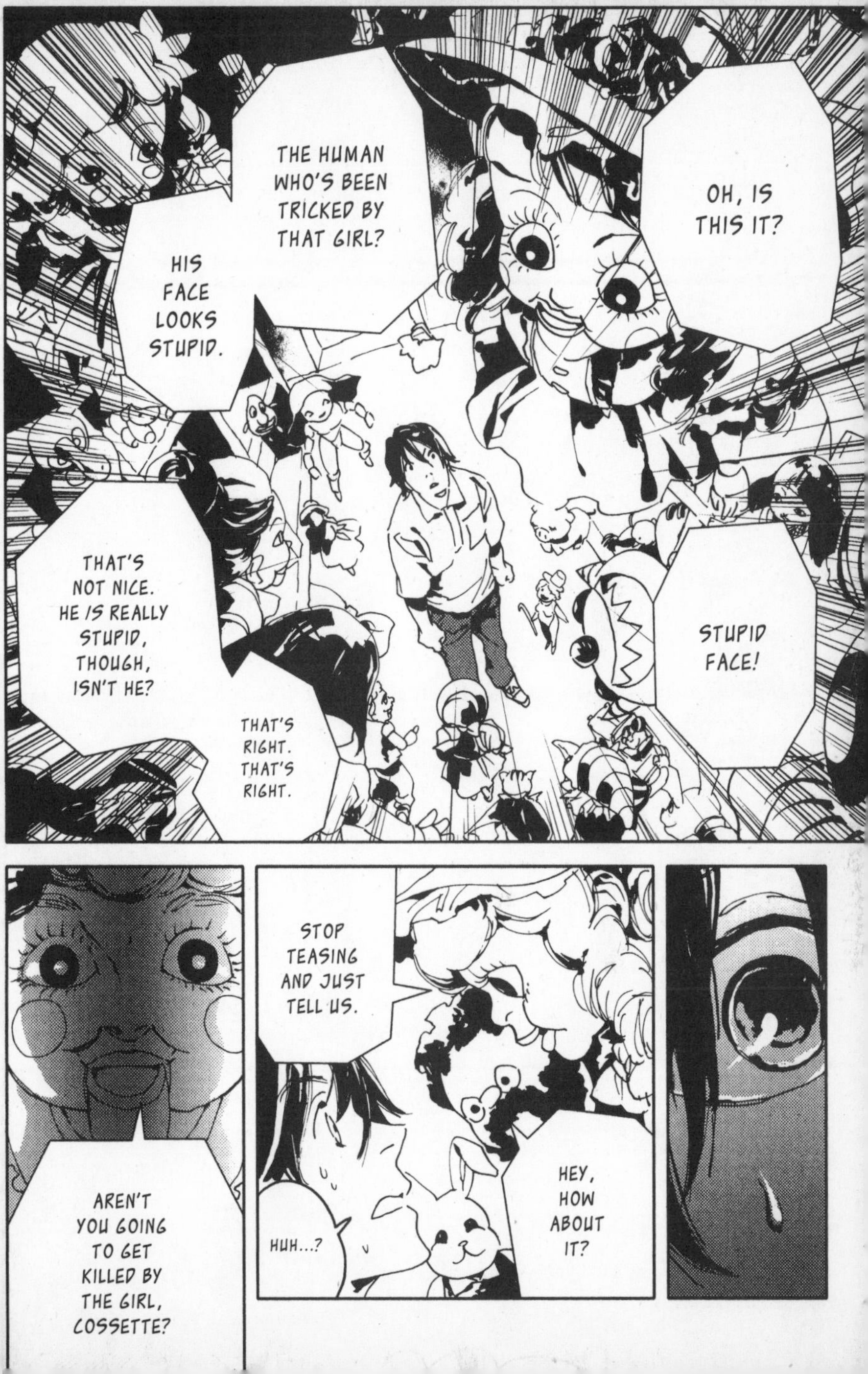
OH, IS THIS IT?
THE HUMAN WHO'S BEEN TRICKED BY THAT GIRL?
HIS FACE LOOKS STUPID.
STUPID FACE!
THAT'S NOT NICE. HE IS REALLY STUPID, THOUGH, ISN'T HE?
THAT'S RIGHT. THAT'S RIGHT.
STOP TEASING AND JUST TELL US.
HEY, HOW ABOUT IT?
HUH...?
AREN'T YOU GOING TO GET KILLED BY THE GIRL, COSSETTE?

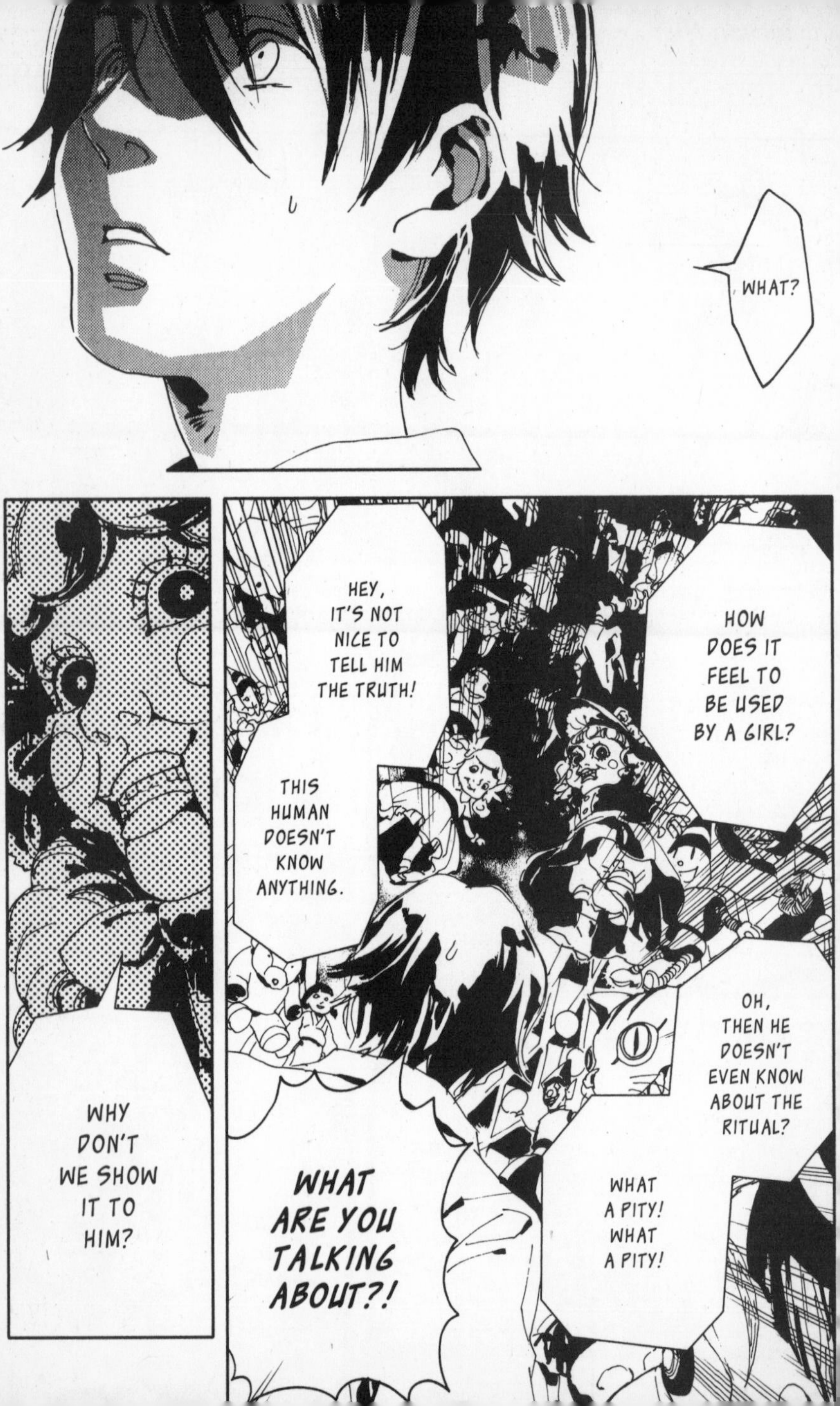
WHAT?
HOW DOES IT FEEL TO BE USED BY A GIRL?
HEY, IT'S NOT NICE TO TELL HIM THE TRUTH!
THIS HUMAN DOESN'T KNOW ANYTHING.
OH, THEN HE DOESN'T EVEN KNOW ABOUT THE RITUAL?
WHAT A PITY! WHAT A PITY!
WHAT ARE YOU TALKING ABOUT?!
WHY DON'T WE SHOW IT TO HIM?

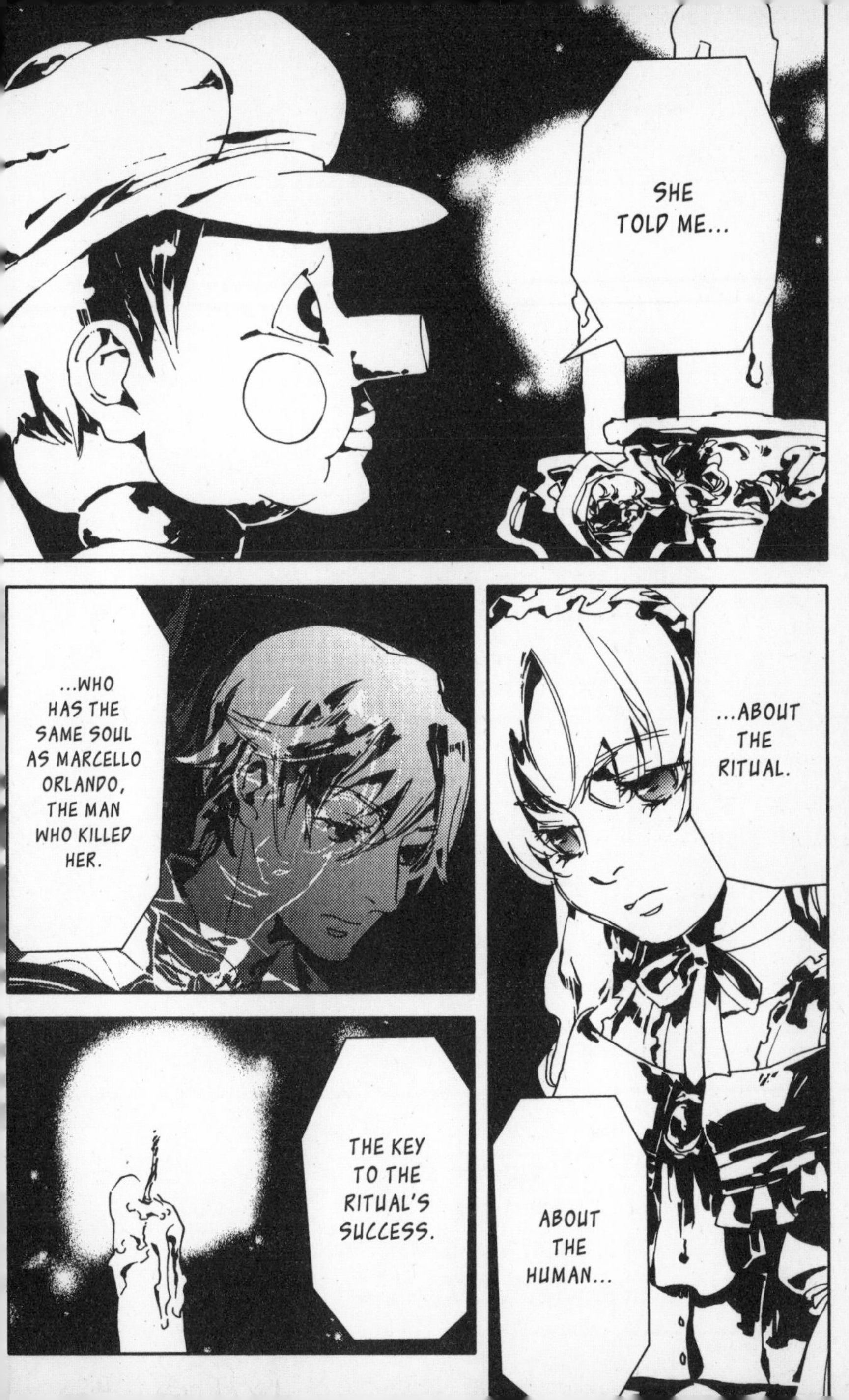
SHE TOLD ME...
...ABOUT THE RITUAL.
ABOUT THE HUMAN...
...WHO HAS THE SAME SOUL AS MARCELLO ORLANDO, THE MAN WHO KILLED HER.
THE KEY TO THE RITUAL'S SUCCESS.

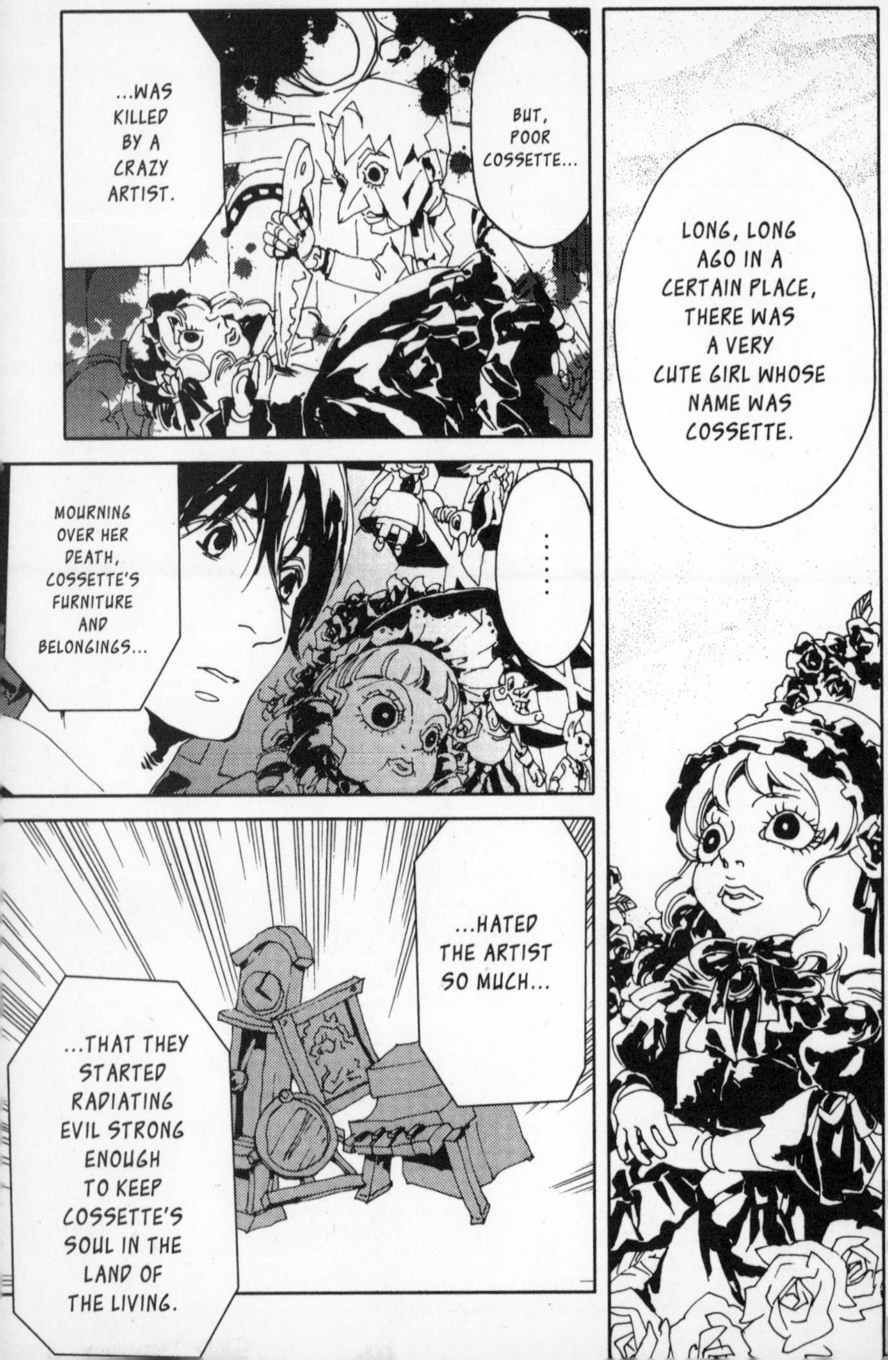
LONG, LONG AGO IN A CERTAIN PLACE, THERE WAS A VERY CUTE GIRL WHOSE NAME WAS COSSETTE.
BUT, POOR COSSETTE...
...WAS KILLED BY A CRAZY ARTIST.
......
MOURNING OVER HER DEATH, COSSETTE'S FURNITURE AND BELONGINGS...
...HATED THE ARTIST SO MUCH...
...THAT THEY STARTED RADIATING EVIL STRONG ENOUGH TO KEEP COSSETTE'S SOUL IN THE LAND OF THE LIVING.

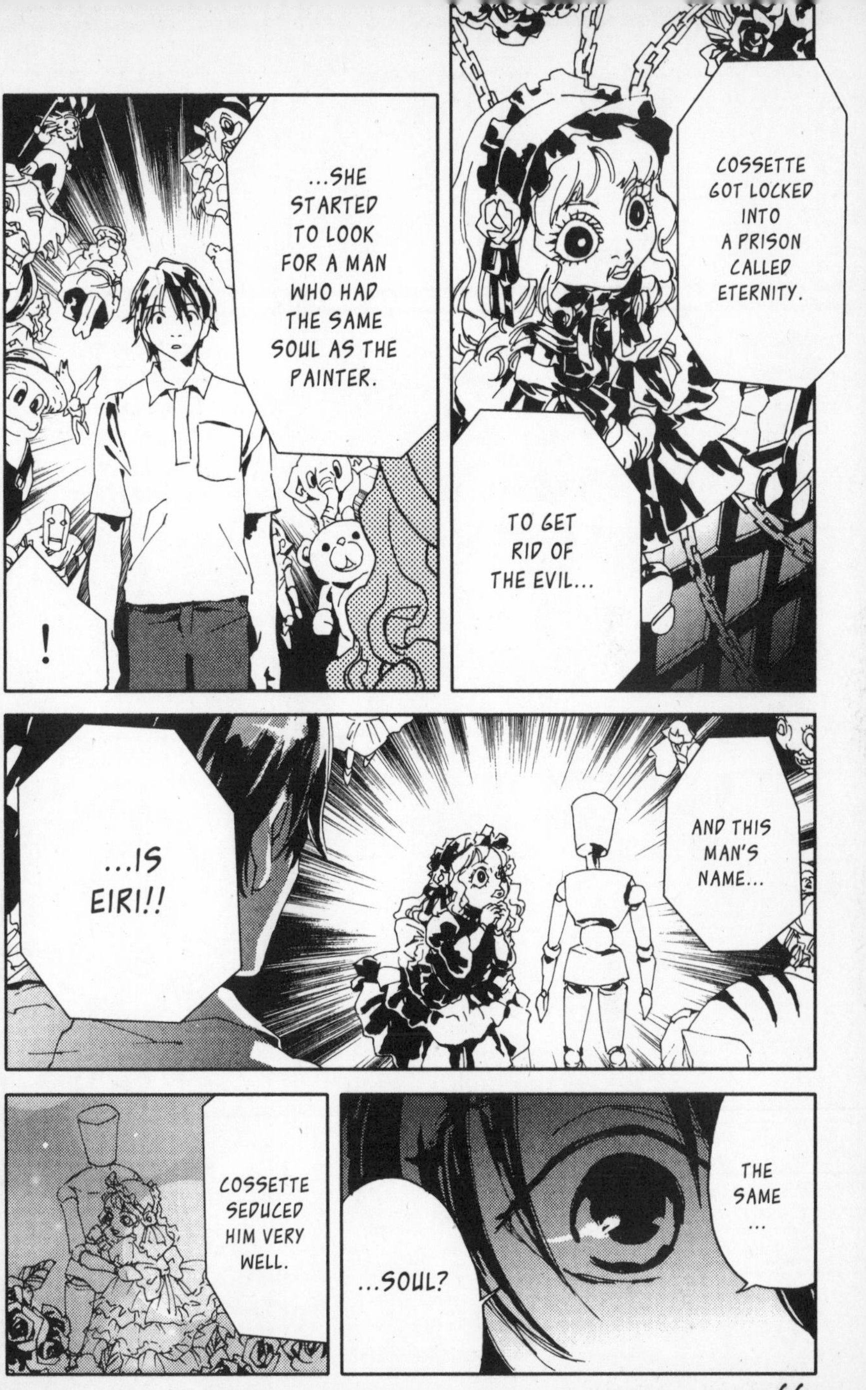
COSSETTE GOT LOCKED INTO A PRISON CALLED ETERNITY.
TO GET RID OF THE EVIL...
...SHE STARTED TO LOOK FOR A MAN WHO HAD THE SAME SOUL AS THE PAINTER.
!
AND THIS MAN'S NAME...
...IS EIRI!!
THE SAME ...
...SOUL?
COSSETTE SEDUCED HIM VERY WELL.

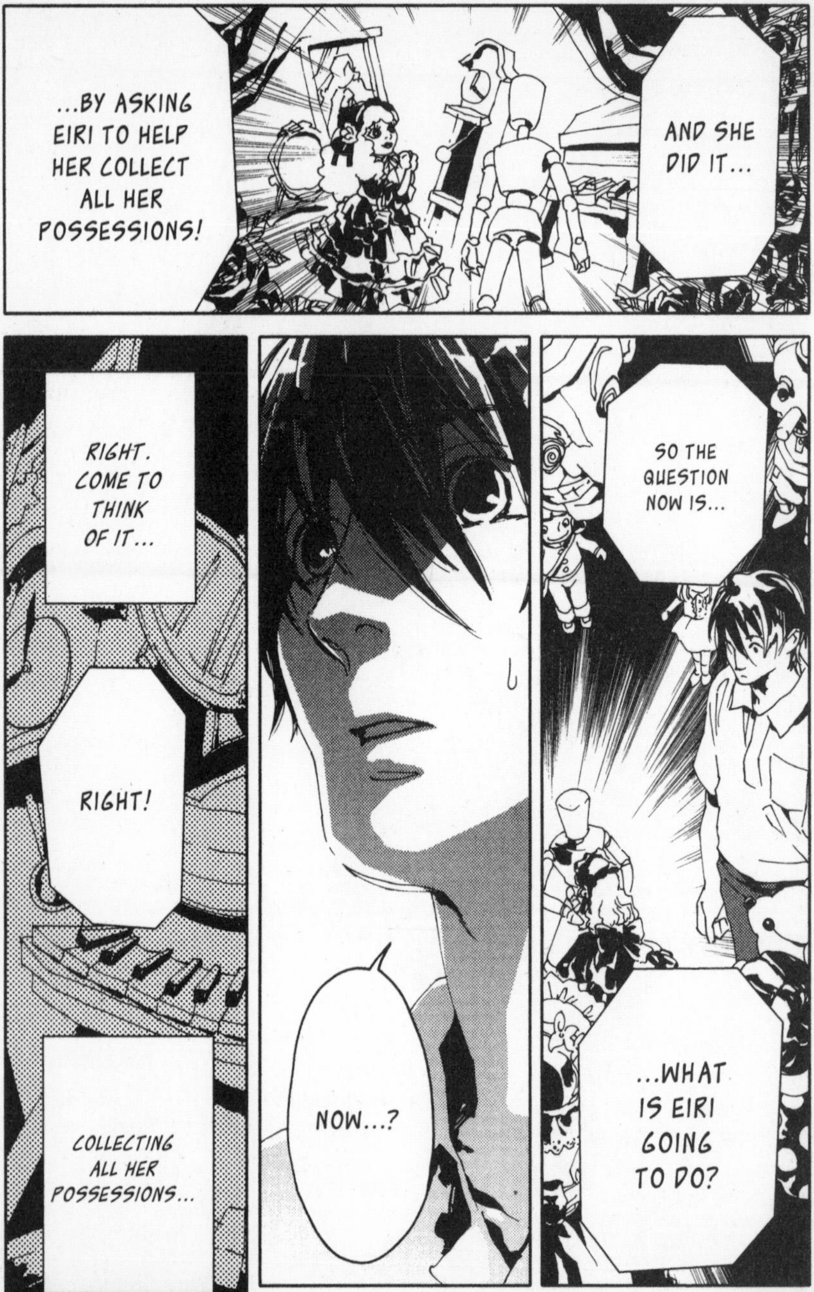
...BY ASKING EIRI TO HELP HER COLLECT ALL HER POSSESSIONS!
AND SHE DID IT...
RIGHT. COME TO THINK OF IT...
RIGHT!
COLLECTING ALL HER POSSESSIONS...
NOW...?
SO THE QUESTION NOW IS...
...WHAT IS EIRI GOING TO DO?

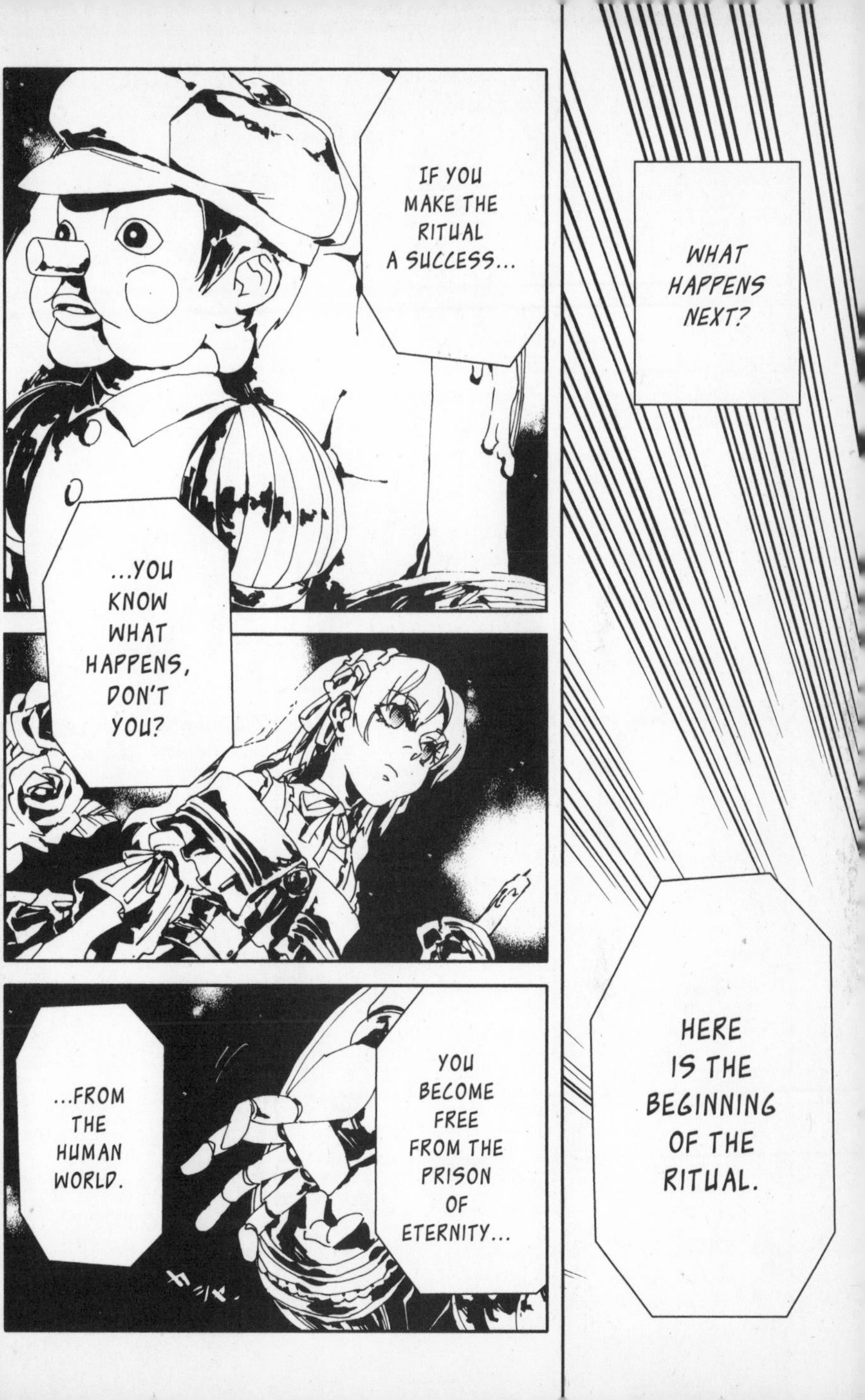
WHAT HAPPENS NEXT?
HERE IS THE BEGINNING OF THE RITUAL.
IF YOU MAKE THE RITUAL A SUCCESS...
...YOU KNOW WHAT HAPPENS, DON'T YOU?
YOU BECOME FREE FROM THE PRISON OF ETERNITY...
...FROM THE HUMAN WORLD.

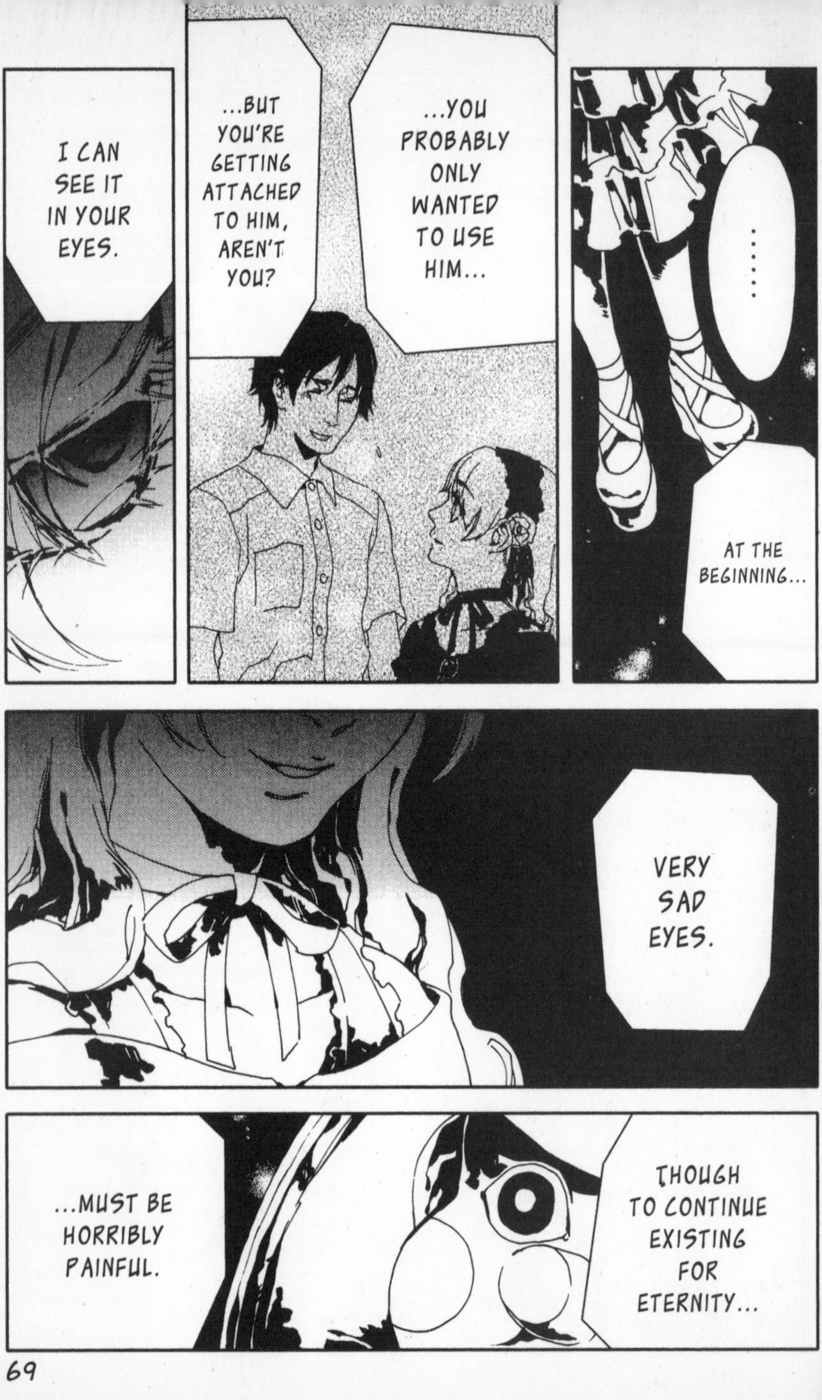
....
AT THE BEGINNING...
...YOU PROBABLY ONLY WANTED TO USE HIM...
...BUT YOU'RE GETTING ATTACHED TO HIM, AREN'T YOU?
I CAN SEE IT IN YOUR EYES.
VERY SAD EYES.
THOUGH TO CONTINUE EXISTING FOR ETERNITY...
...MUST BE HORRIBLY PAINFUL.

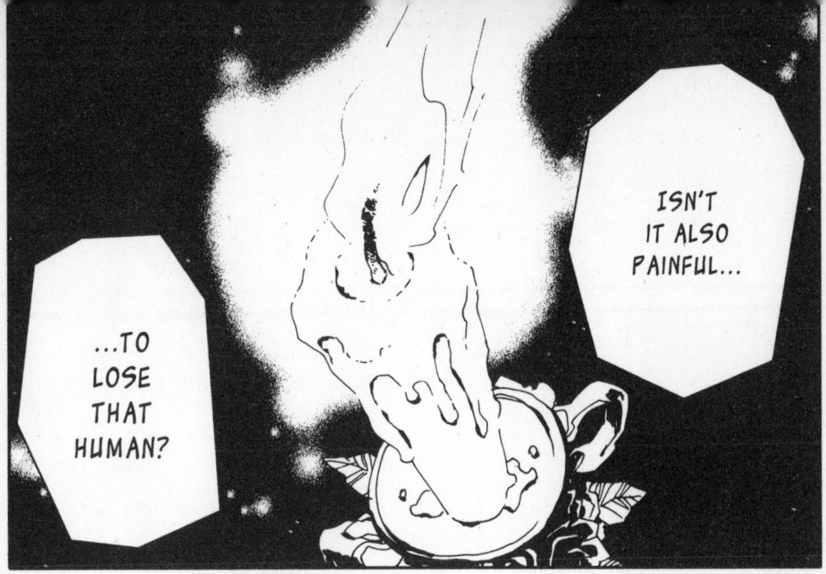
ISN'T IT ALSO PAINFUL...
...TO LOSE THAT HUMAN?

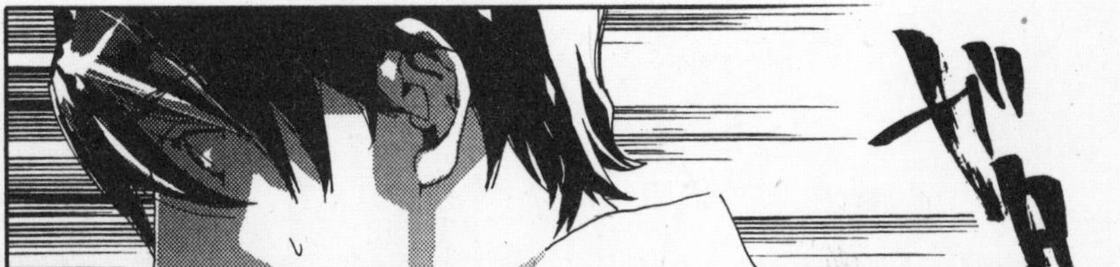

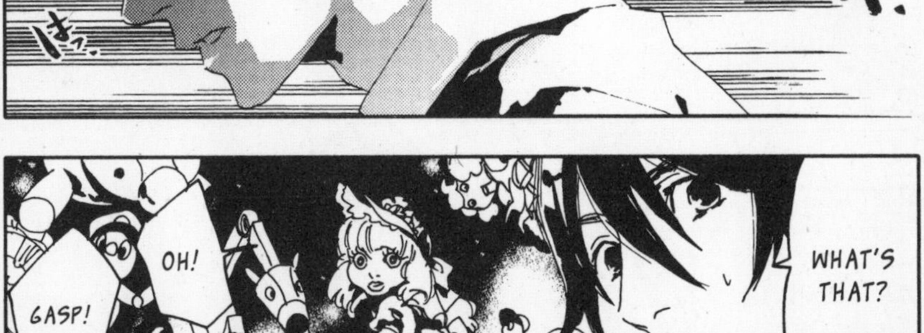
WHAT'S THAT?
OH!
GASP!

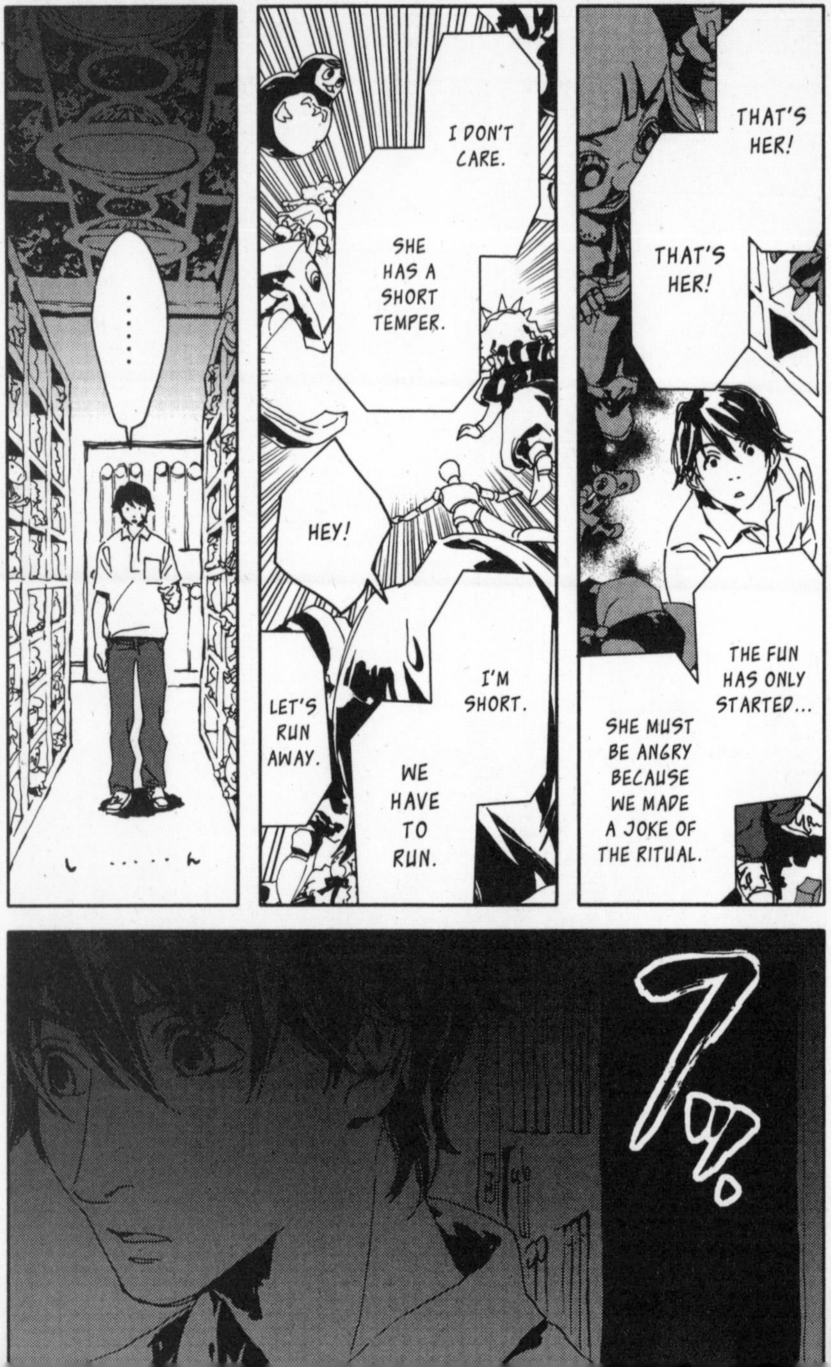
THAT'S HER!
THAT'S HER!
THE FUN HAS ONLY STARTED...
SHE MUST BE ANGRY BECAUSE WE MADE A JOKE OF THE RITUAL.
I DON'T CARE.
SHE HAS A SHORT TEMPER.
HEY!
I'M SHORT.
WE HAVE TO RUN.
LET'S RUN AWAY.
......
し……ん

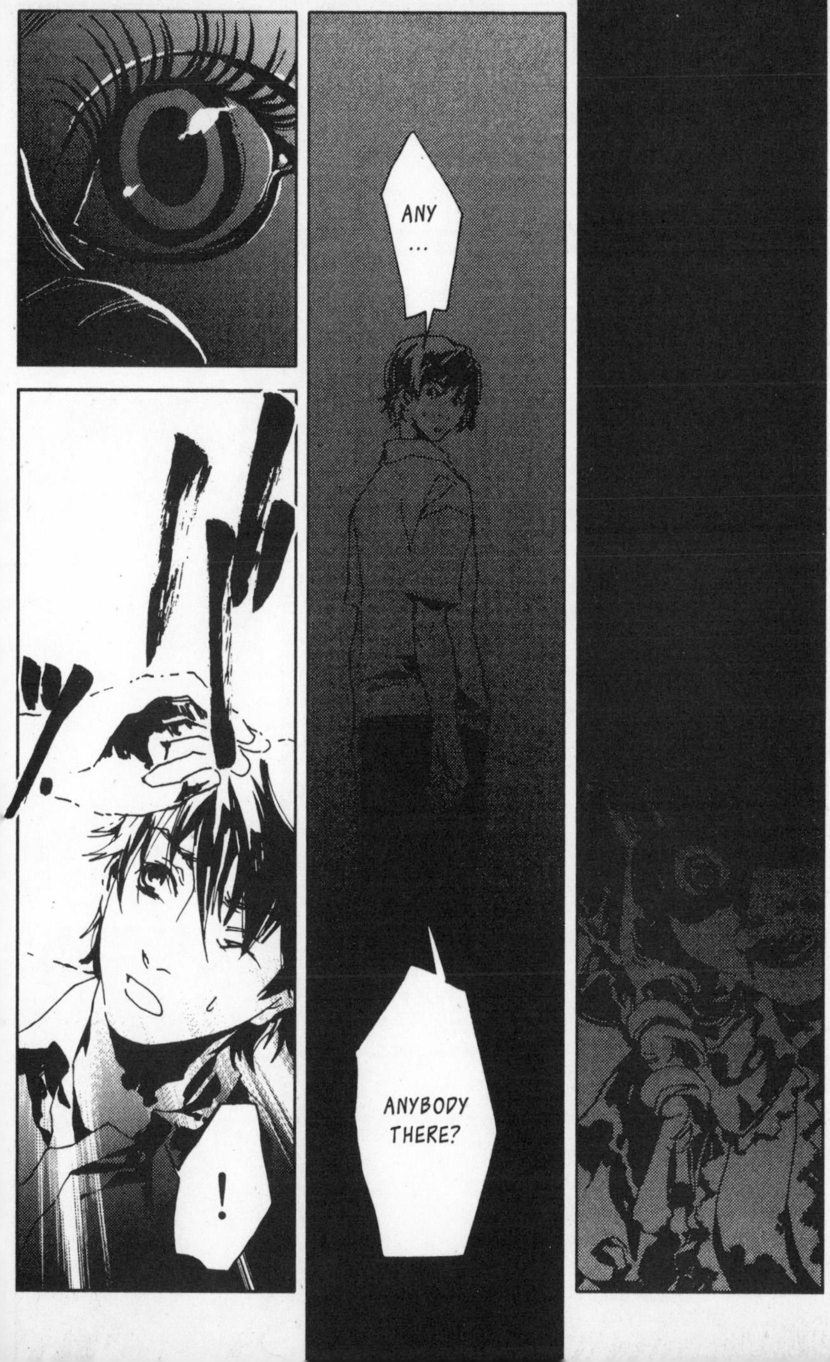
ANY ...
ANYBODY THERE?
!

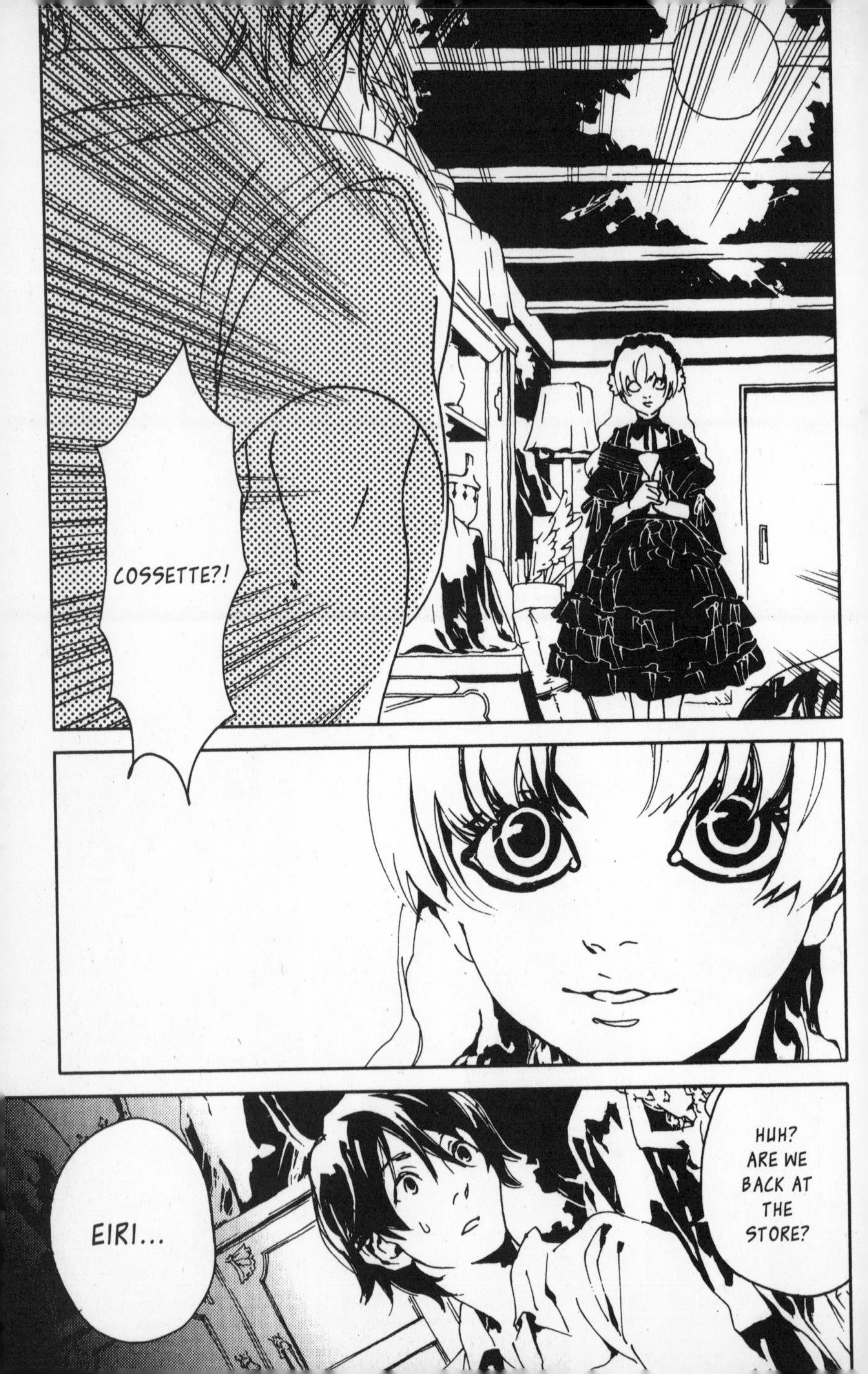
COSSETTE?!
HUH? ARE WE BACK AT THE STORE?
EIRI...

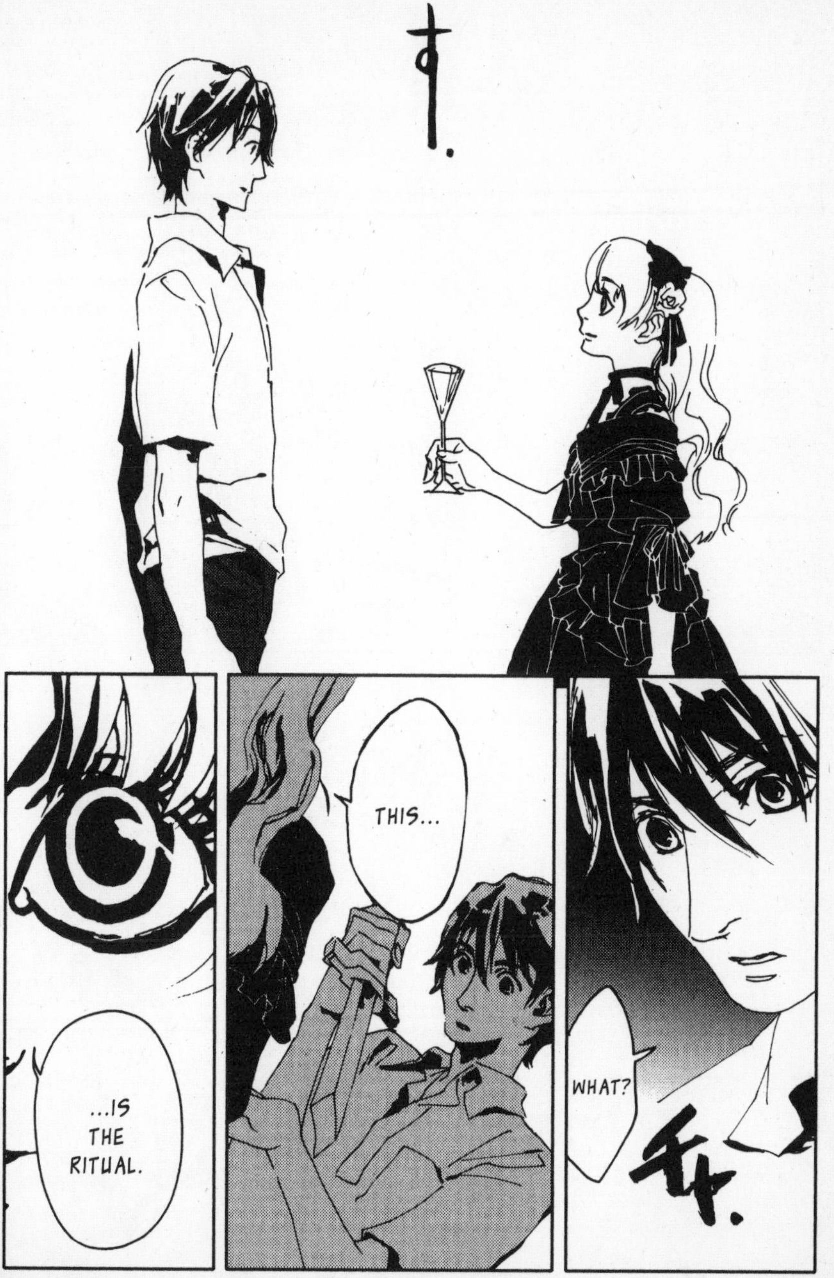
す.
WHAT?
チャ.
THIS...
...IS THE RITUAL.

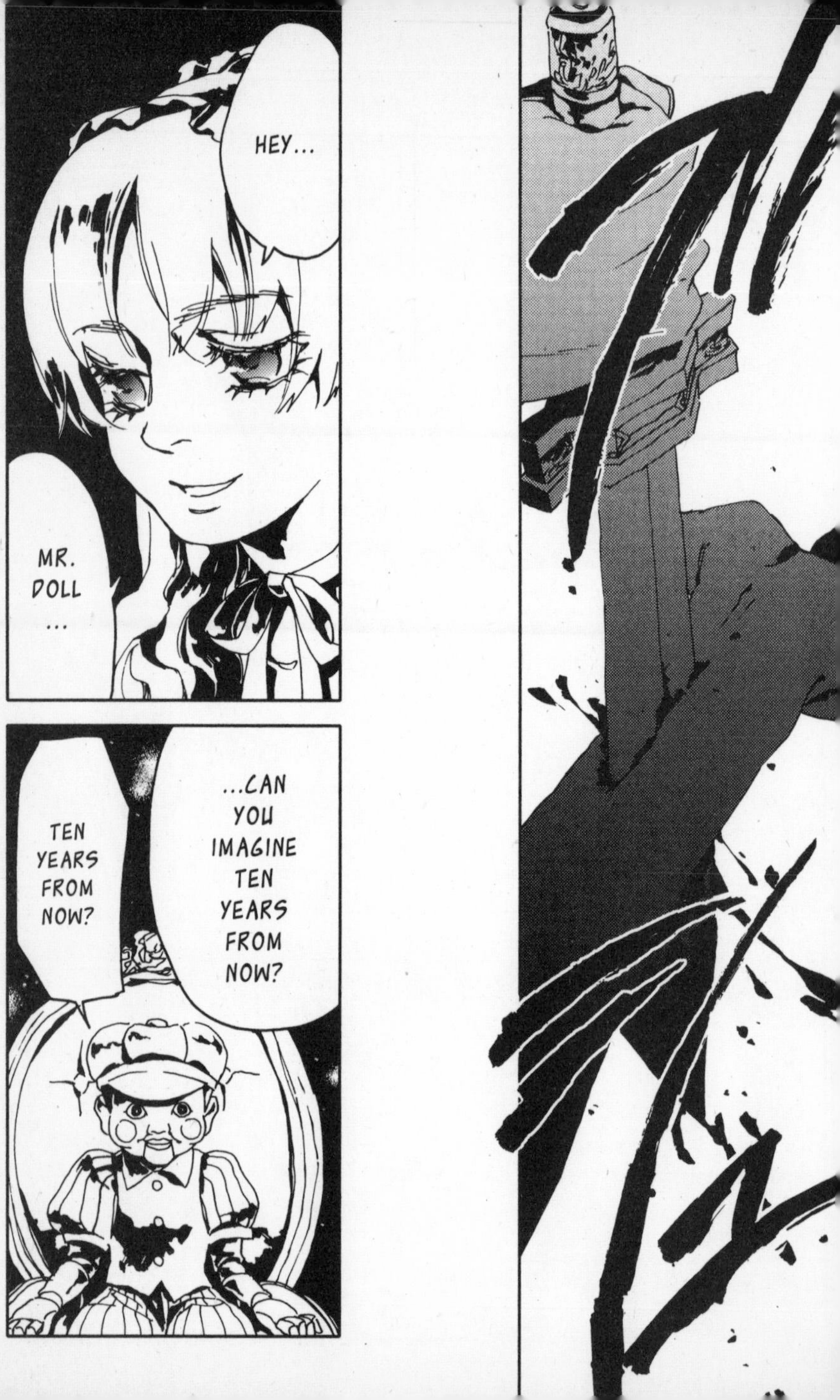
HEY...
MR. DOLL ...
...CAN YOU IMAGINE TEN YEARS FROM NOW?
TEN YEARS FROM NOW?

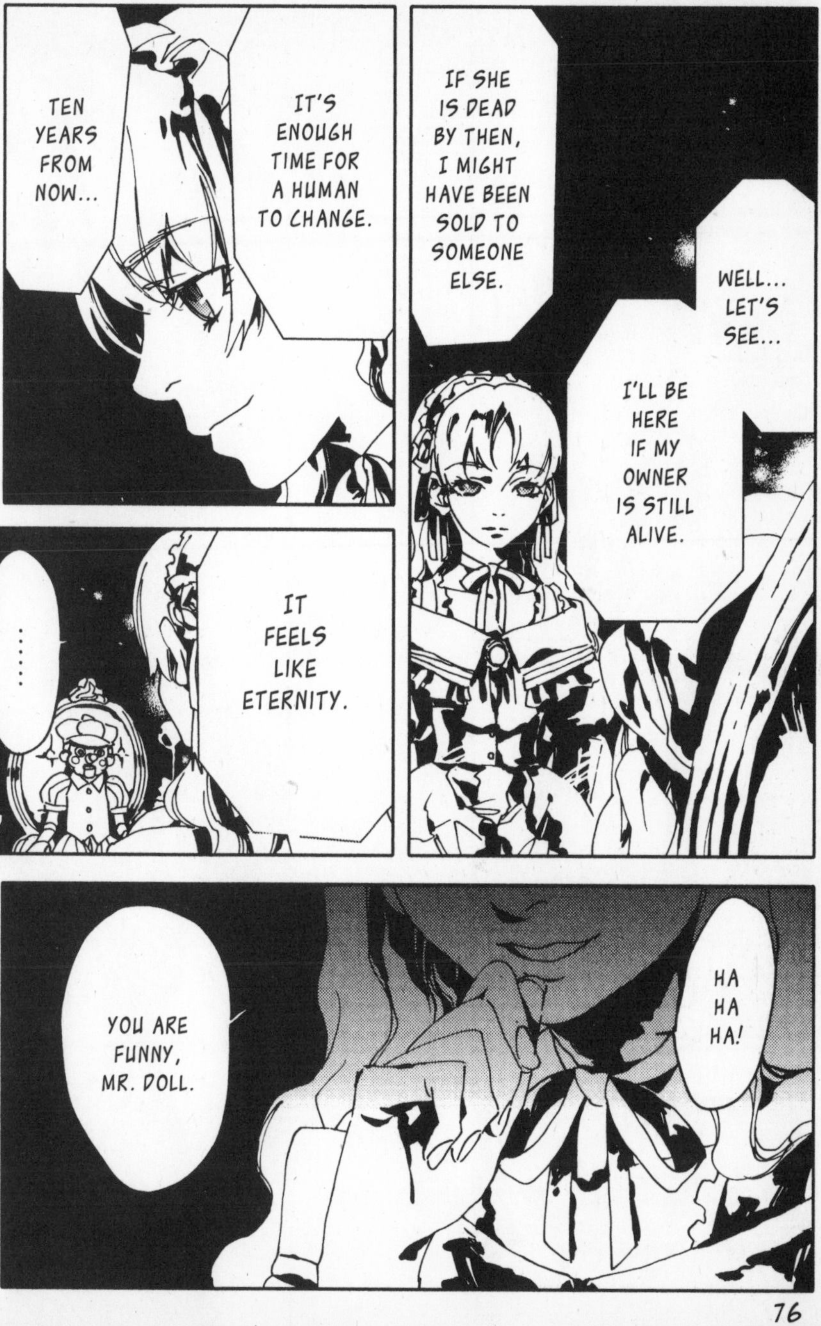
TEN YEARS FROM NOW...
IT'S ENOUGH TIME FOR A HUMAN TO CHANGE.
WELL... LET'S SEE...
I'LL BE HERE IF MY OWNER IS STILL ALIVE.
IF SHE IS DEAD BY THEN, I MIGHT HAVE BEEN SOLD TO SOMEONE ELSE.
......
IT FEELS LIKE ETERNITY.
HA HA HA!
YOU ARE FUNNY, MR. DOLL.

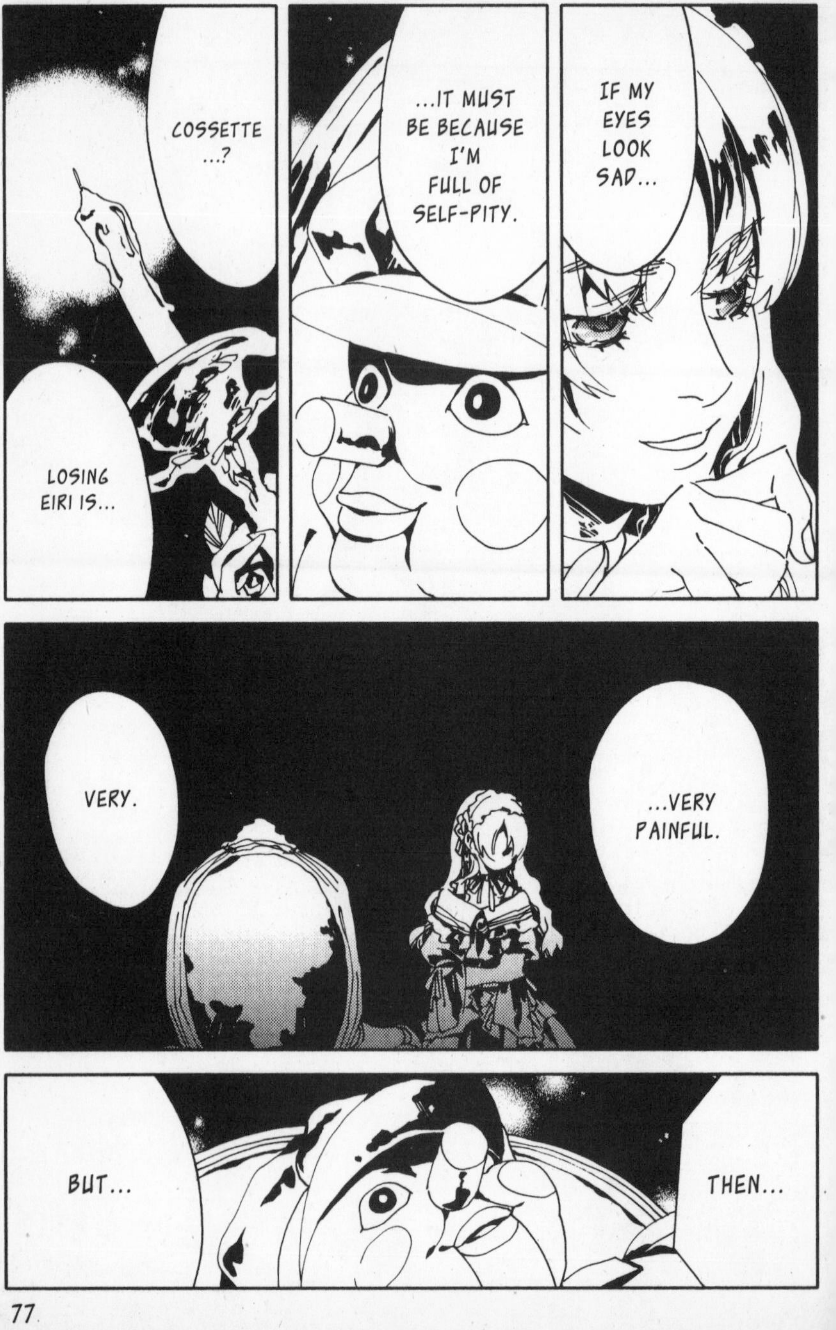
IF MY EYES LOOK SAD...
...IT MUST BE BECAUSE I'M FULL OF SELF-PITY.
COSSETTE ...?
LOSING EIRI IS...
...VERY PAINFUL.
VERY.
THEN...
BUT...

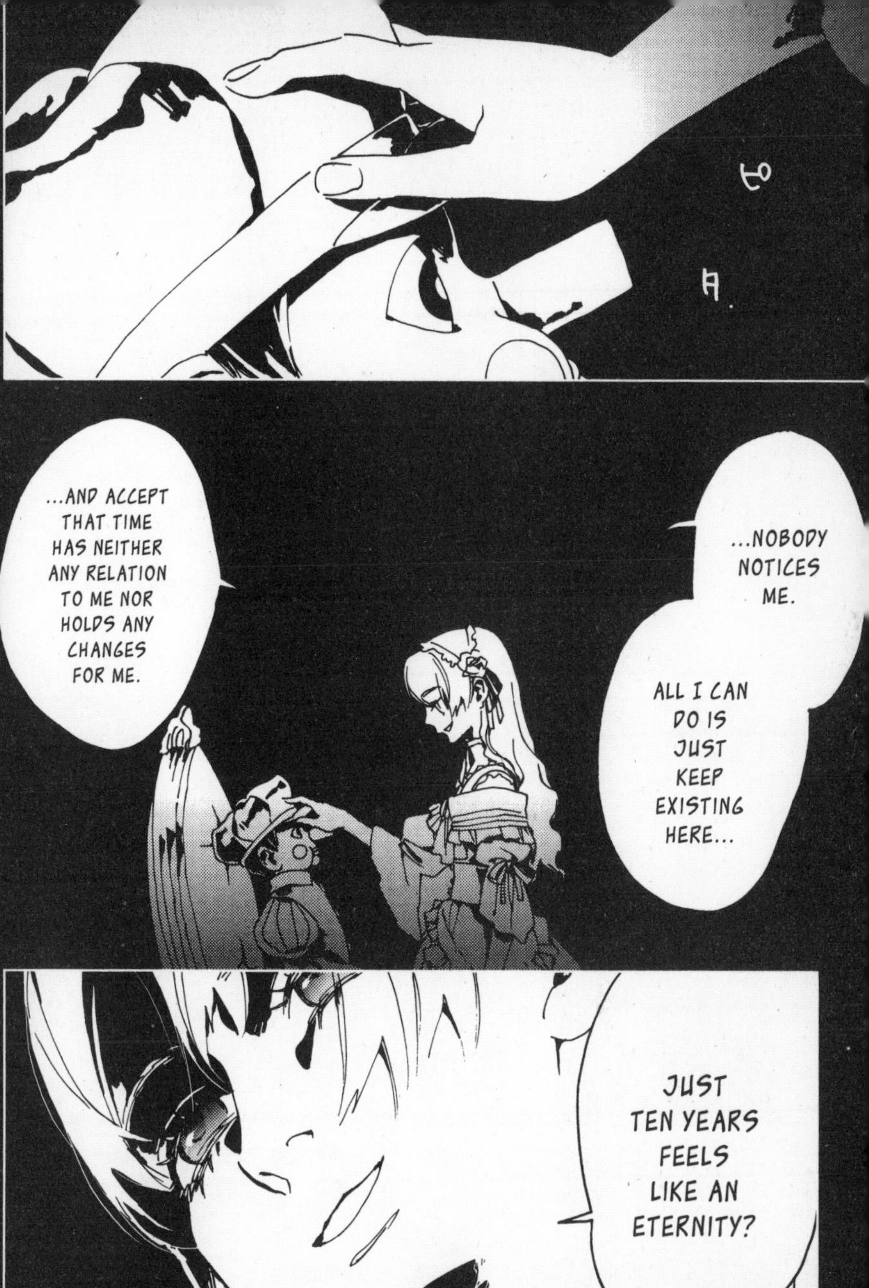
...NOBODY NOTICES ME.
ALL I CAN DO IS JUST KEEP EXISTING HERE...
...AND ACCEPT THAT TIME HAS NEITHER ANY RELATION TO ME NOR HOLDS ANY CHANGES FOR ME.
JUST TEN YEARS FEELS LIKE AN ETERNITY?

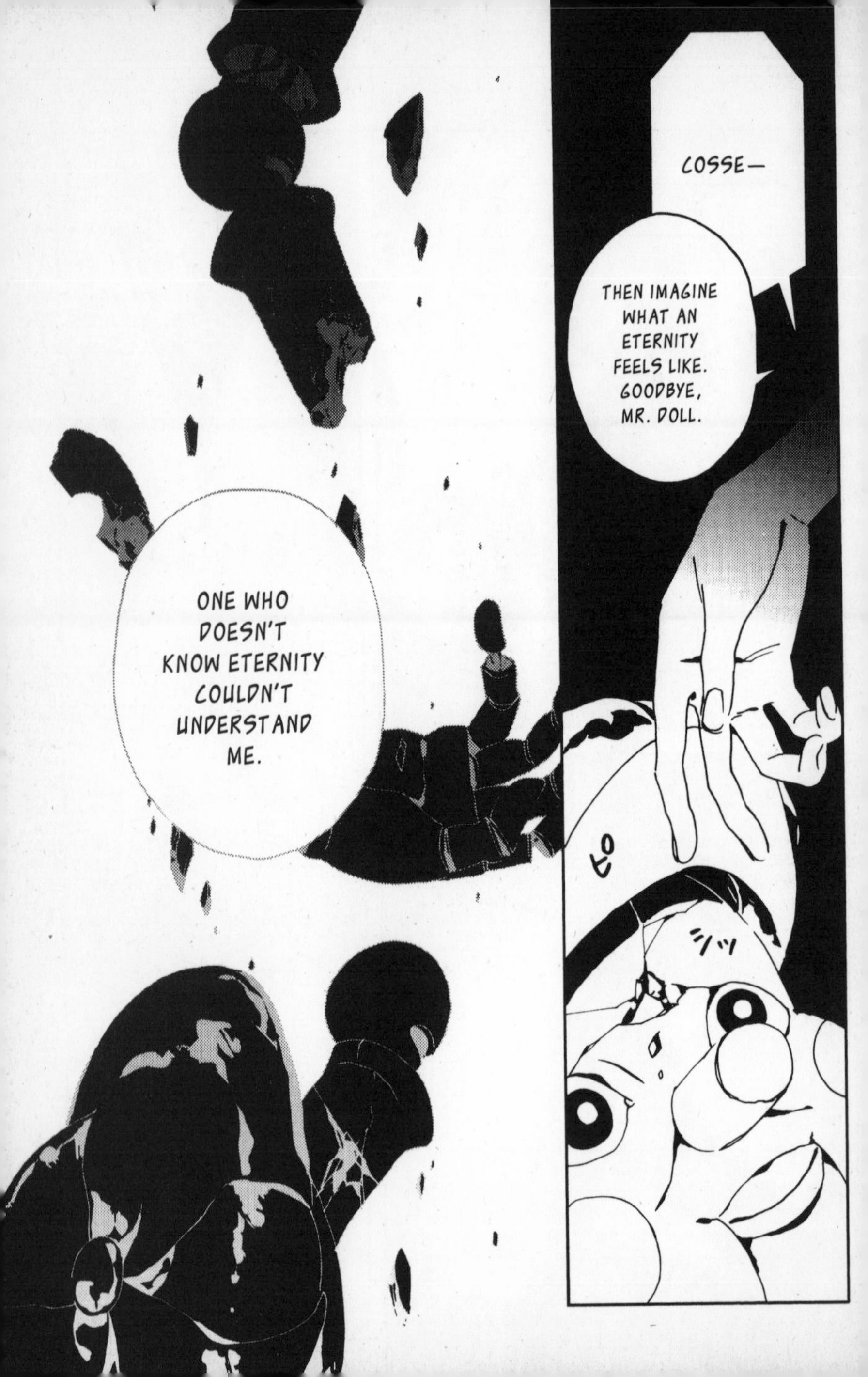
COSSE—
THEN IMAGINE WHAT AN ETERNITY FEELS LIKE. GOODBYE, MR. DOLL.
ONE WHO DOESN'T KNOW ETERNITY COULDN'T UNDERSTAND ME.

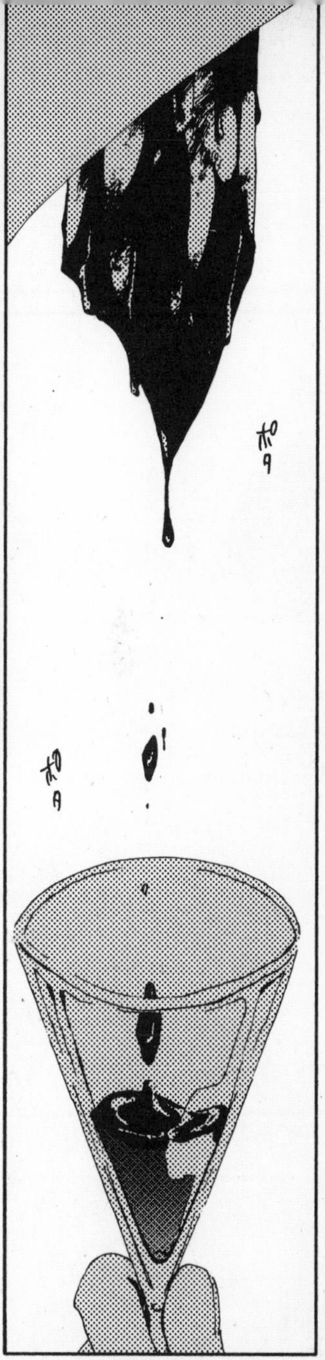
ポタ
ポタ

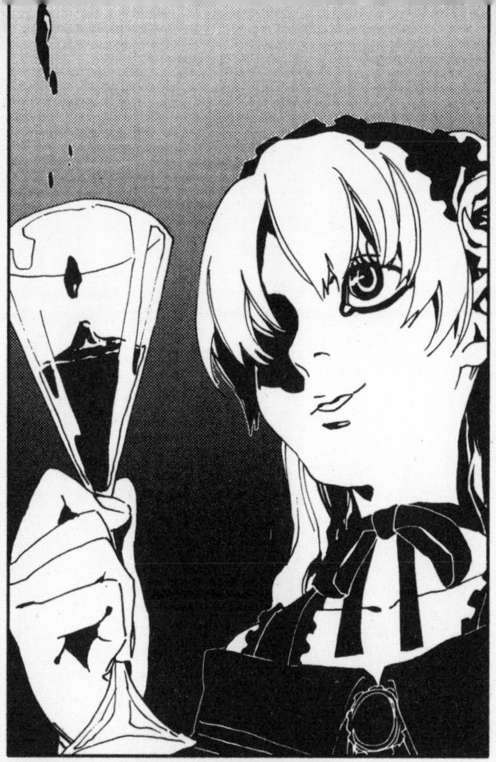

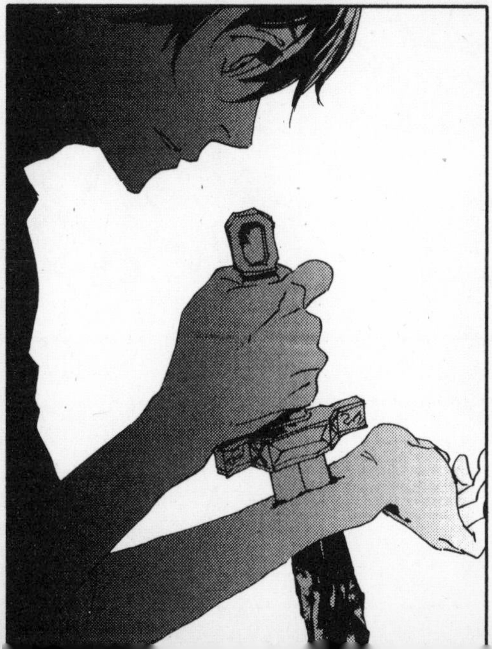

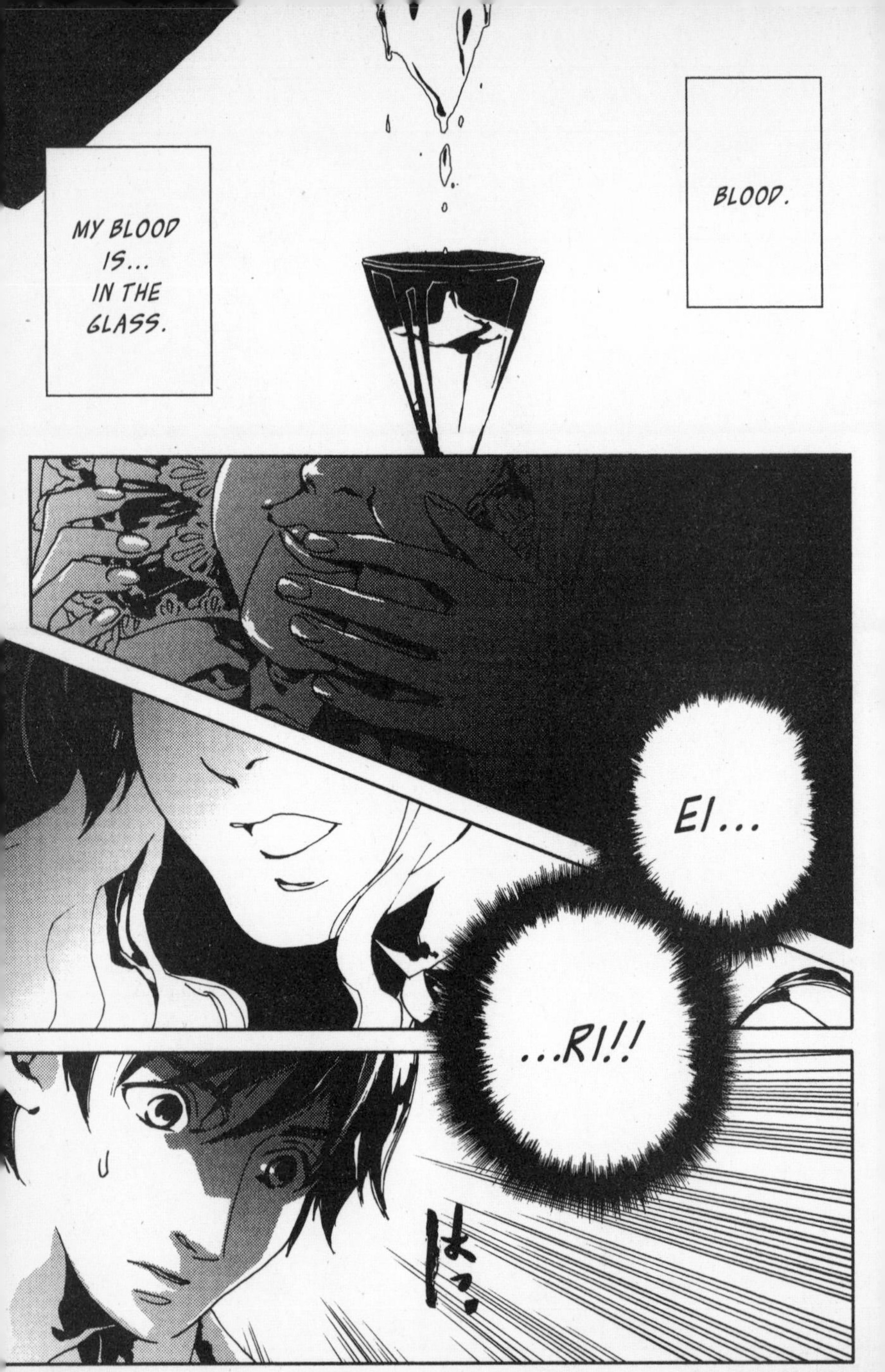
BLOOD.
MY BLOOD IS... IN THE GLASS.
EI...
...RI!!
はっ

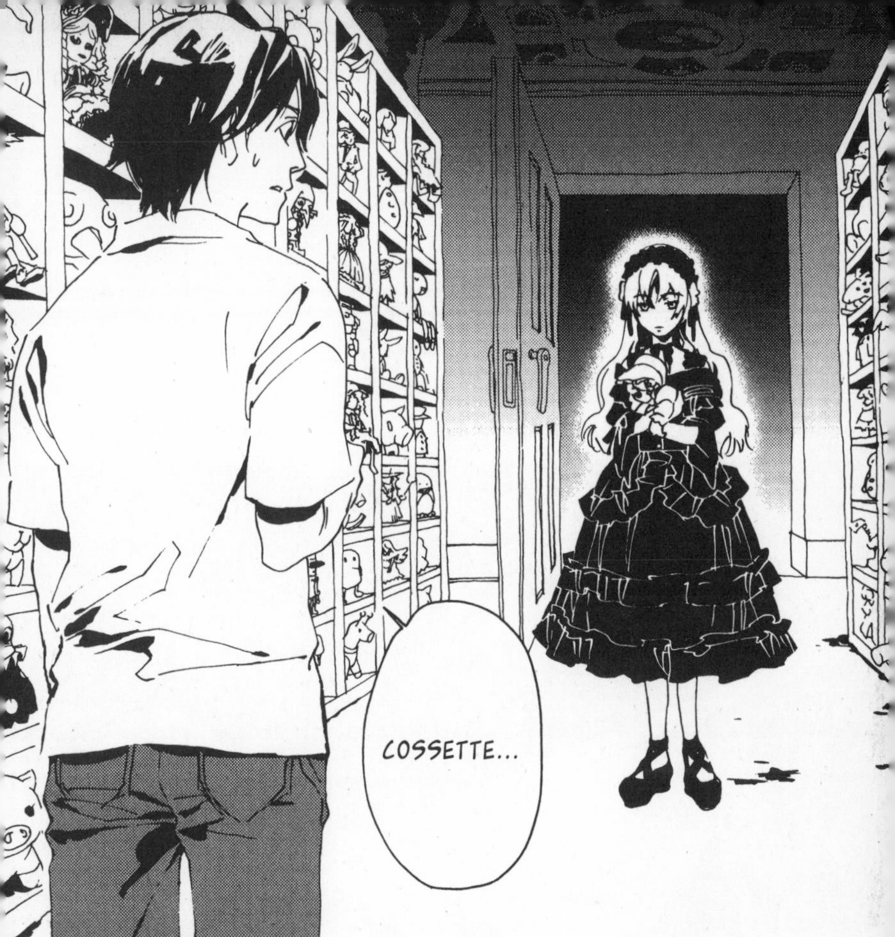
COSSETTE...
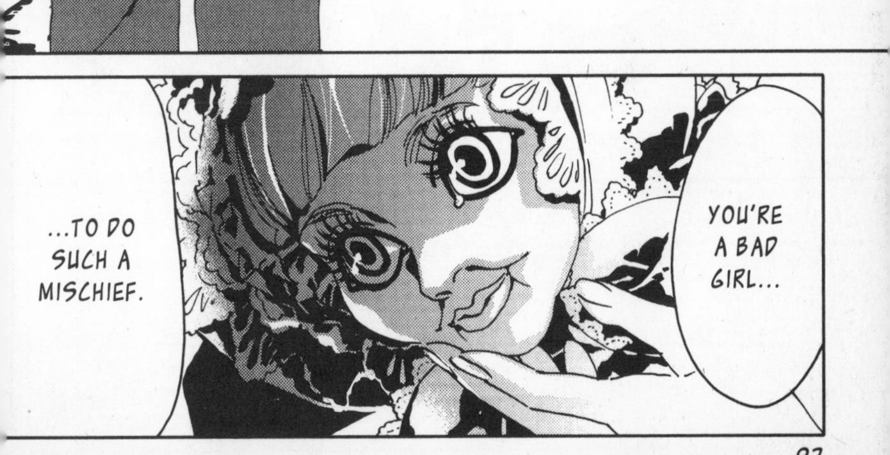
YOU'RE A BAD GIRL...
...TO DO SUCH A MISCHIEF.

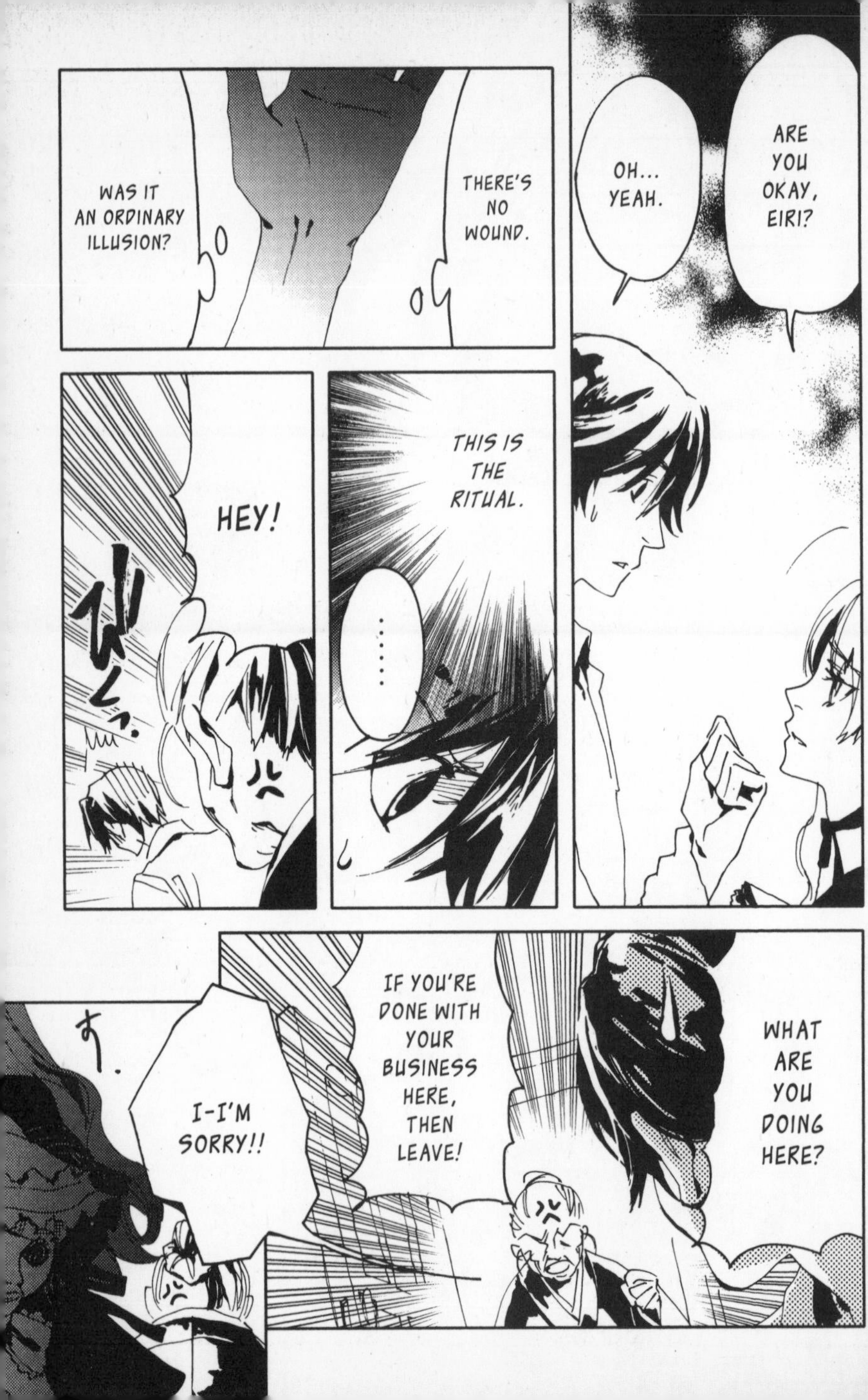
ARE YOU OKAY, EIRI?
OH... YEAH.
THERE'S NO WOUND.
WAS IT AN ORDINARY ILLUSION?
THIS IS THE RITUAL.
......
HEY!
WHAT ARE YOU DOING HERE?
IF YOU'RE DONE WITH YOUR BUSINESS HERE, THEN LEAVE!
I-I'M SORRY!!

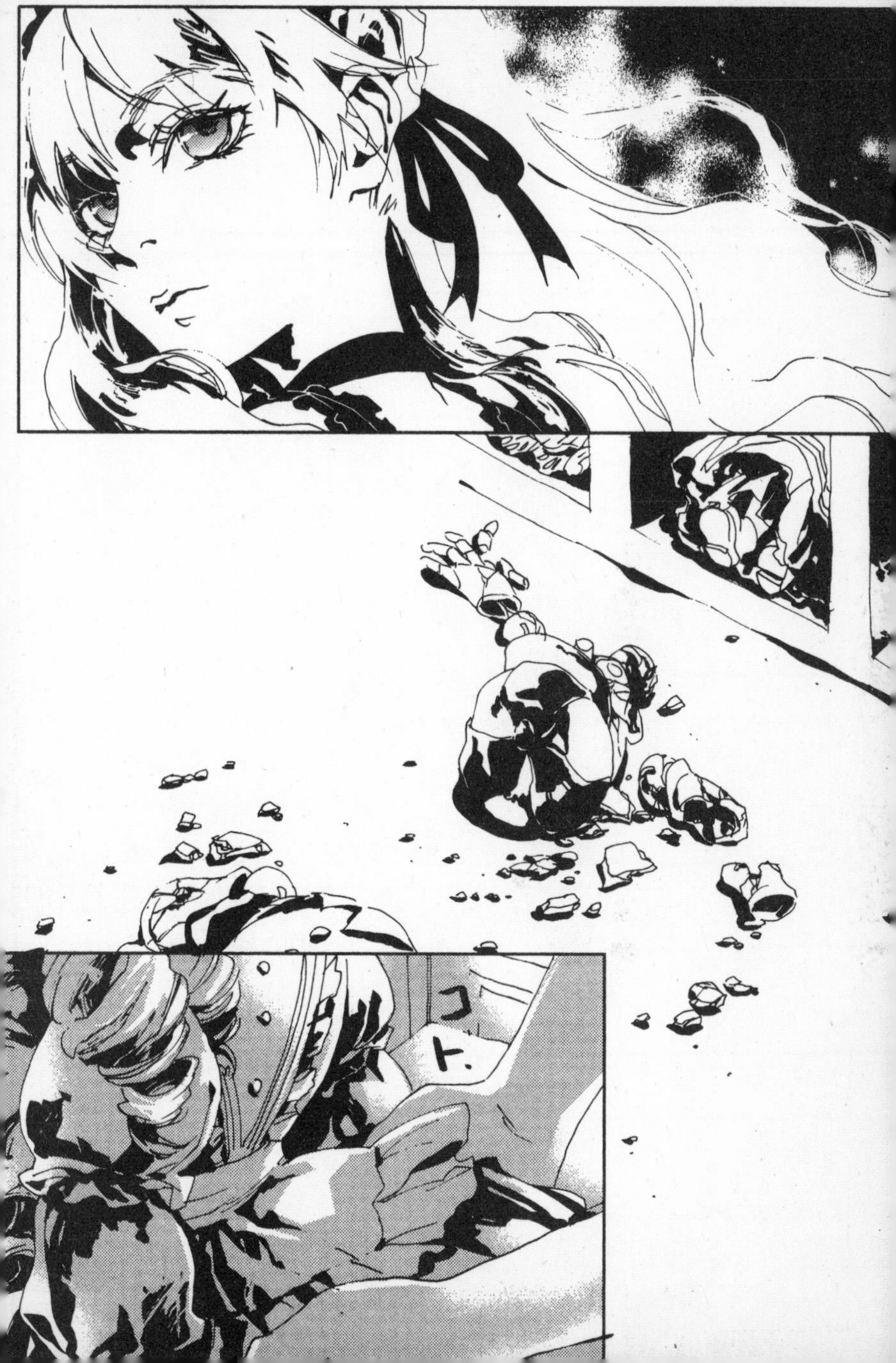
コト.

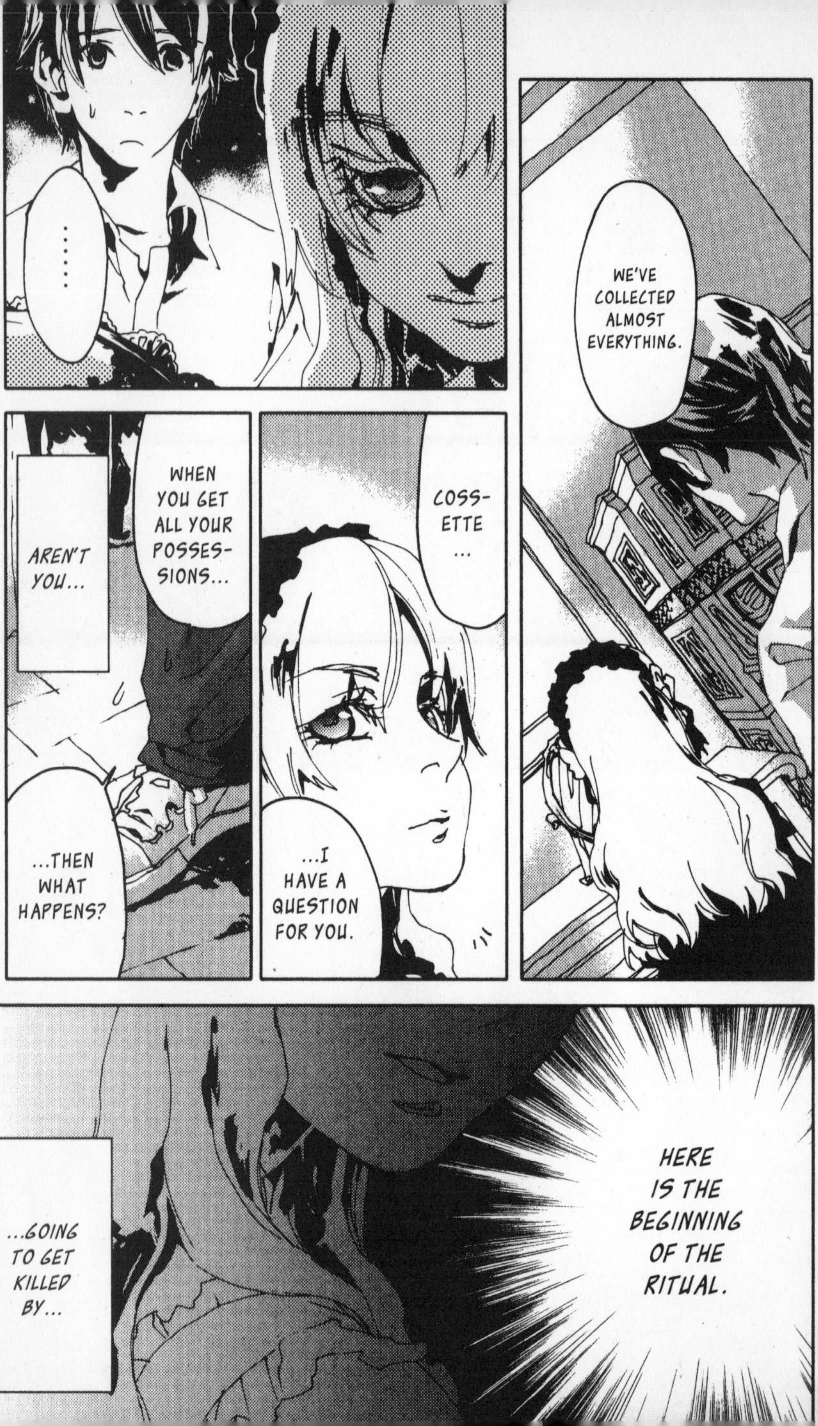
WE'VE COLLECTED ALMOST EVERYTHING.
......
COSS-ETTE ...
...I HAVE A QUESTION FOR YOU.
WHEN YOU GET ALL YOUR POSSES-SIONS...
...THEN WHAT HAPPENS?
AREN'T YOU...
HERE IS THE BEGINNING OF THE RITUAL.
...GOING TO GET KILLED BY...

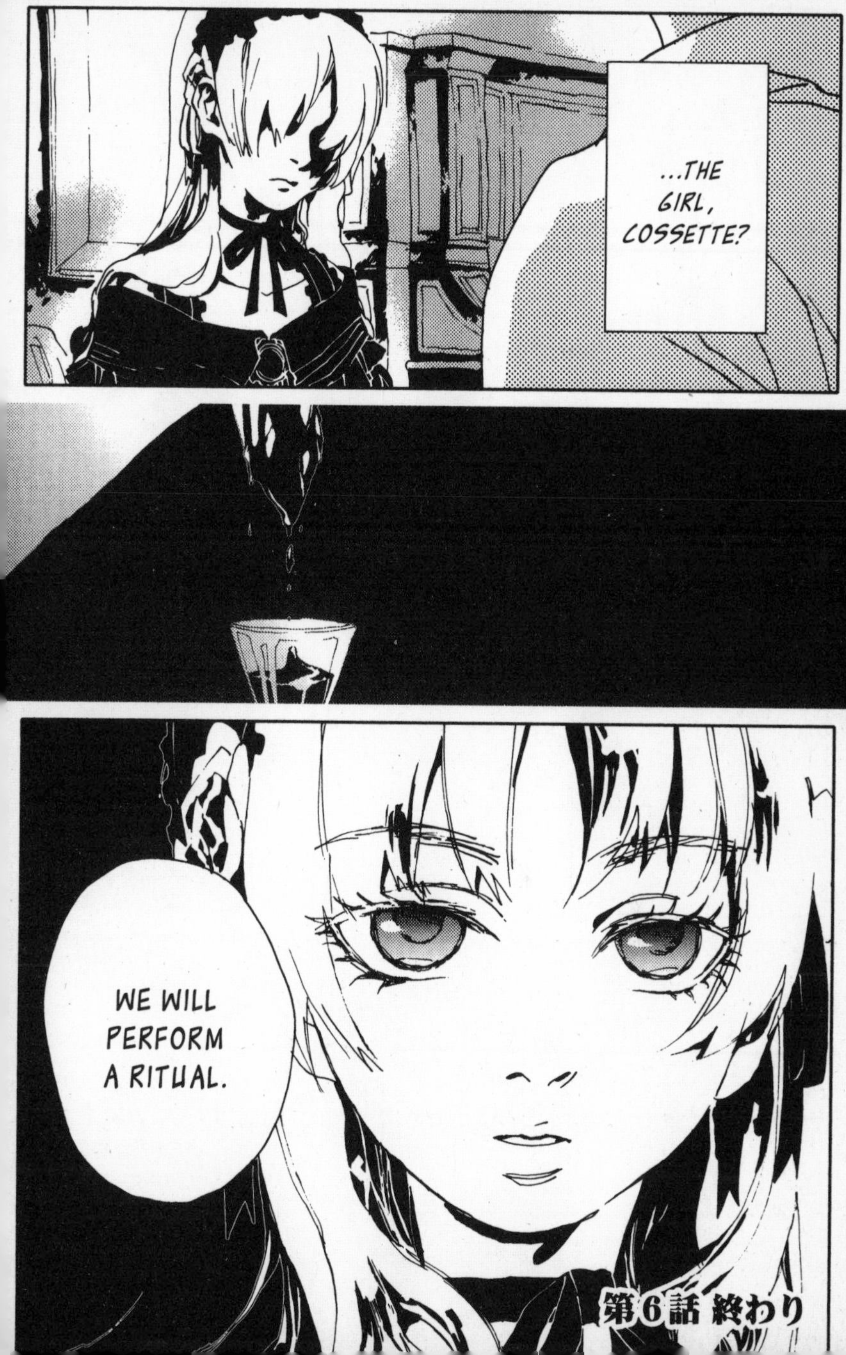
...THE GIRL, COSSETTE?
WE WILL PERFORM A RITUAL.
第6話 終わり

第7話

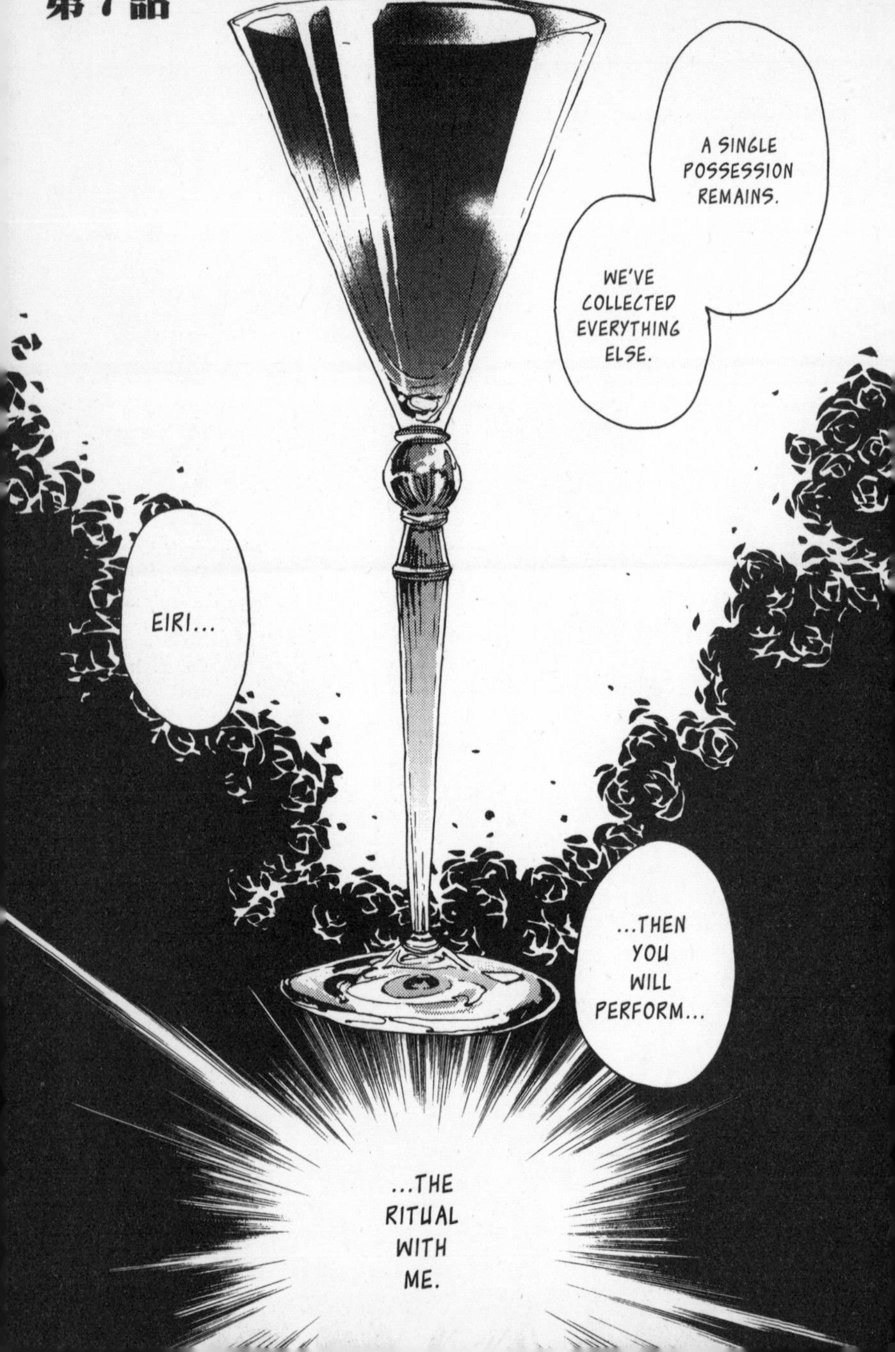
A SINGLE POSSESSION REMAINS.
WE'VE COLLECTED EVERYTHING ELSE.
EIRI...
...THEN YOU WILL PERFORM...
...THE RITUAL WITH ME.

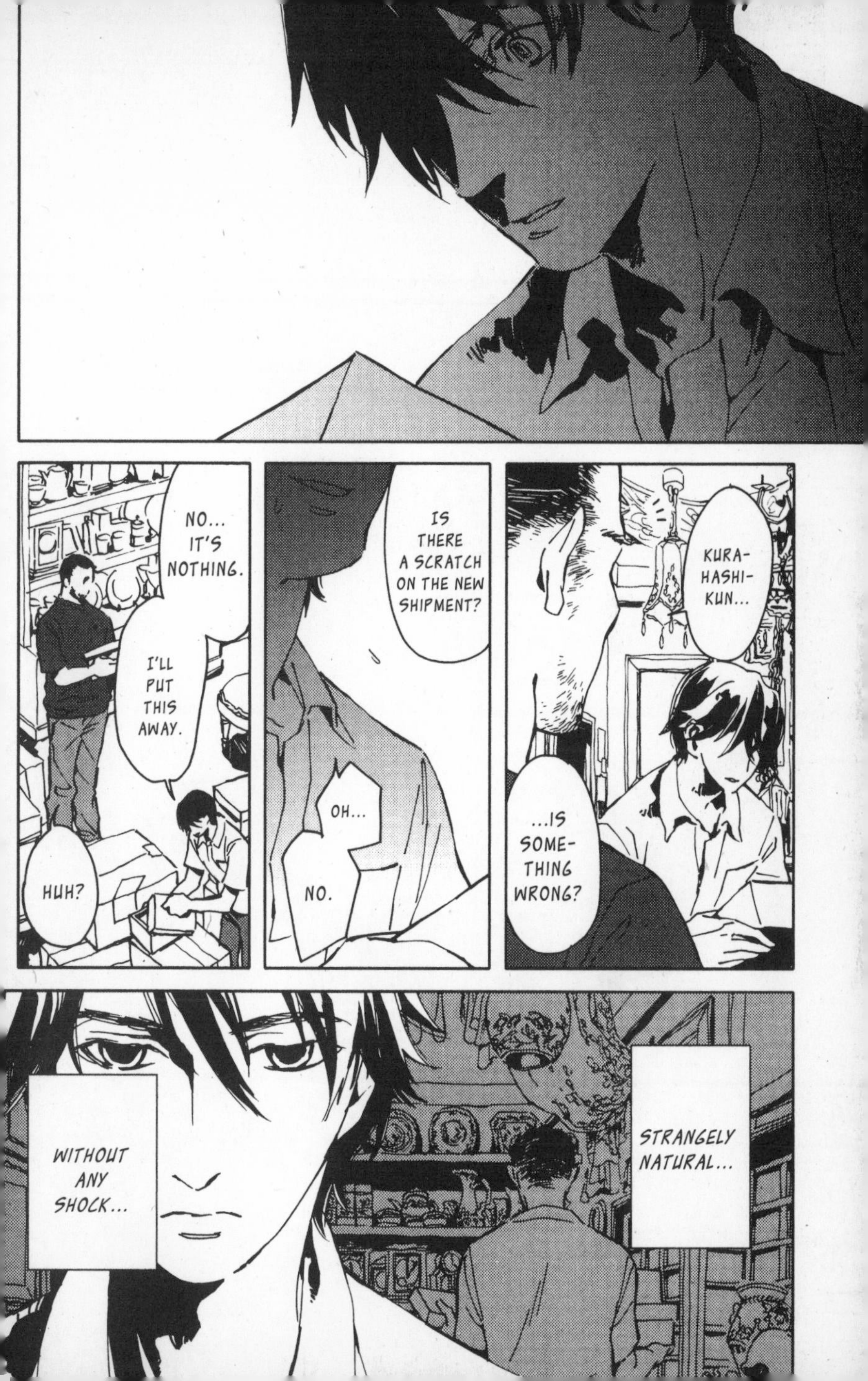
KURA-HASHI-KUN...
...IS SOME-THING WRONG?
IS THERE A SCRATCH ON THE NEW SHIPMENT?
OH...
NO.
NO... IT'S NOTHING.
I'LL PUT THIS AWAY.
HUH?
STRANGELY NATURAL...
WITHOUT ANY SHOCK...

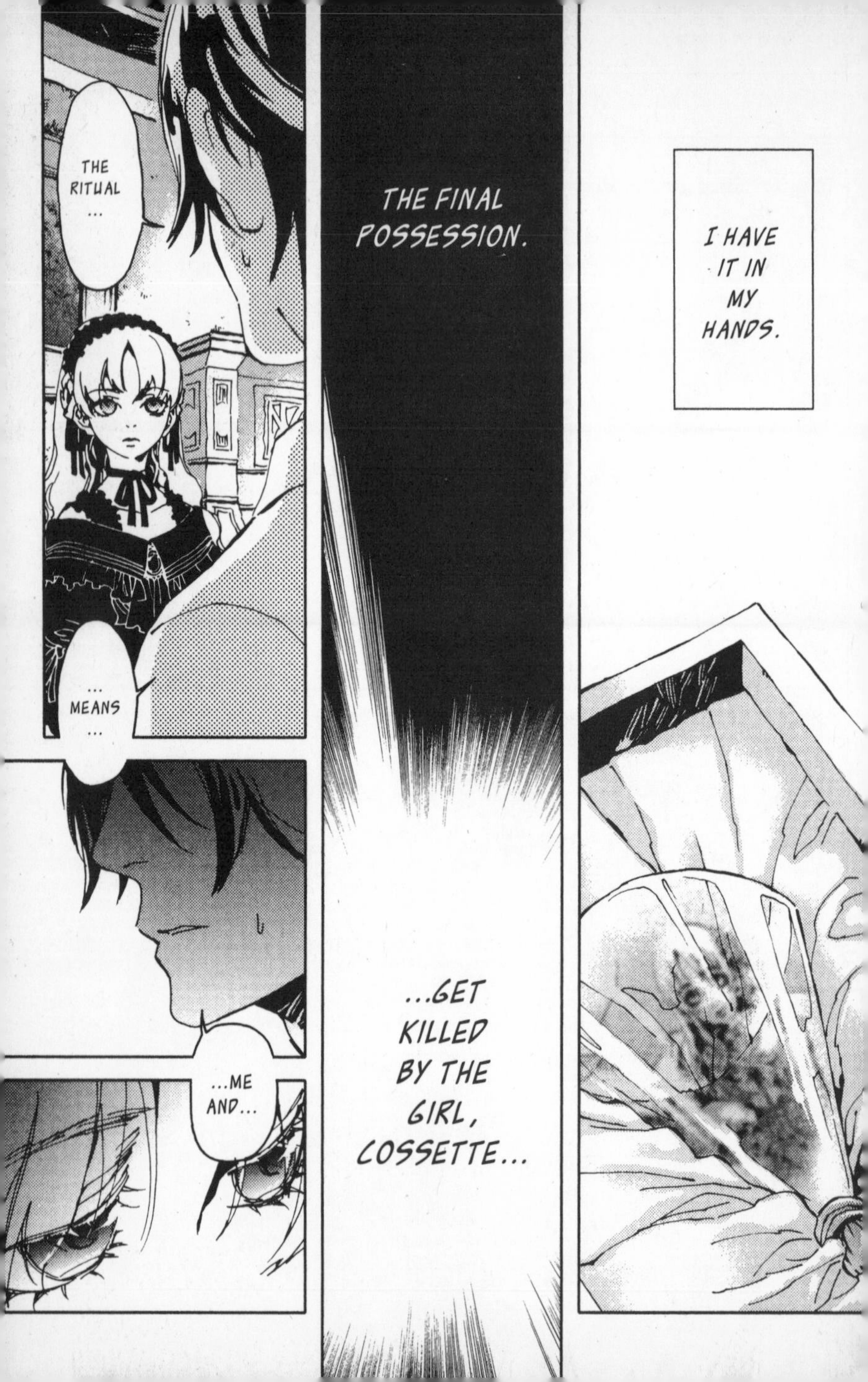
I HAVE IT IN MY HANDS.
THE FINAL POSSESSION.
THE RITUAL ...
... MEANS ...
...ME AND...
...GET KILLED BY THE GIRL, COSSETTE...

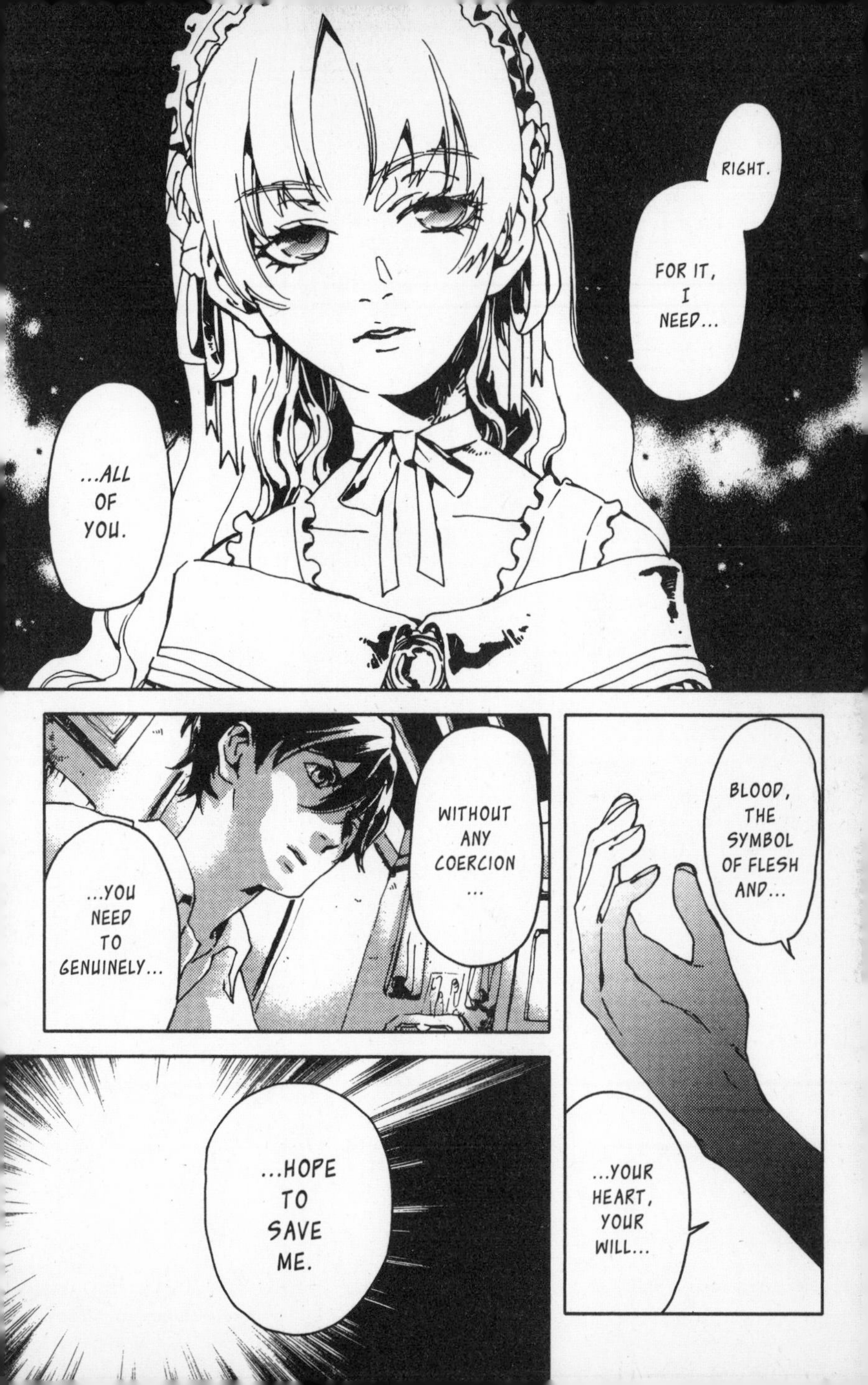
RIGHT.
FOR IT, I NEED...
...ALL OF YOU.
BLOOD, THE SYMBOL OF FLESH AND...
...YOUR HEART, YOUR WILL...
WITHOUT ANY COERCION...
...YOU NEED TO GENUINELY...
...HOPE TO SAVE ME.

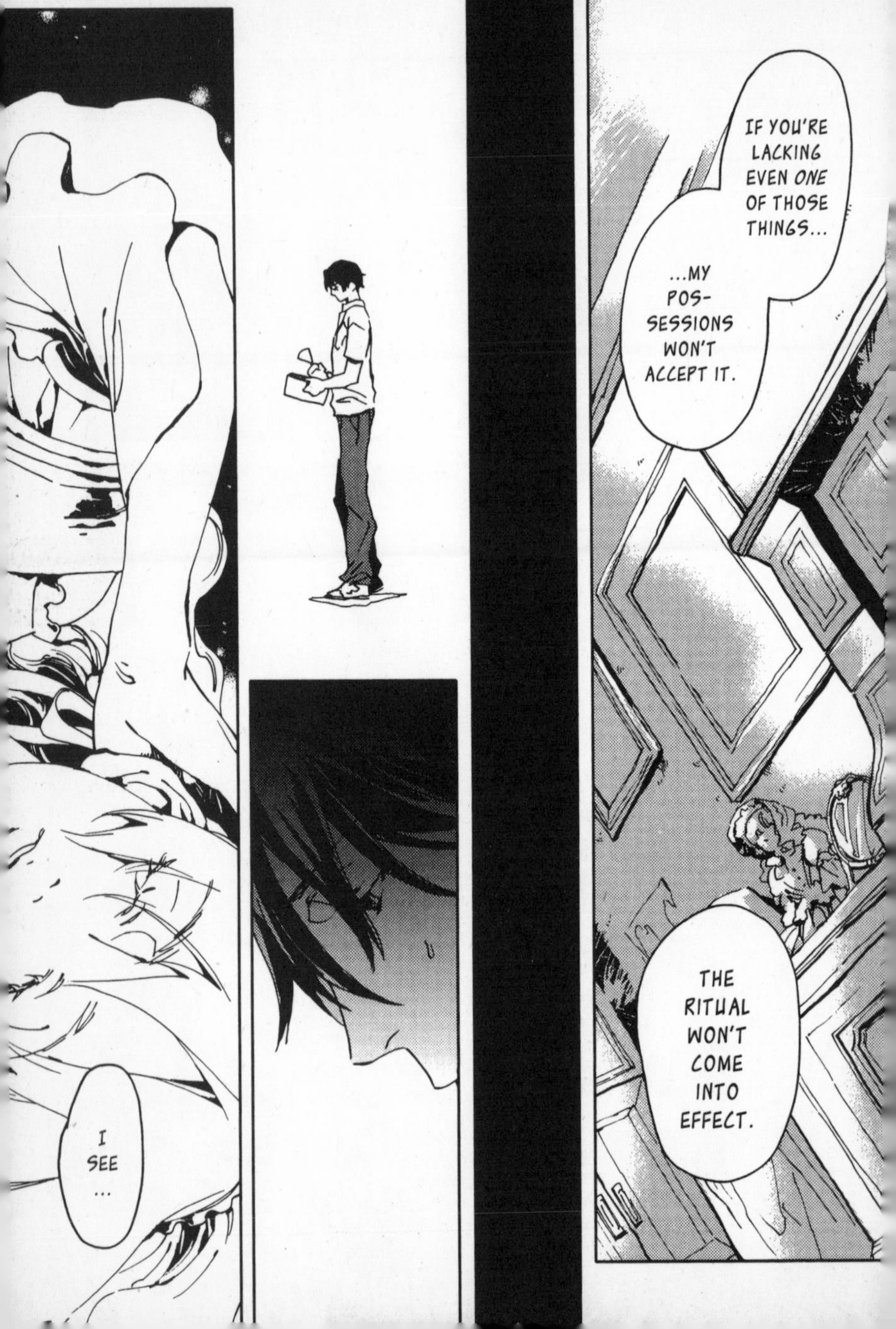
IF YOU'RE LACKING EVEN *ONE* OF THOSE THINGS...
...MY POS-SESSIONS WON'T ACCEPT IT.
THE RITUAL WON'T COME INTO EFFECT.
I SEE ...

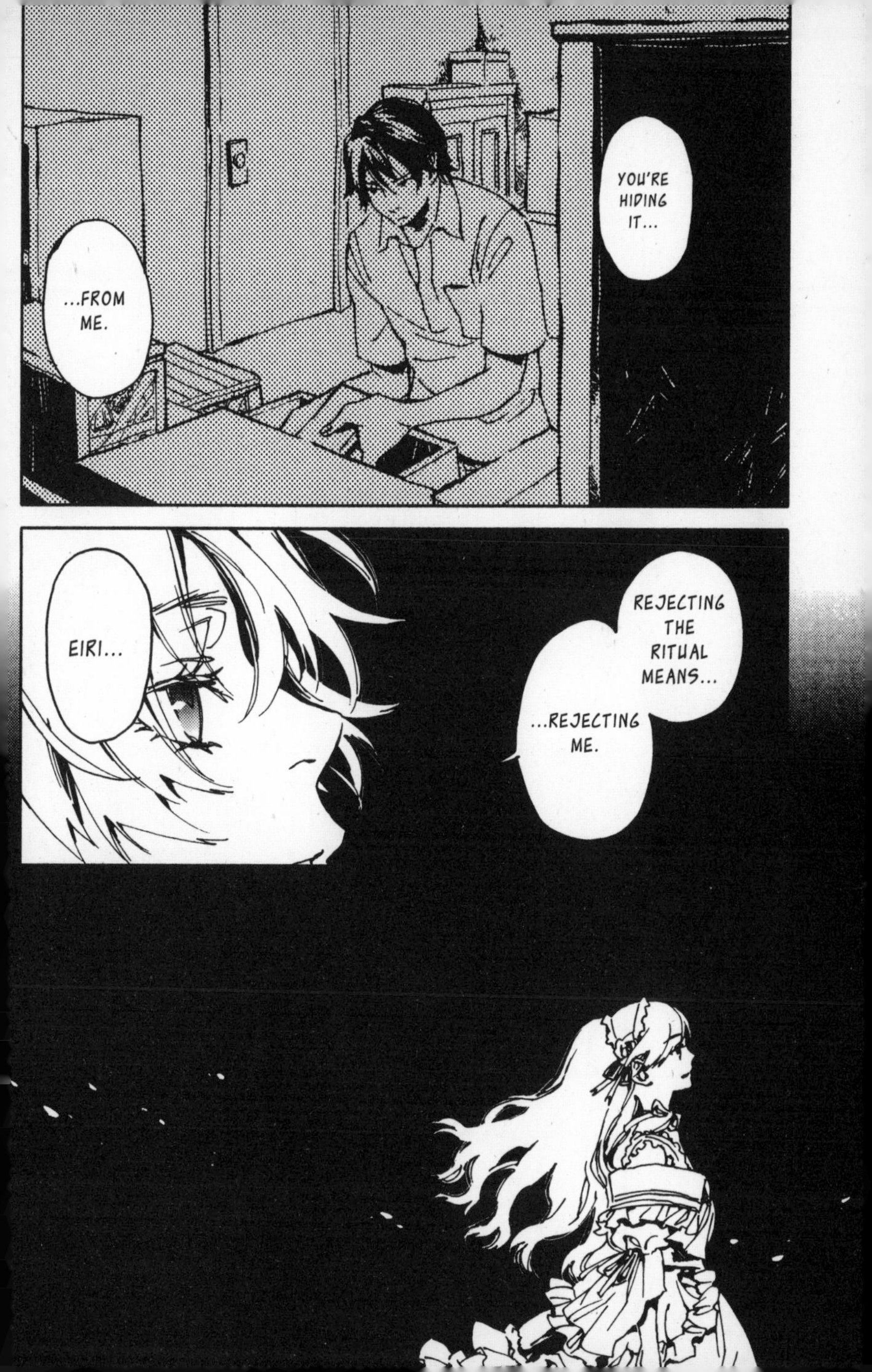
YOU'RE HIDING IT...
...FROM ME.
REJECTING THE RITUAL MEANS...
...REJECTING ME.
EIRI...

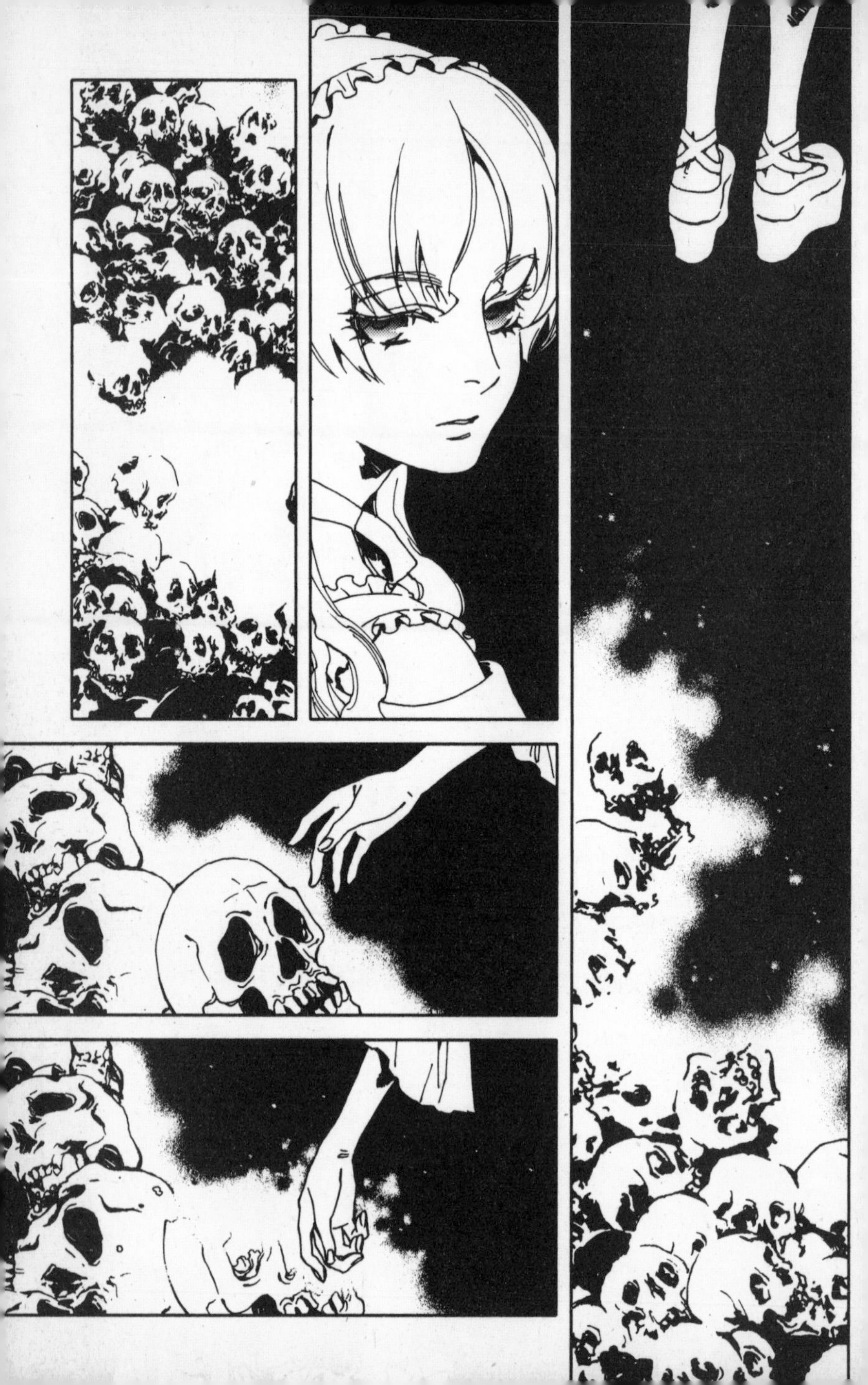

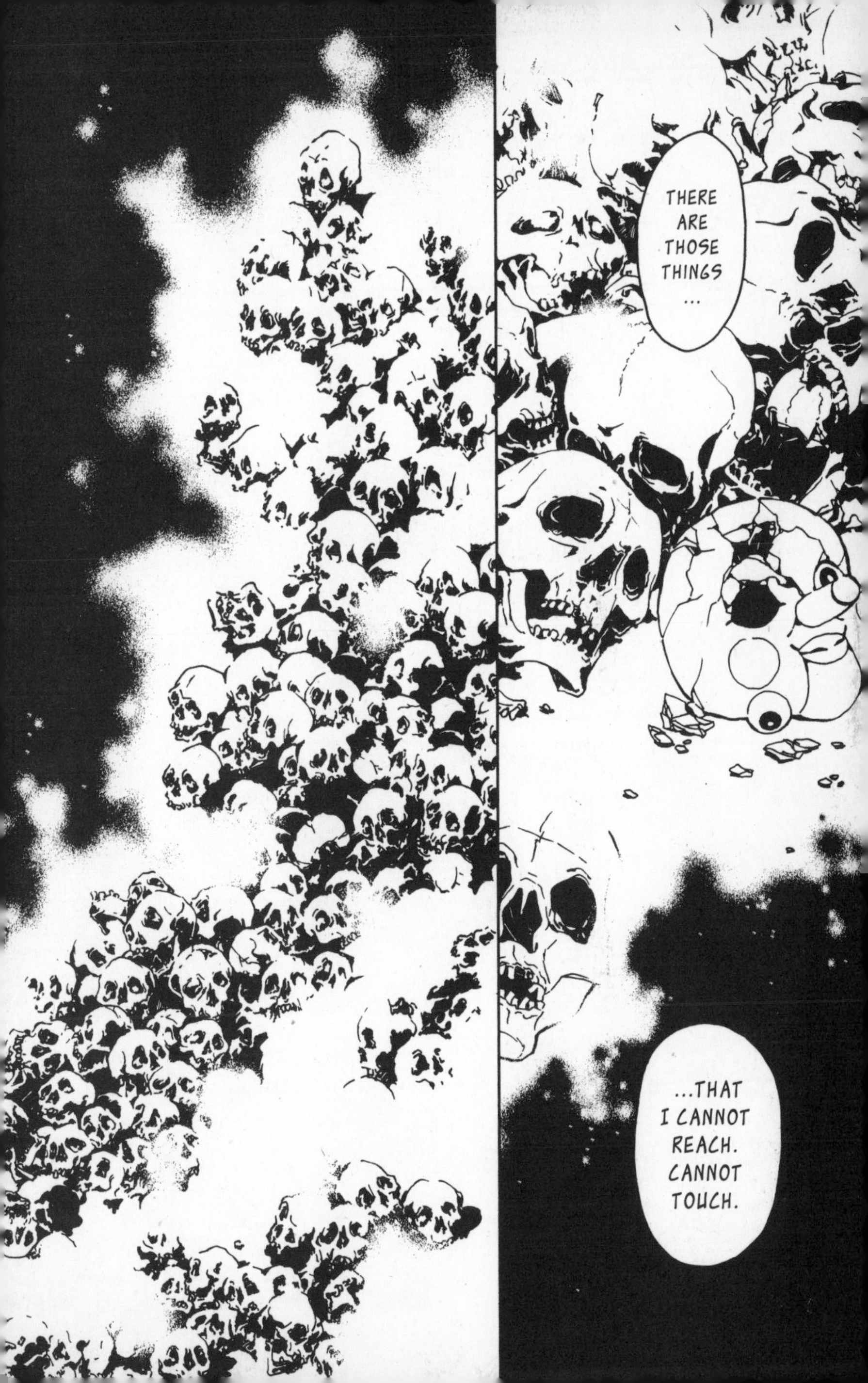
THERE ARE THOSE THINGS ...
...THAT I CANNOT REACH. CANNOT TOUCH.

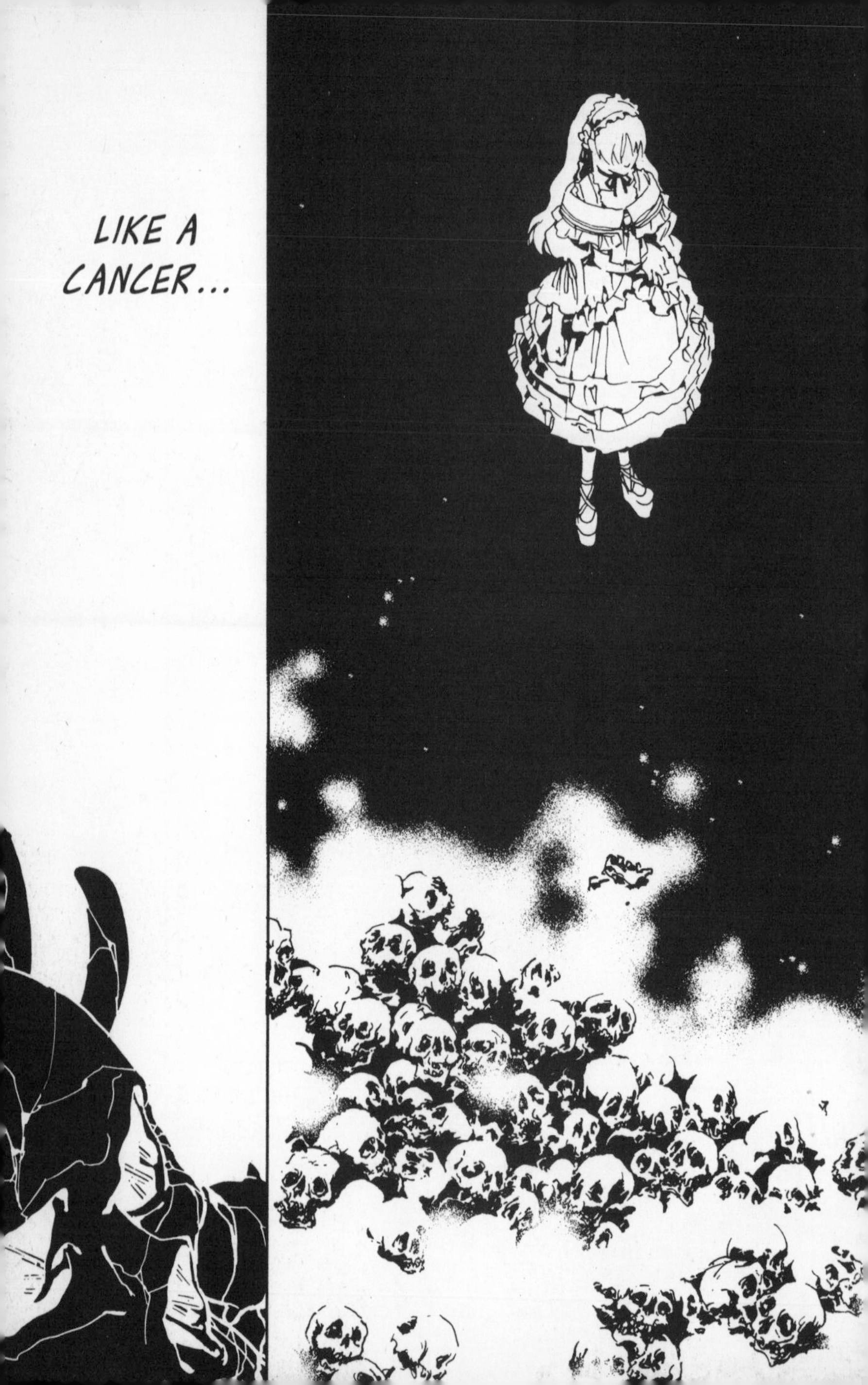
LIKE A CANCER...

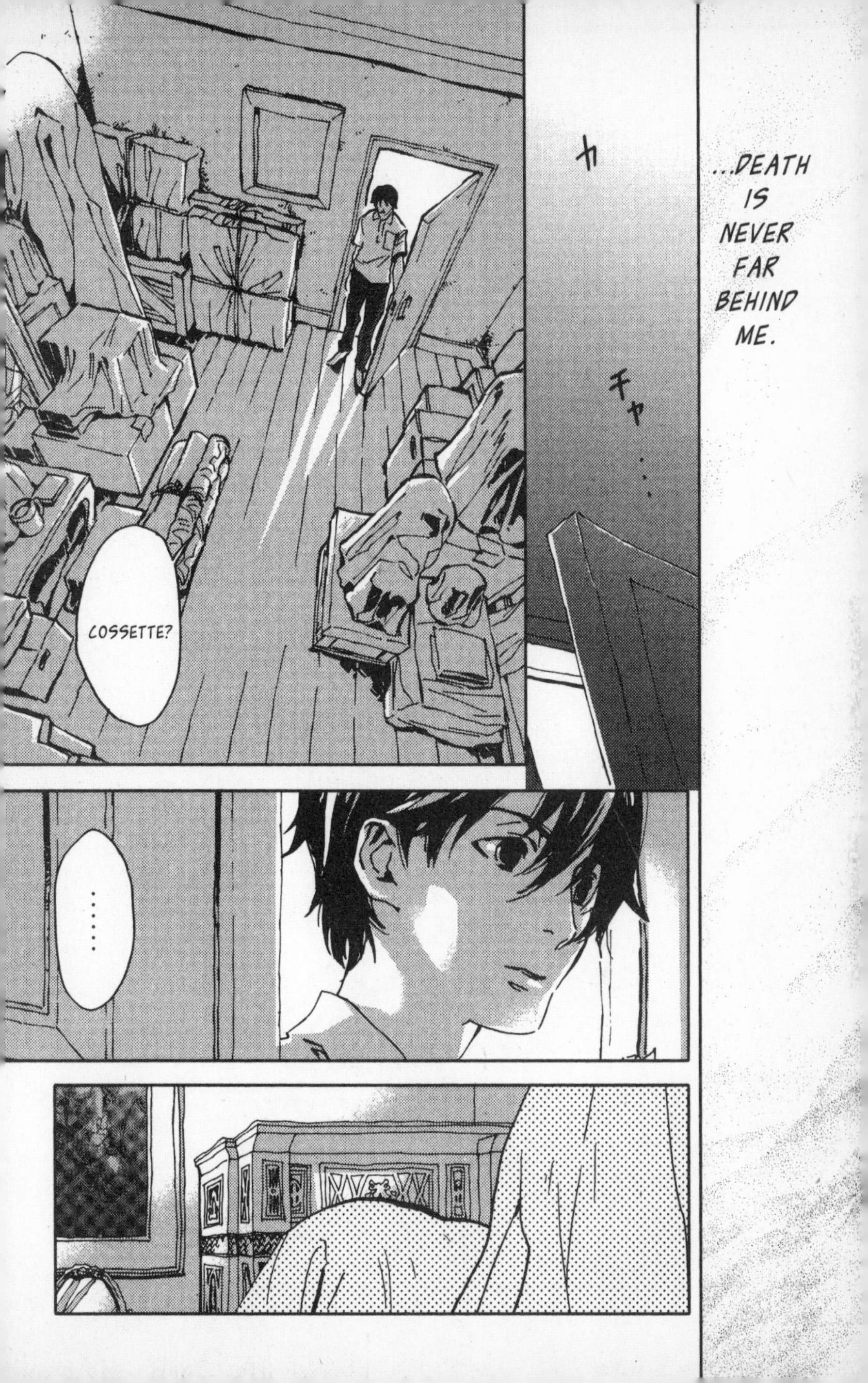
...DEATH IS NEVER FAR BEHIND ME.
カチャ...
COSSETTE?
......

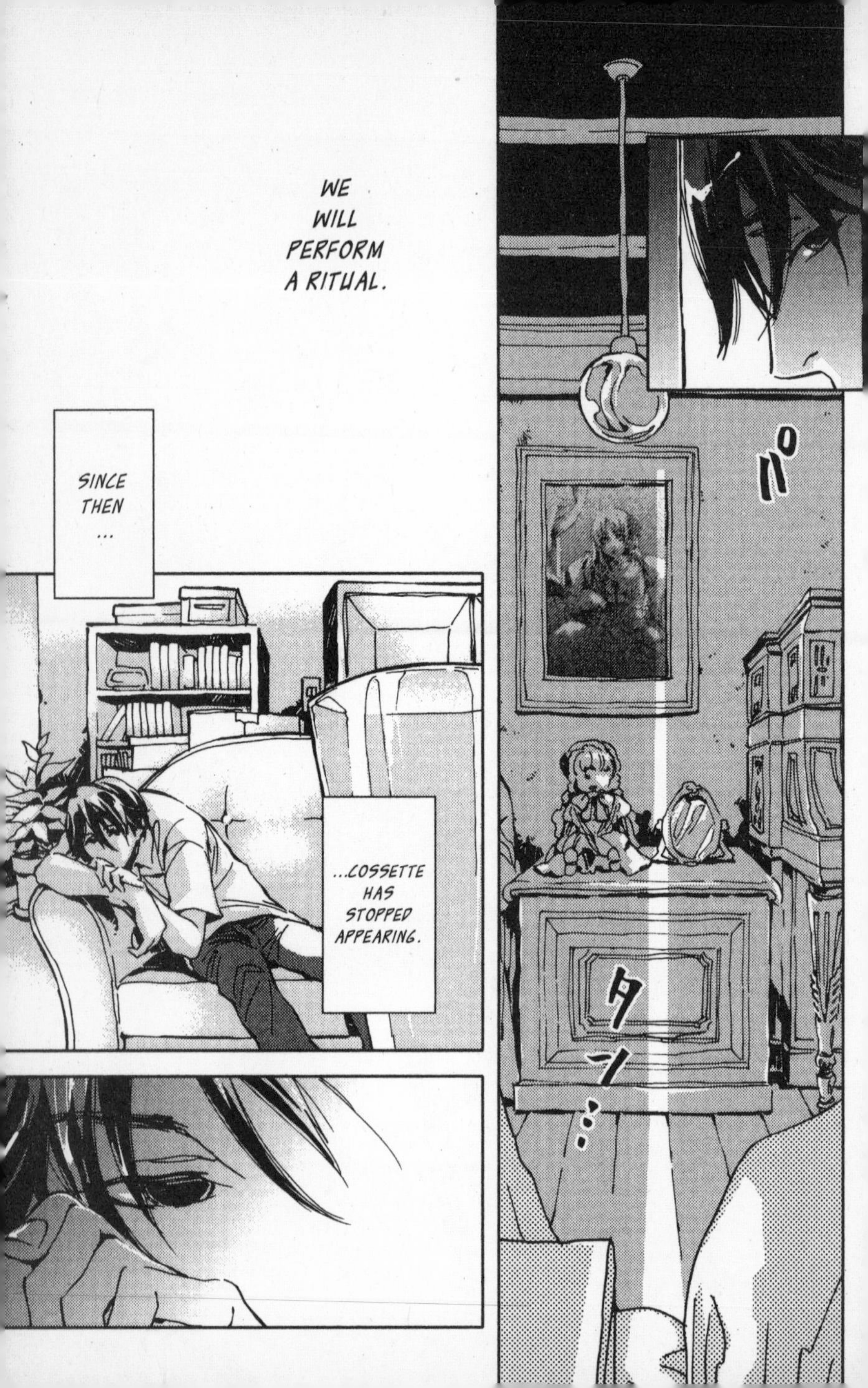
パ
タン…
WE WILL PERFORM A RITUAL.
SINCE THEN ...
...COSSETTE HAS STOPPED APPEARING.

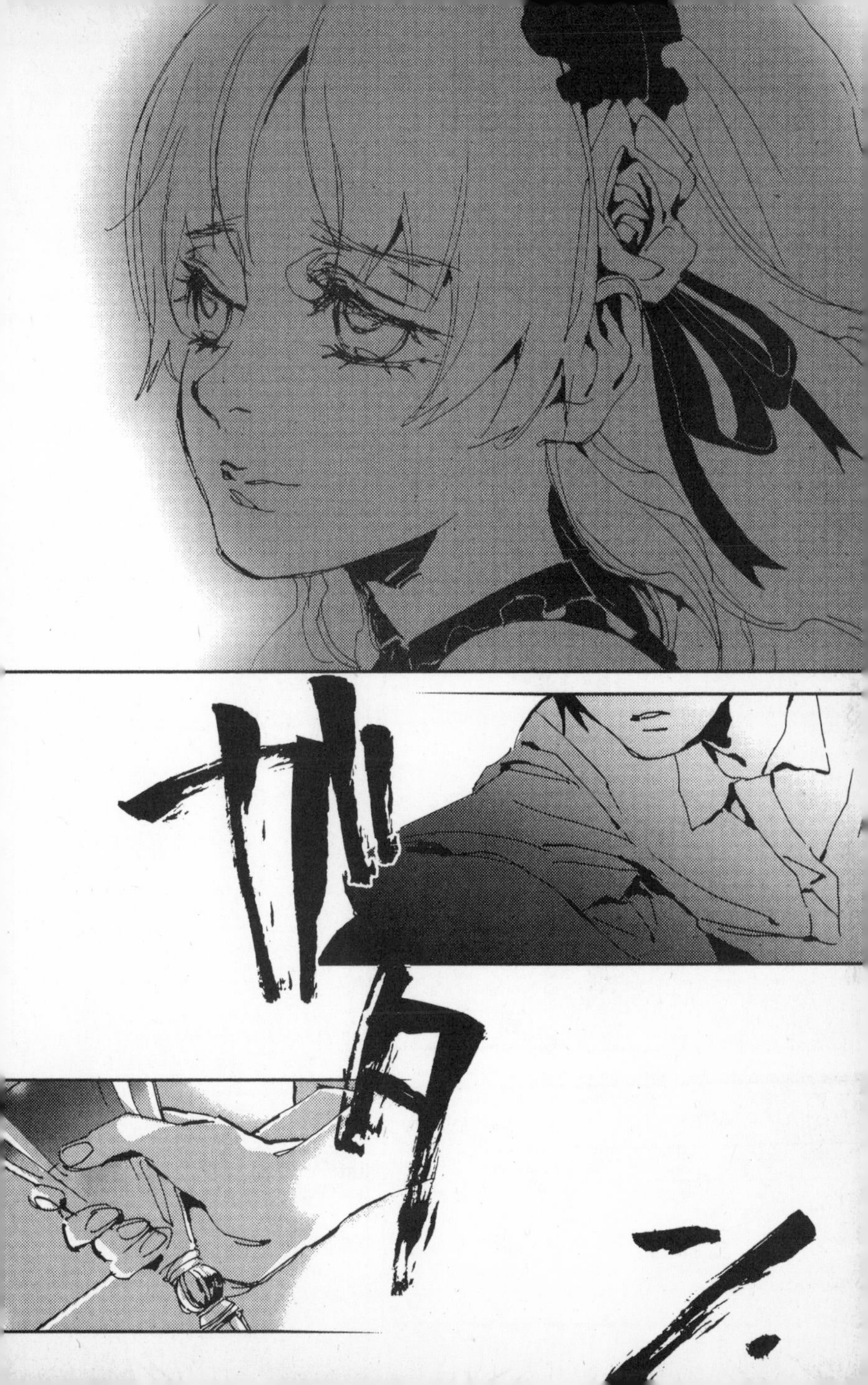
ザクッ

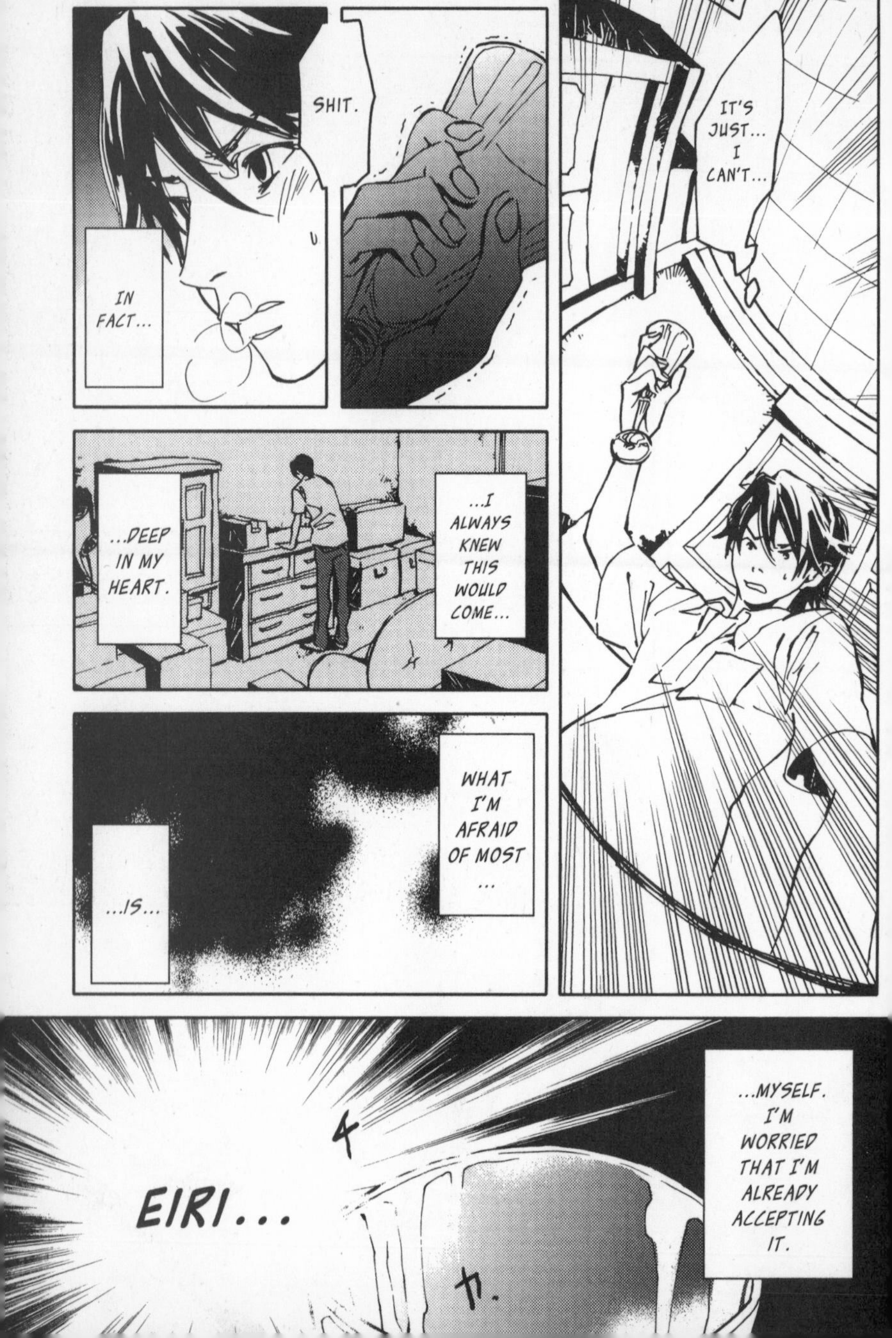
IT'S JUST... I CAN'T...
SHIT.
IN FACT...
...I ALWAYS KNEW THIS WOULD COME...
...DEEP IN MY HEART.
WHAT I'M AFRAID OF MOST ...
...IS...
...MYSELF. I'M WORRIED THAT I'M ALREADY ACCEPTING IT.
EIRI...

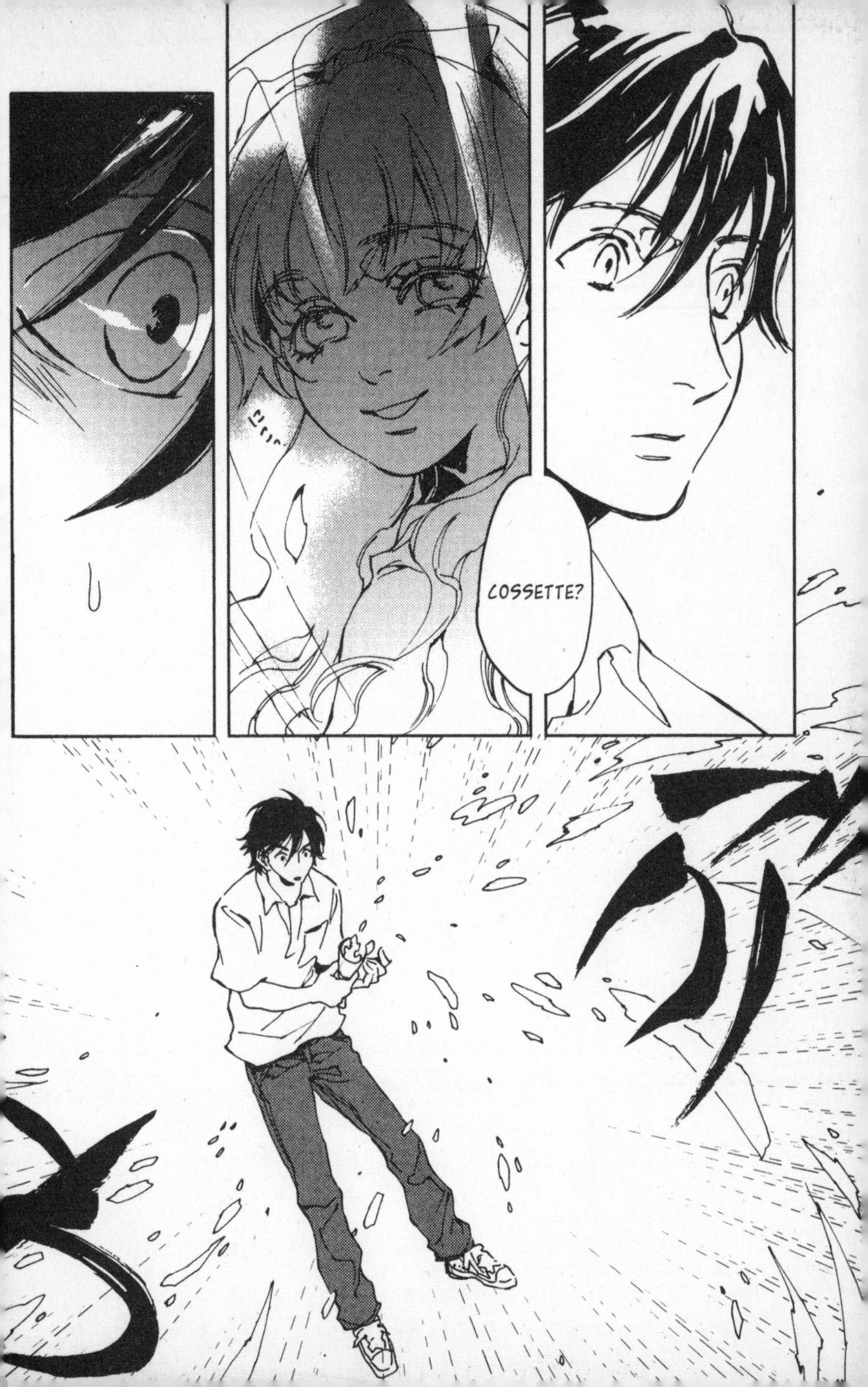
COSSETTE?

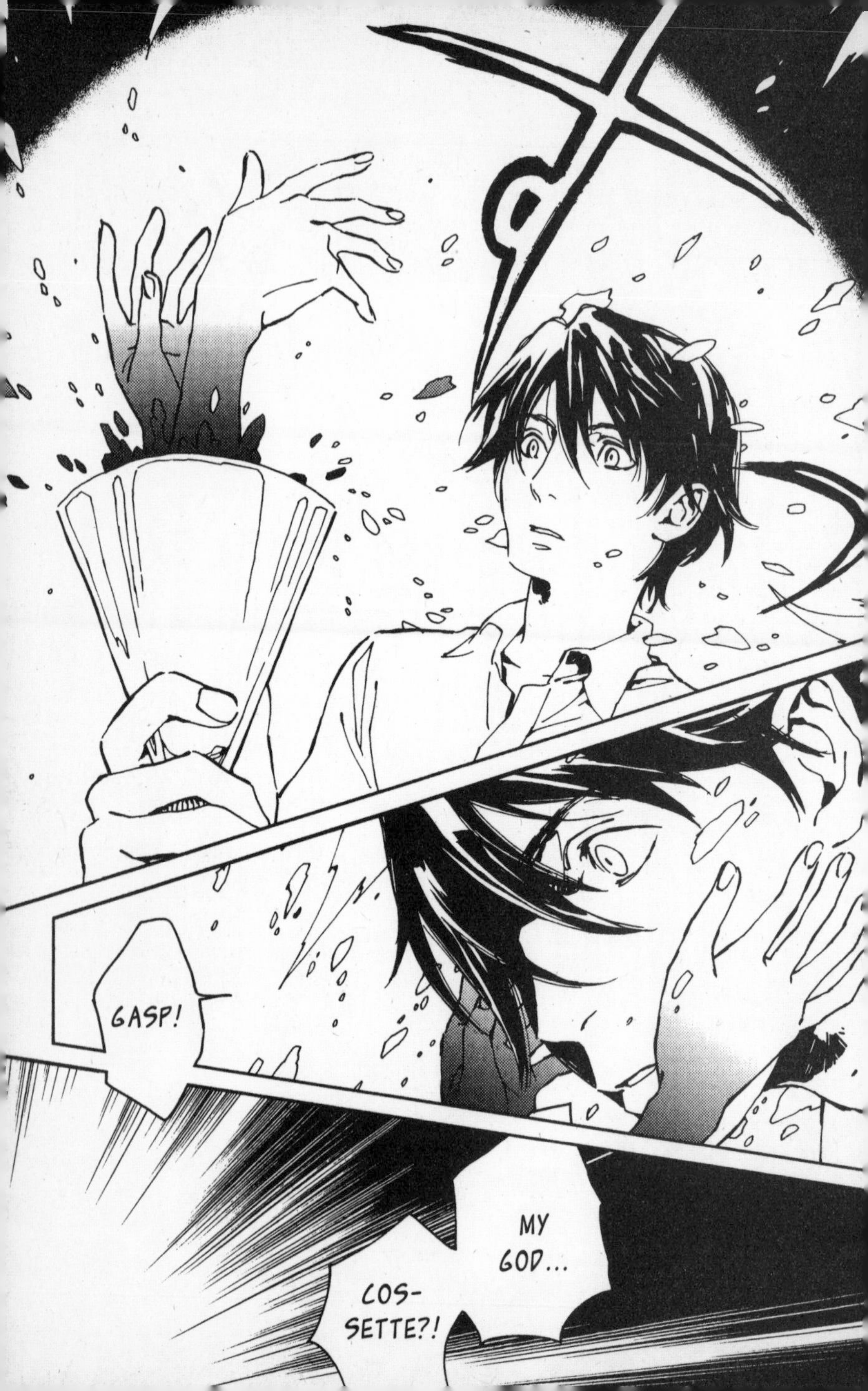
GASP!
MY GOD...
COS-
SETTE?!

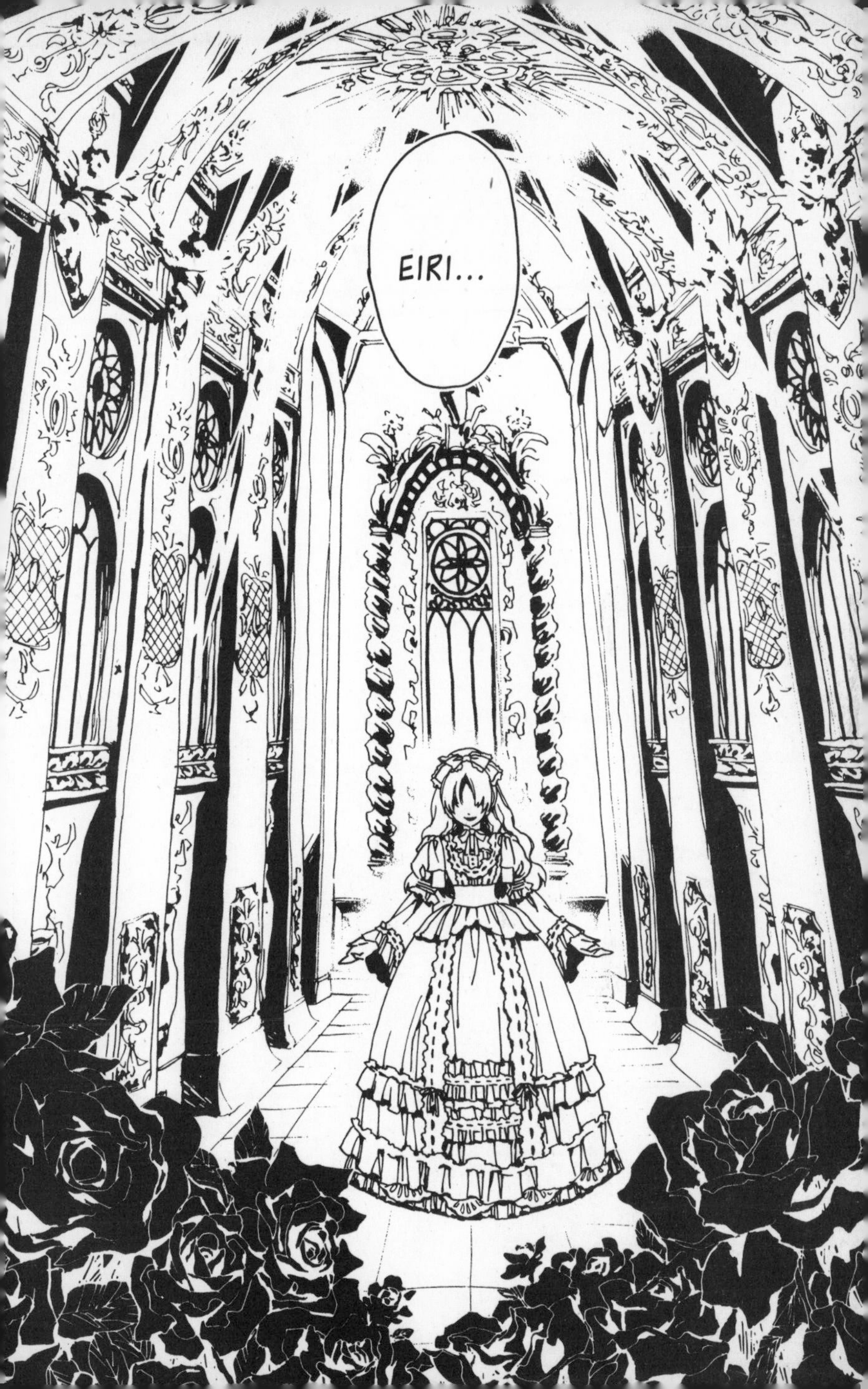
EIRI...

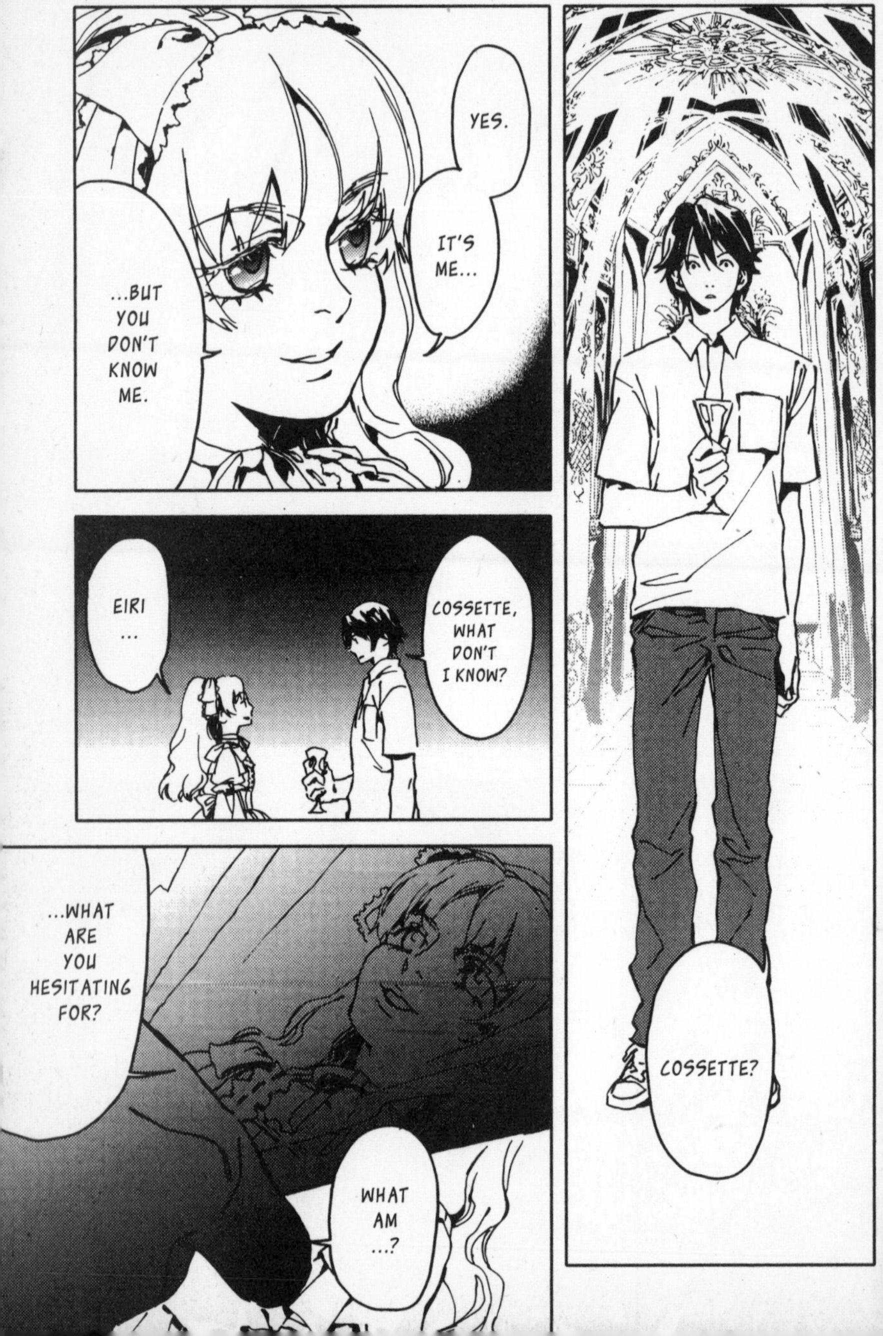
COSSETTE?
YES.
IT'S ME...
...BUT YOU DON'T KNOW ME.
COSSETTE, WHAT DON'T I KNOW?
EIRI ...
...WHAT ARE YOU HESITATING FOR?
WHAT AM ...?

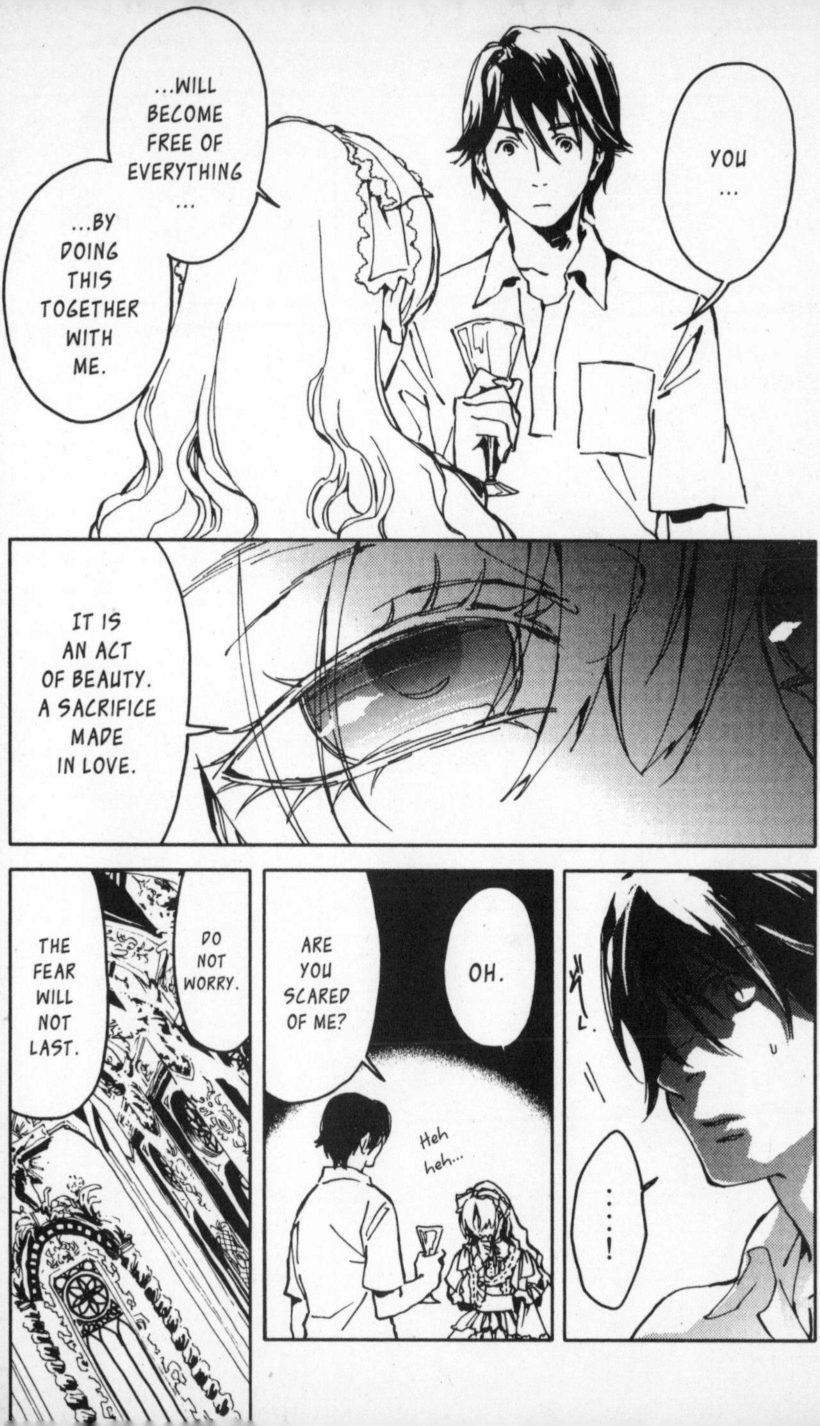
YOU ...
...WILL BECOME FREE OF EVERYTHING ...
...BY DOING THIS TOGETHER WITH ME.
IT IS AN ACT OF BEAUTY. A SACRIFICE MADE IN LOVE.
...!
OH.
ARE YOU SCARED OF ME?
Heh heh...
DO NOT WORRY.
THE FEAR WILL NOT LAST.

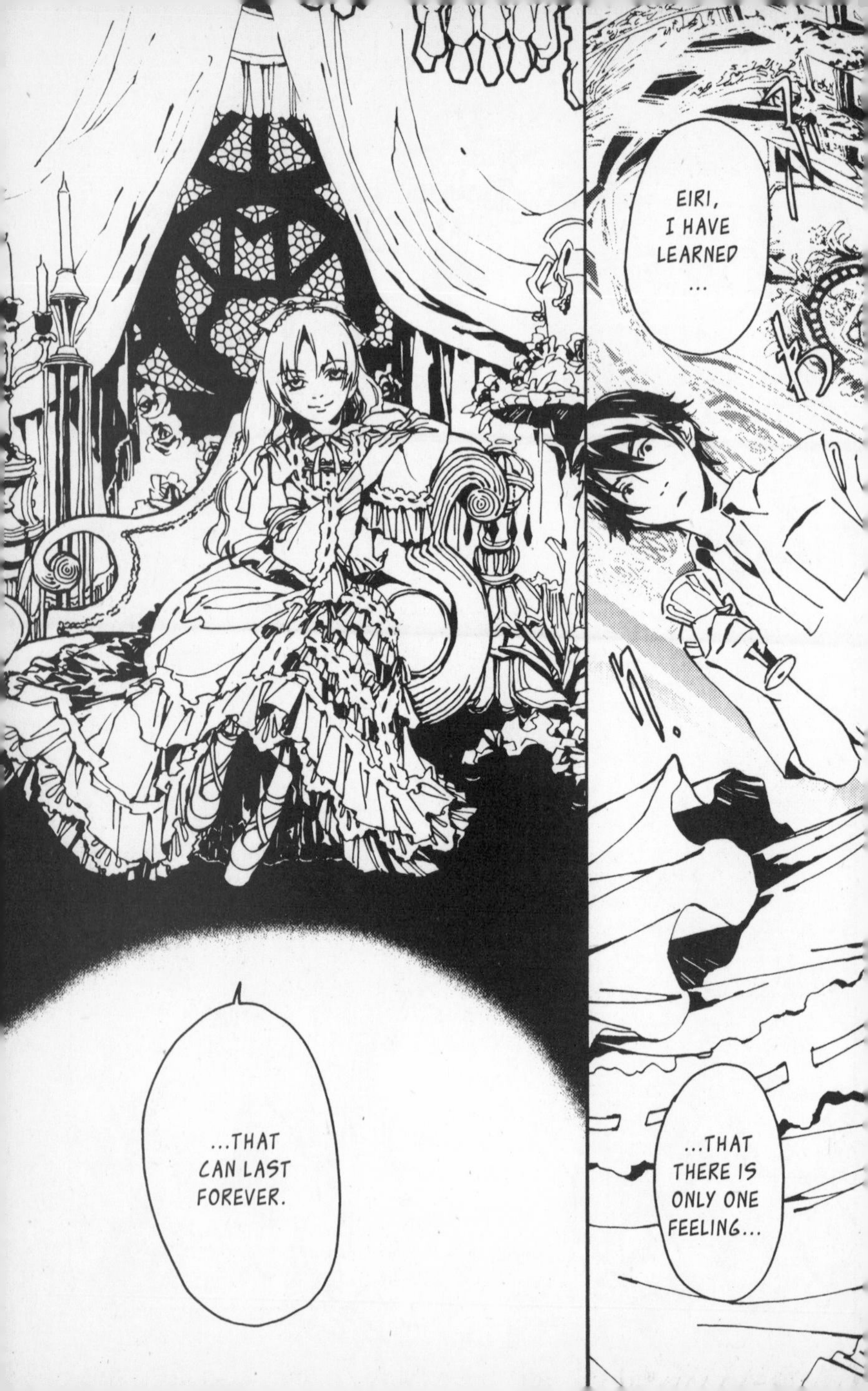
EIRI, I HAVE LEARNED ...
...THAT THERE IS ONLY ONE FEELING...
...THAT CAN LAST FOREVER.

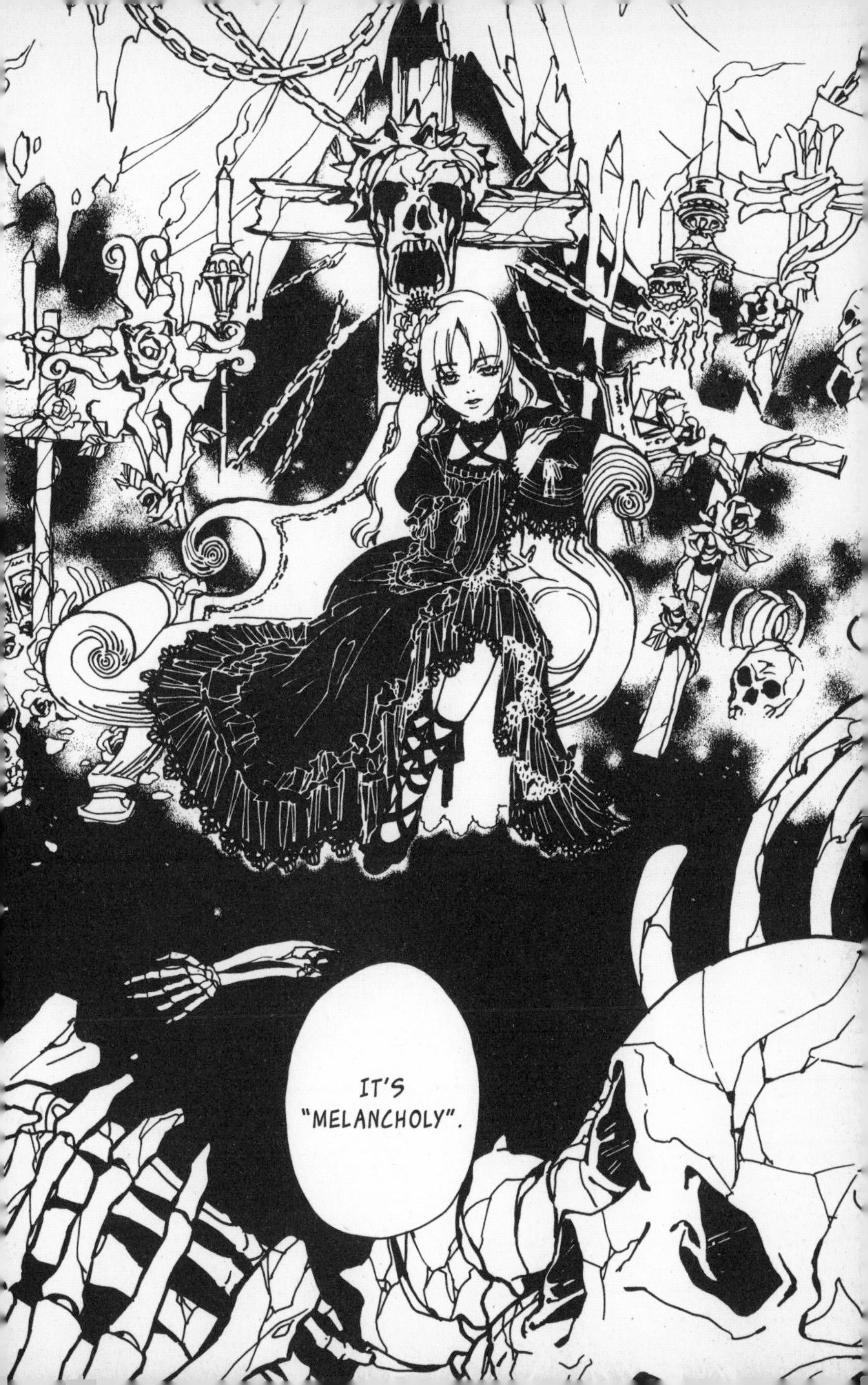
IT'S
"MELANCHOLY".

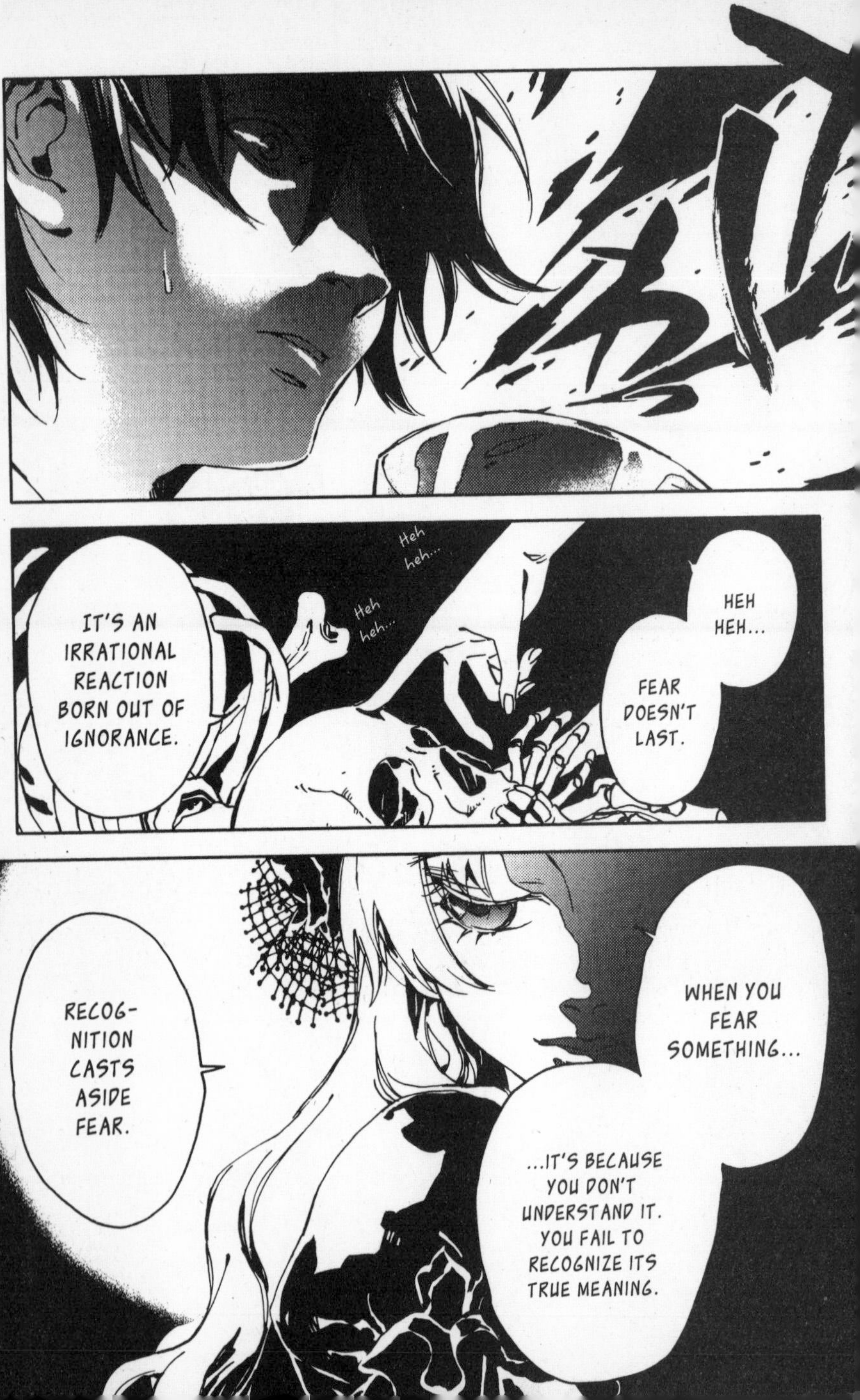
HEH HEH...
FEAR DOESN'T LAST.
Heh heh...
Heh heh...
IT'S AN IRRATIONAL REACTION BORN OUT OF IGNORANCE.
WHEN YOU FEAR SOMETHING...
...IT'S BECAUSE YOU DON'T UNDERSTAND IT. YOU FAIL TO RECOGNIZE ITS TRUE MEANING.
RECOG-NITION CASTS ASIDE FEAR.

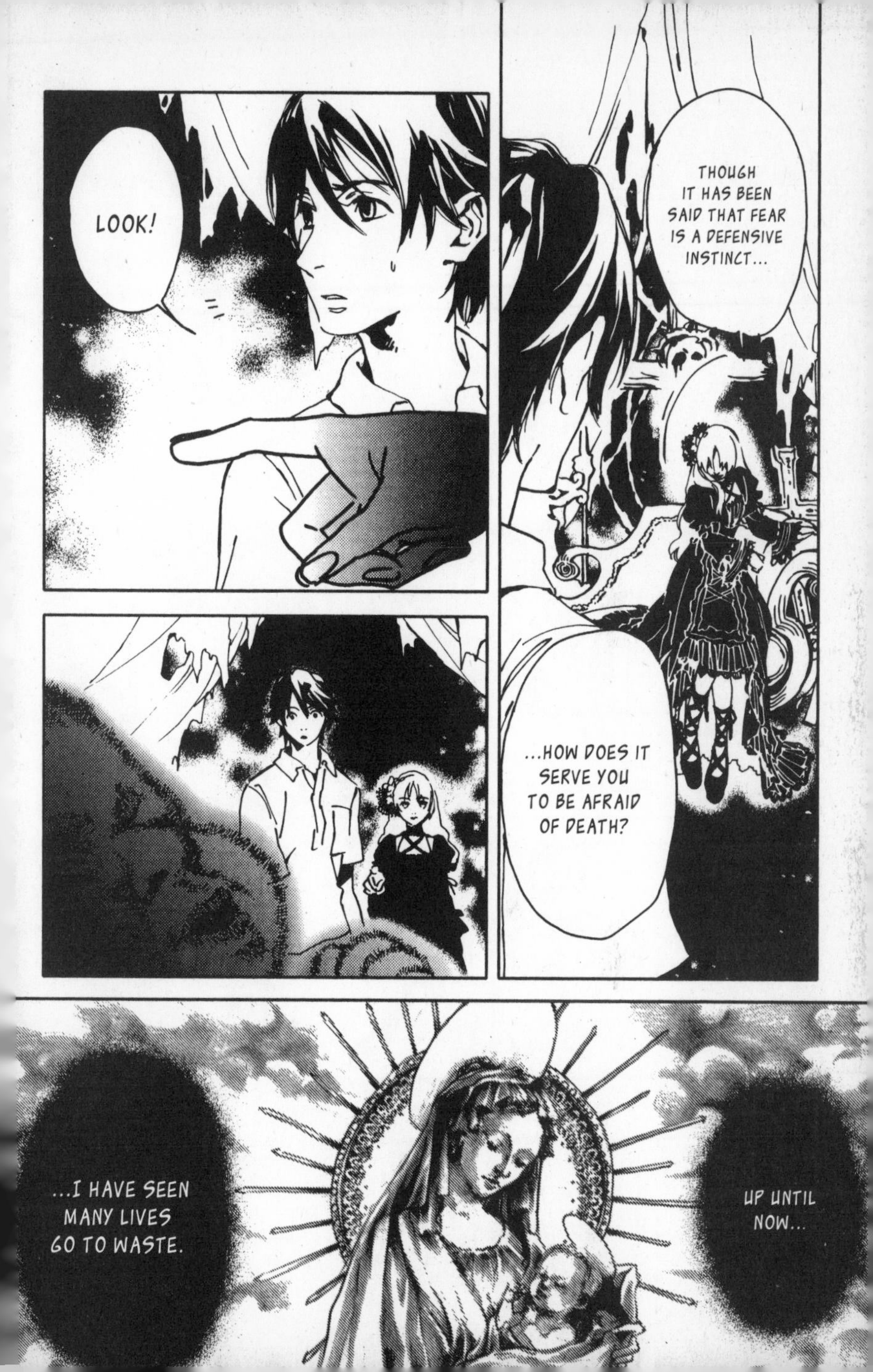
THOUGH IT HAS BEEN SAID THAT FEAR IS A DEFENSIVE INSTINCT...
...HOW DOES IT SERVE YOU TO BE AFRAID OF DEATH?
LOOK!
UP UNTIL NOW...
...I HAVE SEEN MANY LIVES GO TO WASTE.

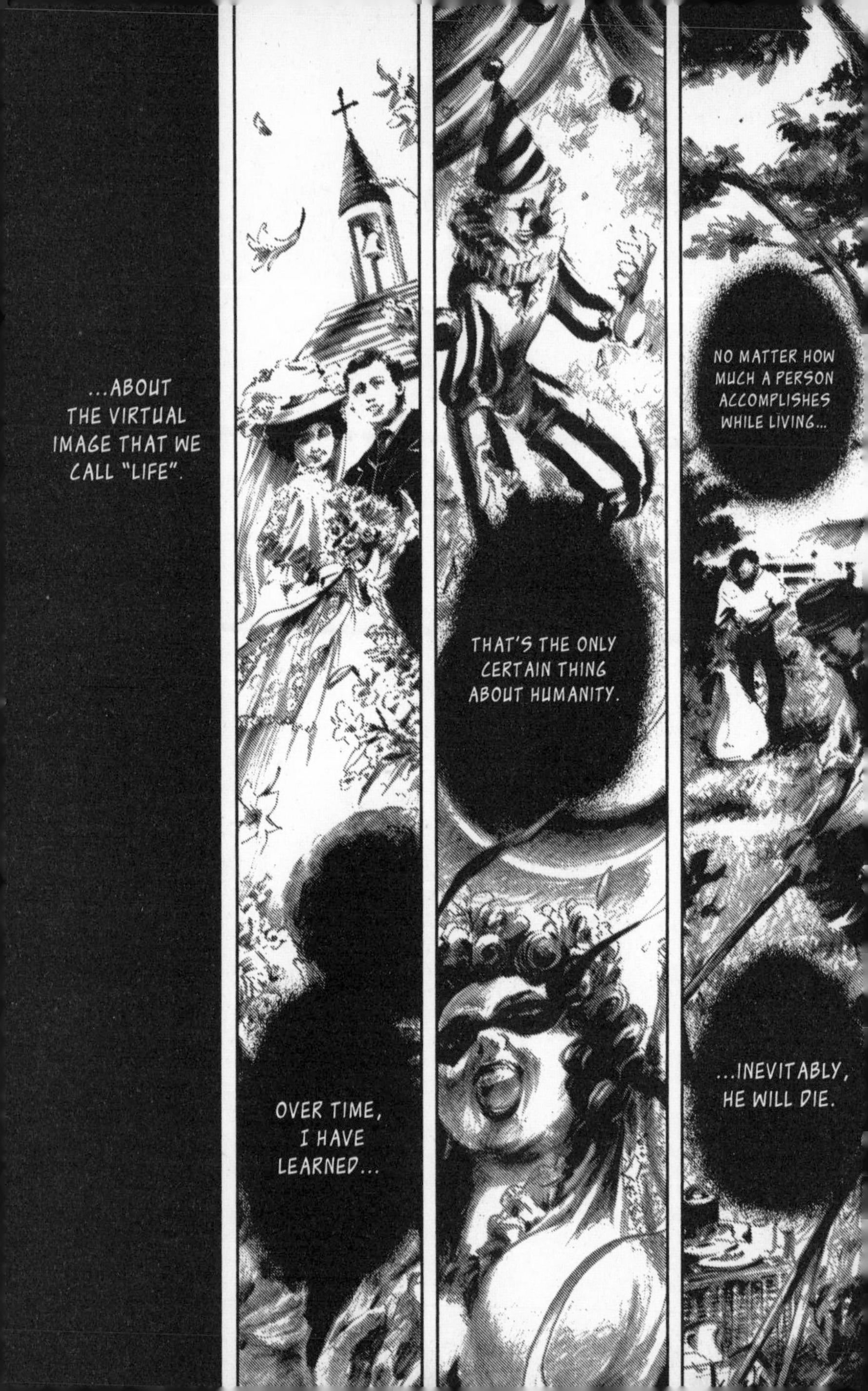
NO MATTER HOW MUCH A PERSON ACCOMPLISHES WHILE LIVING...
...INEVITABLY, HE WILL DIE.
THAT'S THE ONLY CERTAIN THING ABOUT HUMANITY.
OVER TIME, I HAVE LEARNED...
...ABOUT THE VIRTUAL IMAGE THAT WE CALL "LIFE".

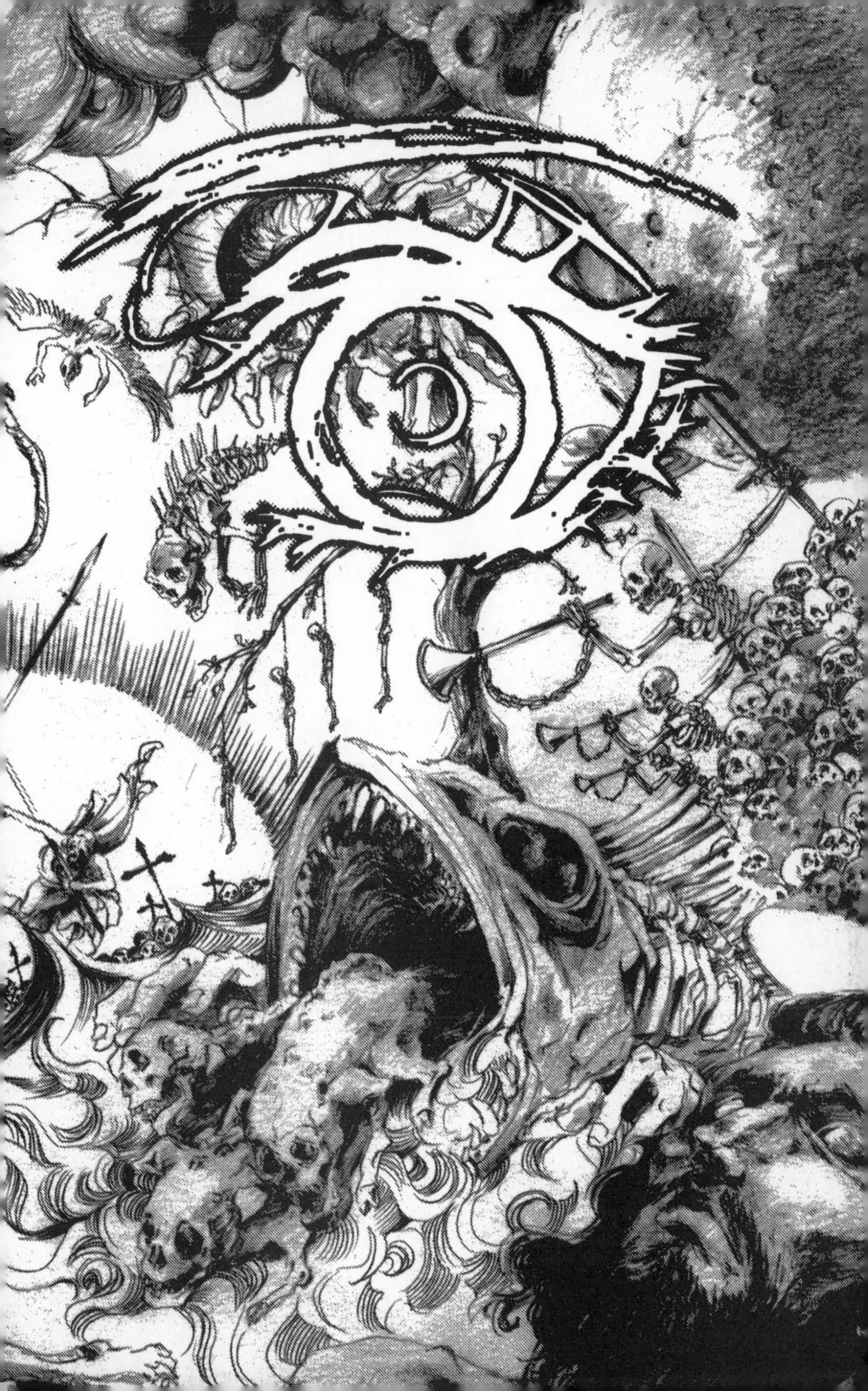

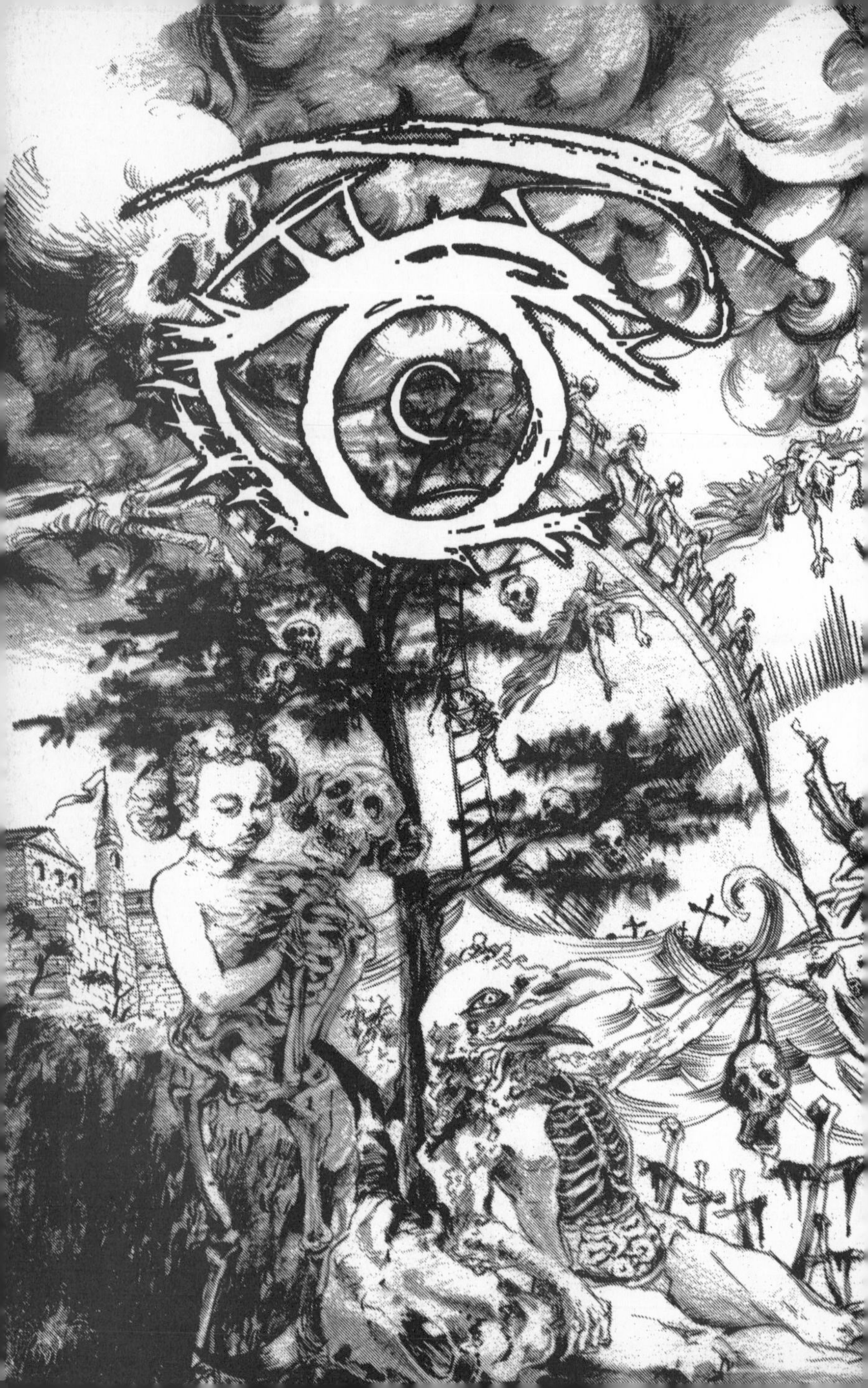

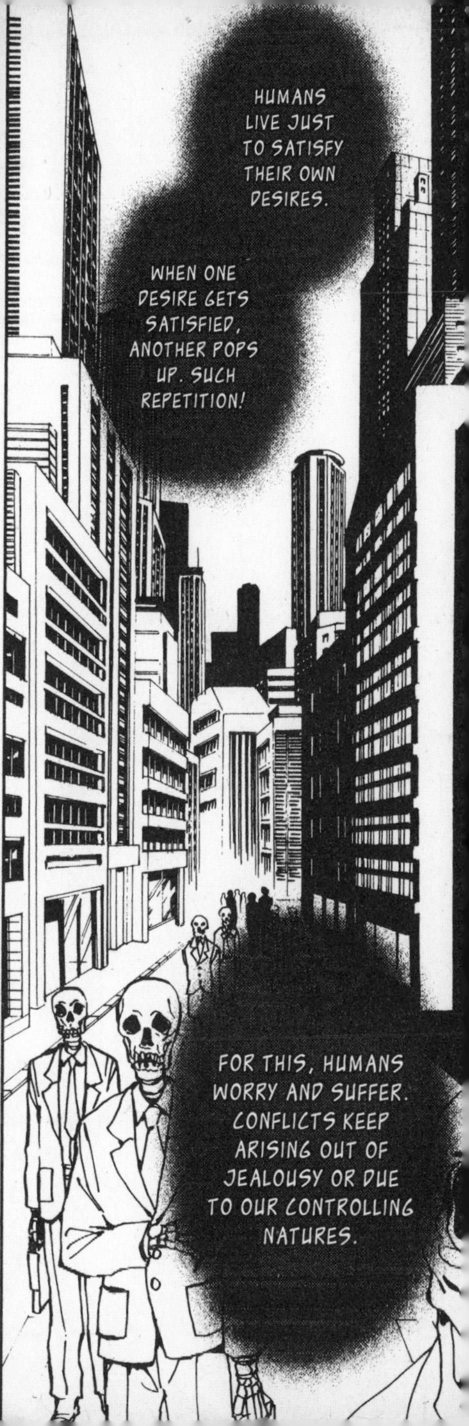
HUMANS LIVE JUST TO SATISFY THEIR OWN DESIRES.
WHEN ONE DESIRE GETS SATISFIED, ANOTHER POPS UP. SUCH REPETITION!
FOR THIS, HUMANS WORRY AND SUFFER. CONFLICTS KEEP ARISING OUT OF JEALOUSY OR DUE TO OUR CONTROLLING NATURES.
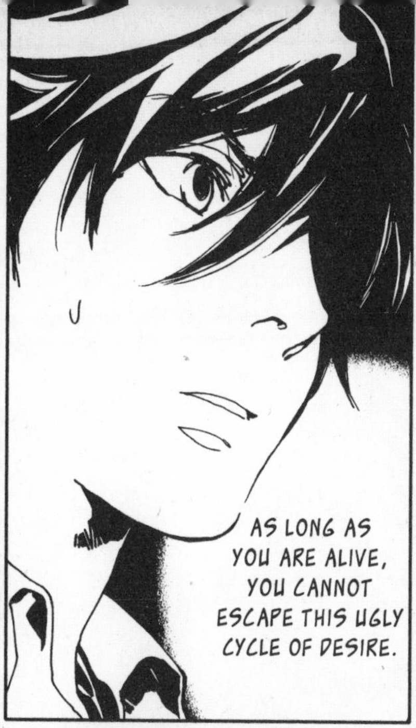
AS LONG AS YOU ARE ALIVE, YOU CANNOT ESCAPE THIS UGLY CYCLE OF DESIRE.
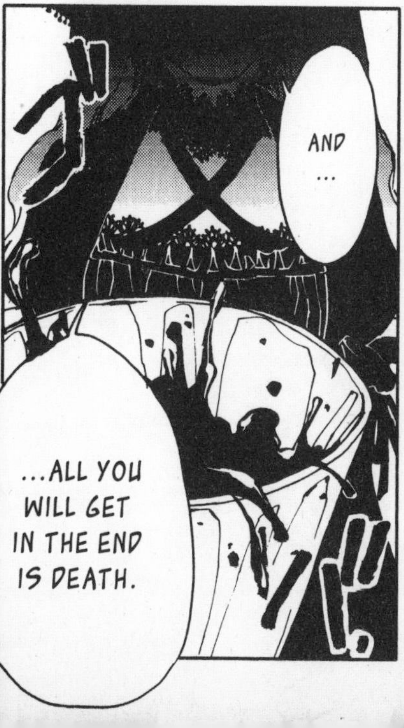
AND ...
...ALL YOU WILL GET IN THE END IS DEATH.

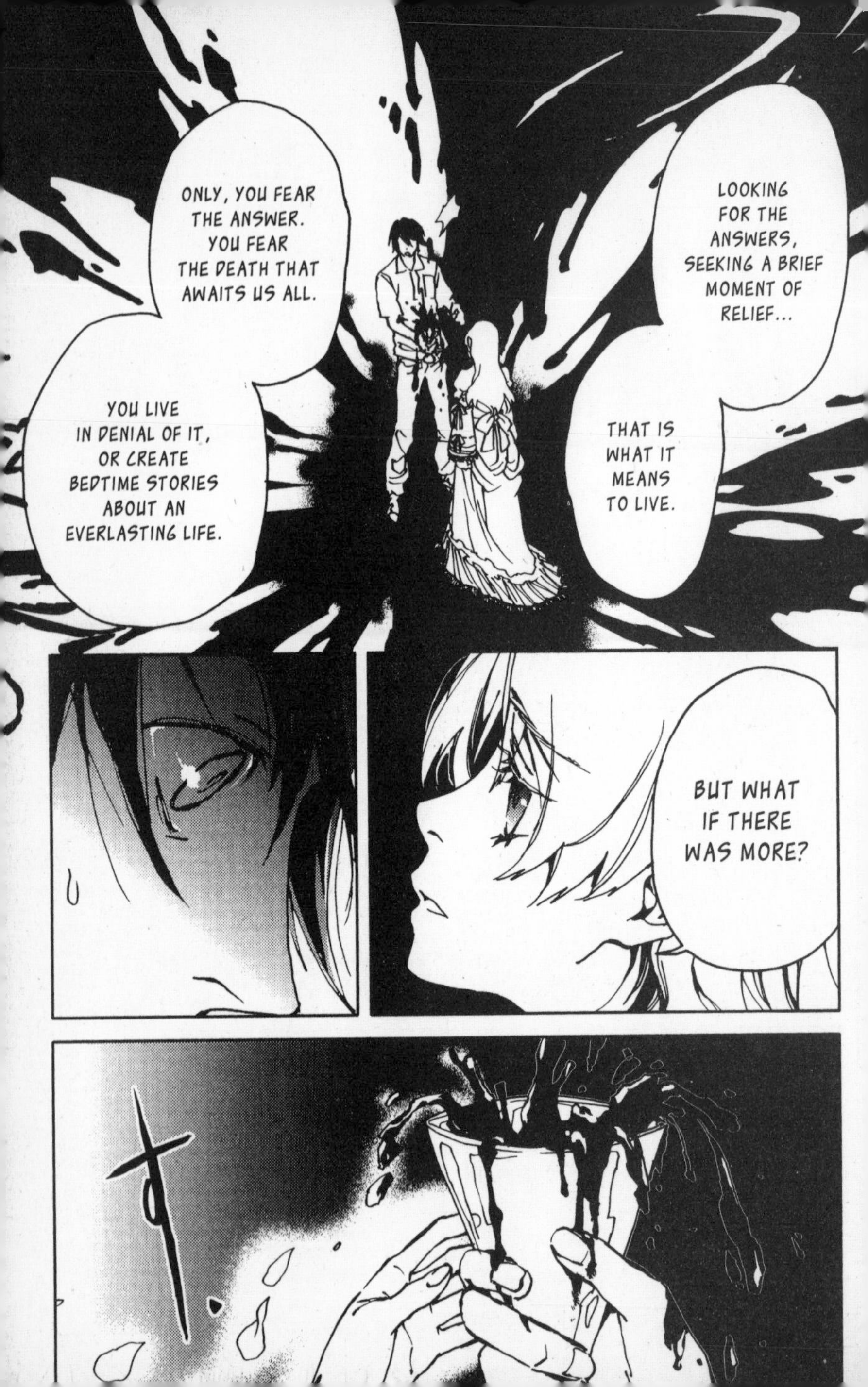
LOOKING FOR THE ANSWERS, SEEKING A BRIEF MOMENT OF RELIEF...
THAT IS WHAT IT MEANS TO LIVE.
ONLY, YOU FEAR THE ANSWER. YOU FEAR THE DEATH THAT AWAITS US ALL.
YOU LIVE IN DENIAL OF IT, OR CREATE BEDTIME STORIES ABOUT AN EVERLASTING LIFE.
BUT WHAT IF THERE WAS MORE?

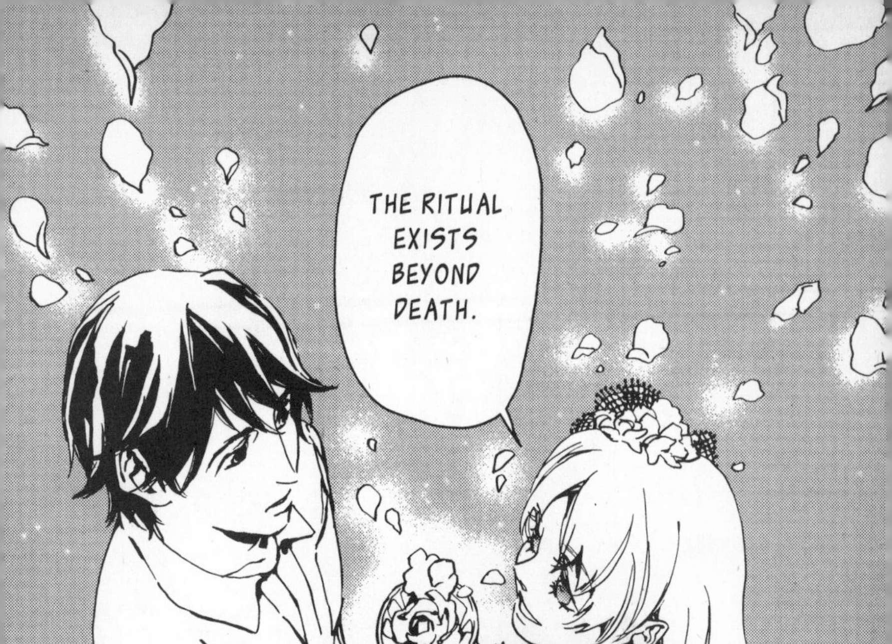
THE RITUAL EXISTS BEYOND DEATH.
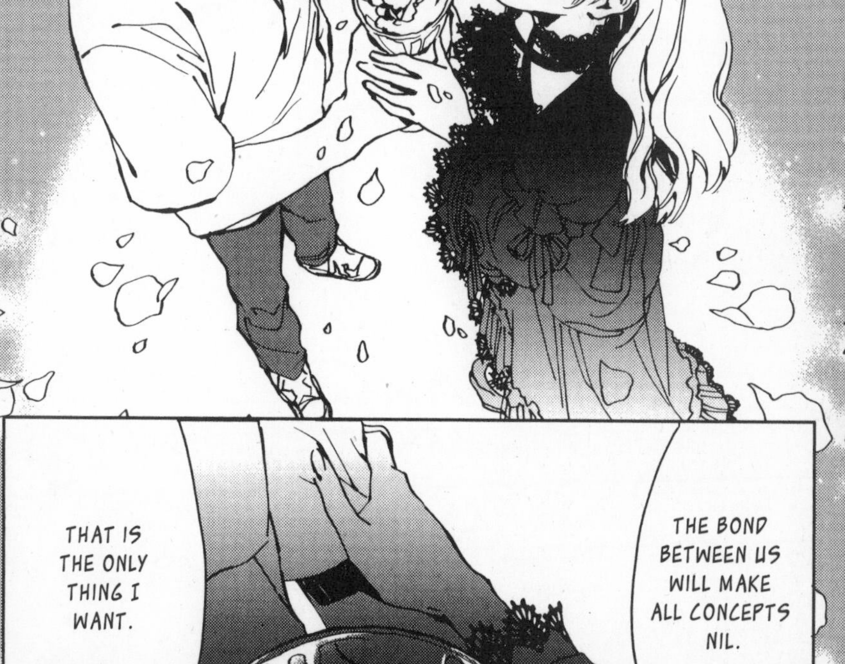
THE BOND BETWEEN US WILL MAKE ALL CONCEPTS NIL.
THAT IS THE ONLY THING I WANT.

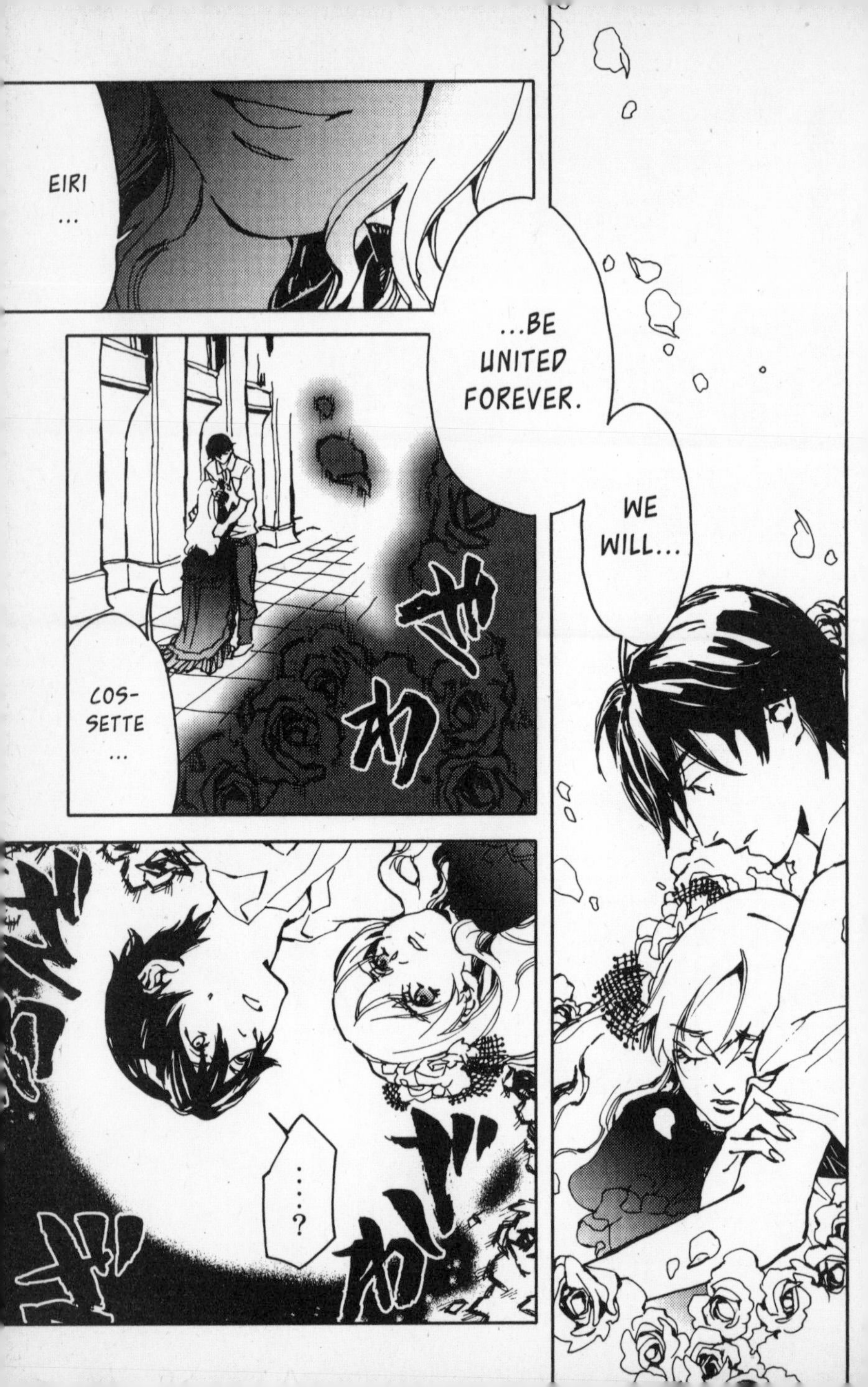
WE WILL...
...BE UNITED FOREVER.
EIRI ...
COS-SETTE ...
...?

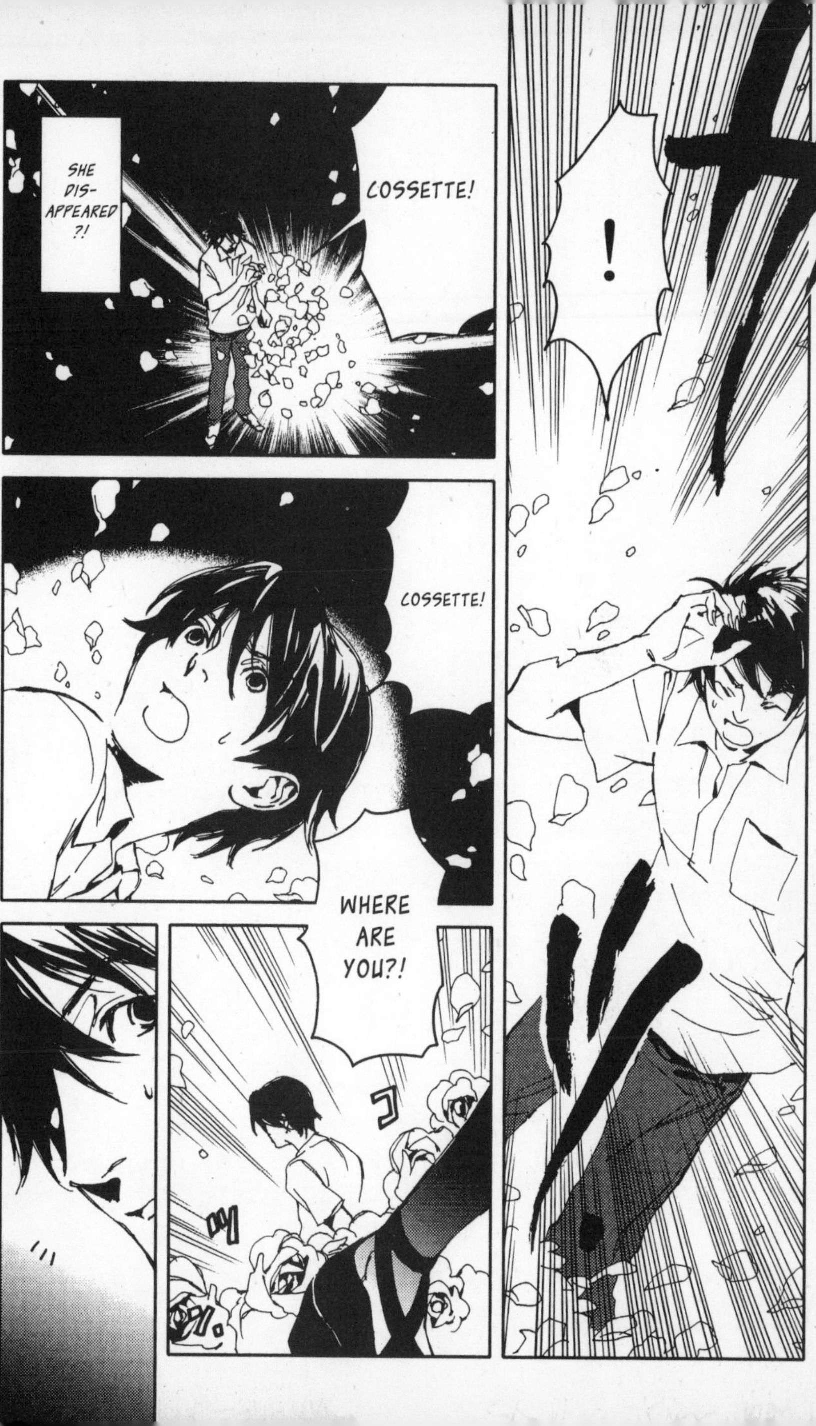
!
COSSETTE!
SHE DIS-APPEARED?!
COSSETTE!
WHERE ARE YOU?!

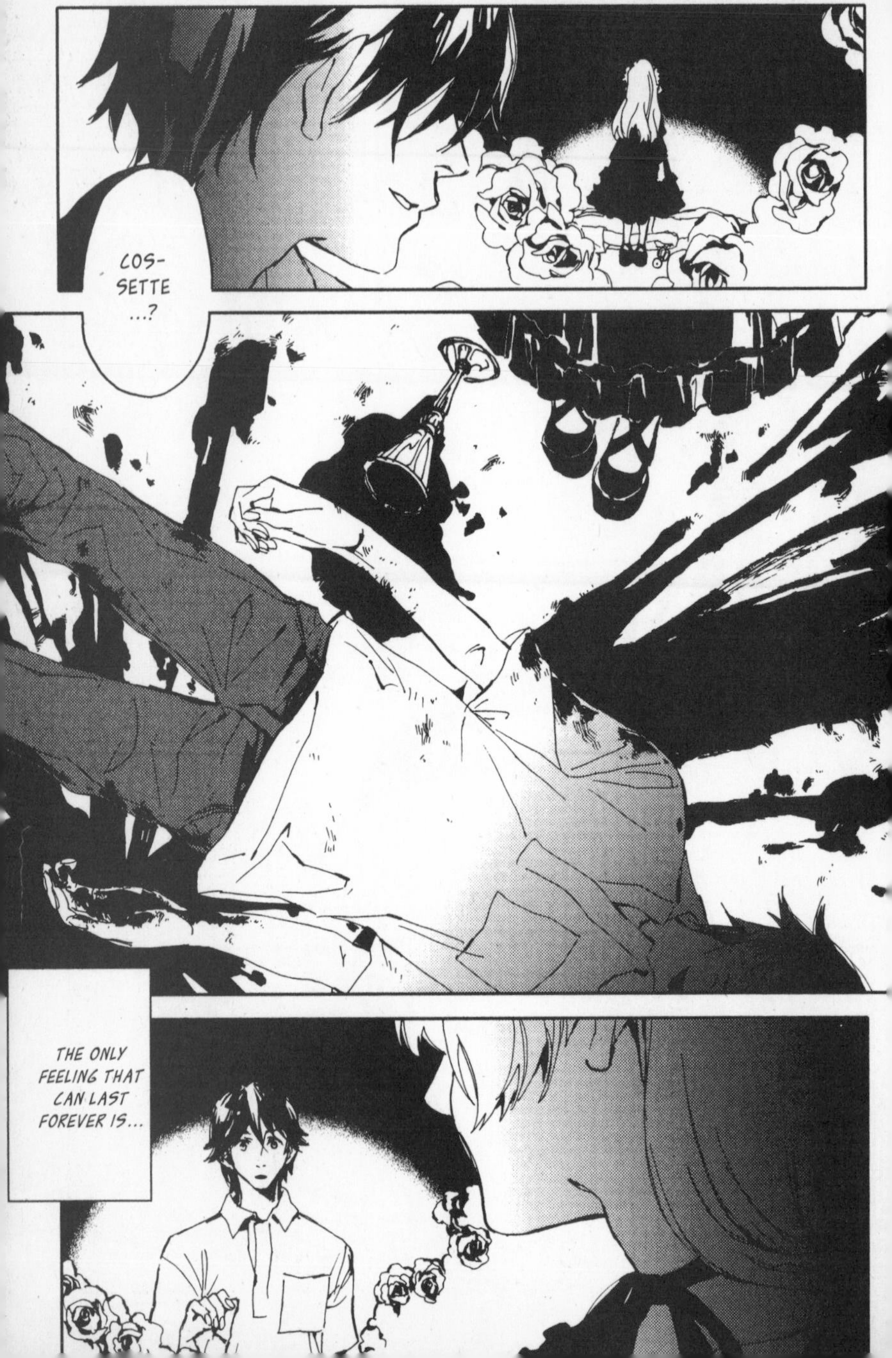
COS-
SETTE
...?
THE ONLY
FEELING THAT
CAN LAST
FOREVER IS...

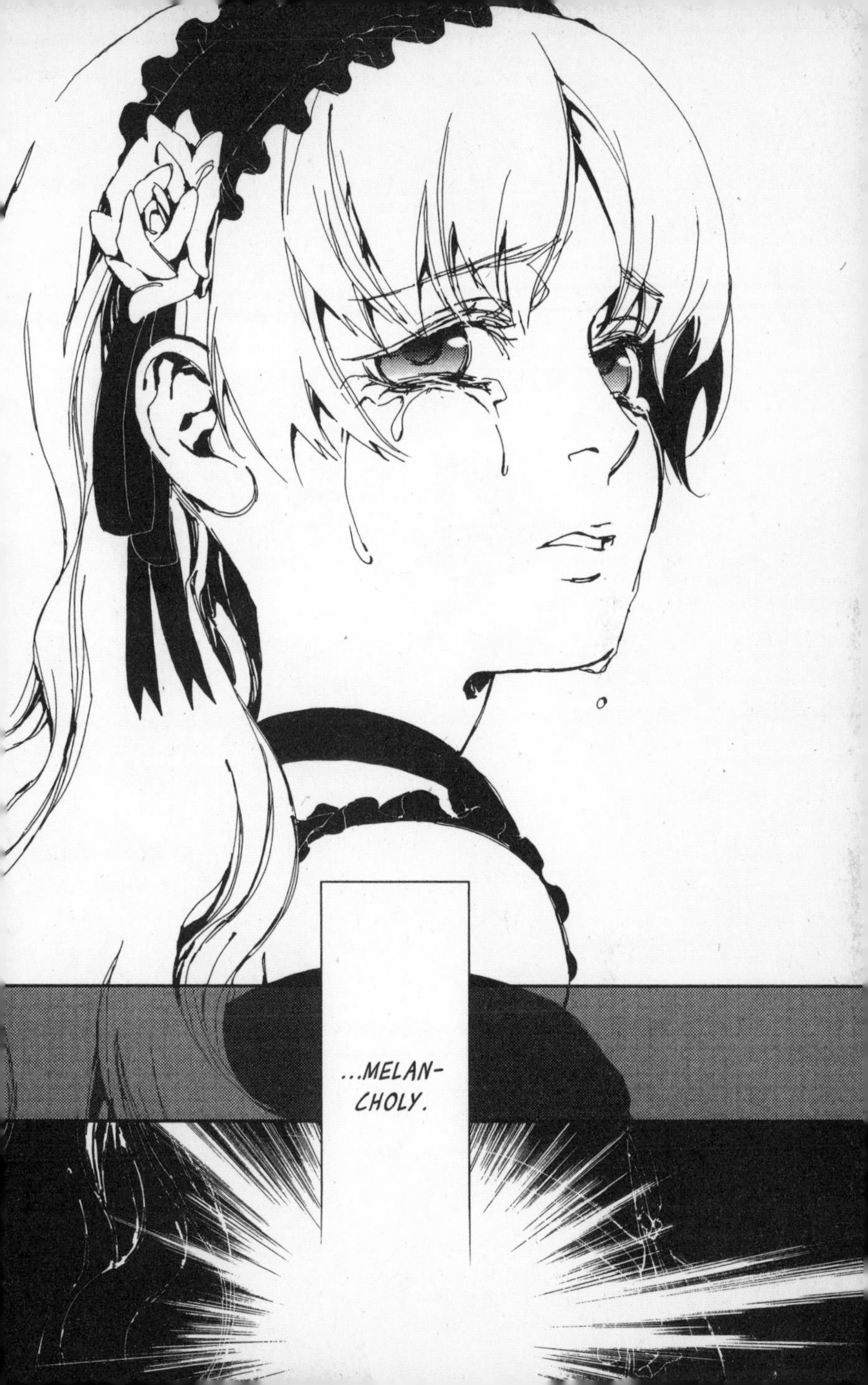
...MELAN-
CHOLY.

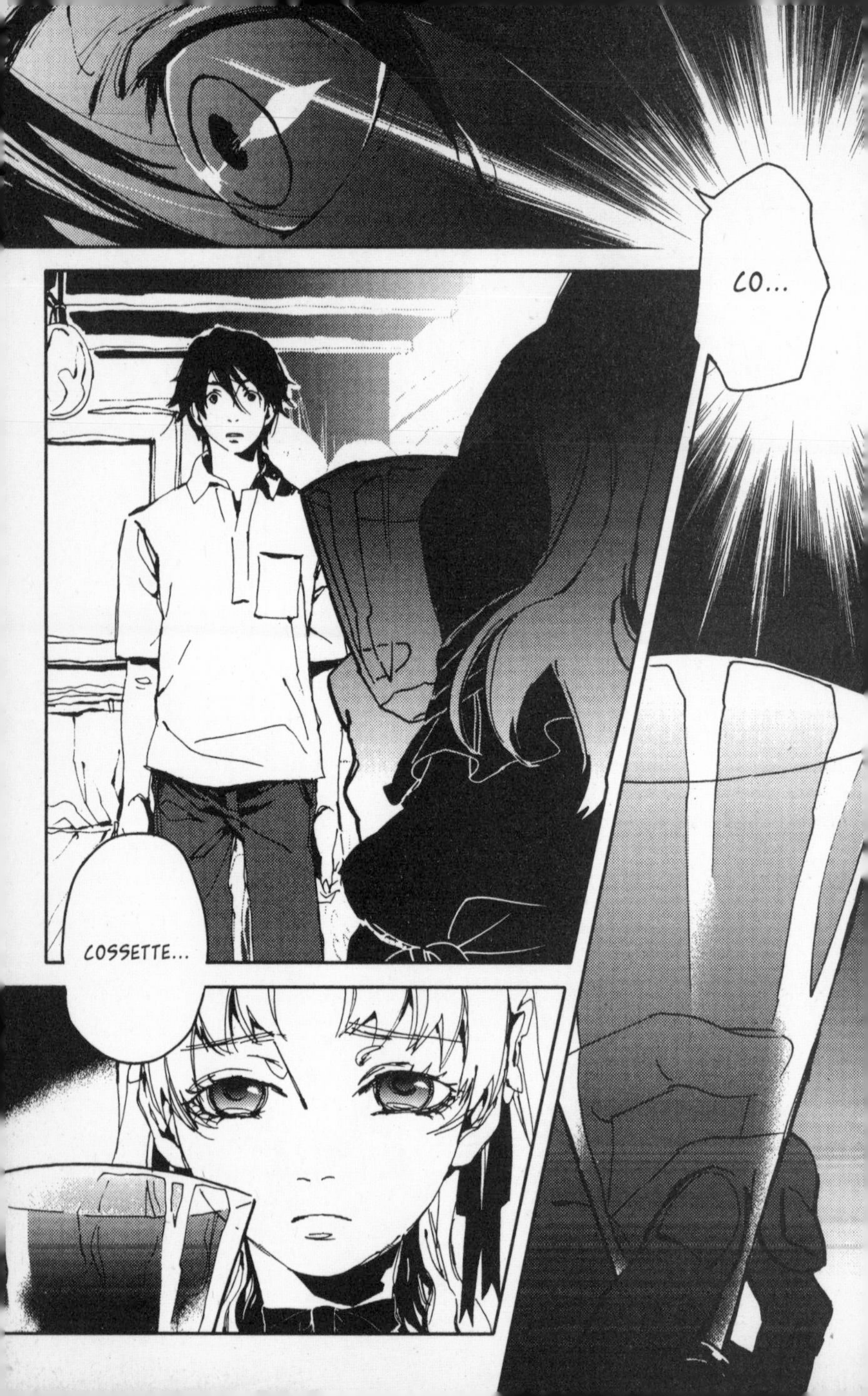
CO...
COSSETTE...

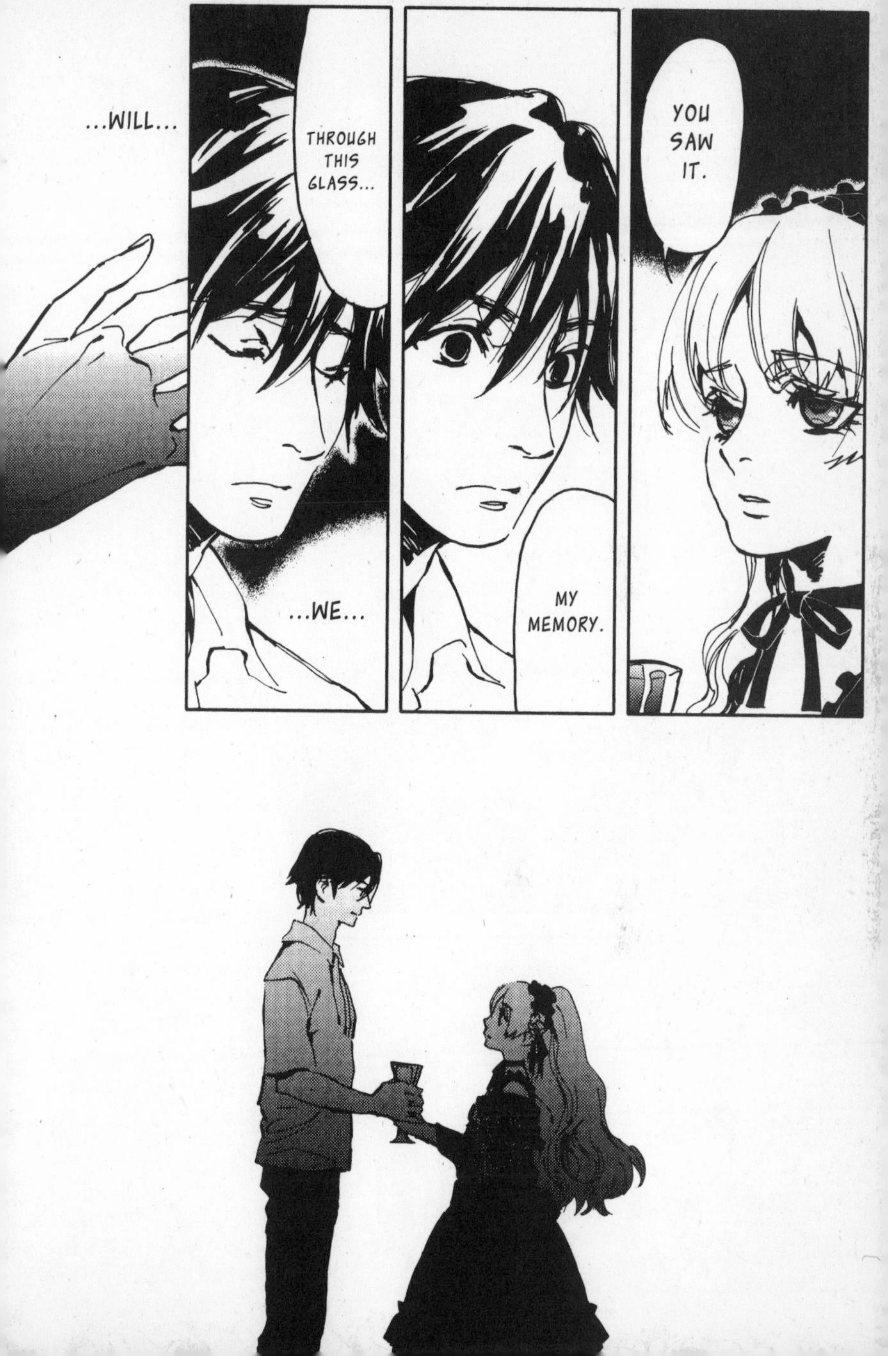
YOU SAW IT.
MY MEMORY.
THROUGH THIS GLASS...
...WE...
...WILL...

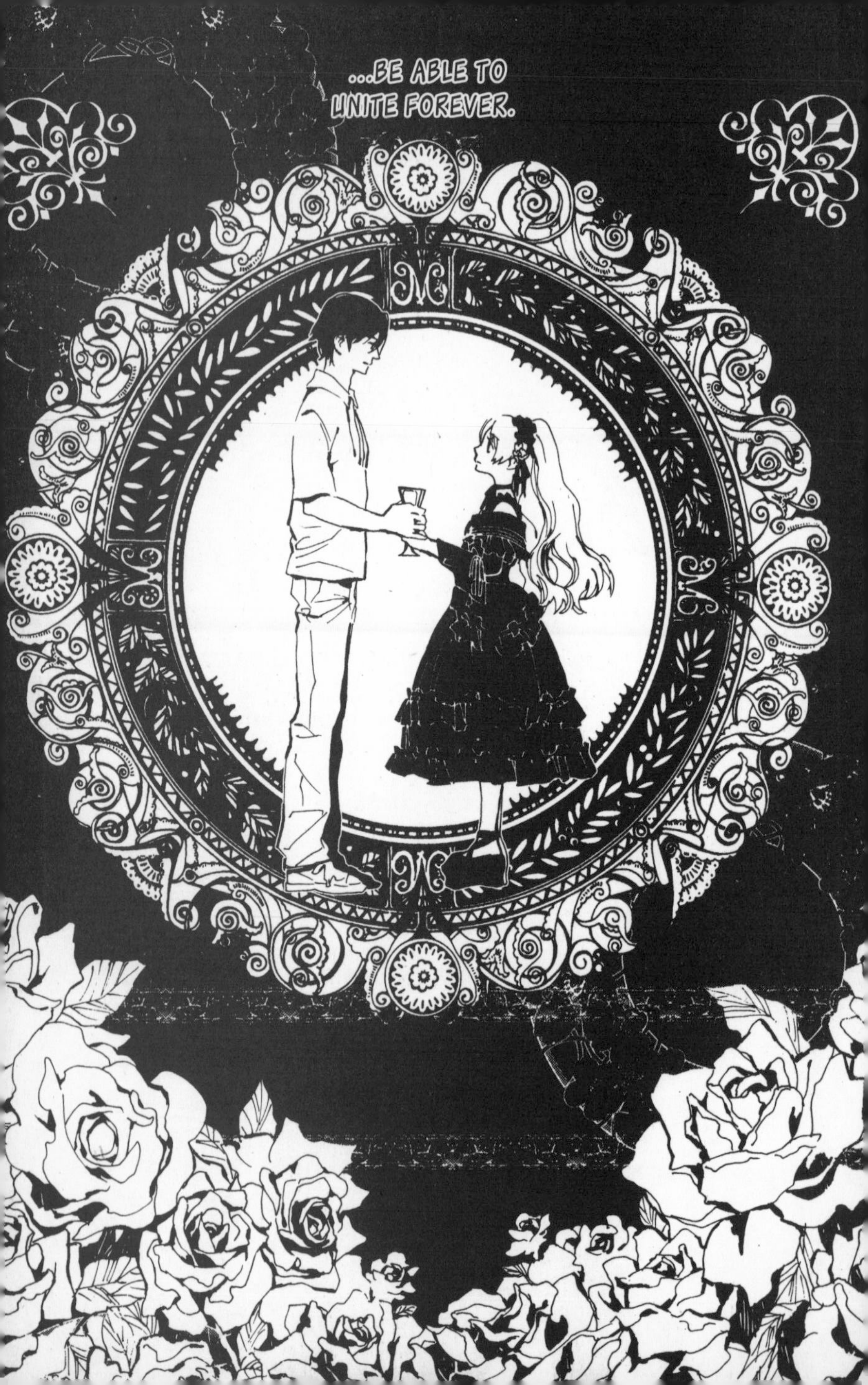
...BE ABLE TO UNITE FOREVER.

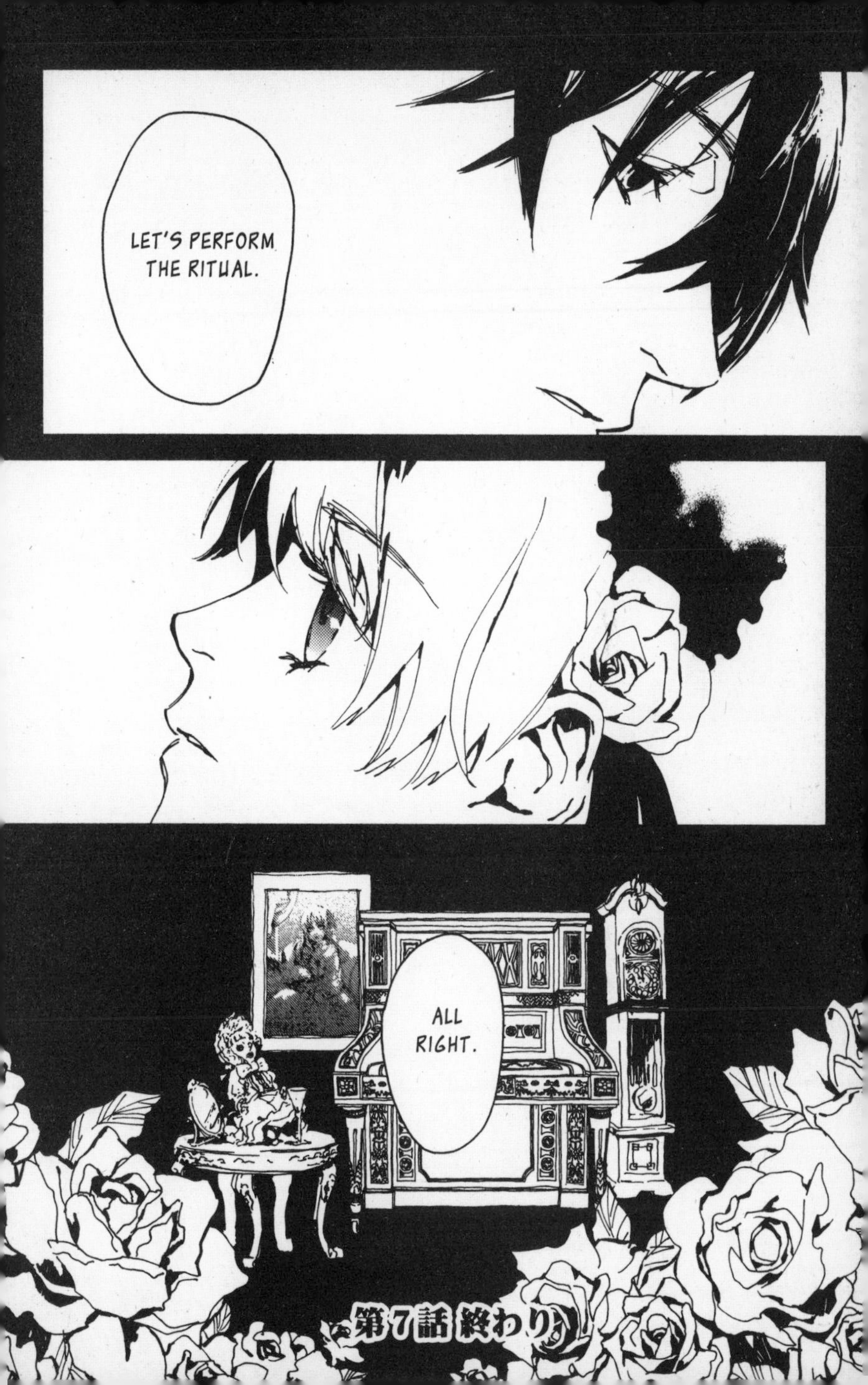
LET'S PERFORM THE RITUAL.
ALL RIGHT.
第7話 終わり

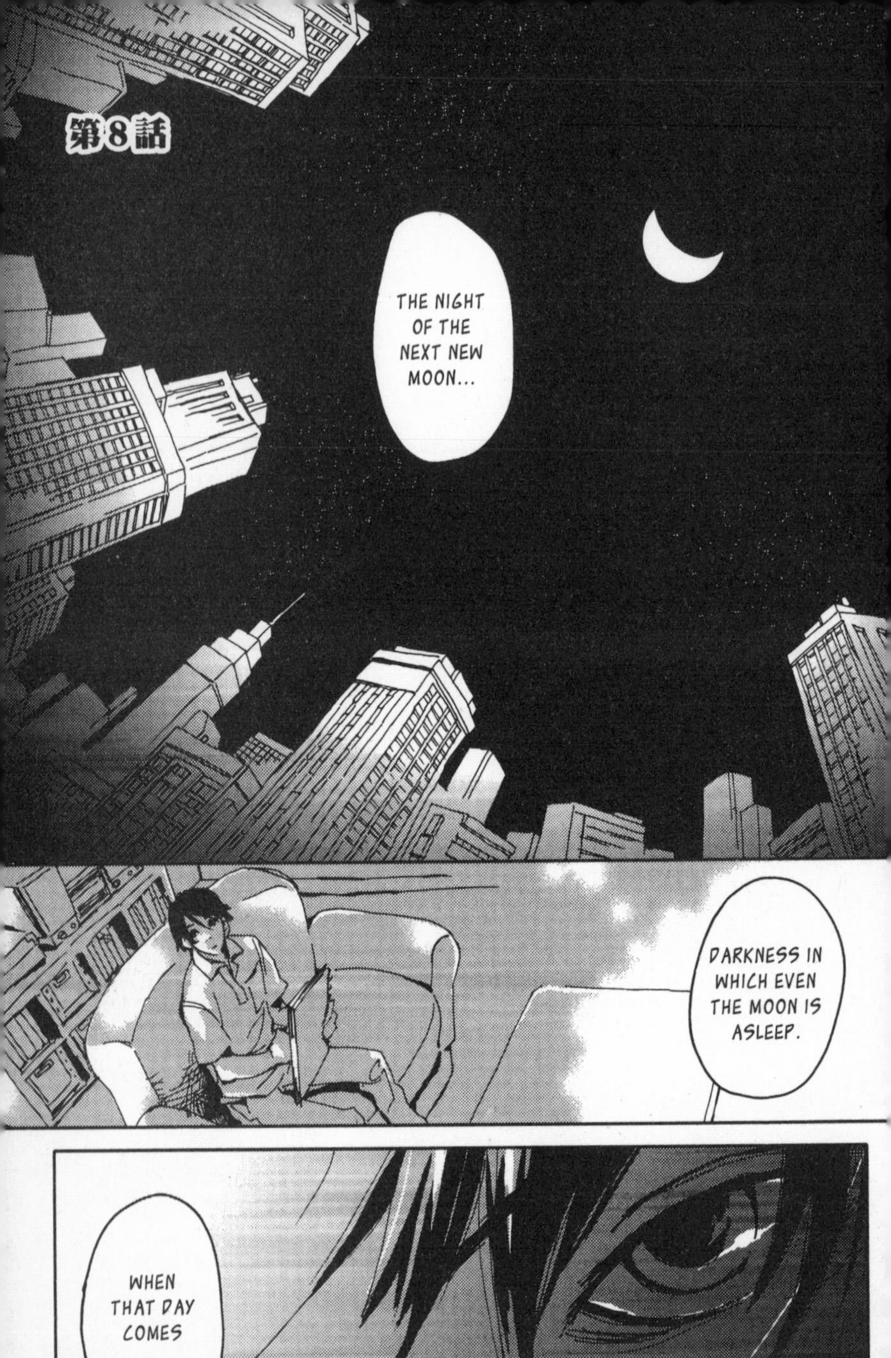
第8話
THE NIGHT OF THE NEXT NEW MOON...
DARKNESS IN WHICH EVEN THE MOON IS ASLEEP.
WHEN THAT DAY COMES ...

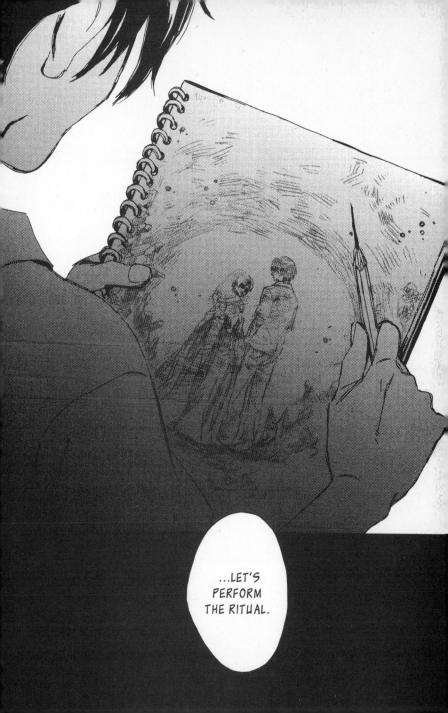

...LET'S
PERFORM
THE RITUAL.

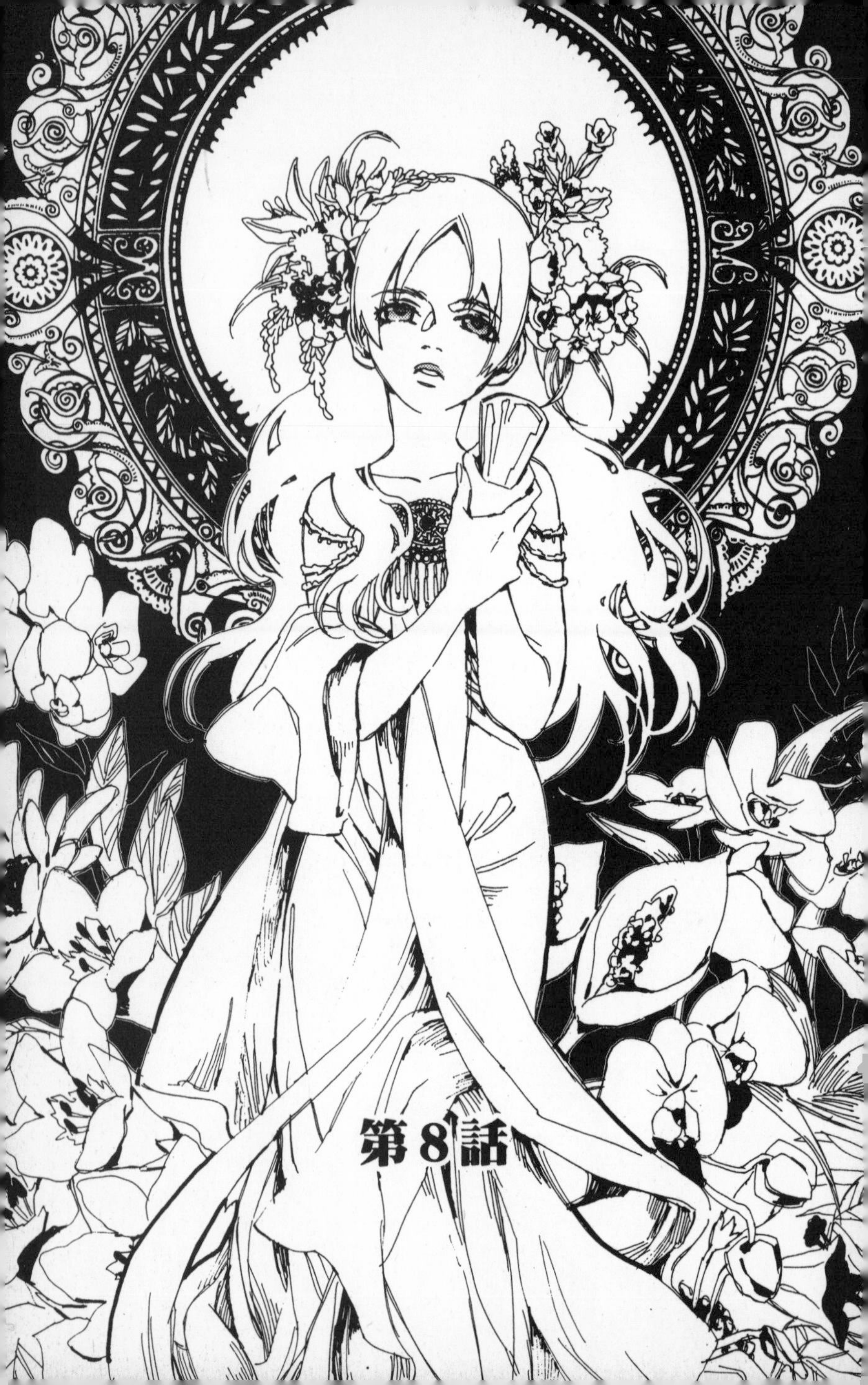
第8話

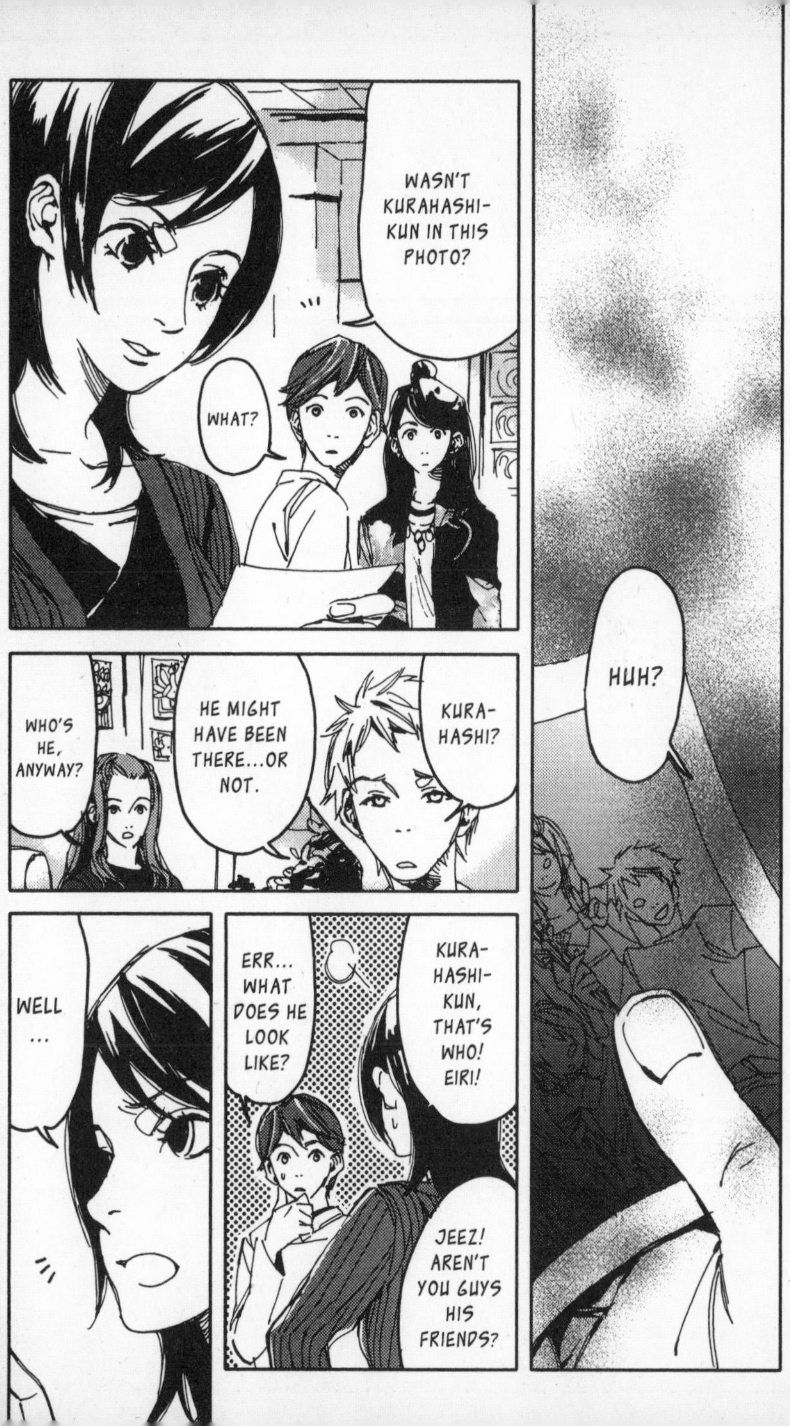
HUH?
WASN'T KURAHASHI-KUN IN THIS PHOTO?
WHAT?
KURA-HASHI?
HE MIGHT HAVE BEEN THERE...OR NOT.
WHO'S HE, ANYWAY?
KURA-HASHI-KUN, THAT'S WHO! EIRI!
ERR... WHAT DOES HE LOOK LIKE?
JEEZ! AREN'T YOU GUYS HIS FRIENDS?
WELL ...

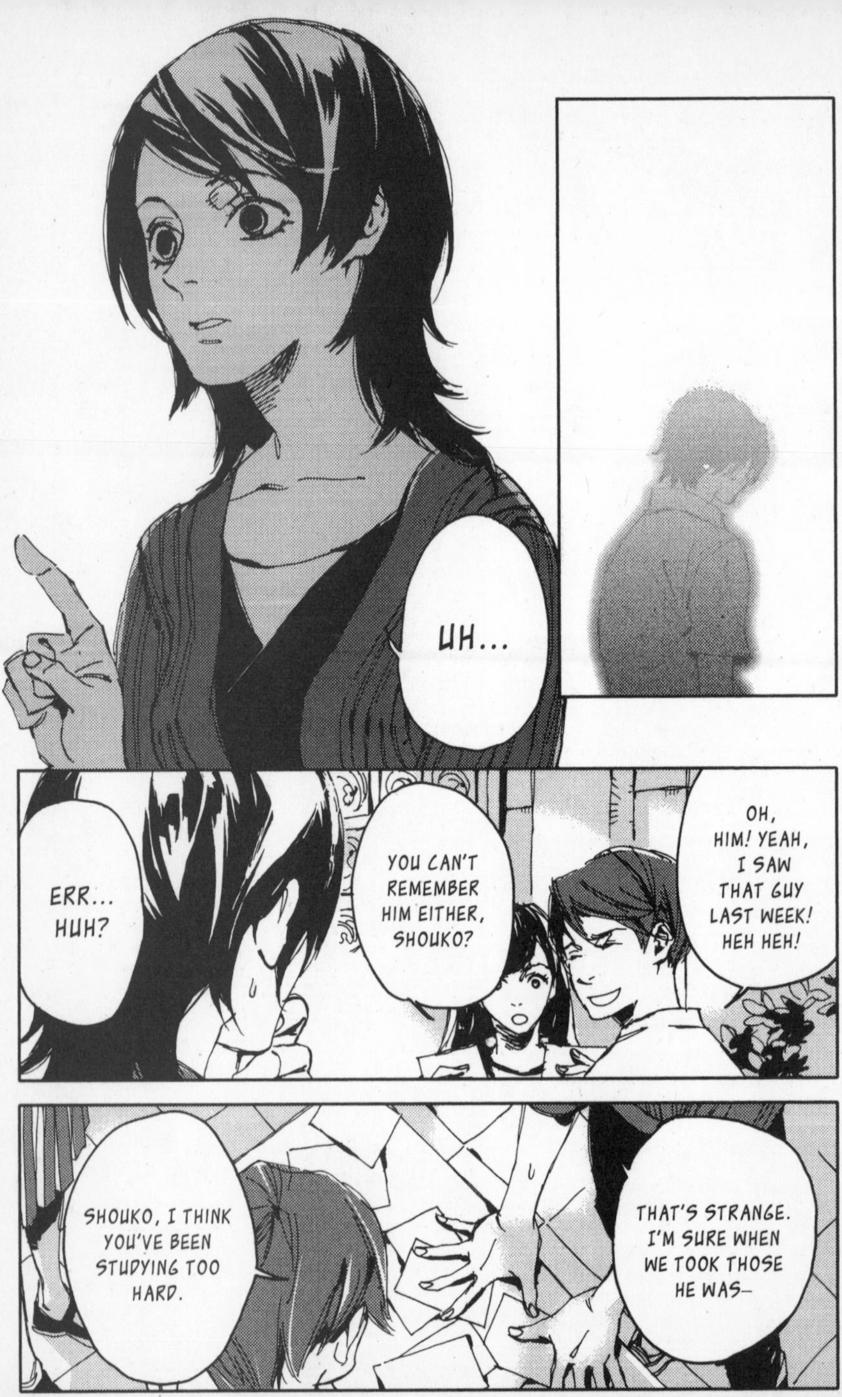
UH...
OH, HIM! YEAH, I SAW THAT GUY LAST WEEK! HEH HEH!
YOU CAN'T REMEMBER HIM EITHER, SHOUKO?
ERR... HUH?
THAT'S STRANGE. I'M SURE WHEN WE TOOK THOSE HE WAS–
SHOUKO, I THINK YOU'VE BEEN STUDYING TOO HARD.

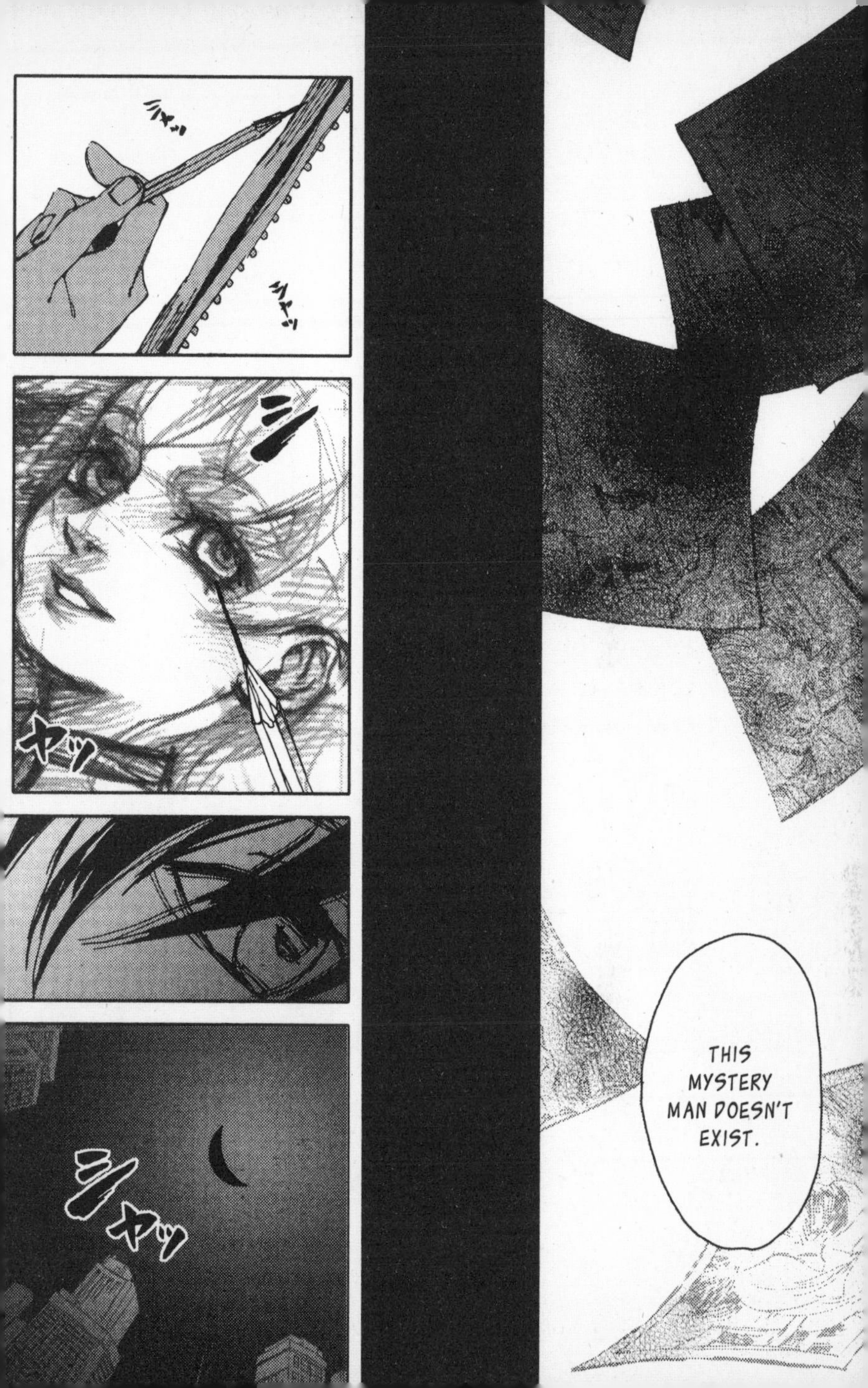
THIS MYSTERY MAN DOESN'T EXIST.

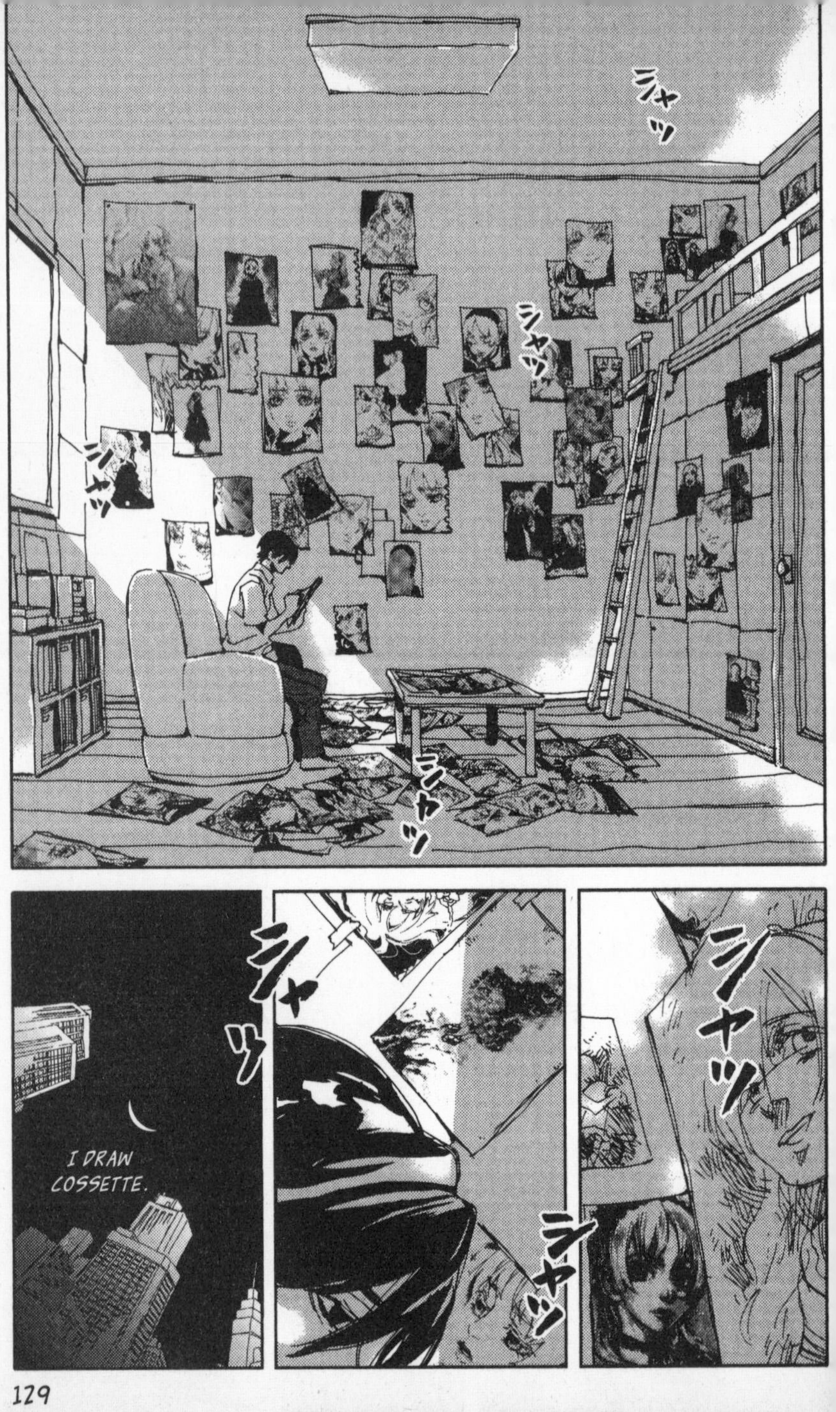
シャッ
シャッ
シャッ
シャッ
シャッ
シャッ
シャッ
I DRAW COSSETTE.

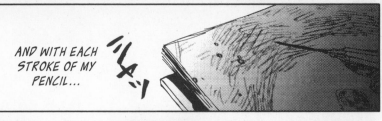

AND WITH EACH STROKE OF MY PENCIL...

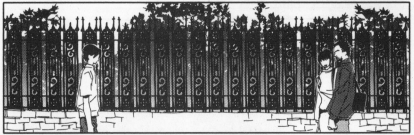

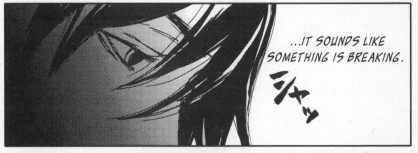

...IT SOUNDS LIKE SOMETHING IS BREAKING.

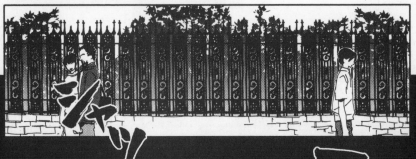

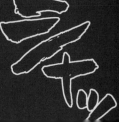

IT SOUNDS LIKE SOMETHING IS ENDING.

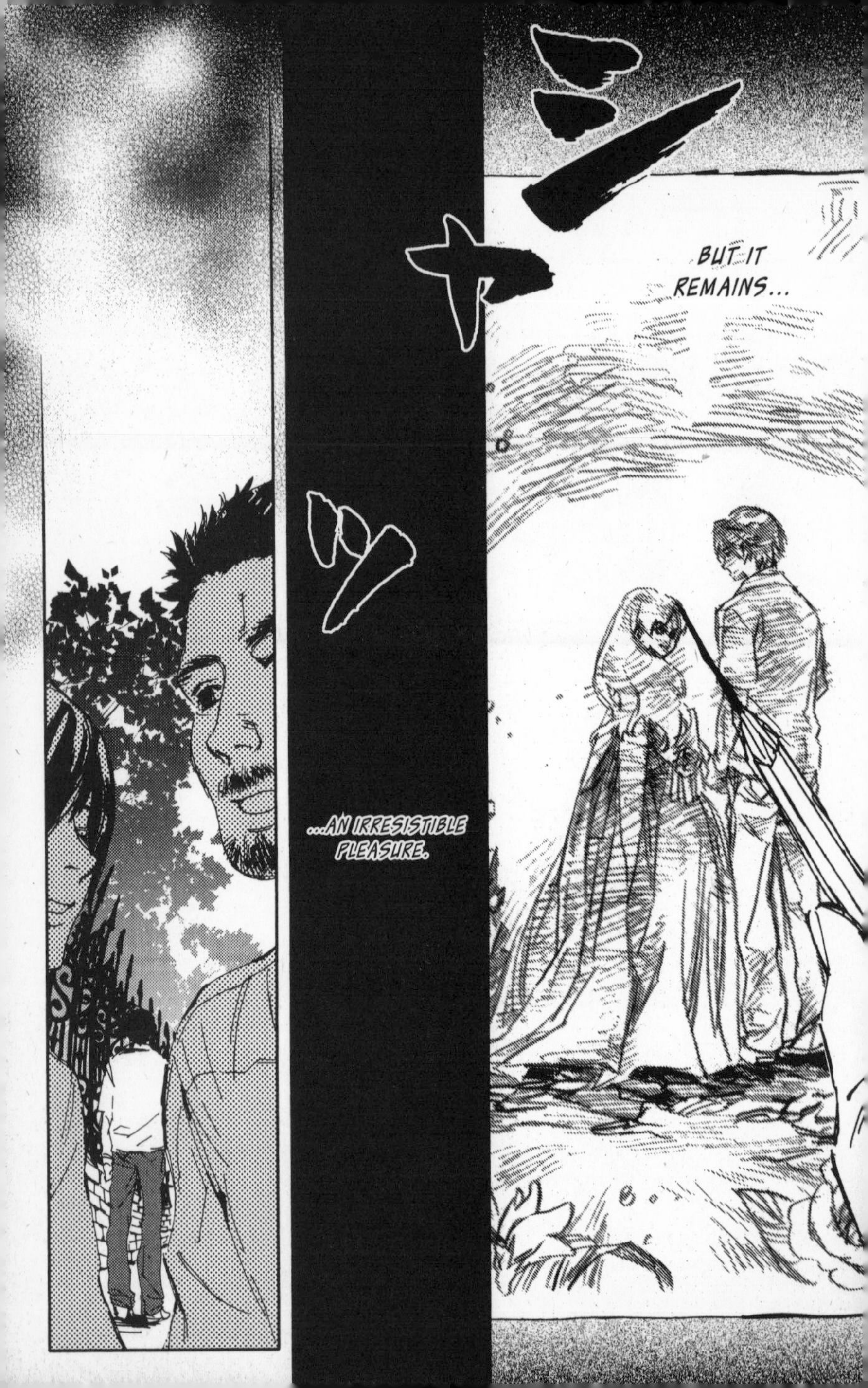
BUT IT REMAINS...
...AN IRRESISTIBLE PLEASURE.

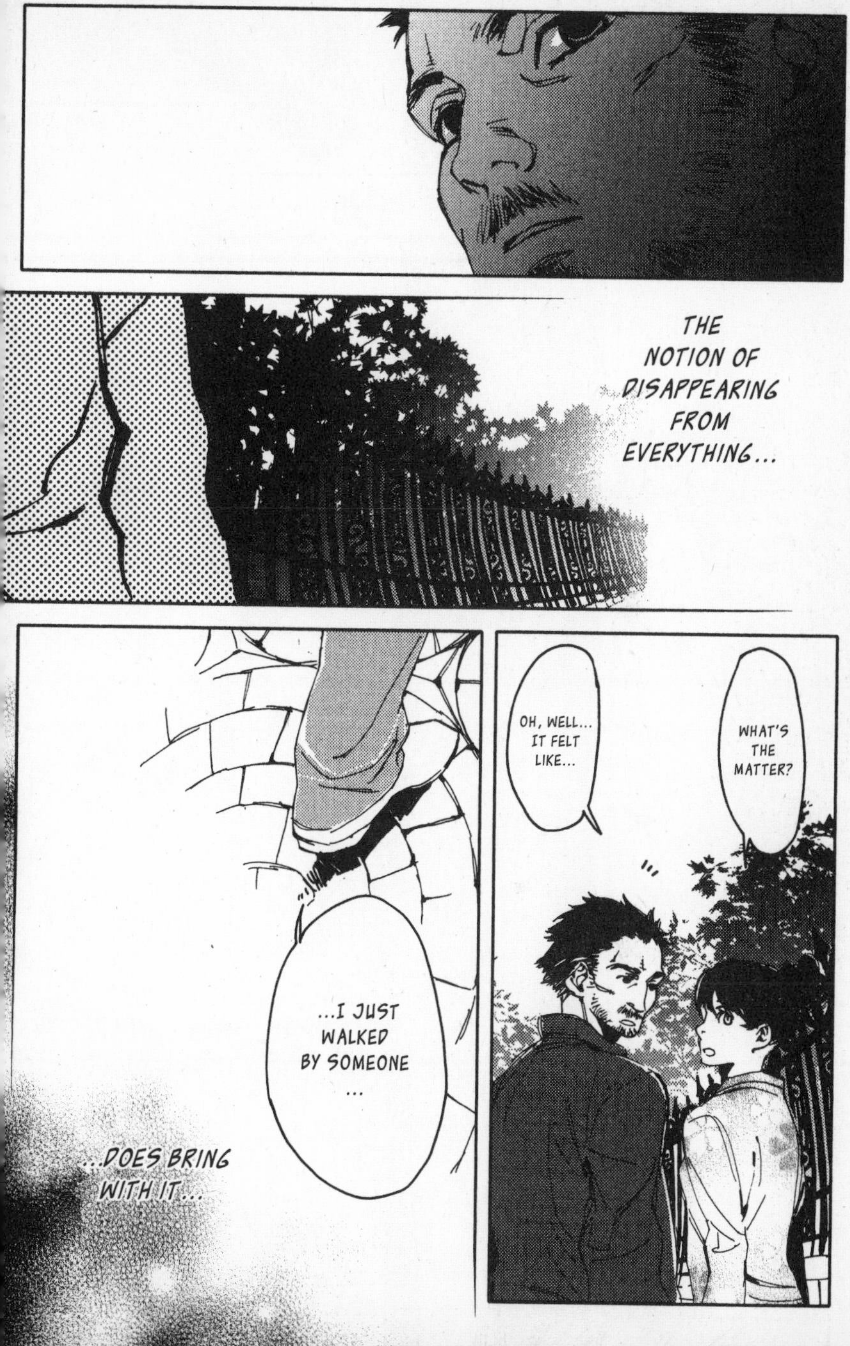
THE NOTION OF DISAPPEARING FROM EVERYTHING...
WHAT'S THE MATTER?
OH, WELL... IT FELT LIKE...
...I JUST WALKED BY SOMEONE ...
...DOES BRING WITH IT...

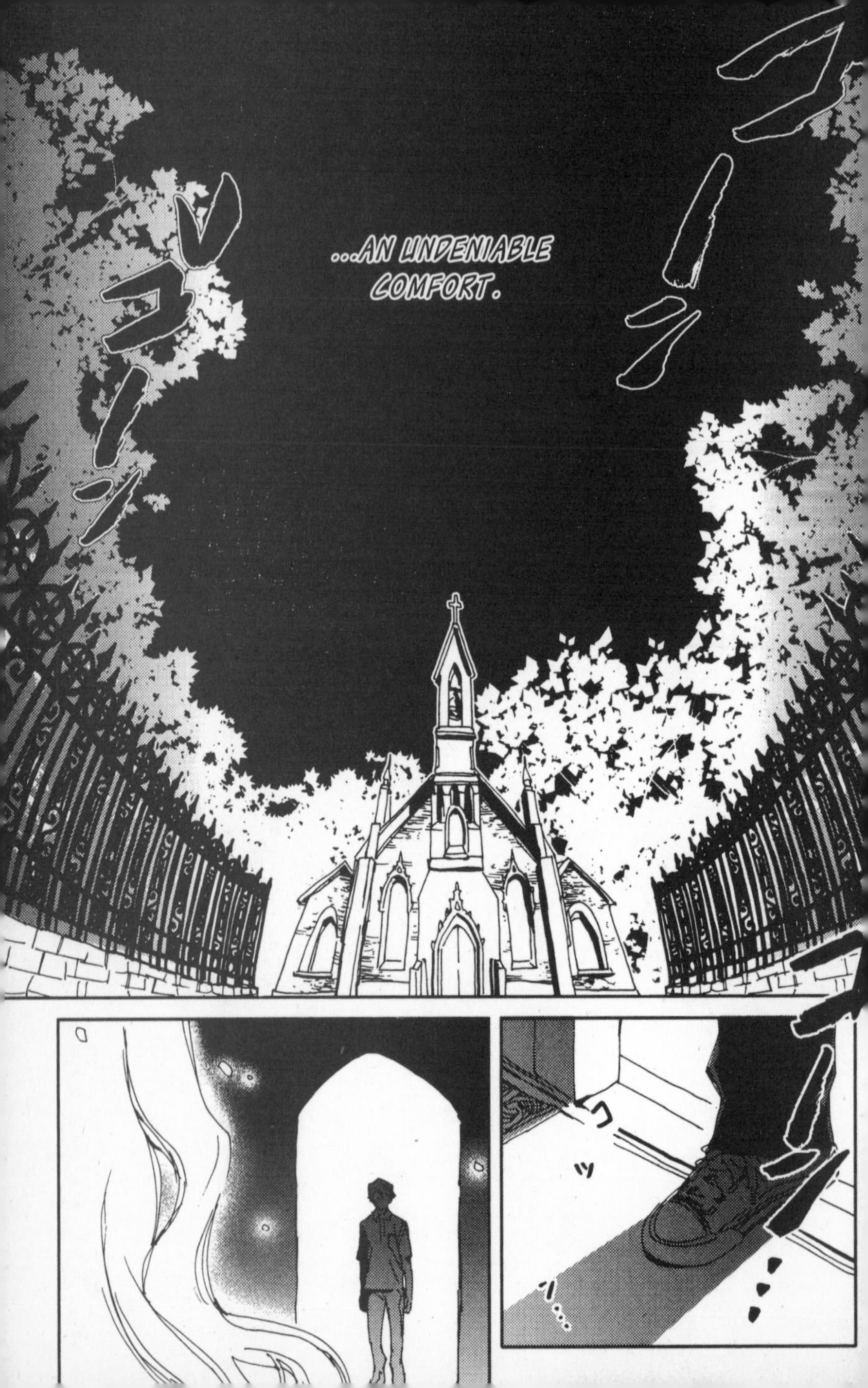
...AN UNDENIABLE COMFORT.

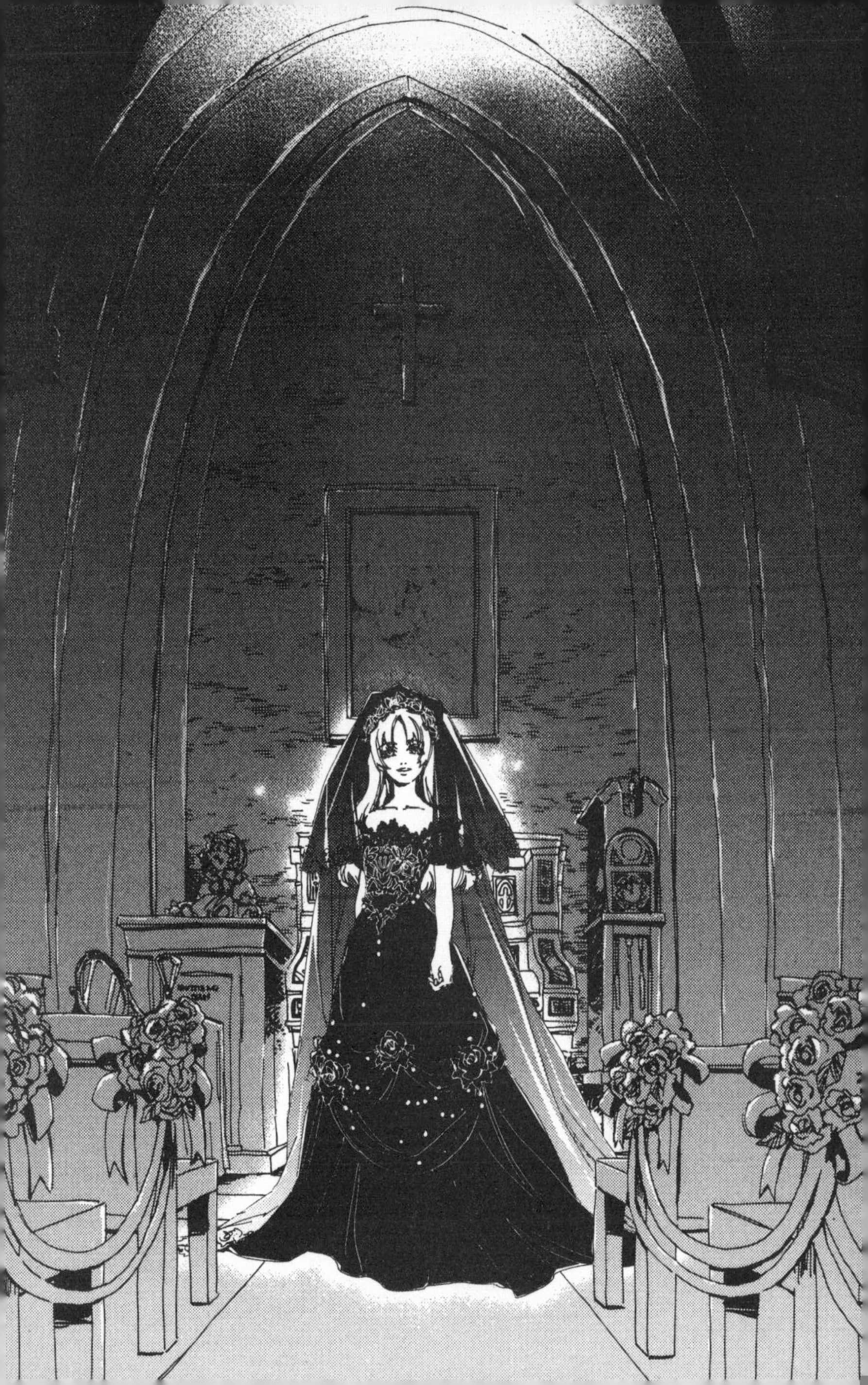

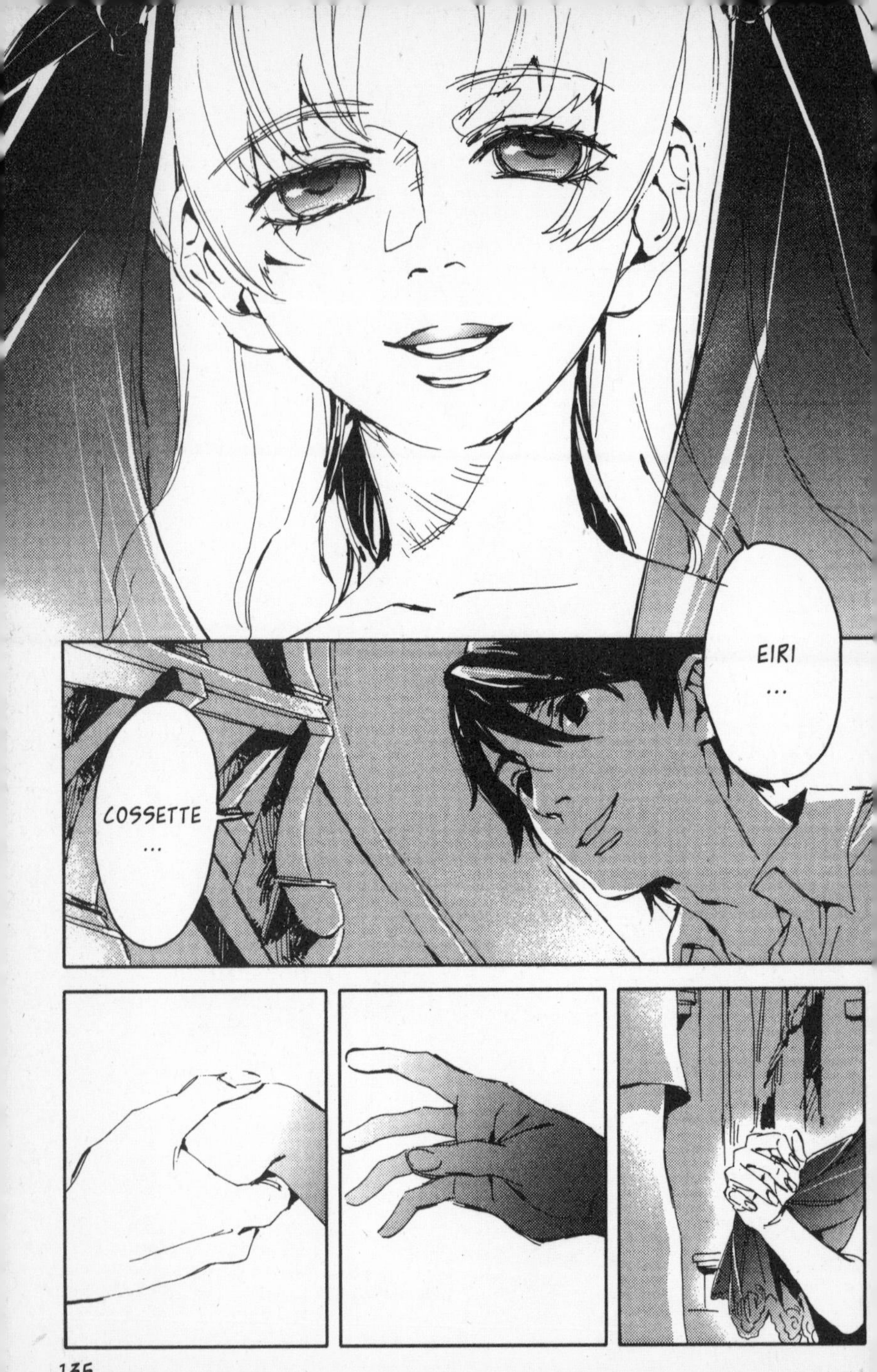
EIRI ...
COSSETTE ...

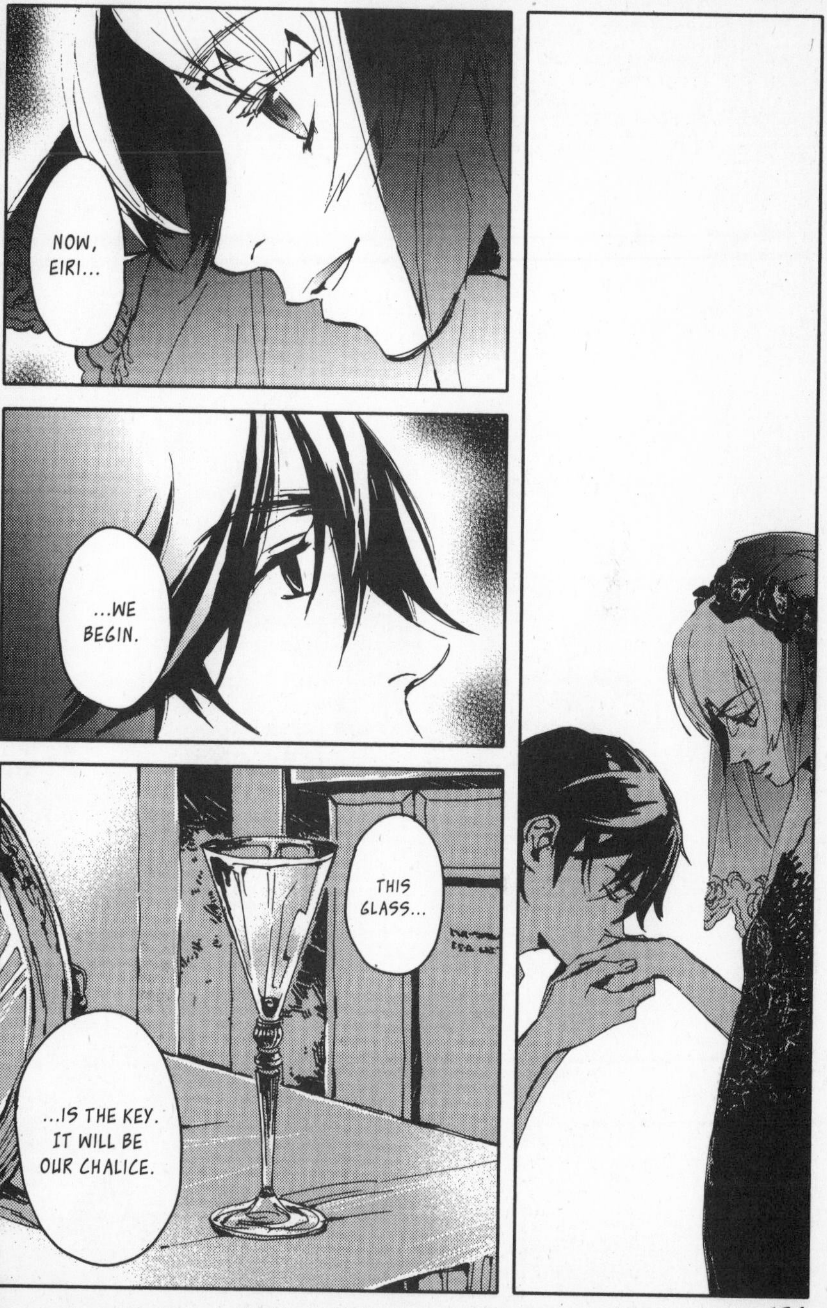
NOW, EIRI...
...WE BEGIN.
THIS GLASS...
...IS THE KEY. IT WILL BE OUR CHALICE.

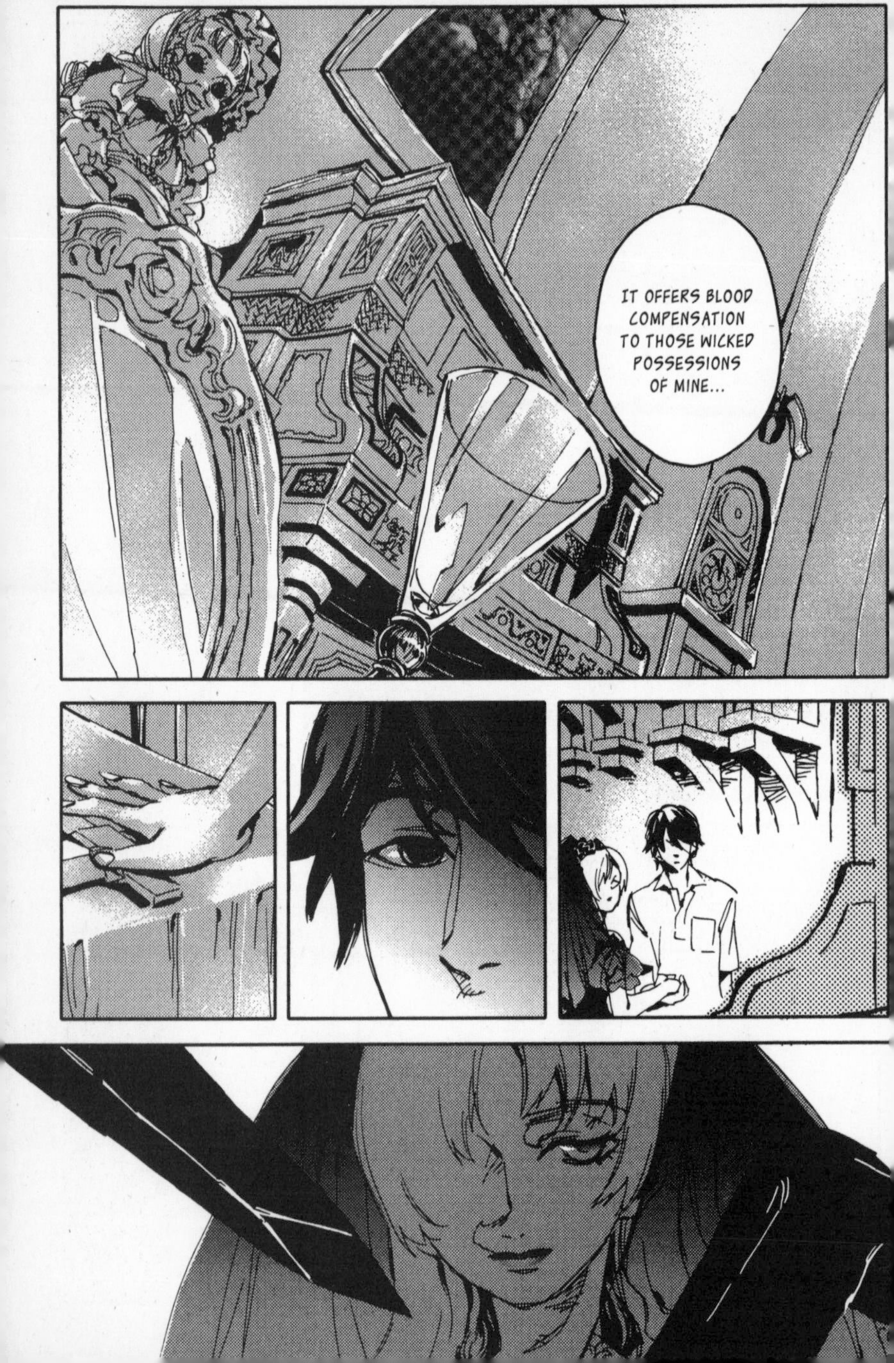
IT OFFERS BLOOD COMPENSATION TO THOSE WICKED POSSESSIONS OF MINE...

THIS IS THE RITUAL.

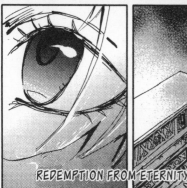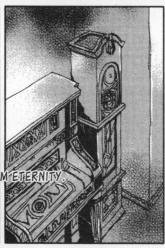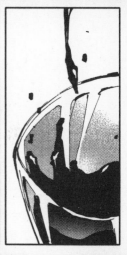

REDEMPTION FROM ETERNITY.

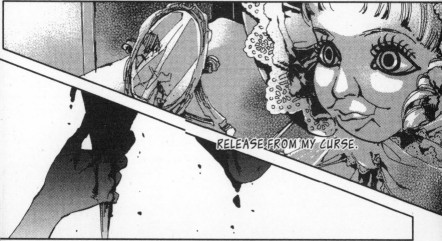

RELEASE FROM MY CURSE.

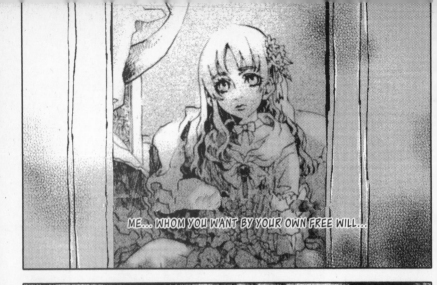

ME... WHOM YOU WANT BY YOUR OWN FREE WILL...

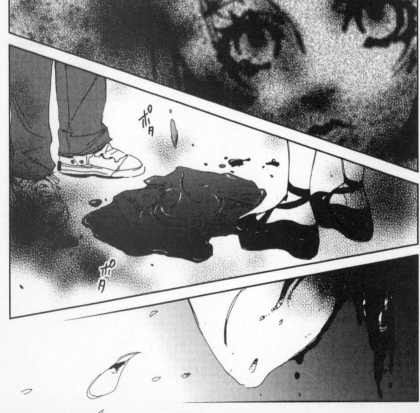

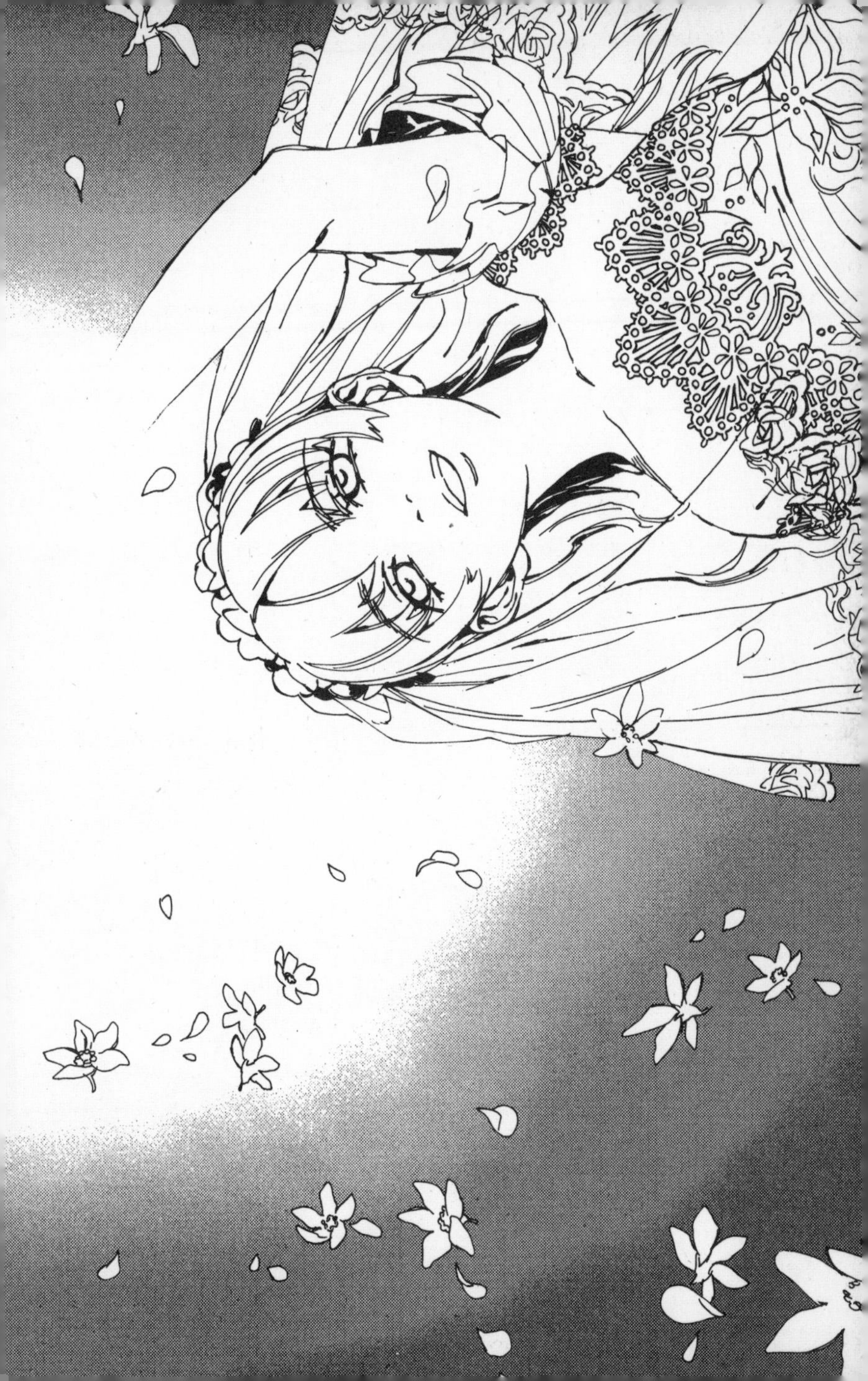

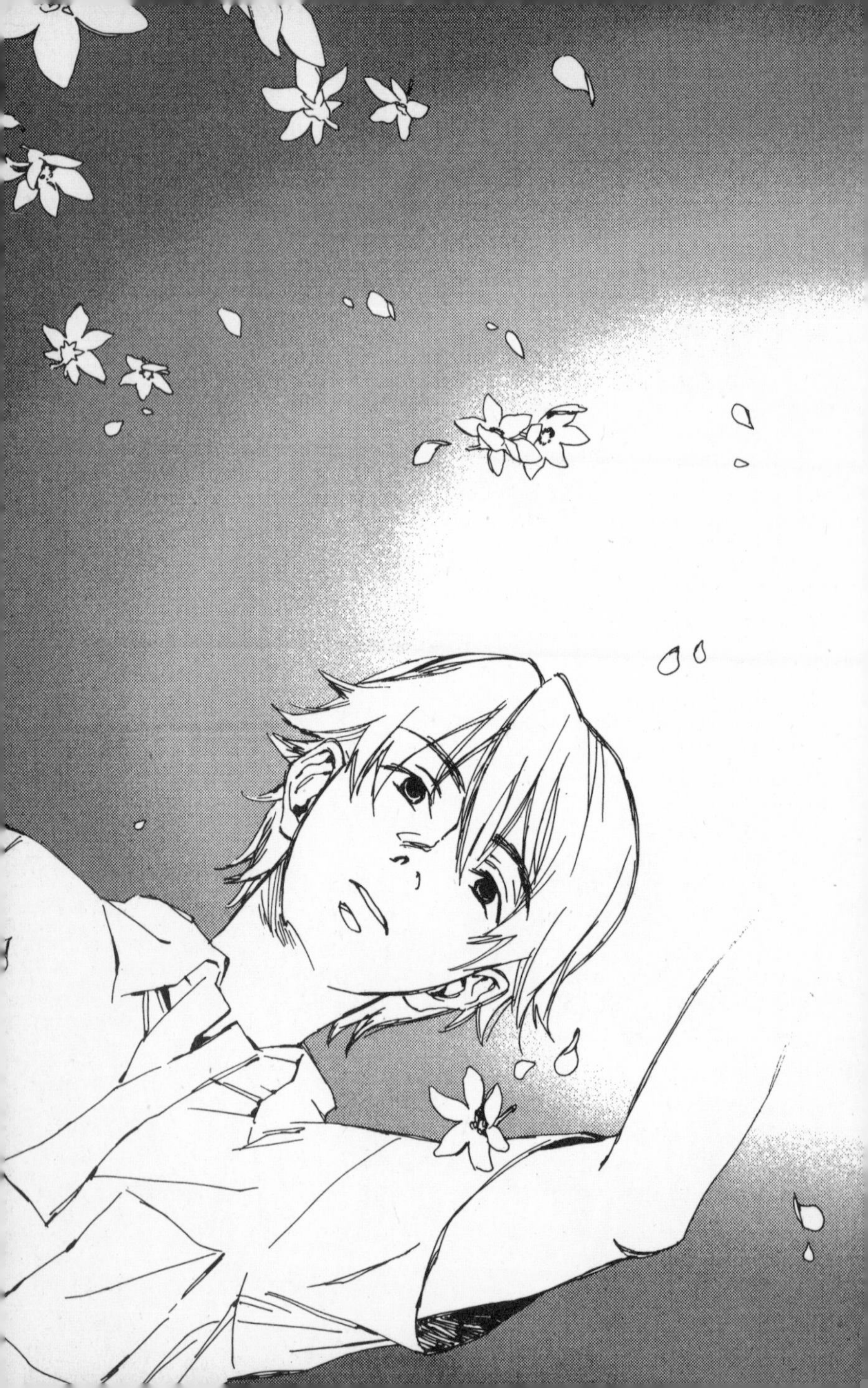

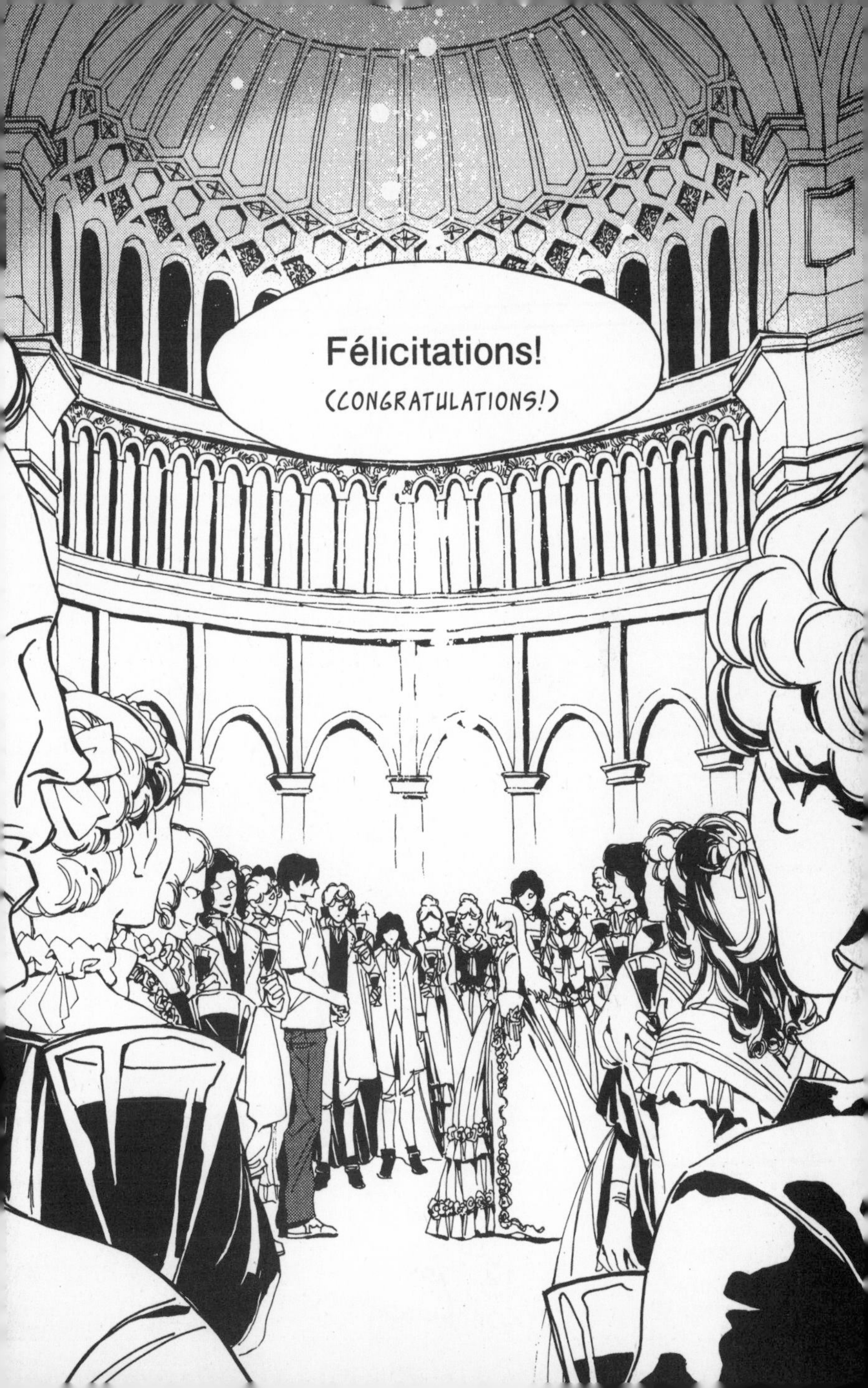
Félicitations!
(CONGRATULATIONS!)

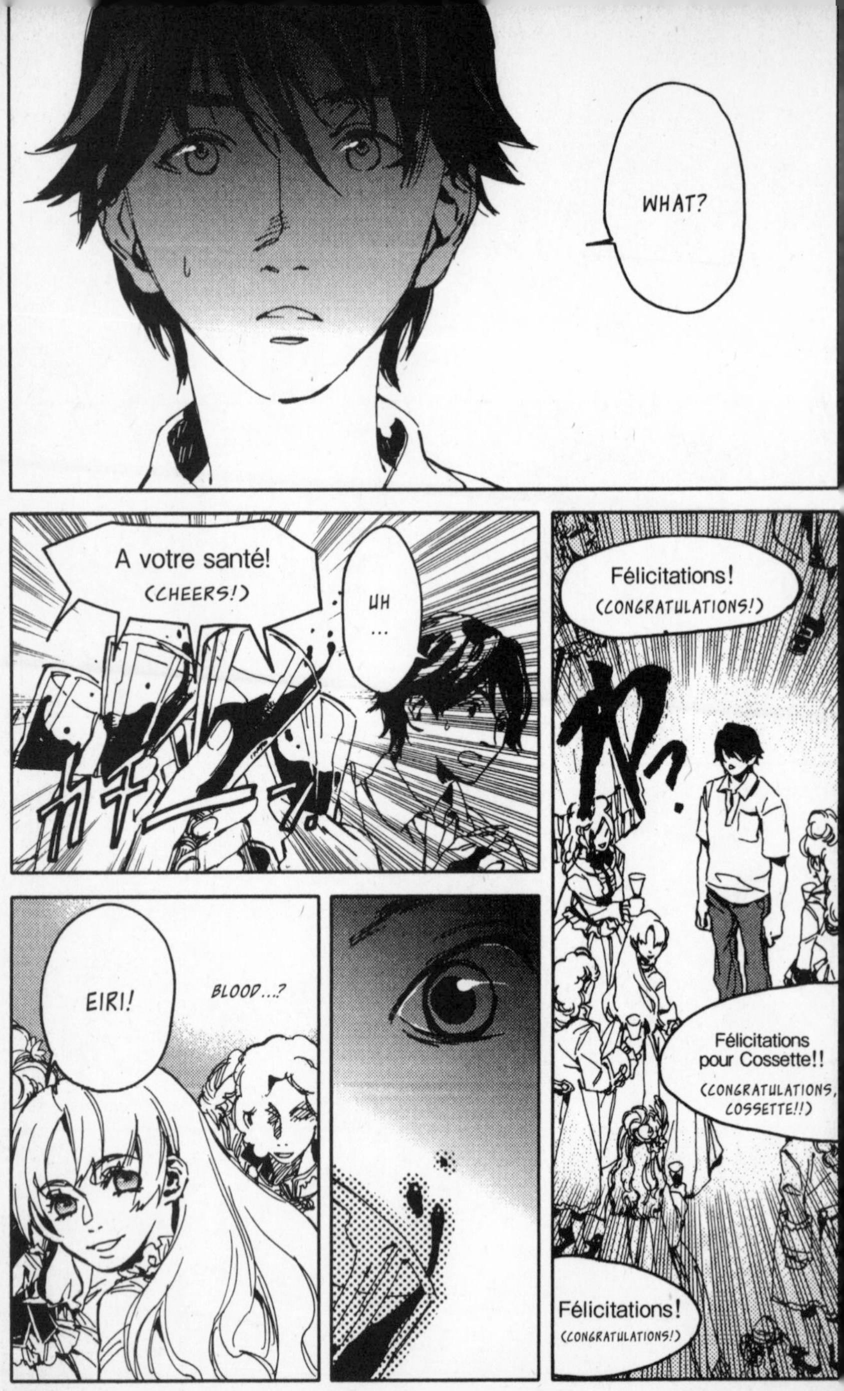
WHAT?
Félicitations! (CONGRATULATIONS!)
Félicitations pour Cossette!! (CONGRATULATIONS, COSSETTE!!)
Félicitations! (CONGRATULATIONS!)
A votre santé! (CHEERS!)
UH ...
BLOOD...?
EIRI!

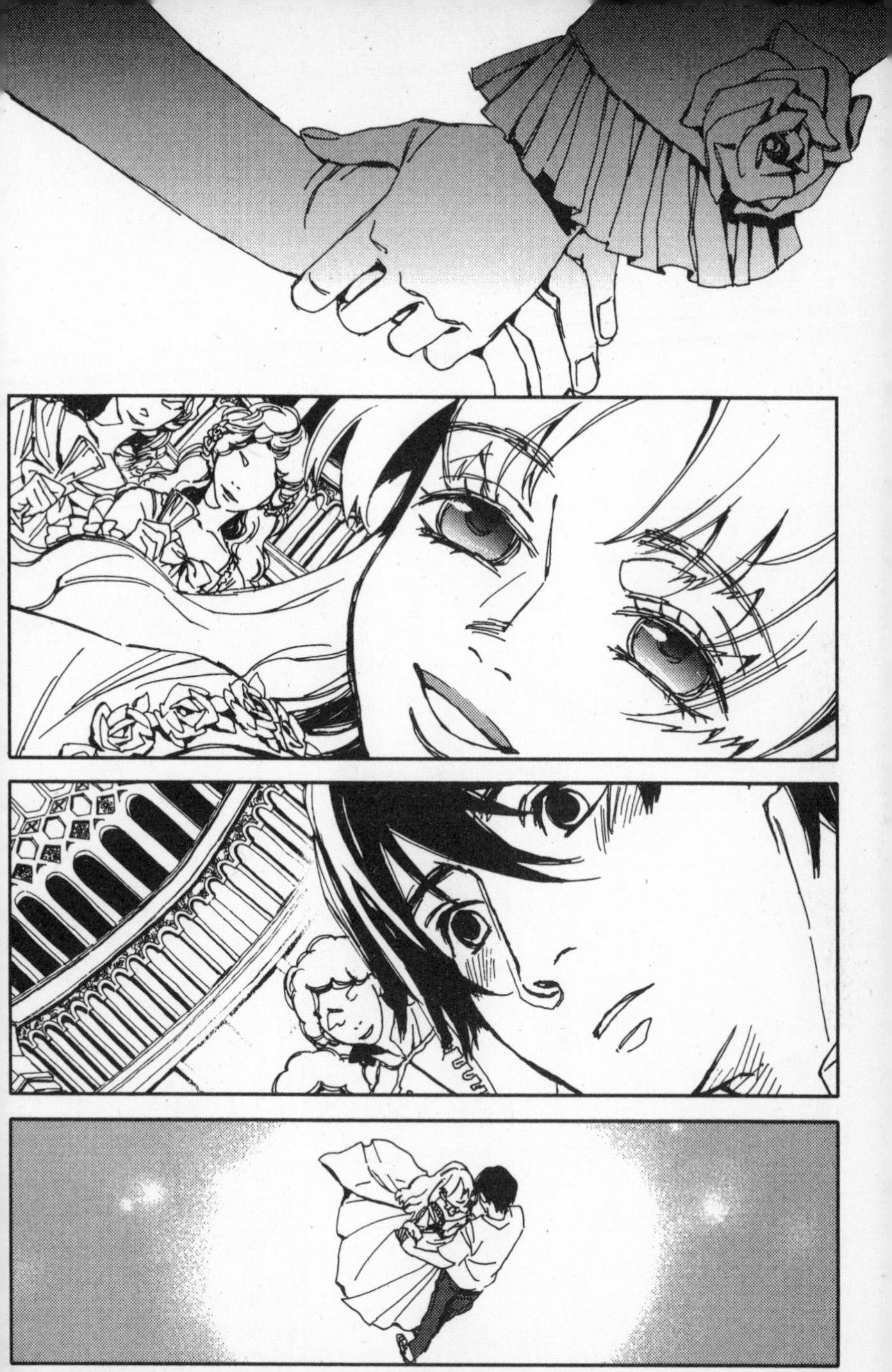

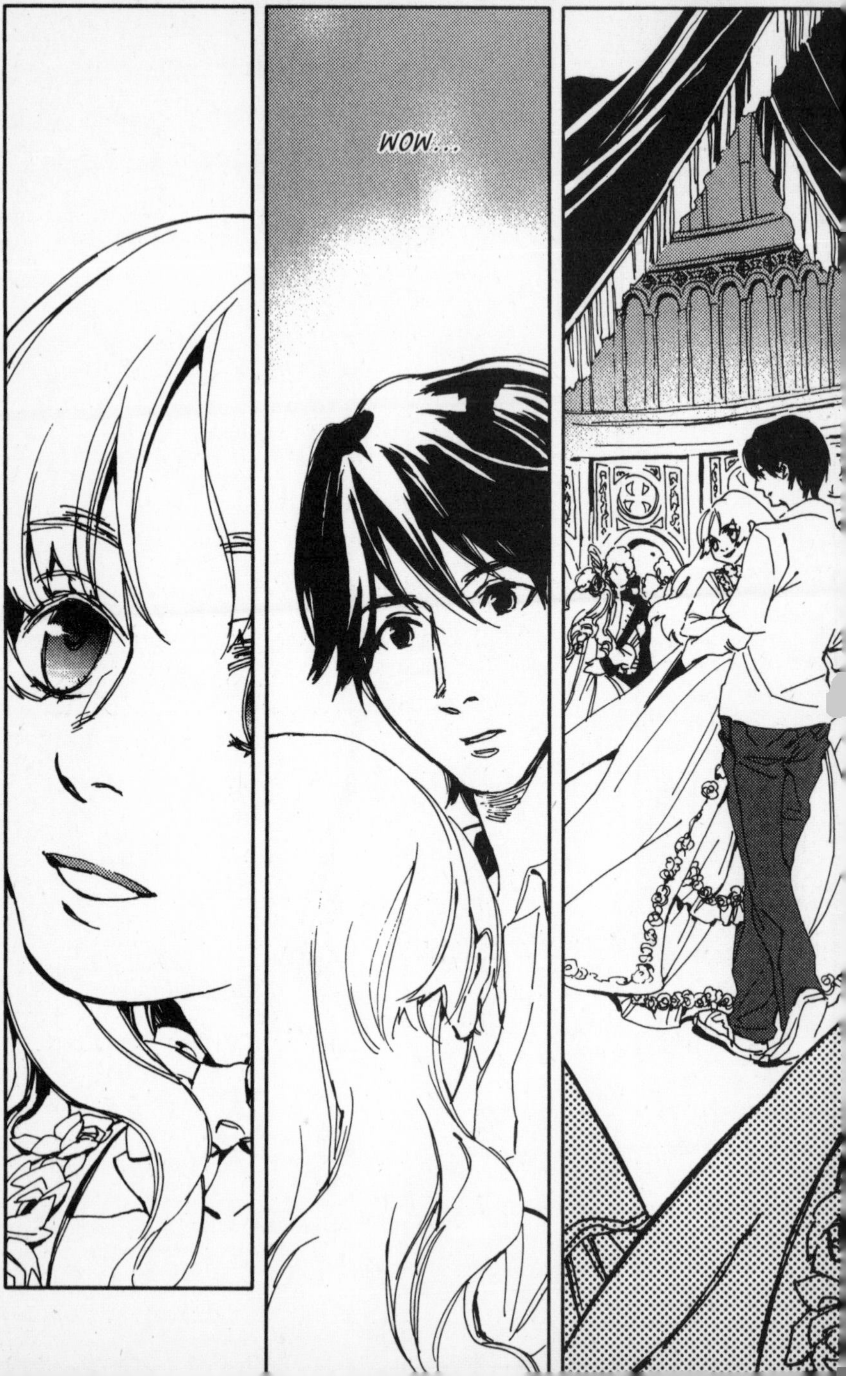
WOW...

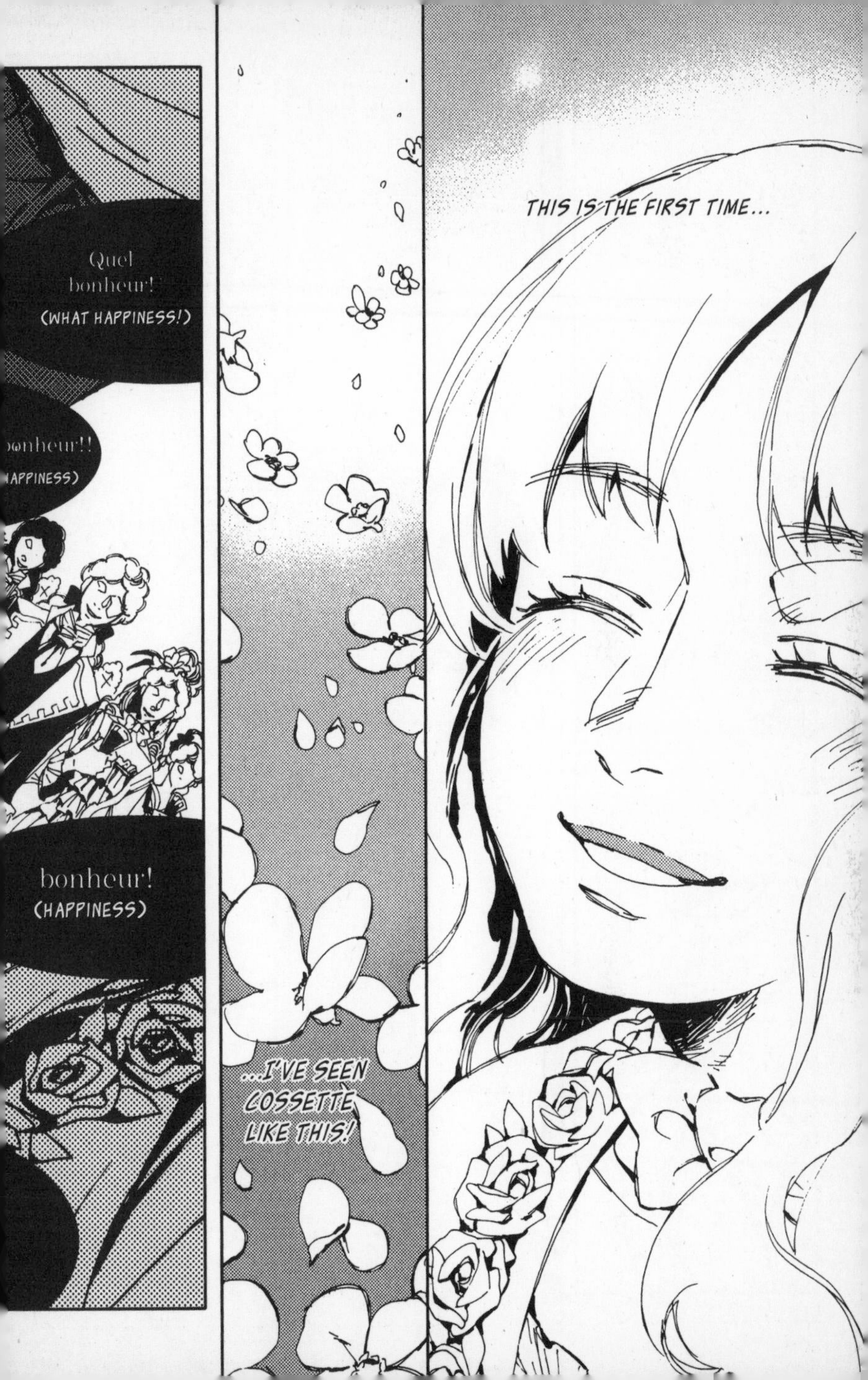
THIS IS THE FIRST TIME...
...I'VE SEEN COSSETTE LIKE THIS!
Quel bonheur! (WHAT HAPPINESS!)
onheur!! APPINESS)
bonheur! (HAPPINESS)

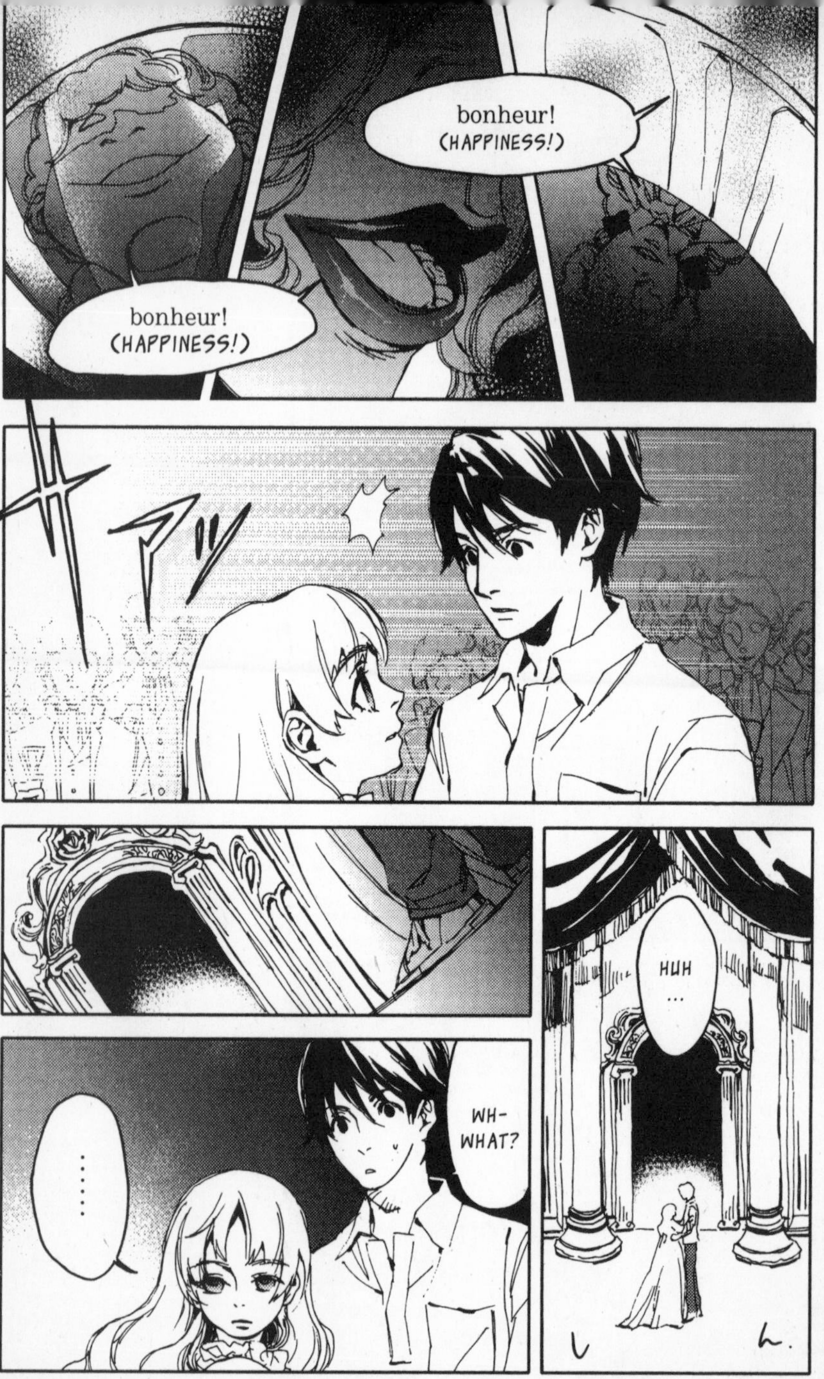

bonheur! (HAPPINESS!)
bonheur! (HAPPINESS!)
ハッ
HUH ...
しん.
WH- WHAT?
......

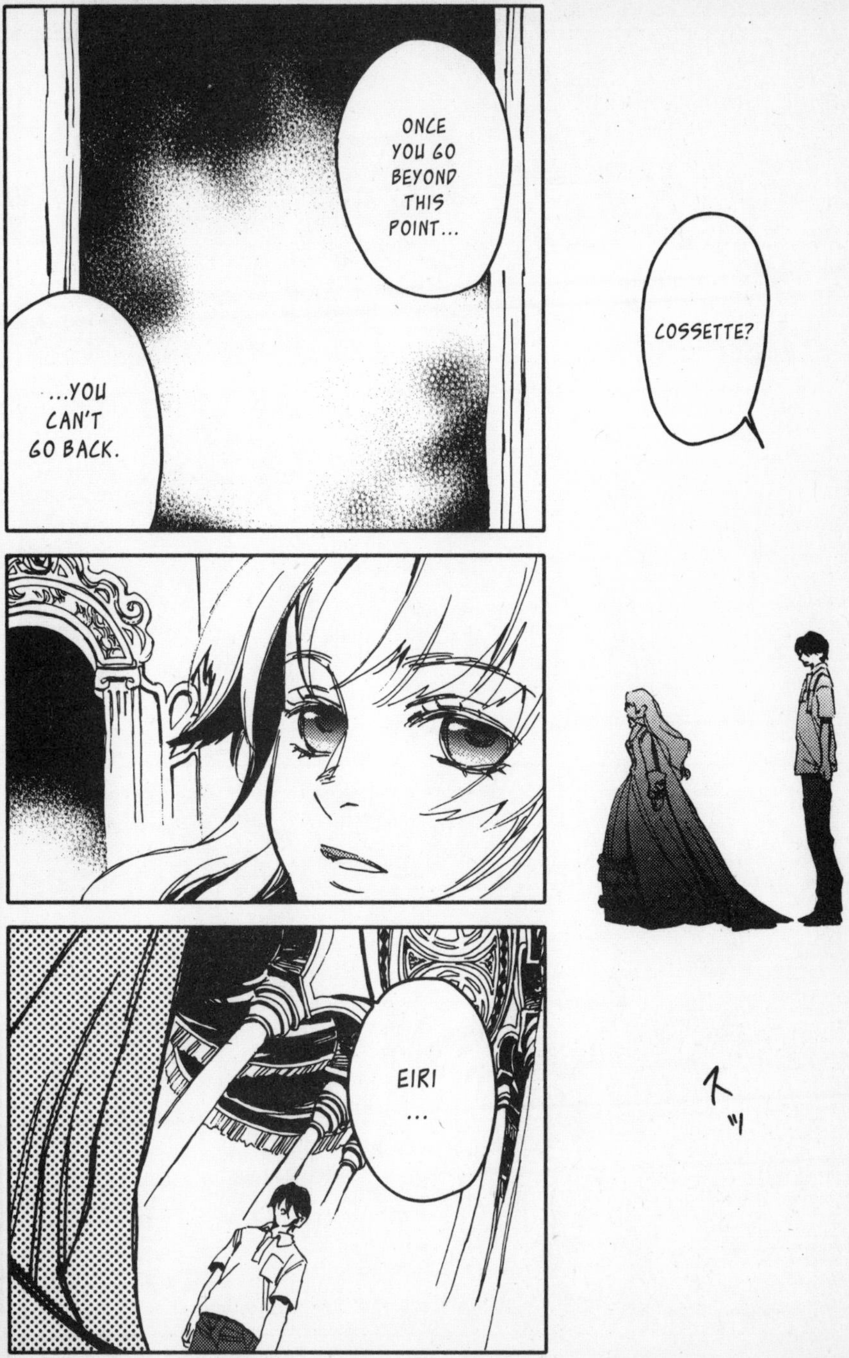
COSSETTE?
スッ
ONCE YOU GO BEYOND THIS POINT...
...YOU CAN'T GO BACK.
EIRI ...

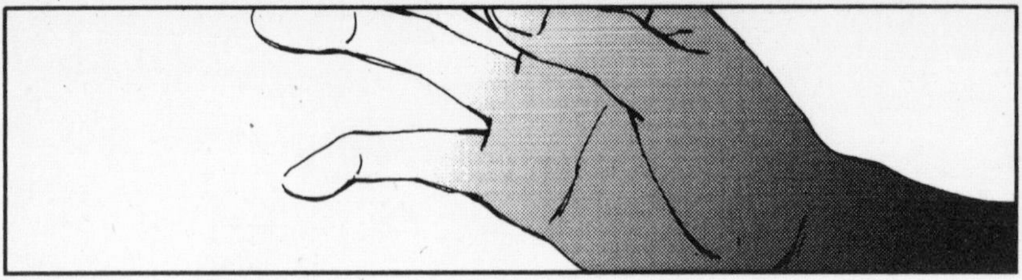

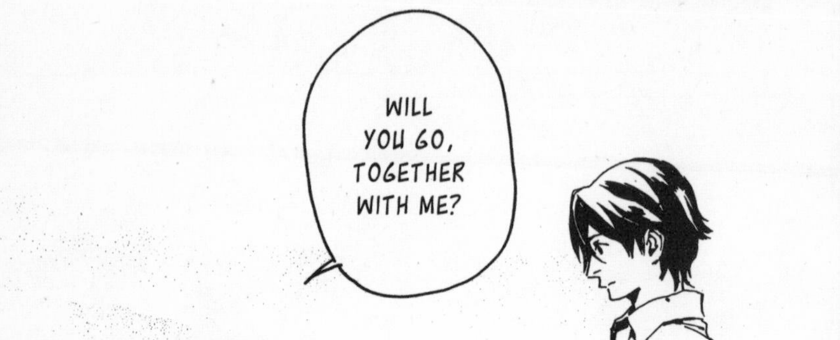
WILL YOU GO, TOGETHER WITH ME?

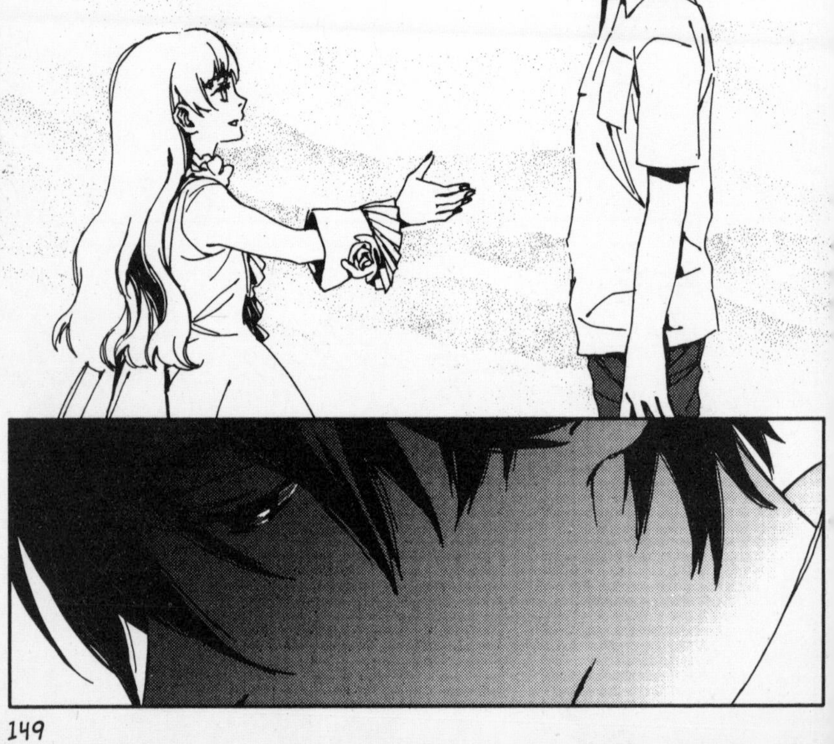

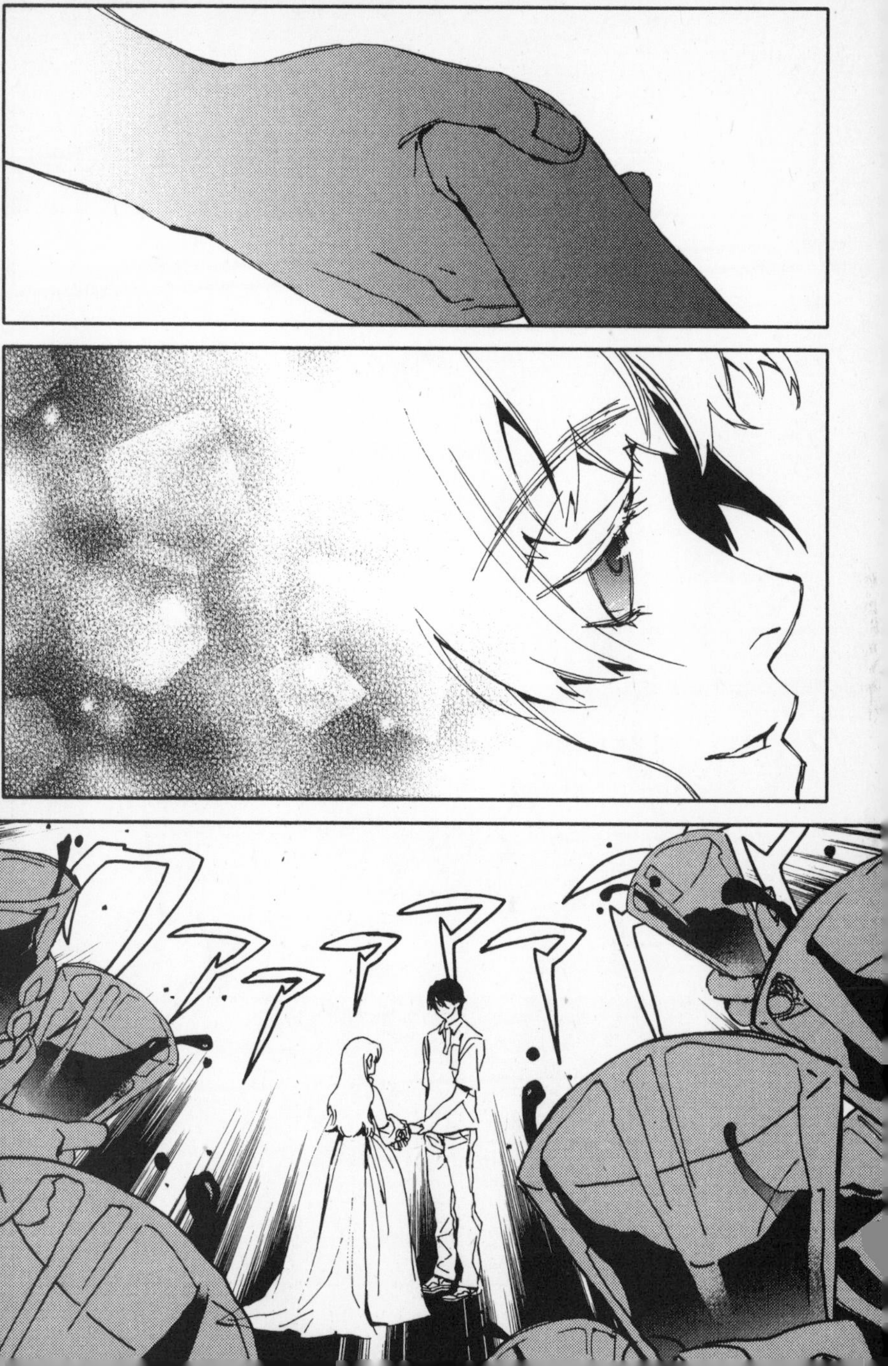
アァァアア

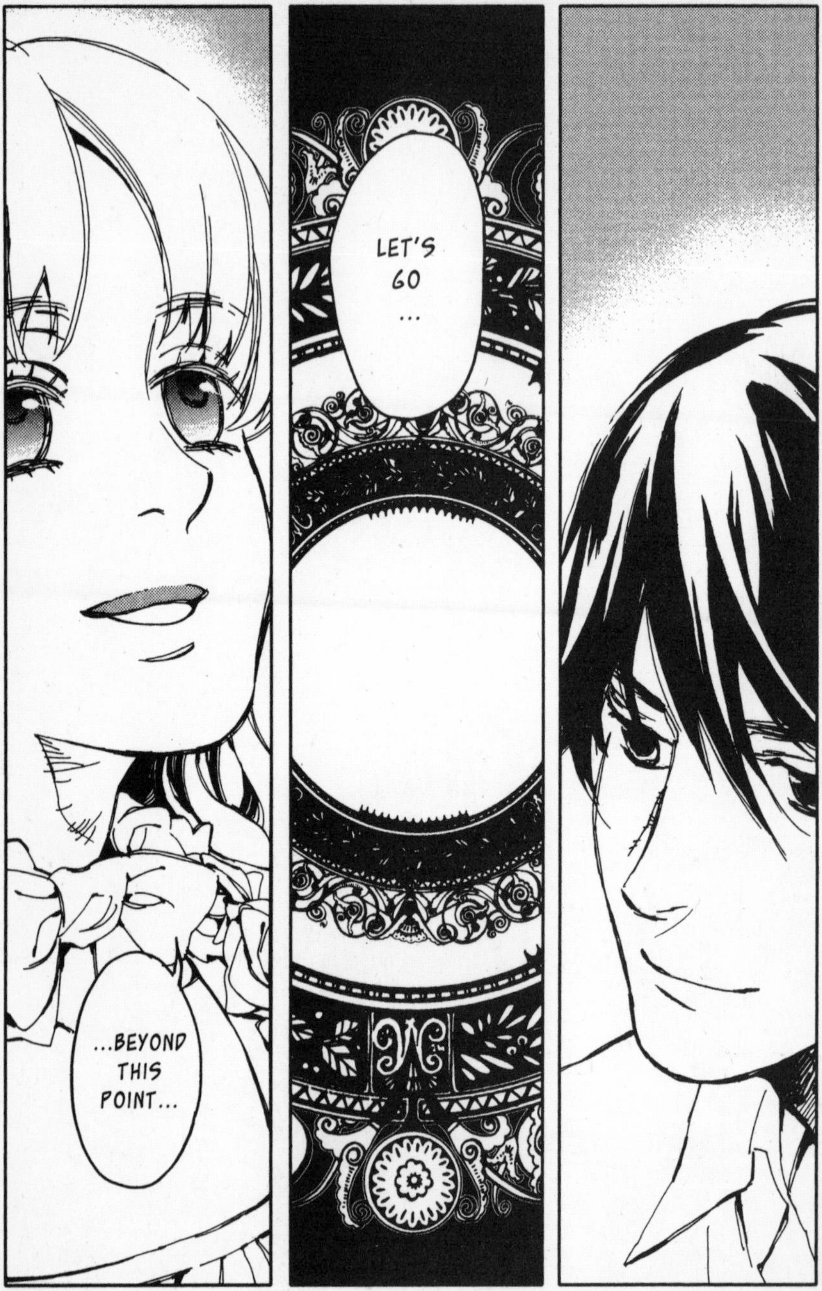
LET'S GO ...
...BEYOND THIS POINT...

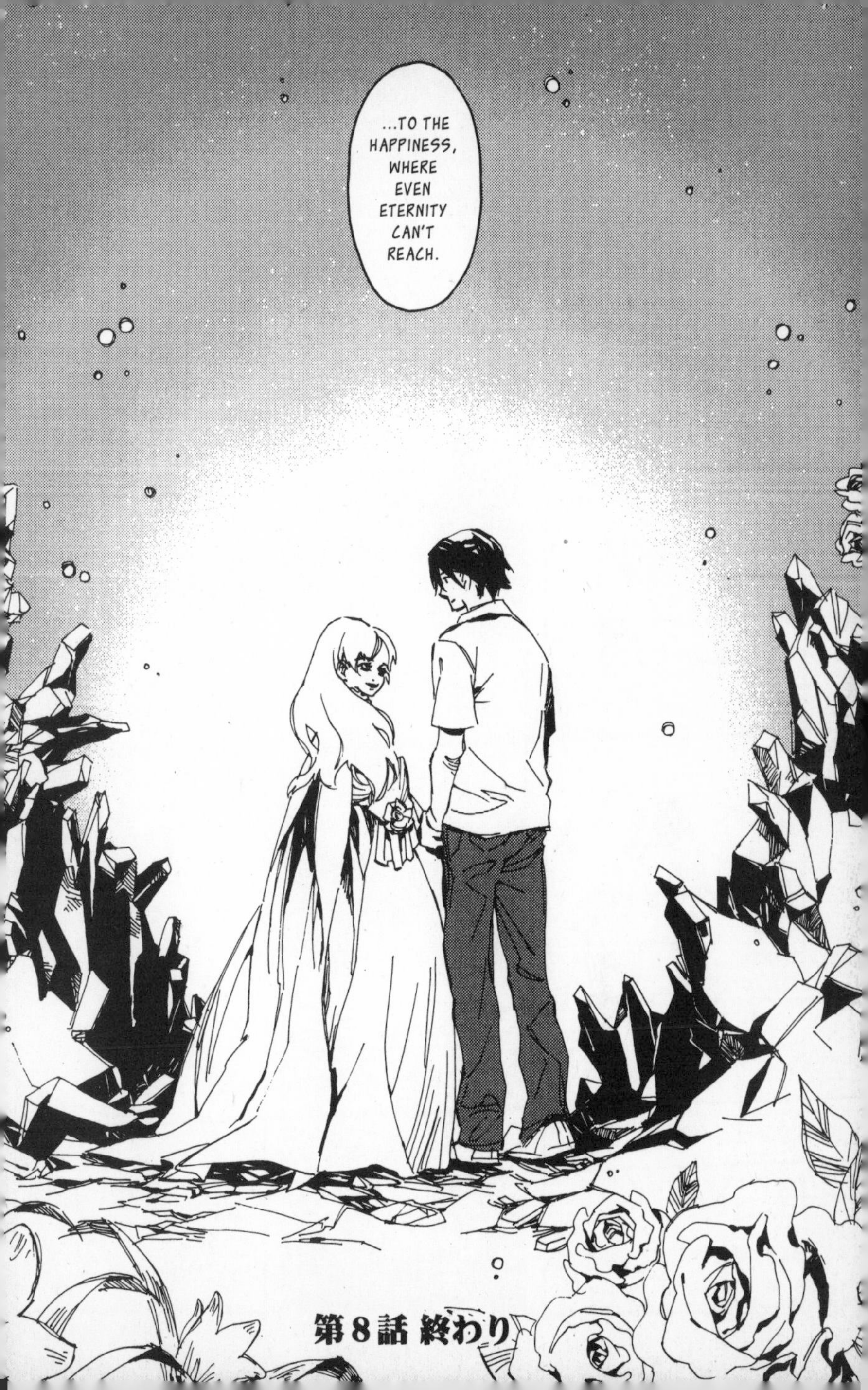
...TO THE HAPPINESS, WHERE EVEN ETERNITY CAN'T REACH.
第8話 終わり

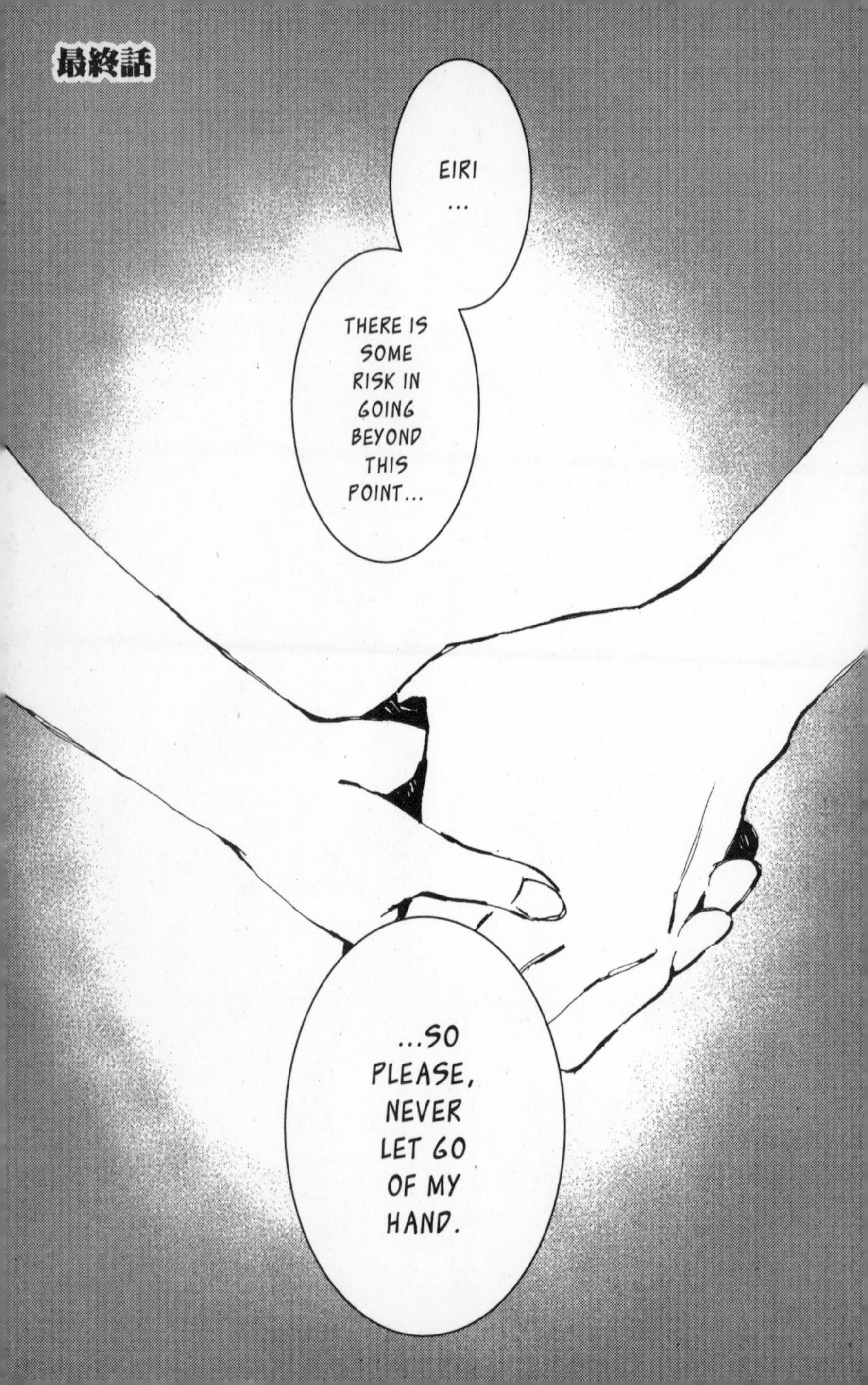
最終話
EIRI ...
THERE IS SOME RISK IN GOING BEYOND THIS POINT...
...SO PLEASE, NEVER LET GO OF MY HAND.

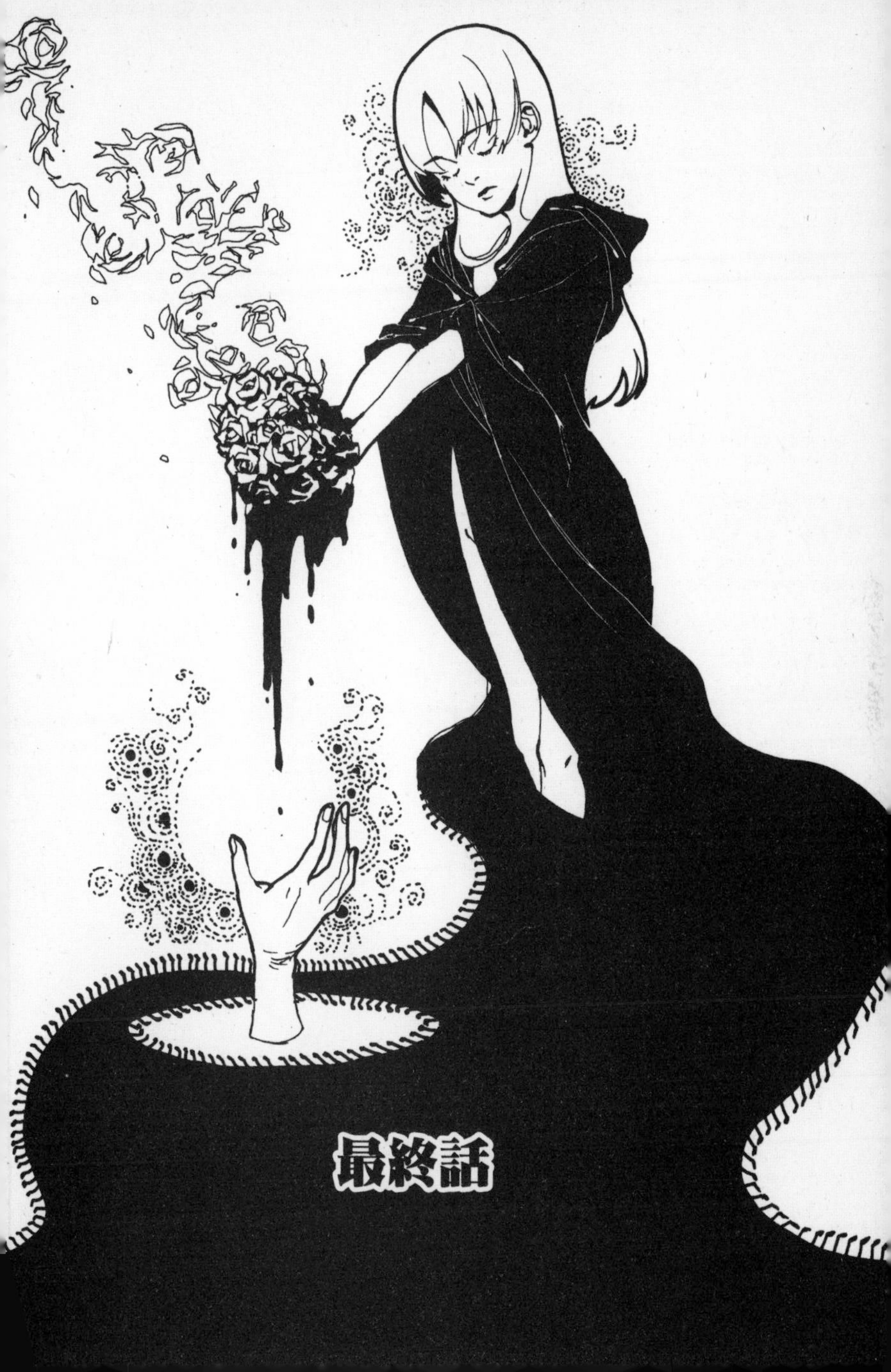
最終話

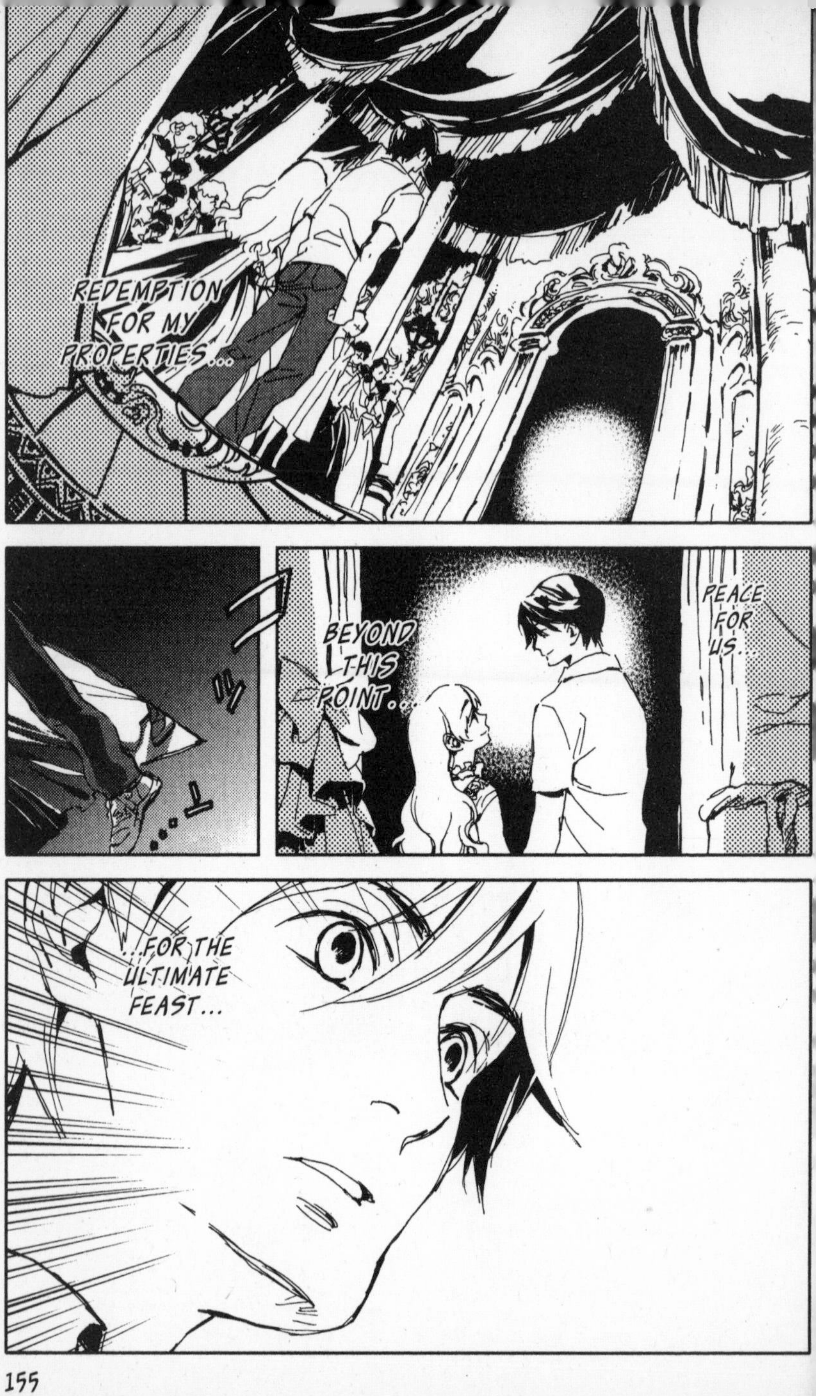
REDEMPTION FOR MY PROPERTIES...
PEACE FOR US...
BEYOND THIS POINT...
...FOR THE ULTIMATE FEAST...

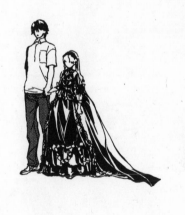

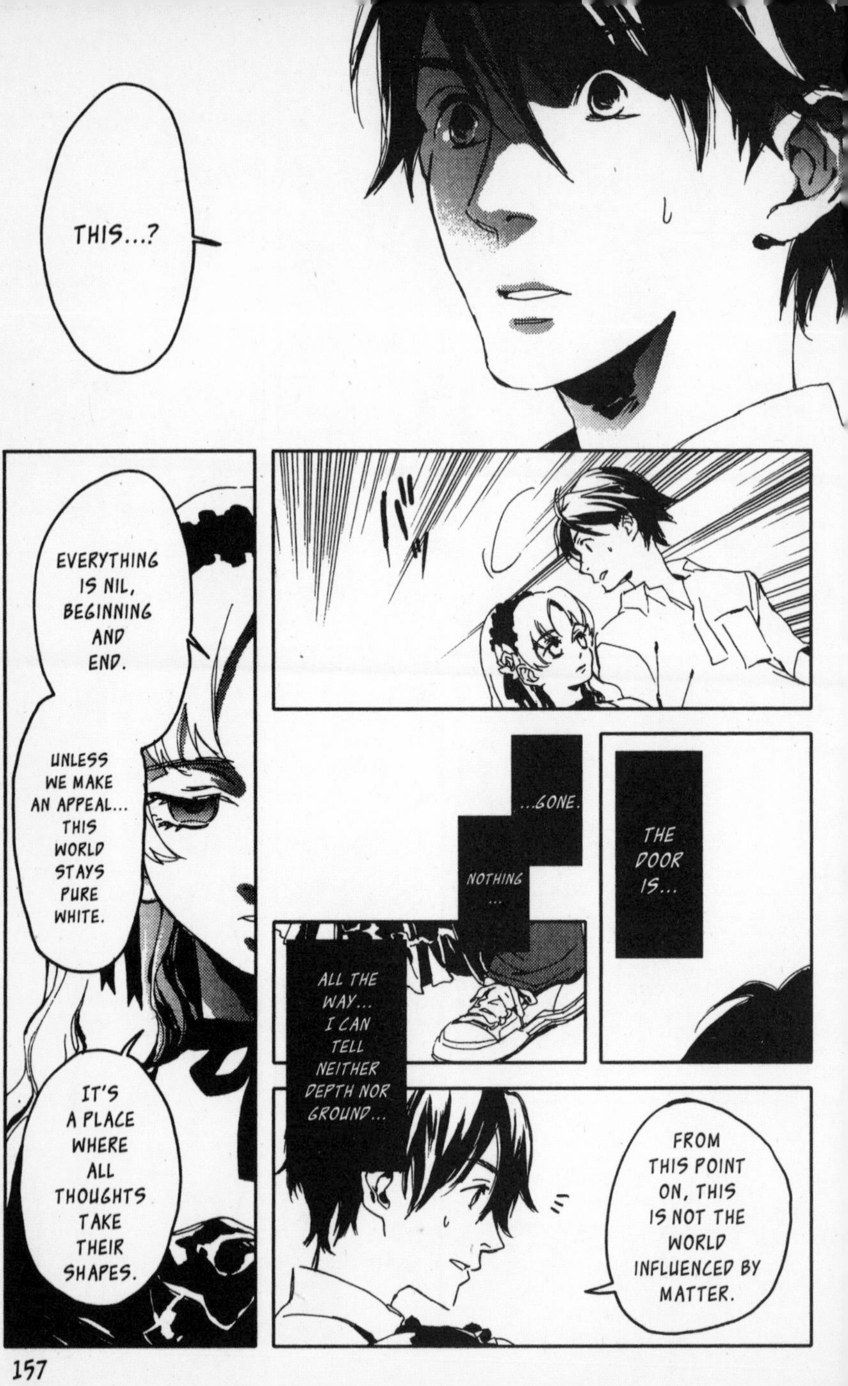
THIS...?
THE DOOR IS...
...GONE.
NOTHING...
ALL THE WAY... I CAN TELL NEITHER DEPTH NOR GROUND...
FROM THIS POINT ON, THIS IS NOT THE WORLD INFLUENCED BY MATTER.
EVERYTHING IS NIL, BEGINNING AND END.
UNLESS WE MAKE AN APPEAL... THIS WORLD STAYS PURE WHITE.
IT'S A PLACE WHERE ALL THOUGHTS TAKE THEIR SHAPES.

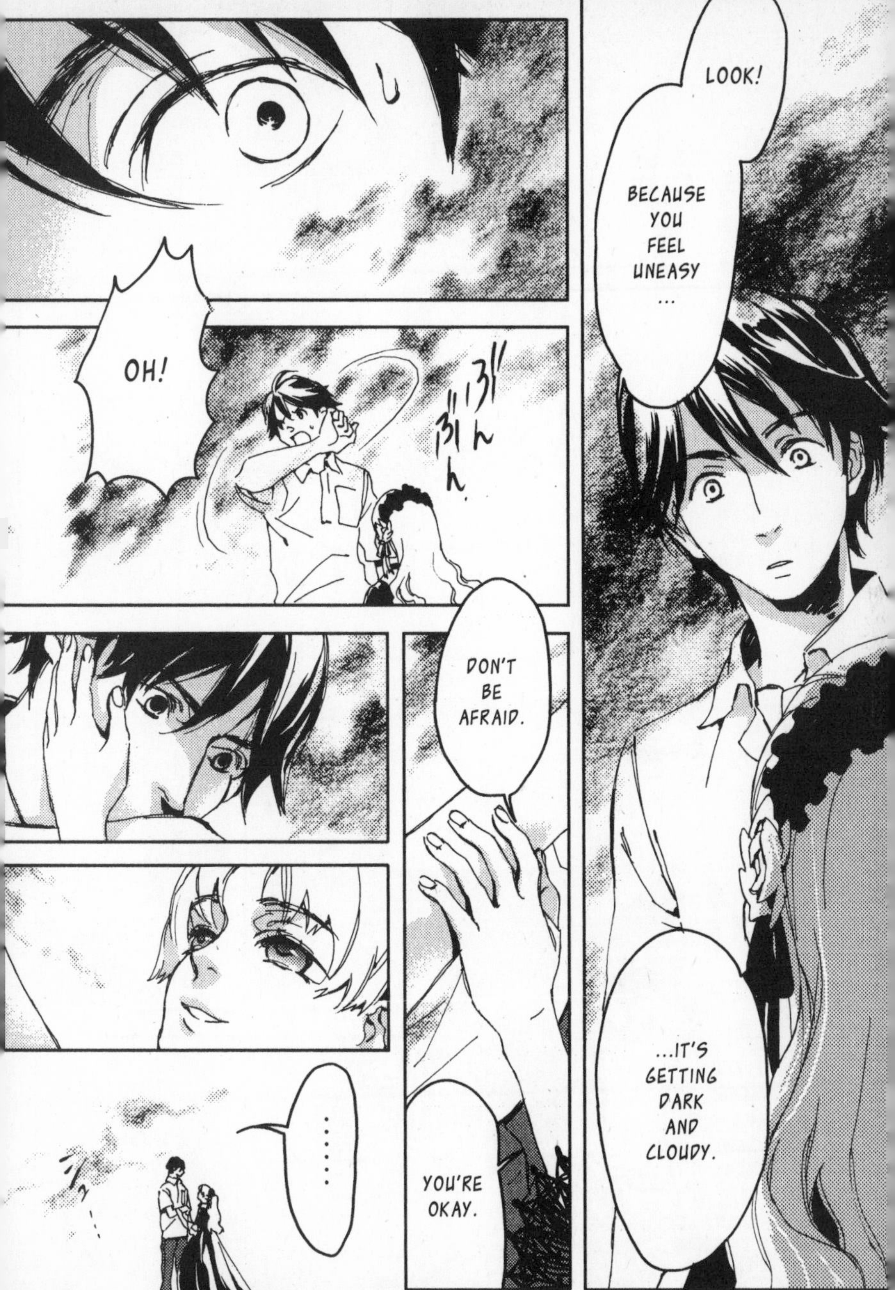
LOOK!
BECAUSE YOU FEEL UNEASY ...
...IT'S GETTING DARK AND CLOUDY.
OH!
ぶん ぶん
DON'T BE AFRAID.
YOU'RE OKAY.
......

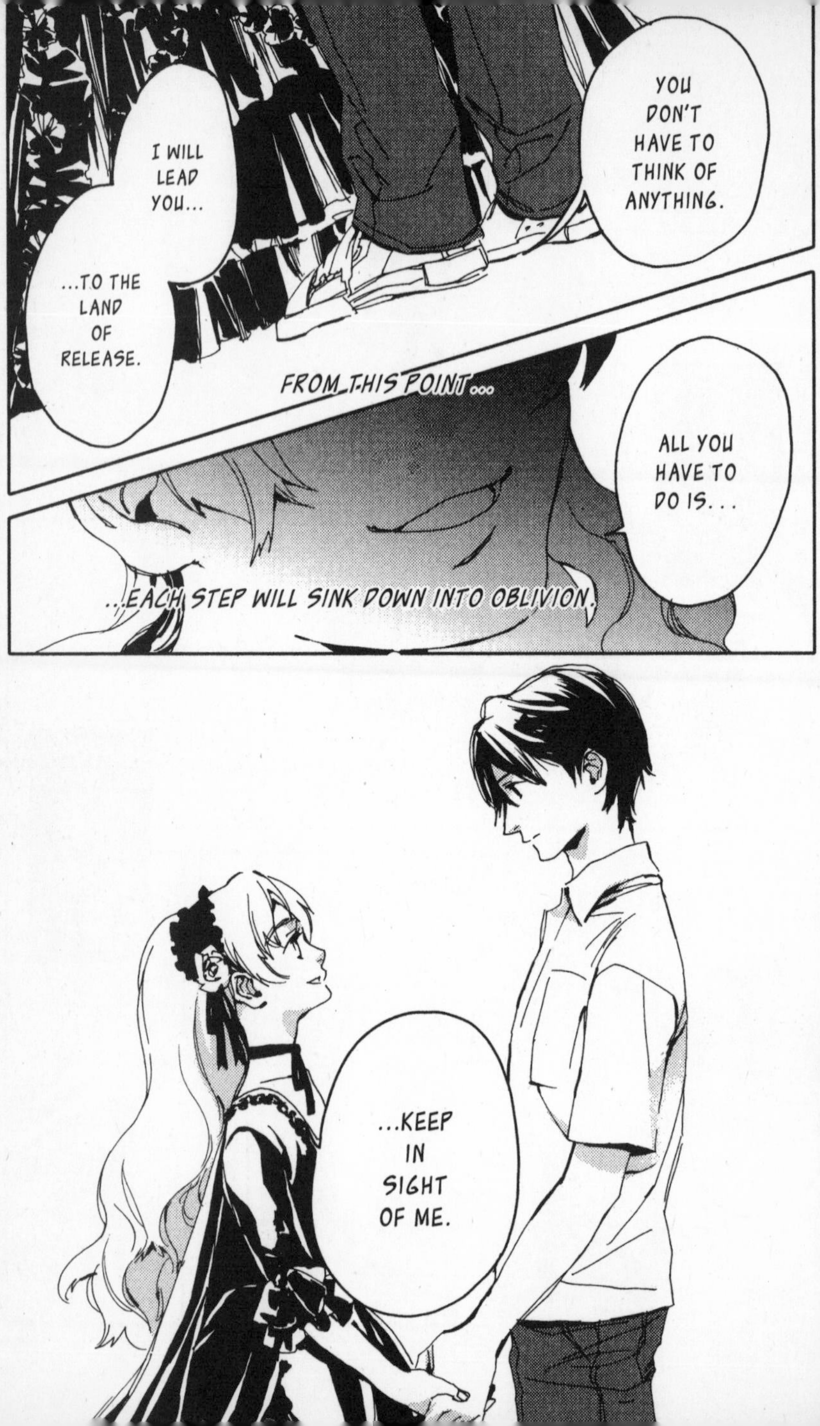
YOU DON'T HAVE TO THINK OF ANYTHING.
I WILL LEAD YOU...
...TO THE LAND OF RELEASE.
FROM THIS POINT...
ALL YOU HAVE TO DO IS...
...EACH STEP WILL SINK DOWN INTO OBLIVION.
...KEEP IN SIGHT OF ME.

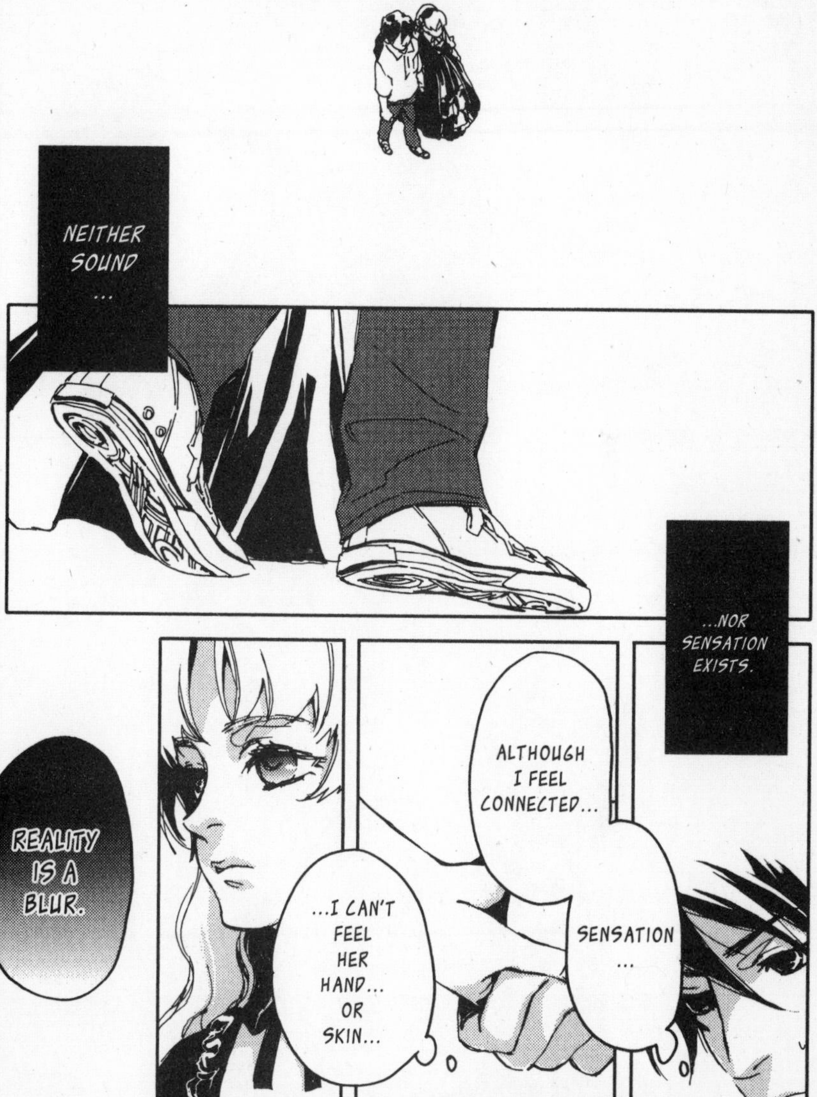

NEITHER SOUND ...
...NOR SENSATION EXISTS.
ALTHOUGH I FEEL CONNECTED...
SENSATION ...
...I CAN'T FEEL HER HAND... OR SKIN...
REALITY IS A BLUR.

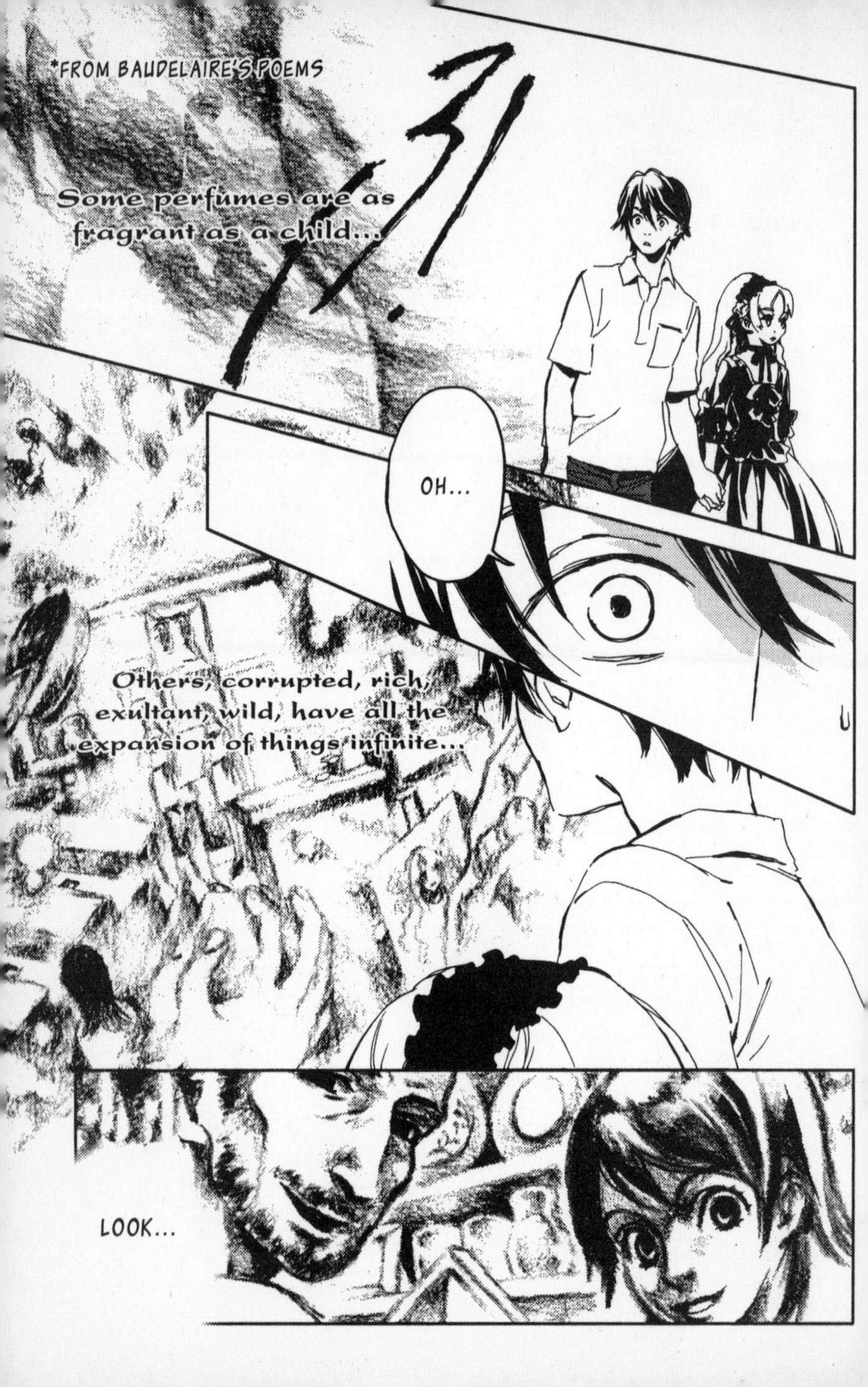
*FROM BAUDELAIRE'S POEMS
Some perfumes are as fragrant as a child...
OH...
Others, corrupted, rich, exultant, wild, have all the expansion of things infinite...
LOOK...

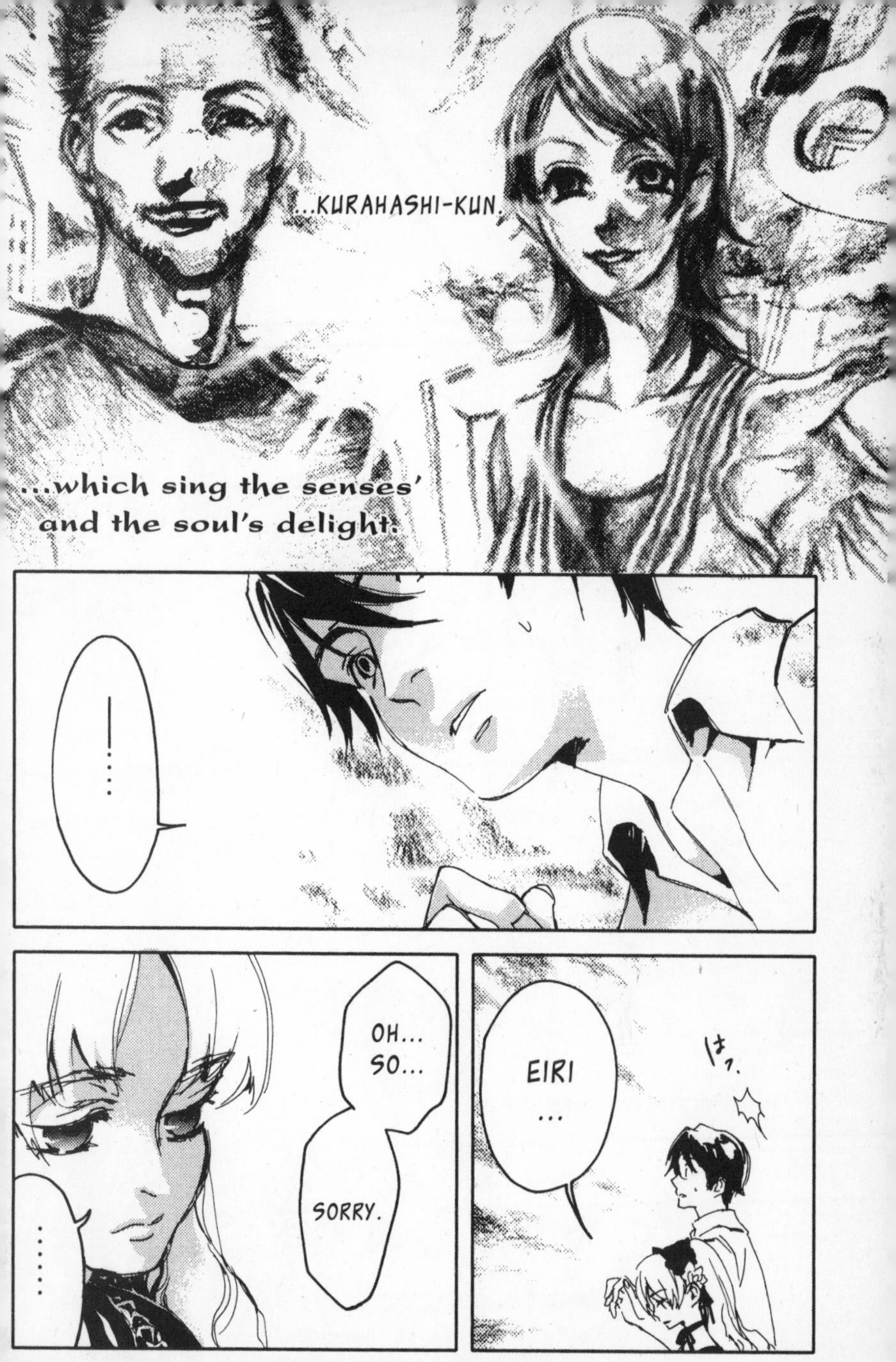
...KURAHASHI-KUN.
...which sing the senses' and the soul's delight:
......
はっ
EIRI ...
OH... SO... SORRY.
......

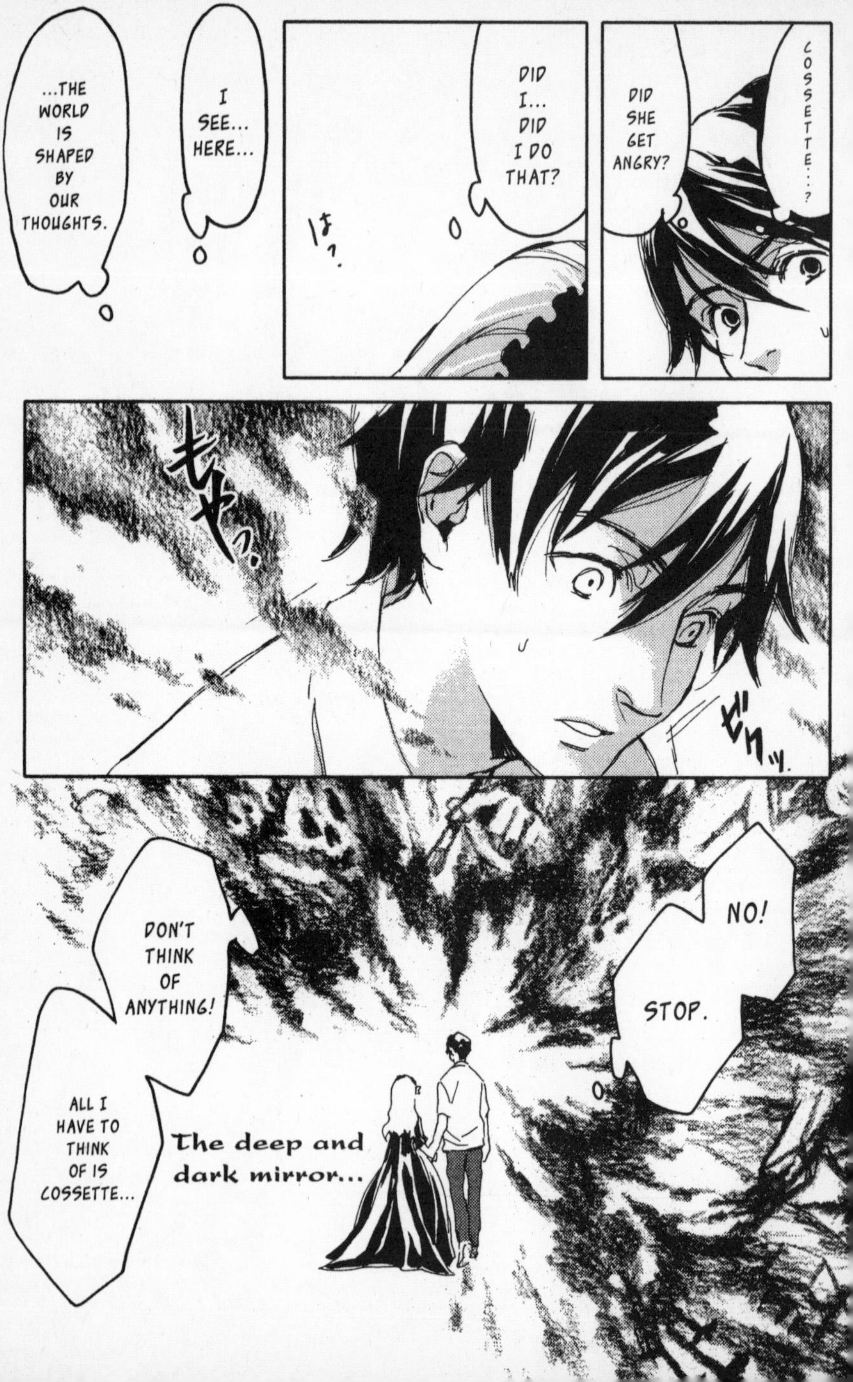
COSSETTE...?
DID SHE GET ANGRY?
DID I... DID I DO THAT?
は？
I SEE... HERE...
...THE WORLD IS SHAPED BY OUR THOUGHTS.
もやっ
ビクッ
NO!
STOP.
DON'T THINK OF ANYTHING!
ALL I HAVE TO THINK OF IS COSSETTE...
The deep and dark mirror...

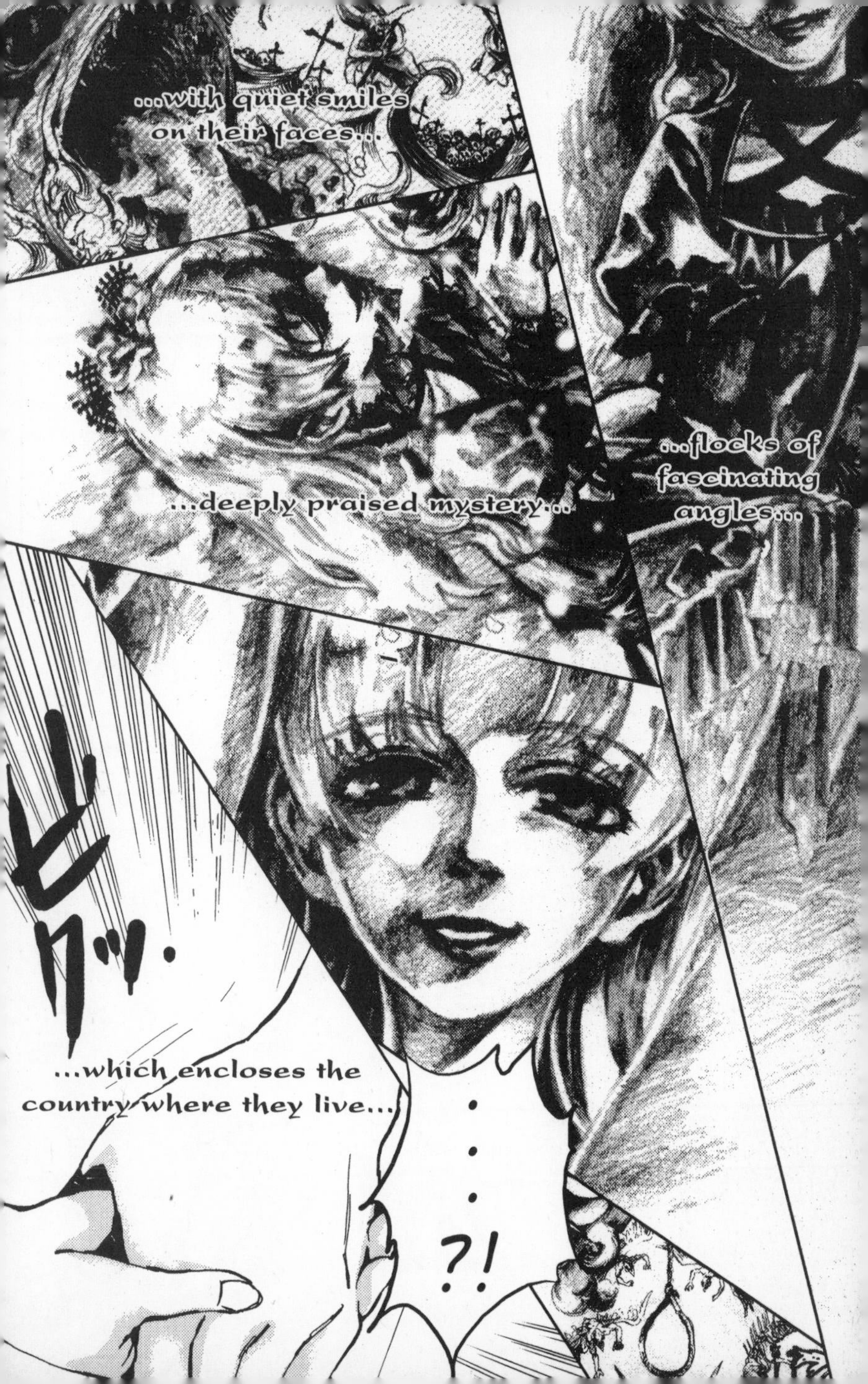
...flocks of fascinating angles...
...with quiet smiles on their faces...
...deeply praised mystery...
ビクッ
...which encloses the country where they live...
...
?!

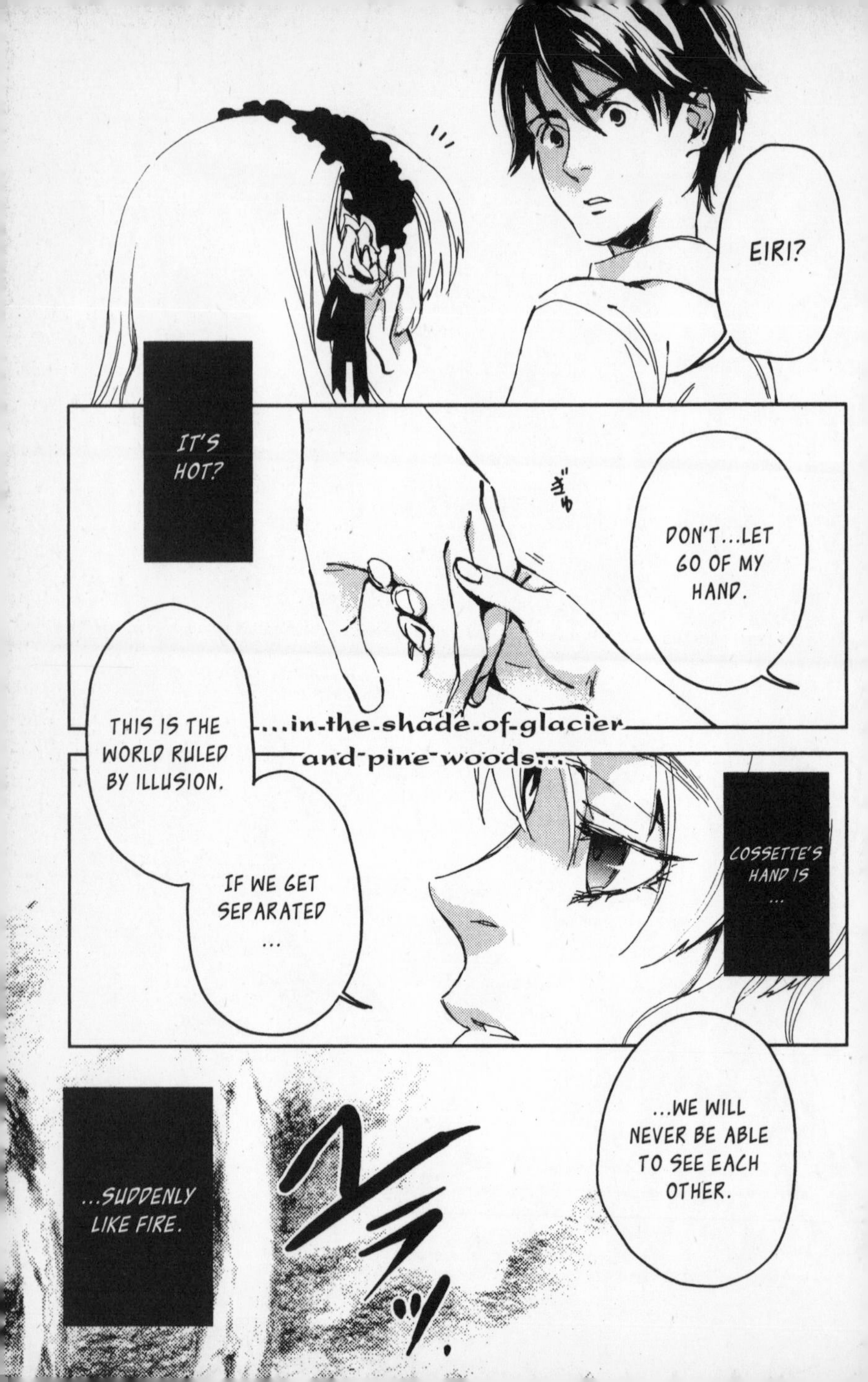
EIRI?
DON'T...LET GO OF MY HAND.
IT'S HOT?
...in-the-shade-of-glacier and-pine-woods...
COSSETTE'S HAND IS ...
THIS IS THE WORLD RULED BY ILLUSION.
IF WE GET SEPARATED ...
...WE WILL NEVER BE ABLE TO SEE EACH OTHER.
...SUDDENLY LIKE FIRE.

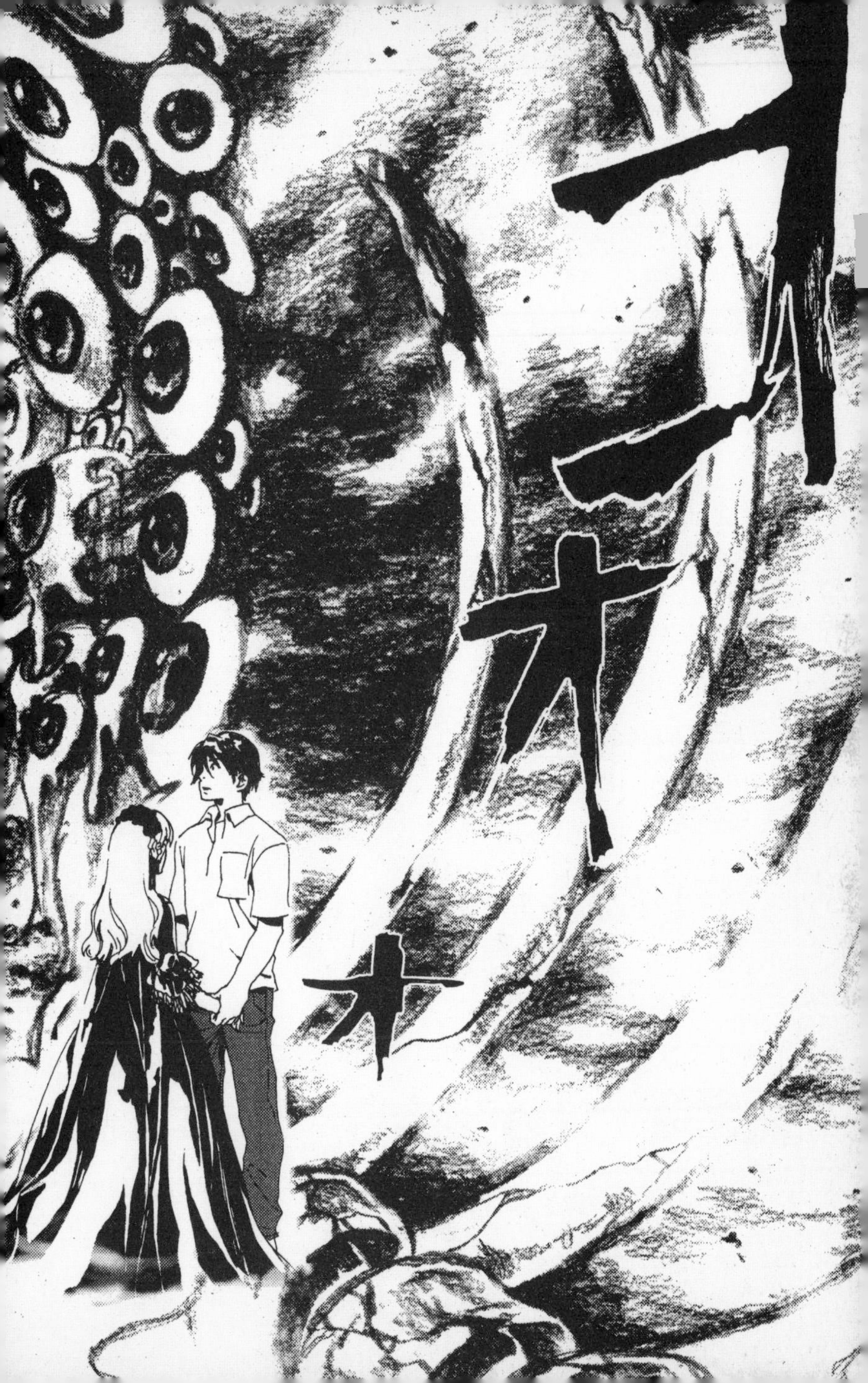
オオオ

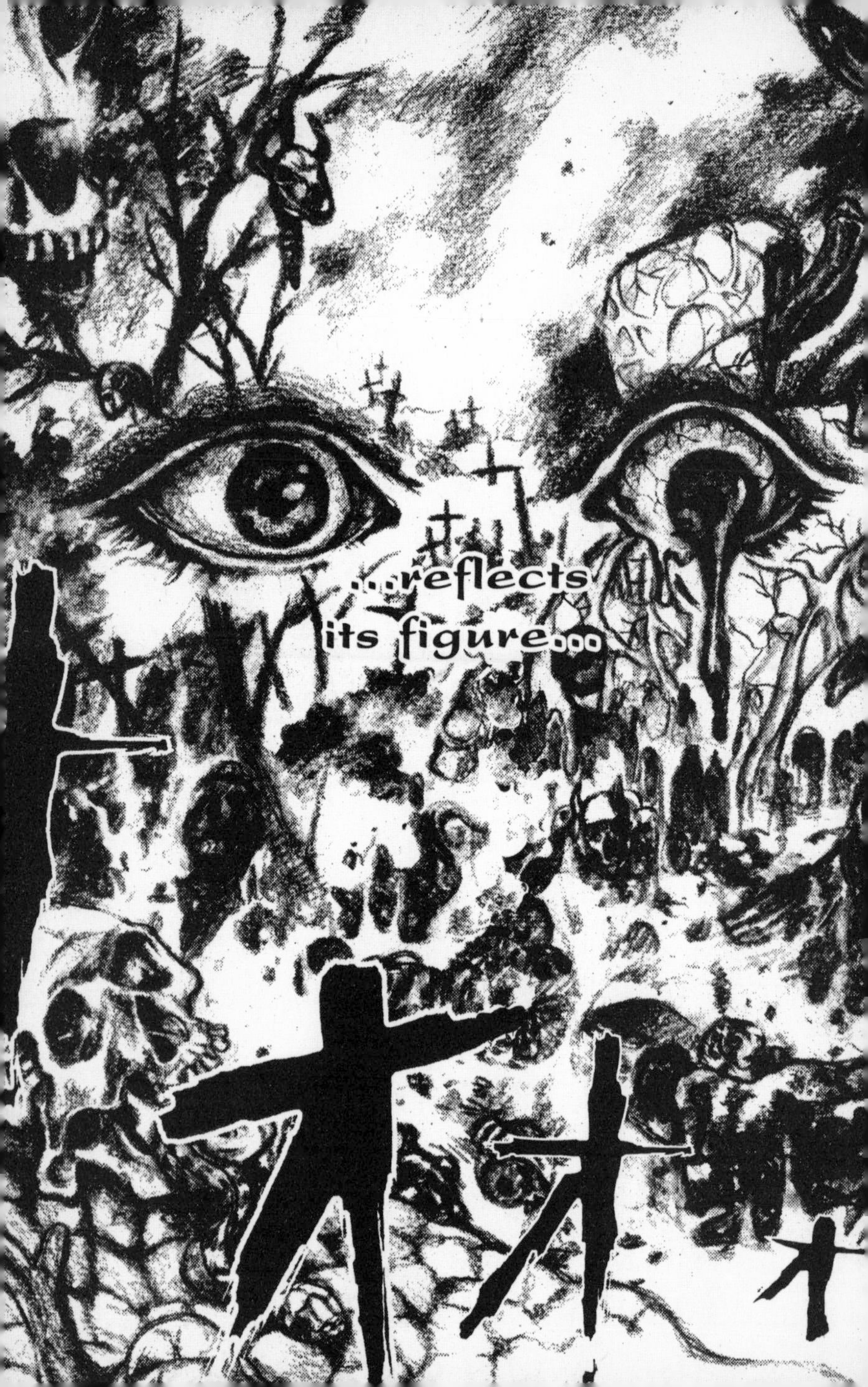
...reflects
its figure...

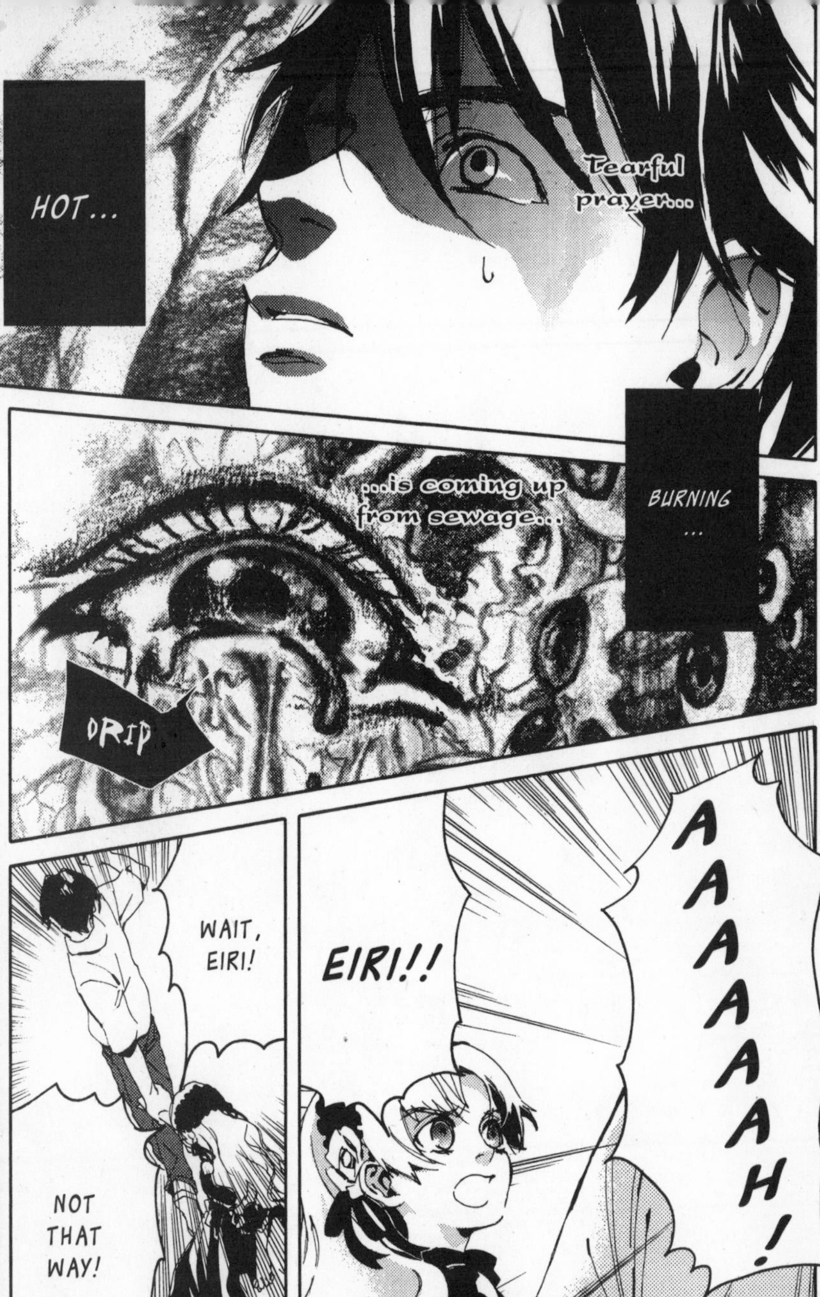
Tearful prayer...
HOT...
BURNING ...
...is coming up from sewage...
DRIP
AAAAAAH!
EIRI!!
WAIT, EIRI!
NOT THAT WAY!

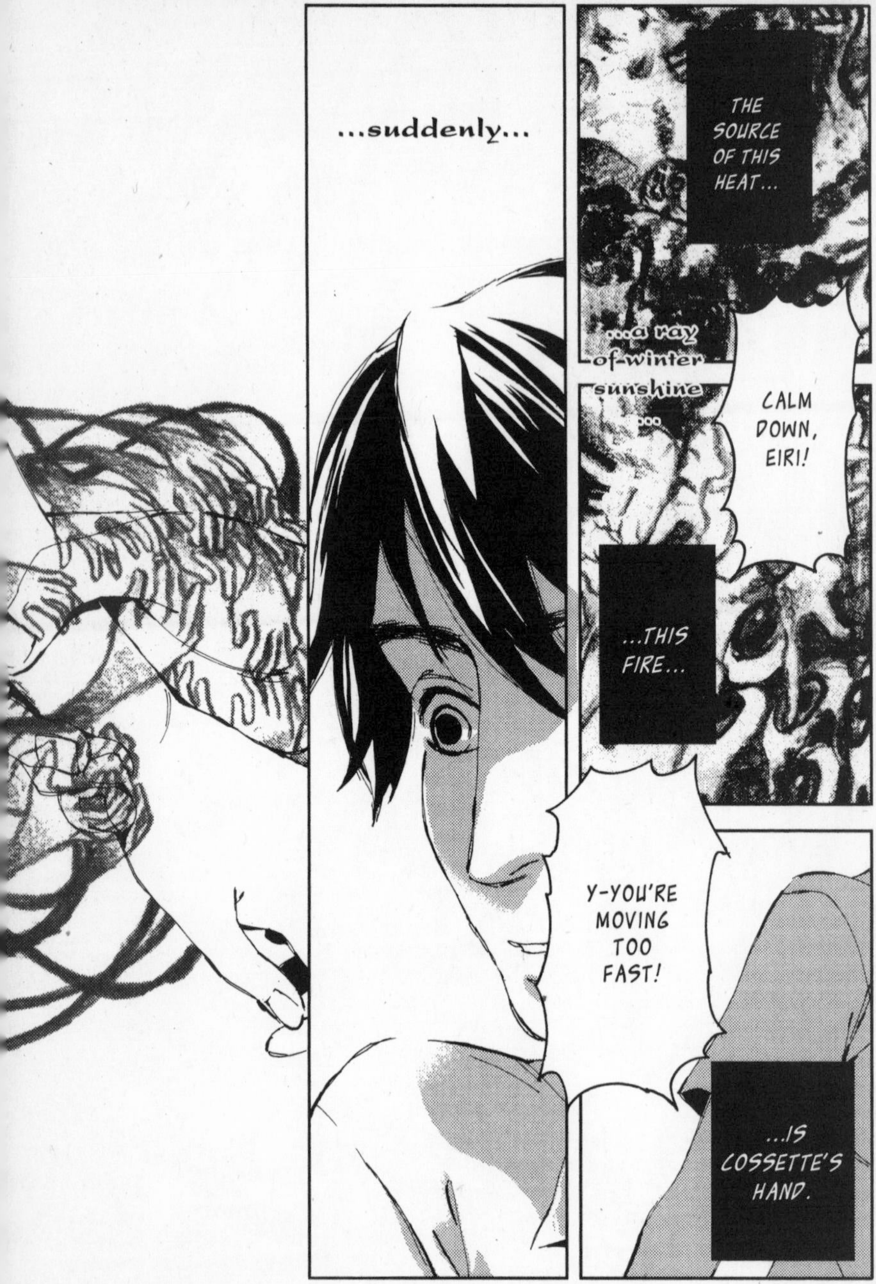
THE SOURCE OF THIS HEAT...
CALM DOWN, EIRI!
...THIS FIRE...
Y-YOU'RE MOVING TOO FAST!
...IS COSSETTE'S HAND.
...suddenly...
...a ray of winter sunshine...

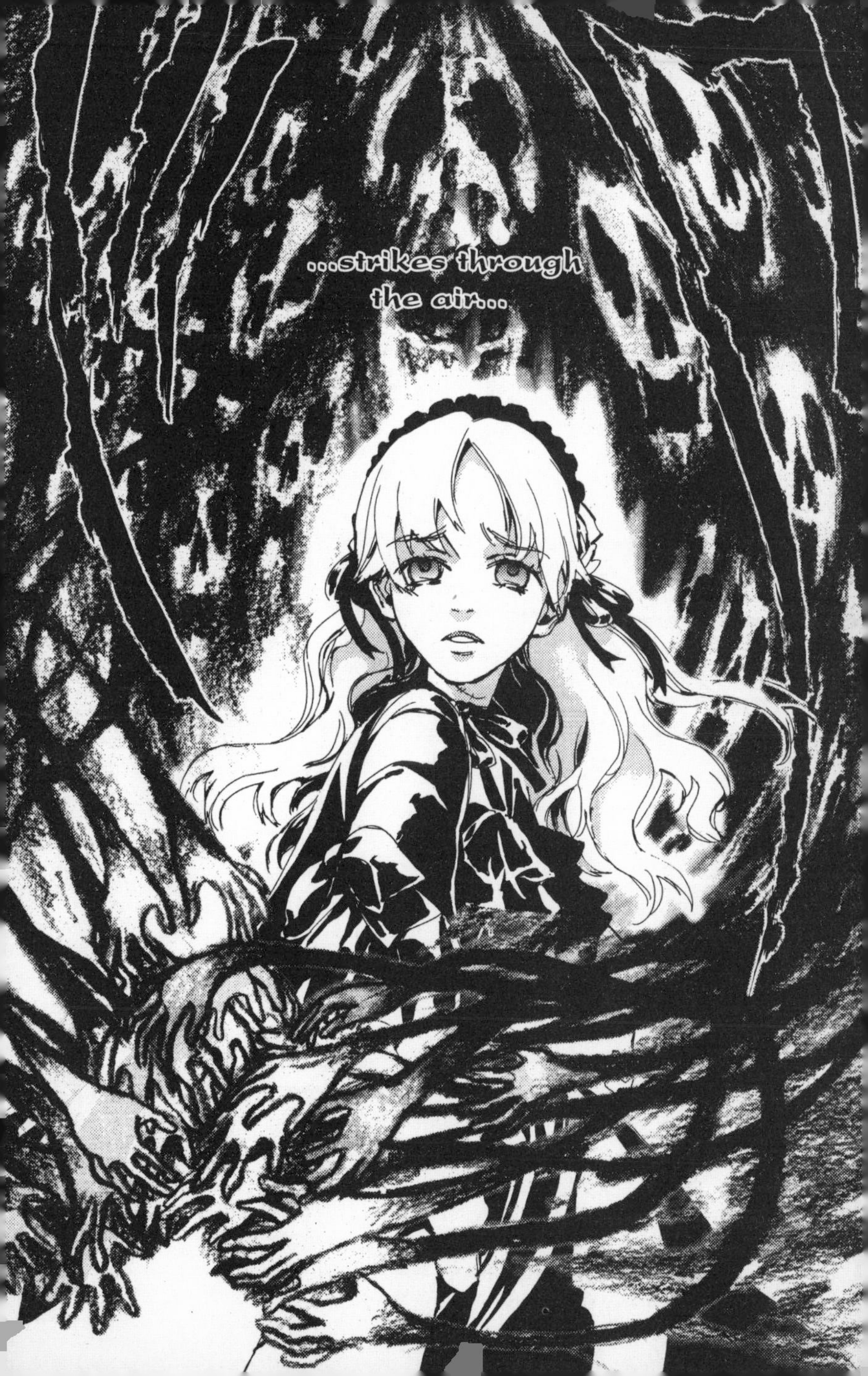
...strikes through
the air...

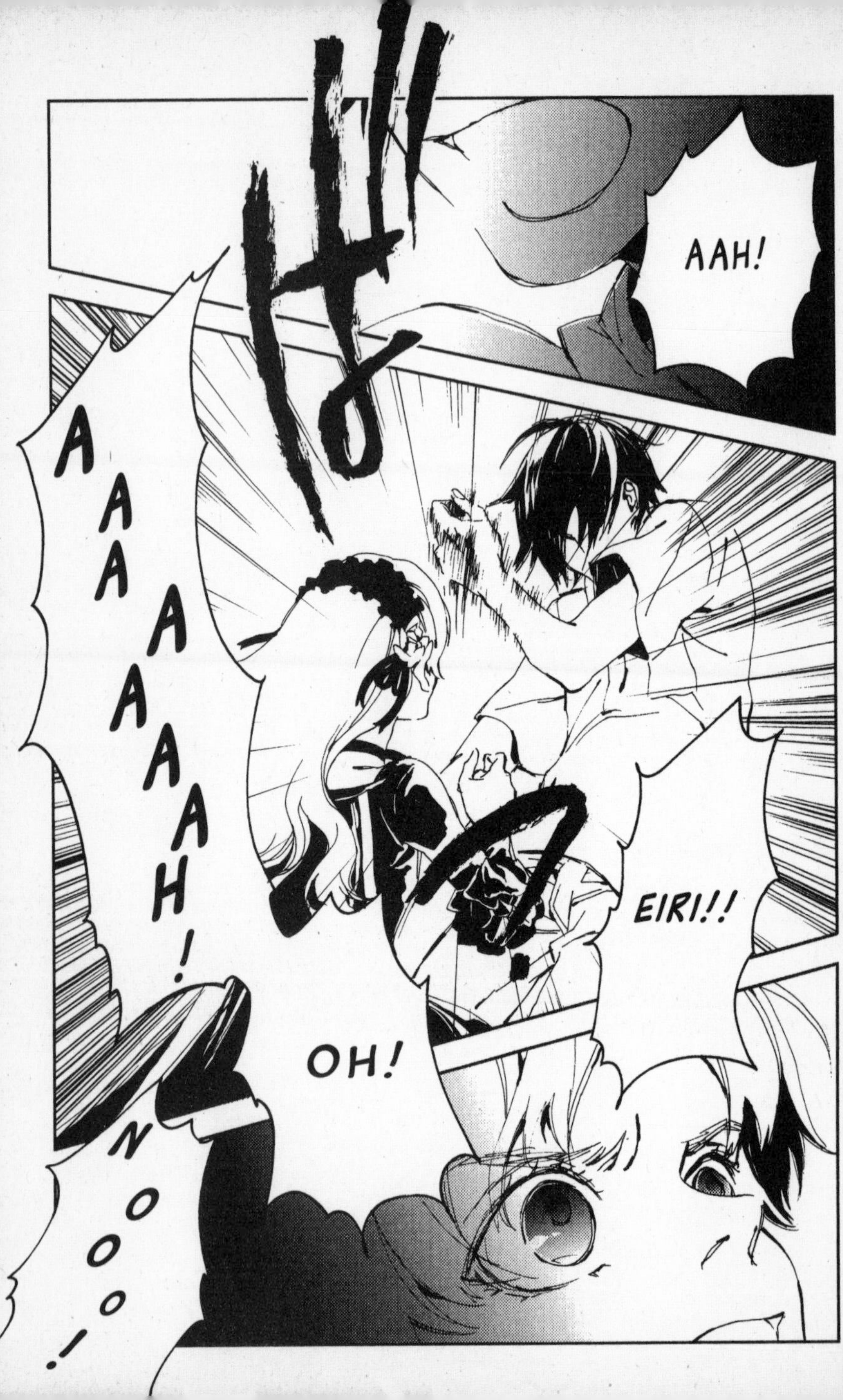

AAH!
AAAAAAAAH!
EIRI!!
OH!
NOOOO!

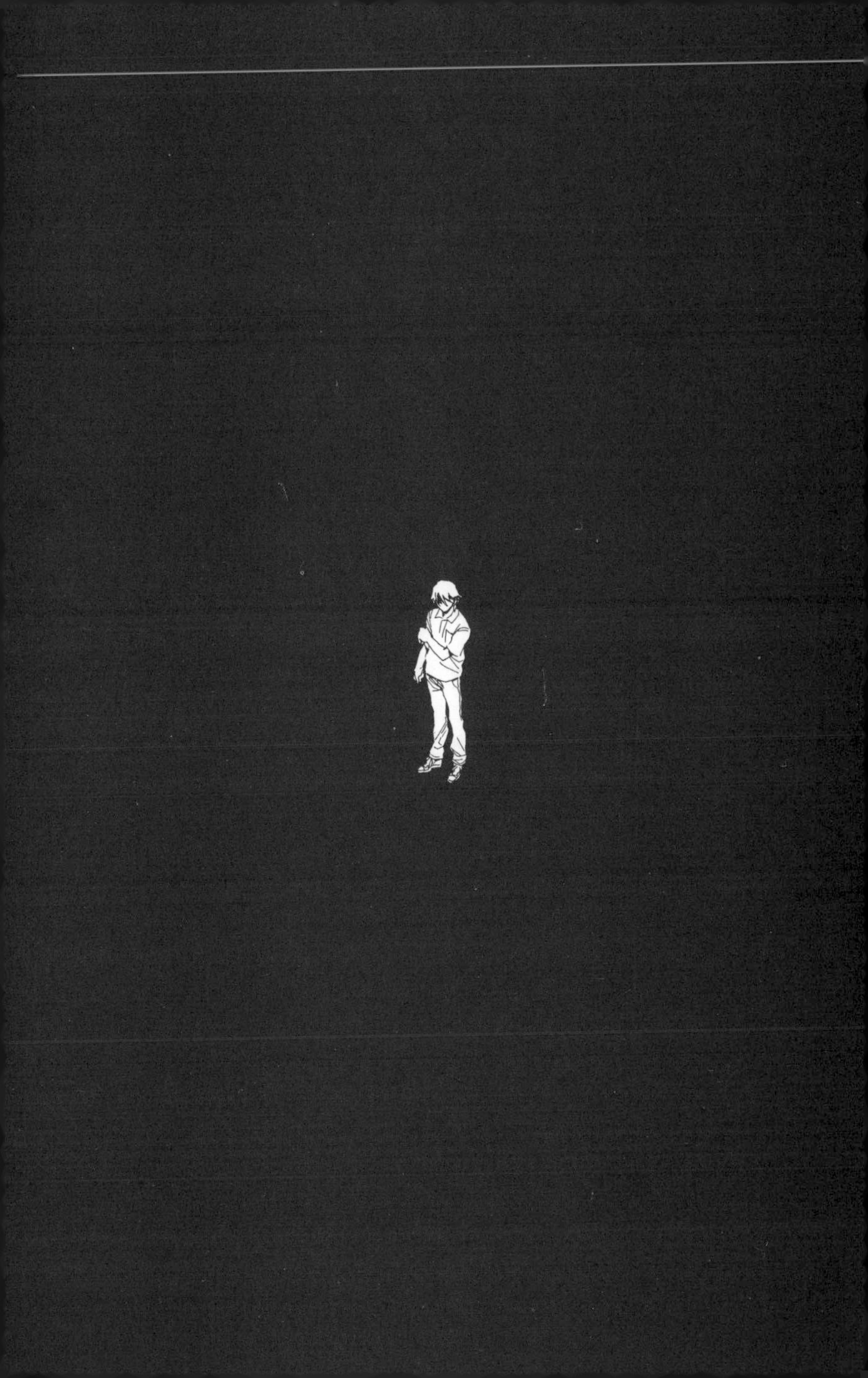

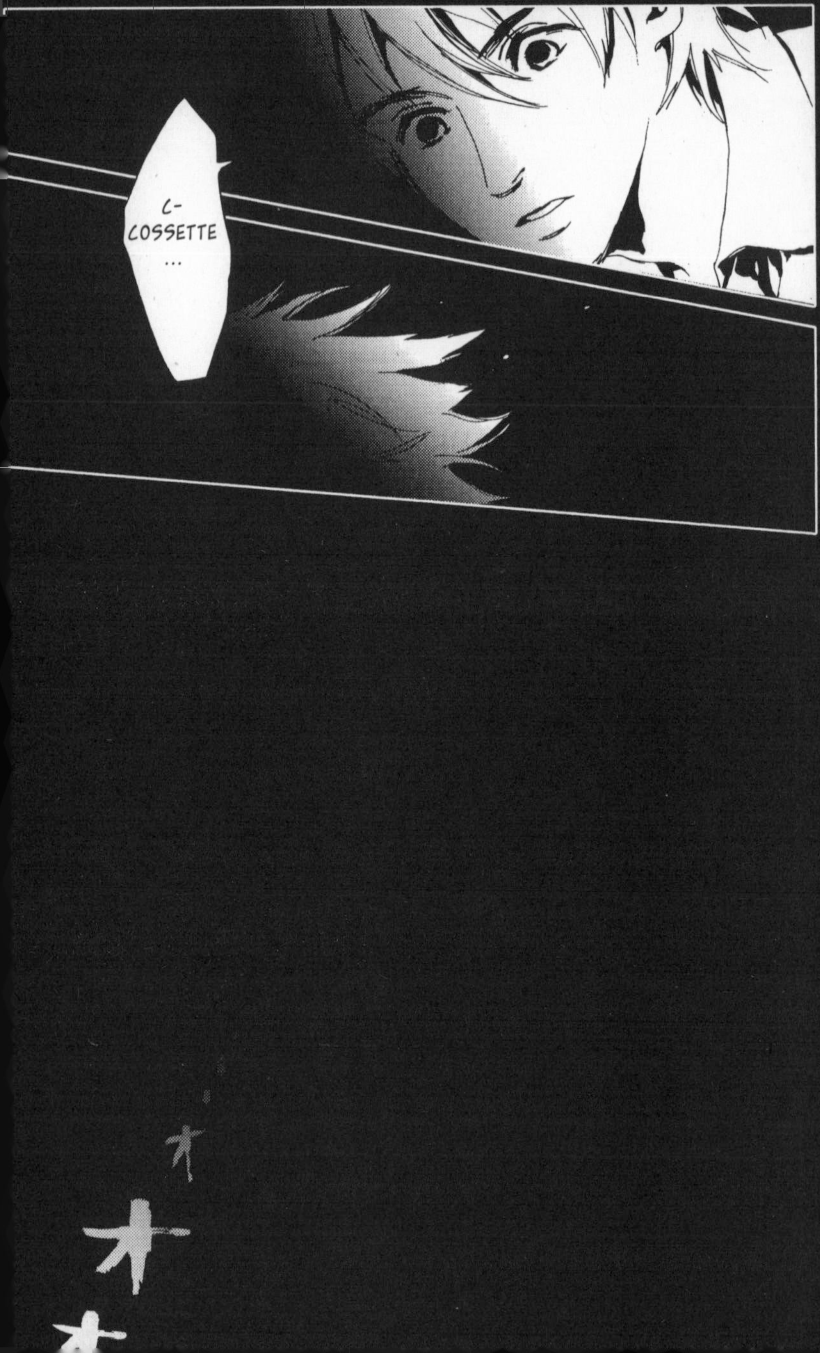
C-COSSETTE ...
オオオ

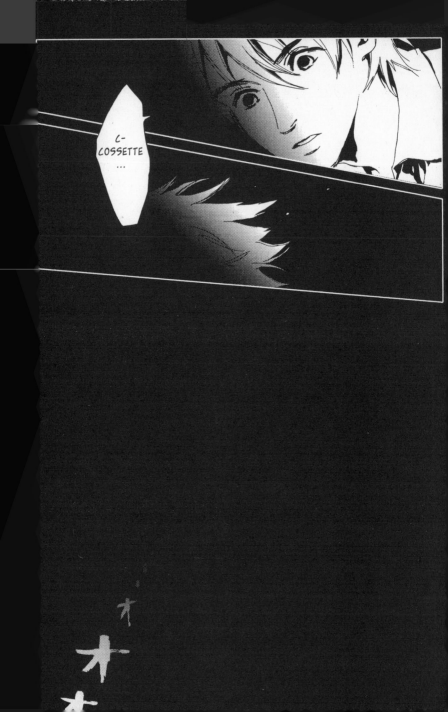

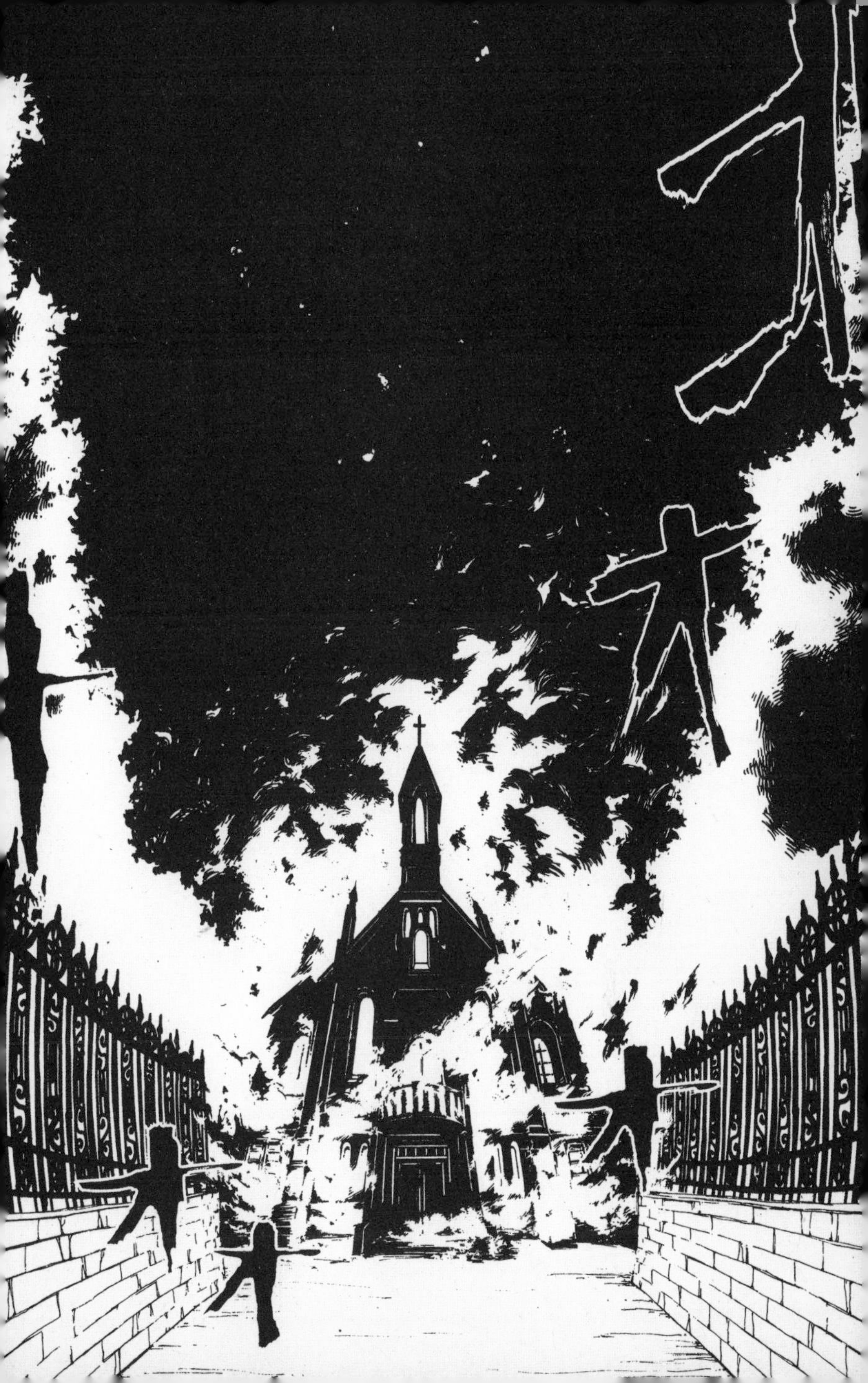

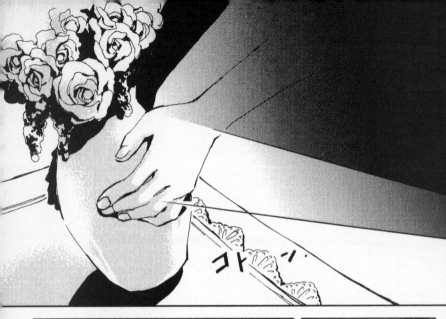

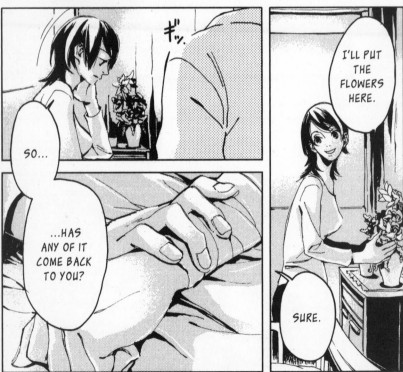

I'LL PUT THE FLOWERS HERE.

SO...

...HAS ANY OF IT COME BACK TO YOU?

SURE.

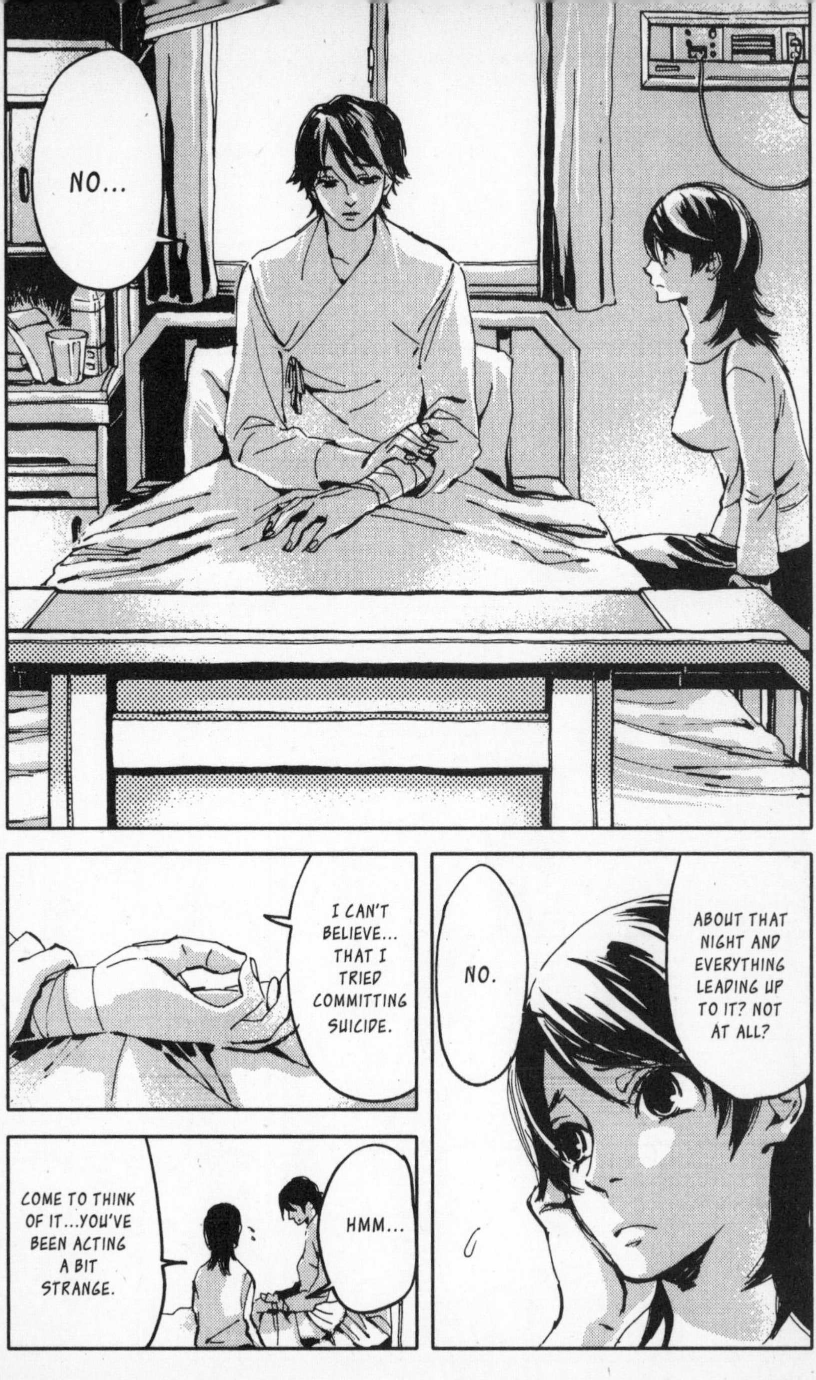
NO...
ABOUT THAT NIGHT AND EVERYTHING LEADING UP TO IT? NOT AT ALL?
NO.
I CAN'T BELIEVE... THAT I TRIED COMMITTING SUICIDE.
HMM...
COME TO THINK OF IT...YOU'VE BEEN ACTING A BIT STRANGE.

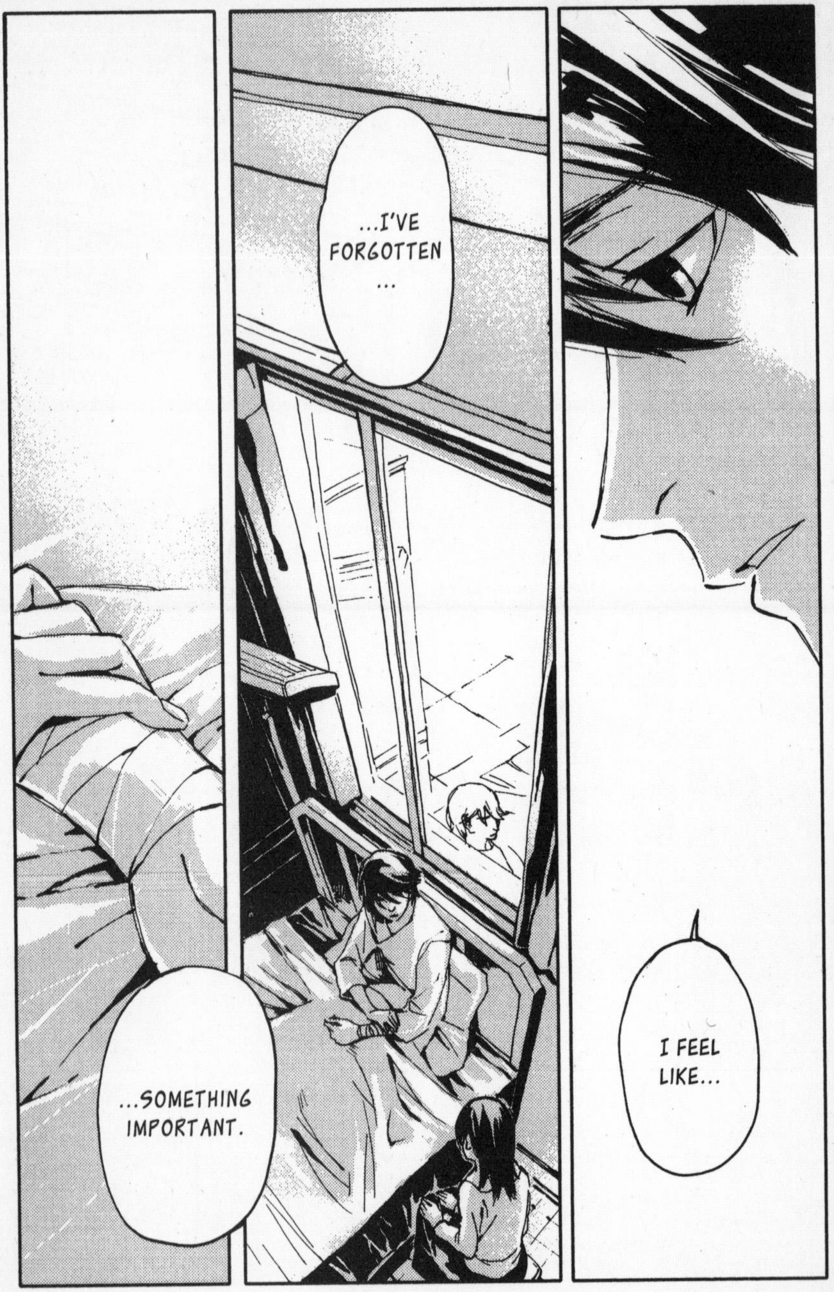
I FEEL LIKE...
...I'VE FORGOTTEN ...
...SOMETHING IMPORTANT.

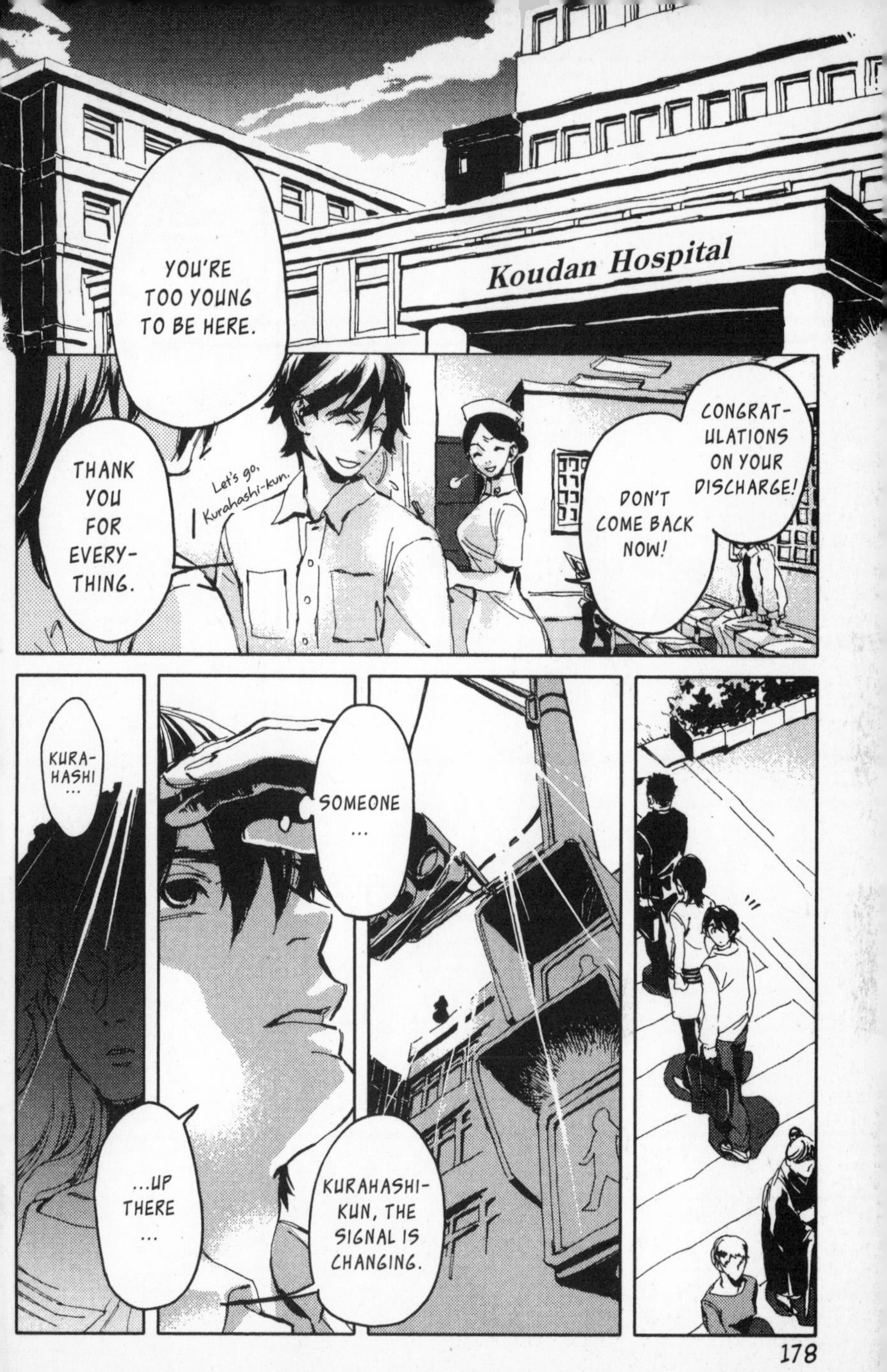
Koudan Hospital
YOU'RE TOO YOUNG TO BE HERE.
CONGRAT-ULATIONS ON YOUR DISCHARGE!
DON'T COME BACK NOW!
Let's go, Kurahashi-kun.
THANK YOU FOR EVERY-THING.
SOMEONE ...
KURAHASHI-KUN, THE SIGNAL IS CHANGING.
...UP THERE ...
KURA-HASHI ...

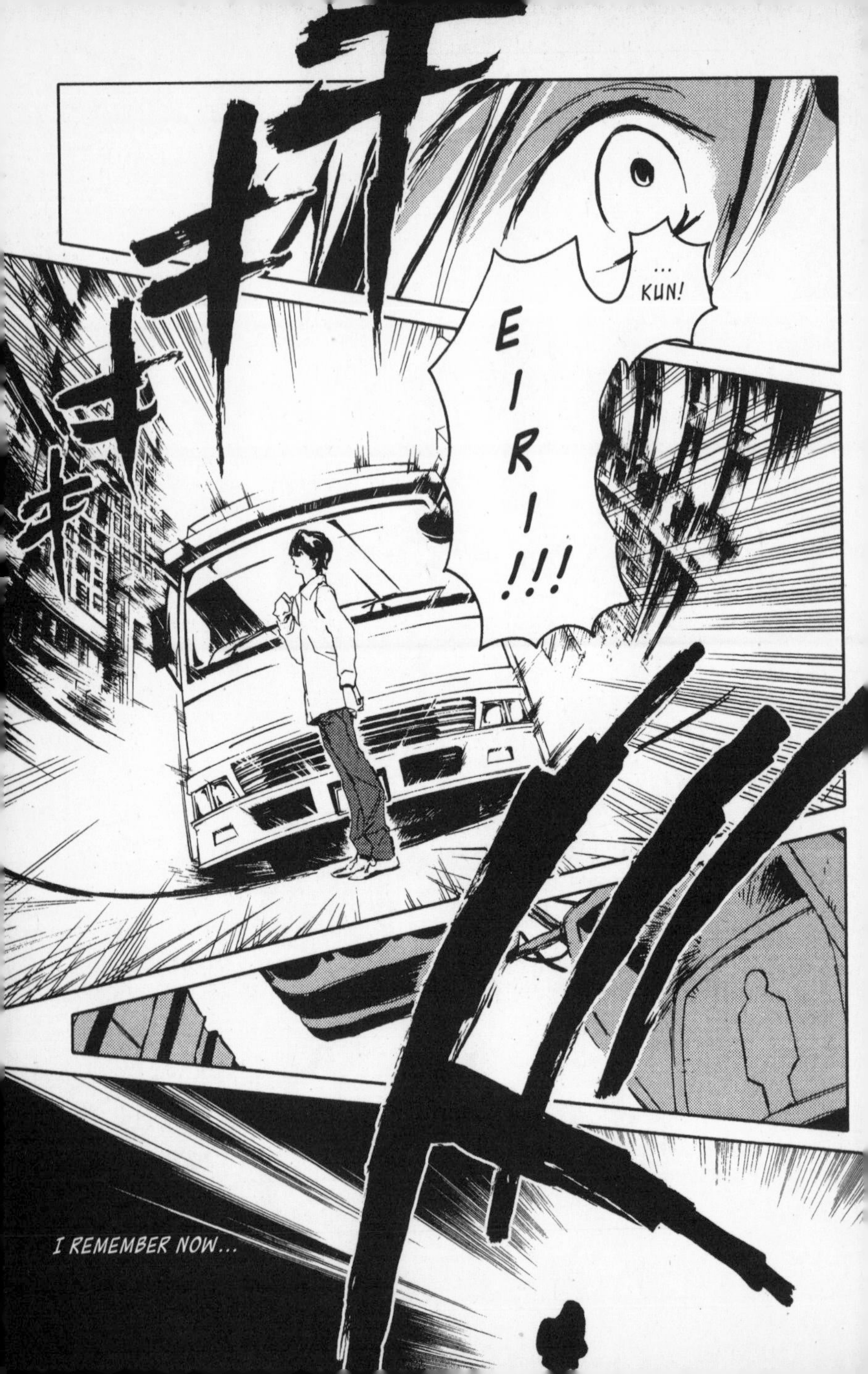

... KUN!
EIRI!!!
I REMEMBER NOW...

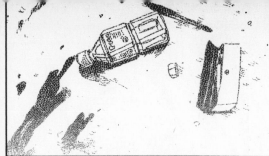

THIS IS THE PICTURE...

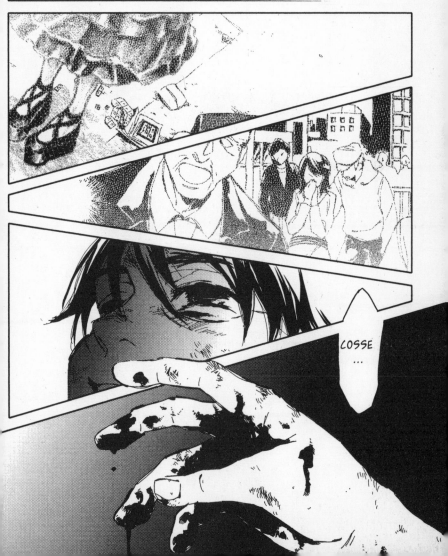

COSSE
...

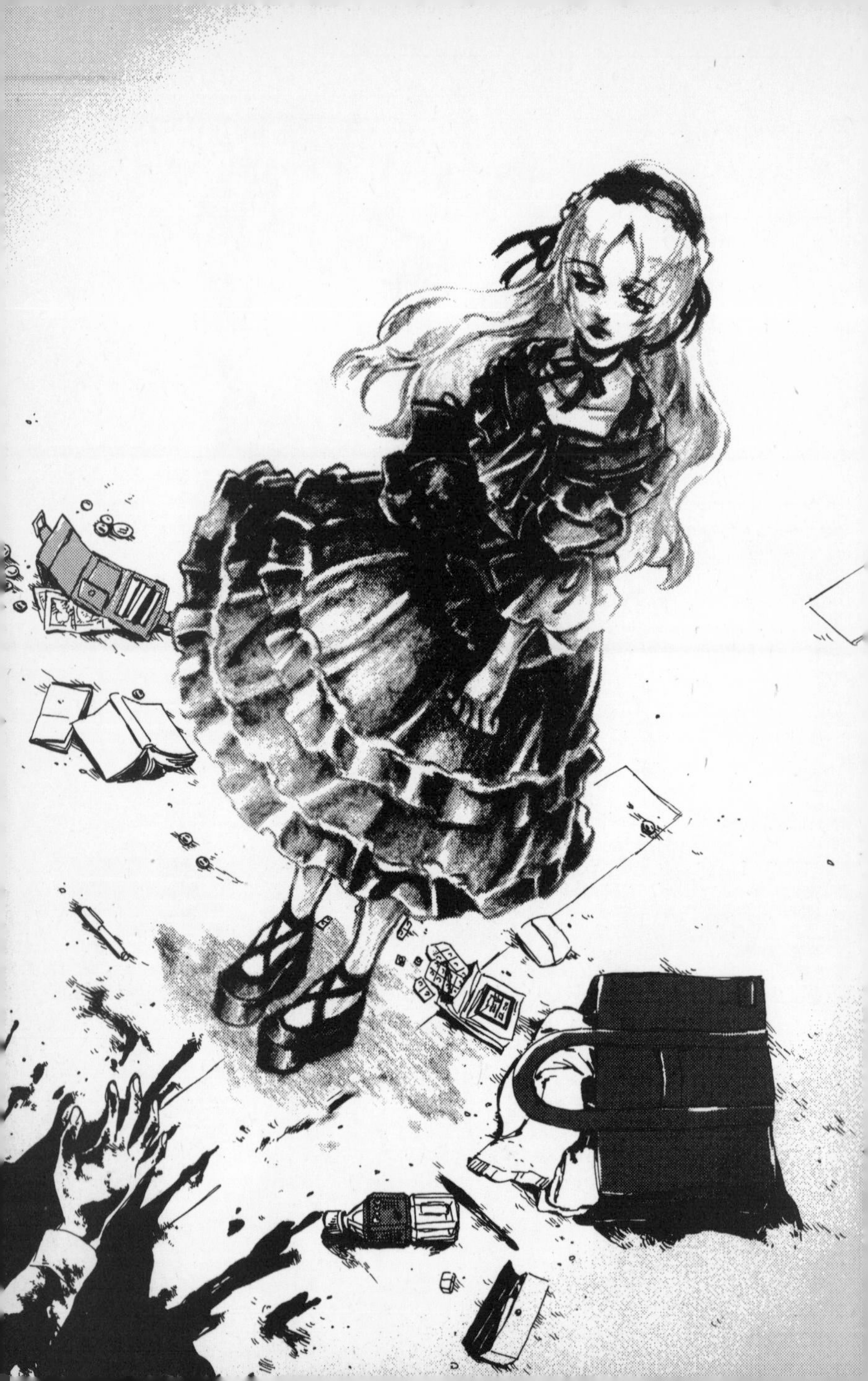

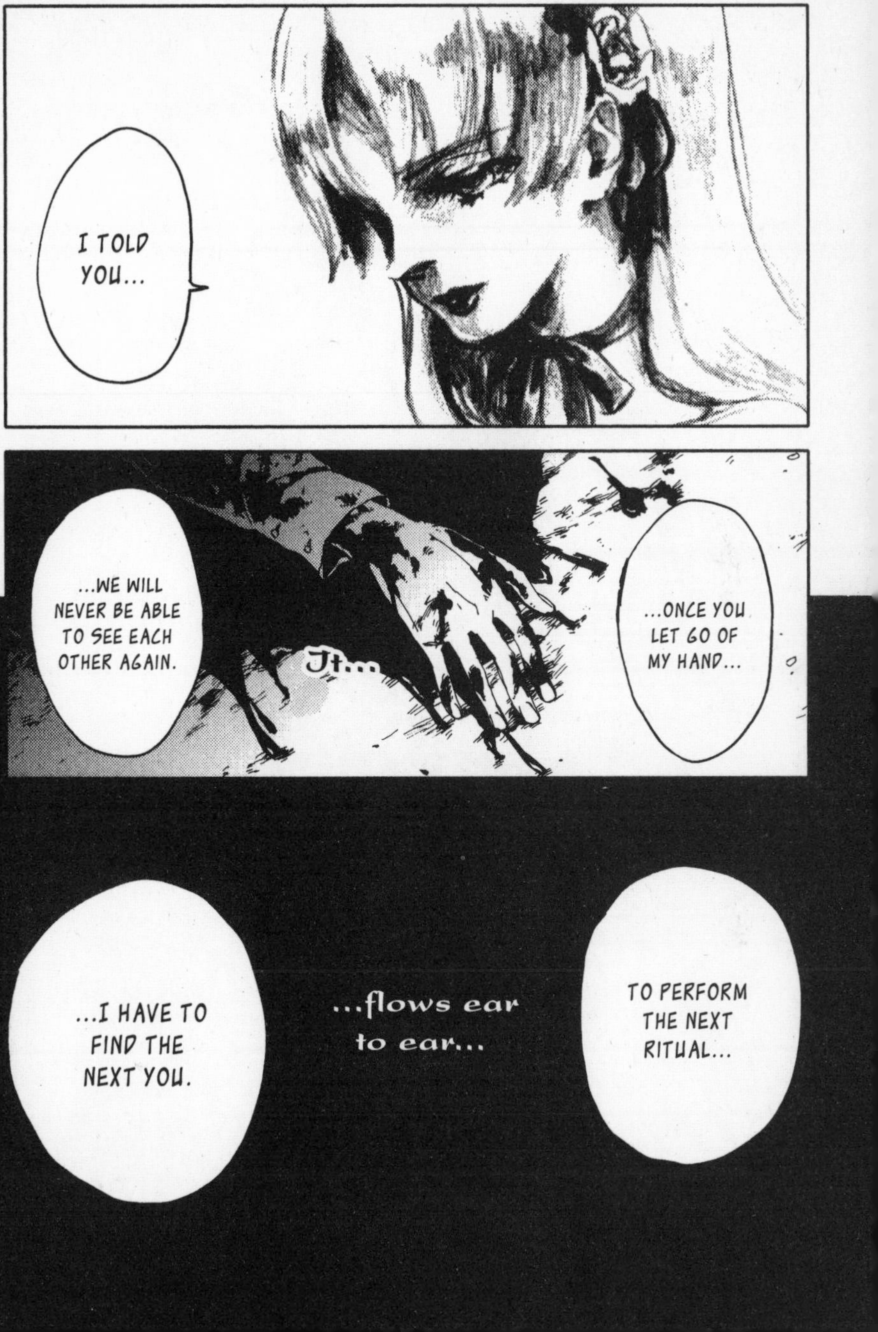
I TOLD YOU...
...ONCE YOU LET GO OF MY HAND...
It...
...WE WILL NEVER BE ABLE TO SEE EACH OTHER AGAIN.
TO PERFORM THE NEXT RITUAL...
...flows ear to ear...
...I HAVE TO FIND THE NEXT YOU.

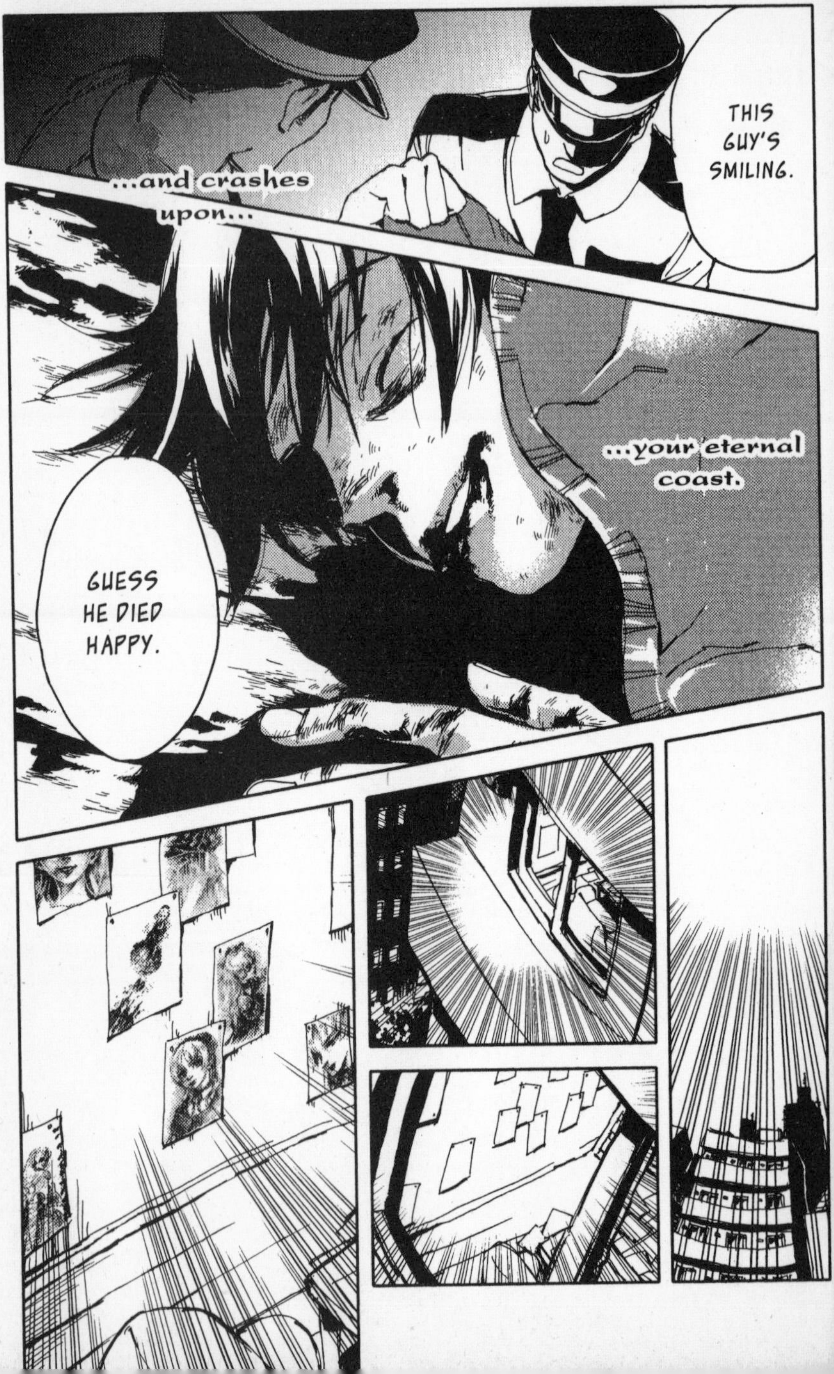
THIS GUY'S SMILING.
...and crashes upon...
...your eternal coast.
GUESS HE DIED HAPPY.

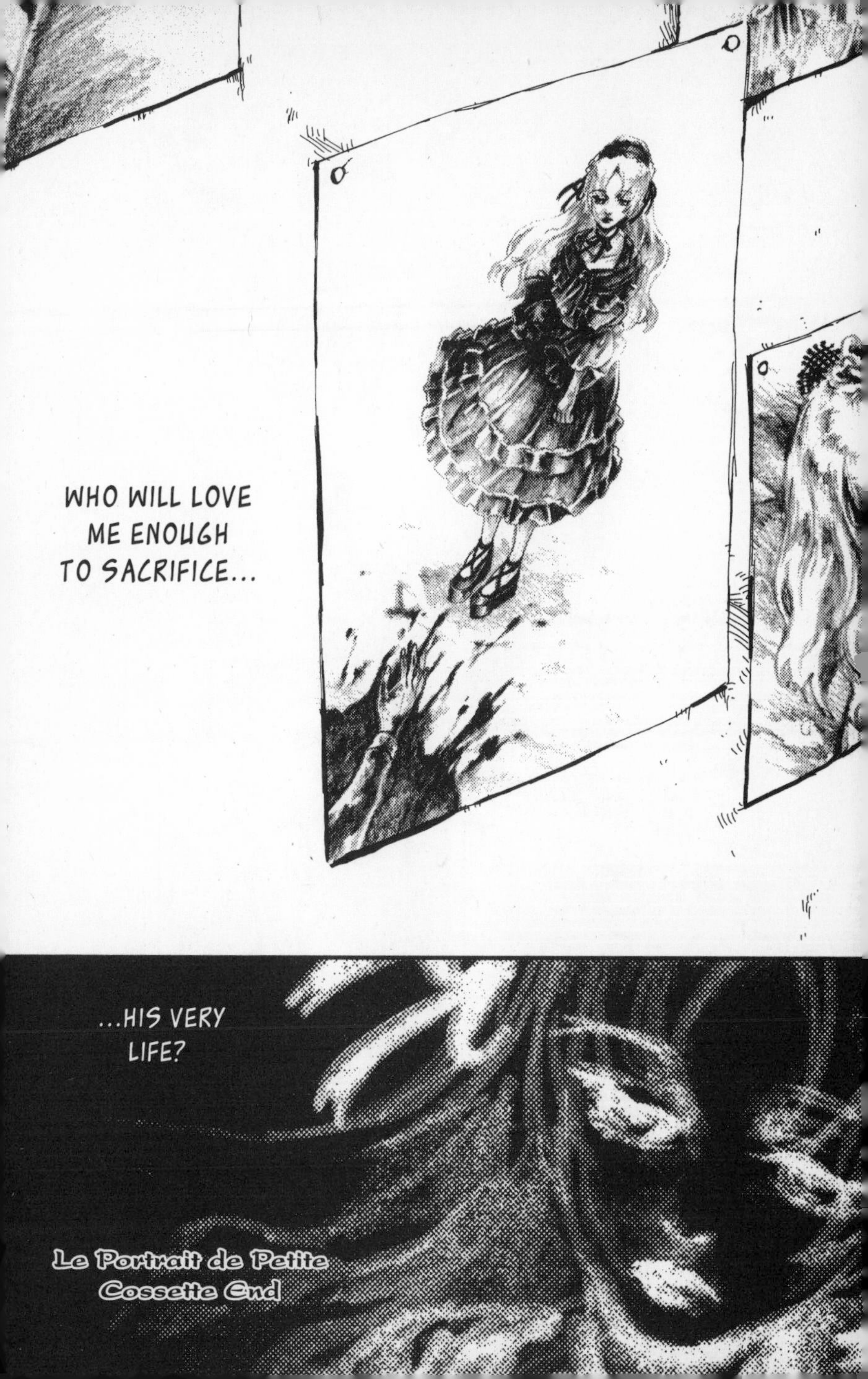
WHO WILL LOVE ME ENOUGH TO SACRIFICE...
...HIS VERY LIFE?
Le Portrait de Petite Cossette End

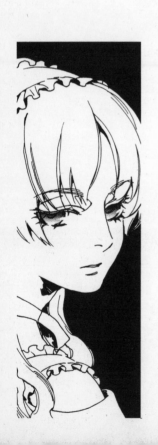

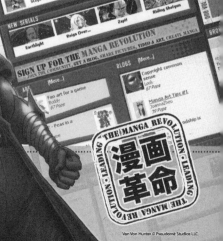

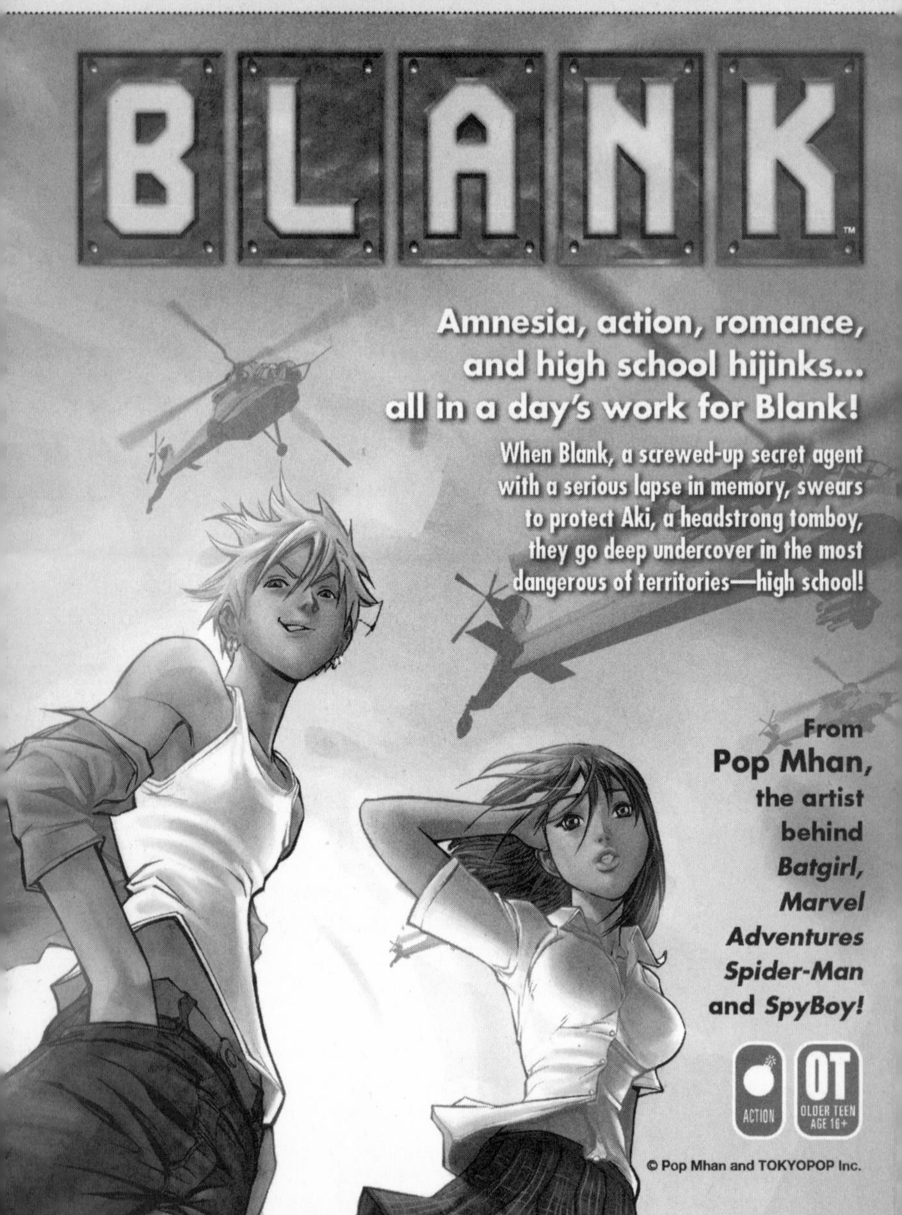
BLANK™
Amnesia, action, romance, and high school hijinks... all in a day's work for Blank!
When Blank, a screwed-up secret agent with a serious lapse in memory, swears to protect Aki, a headstrong tomboy, they go deep undercover in the most dangerous of territories—high school!
From Pop Mhan, the artist behind Batgirl, Marvel Adventures Spider-Man and SpyBoy!
ACTION
OT OLDER TEEN AGE 16+
© Pop Mhan and TOKYOPOP Inc.

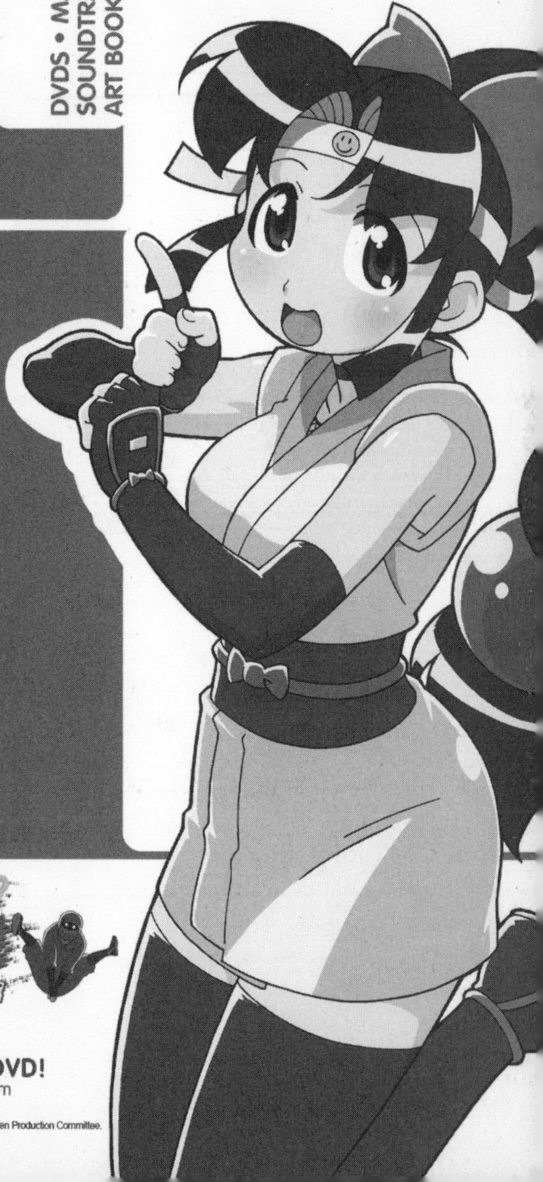

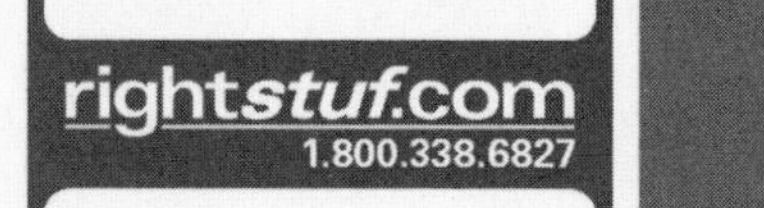
NINJA
NONSENSE
THE LEGEND OF SHINOBU

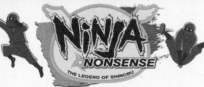

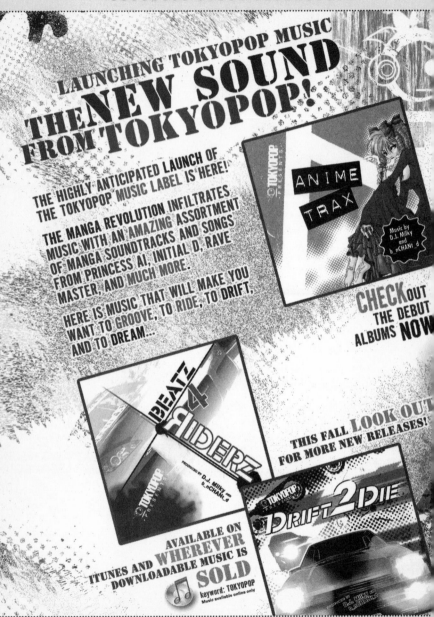

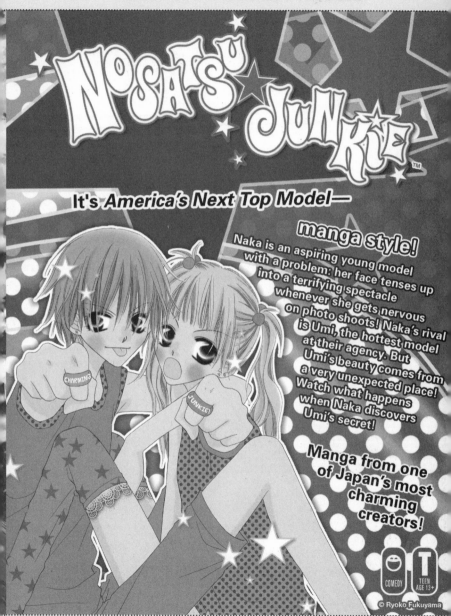

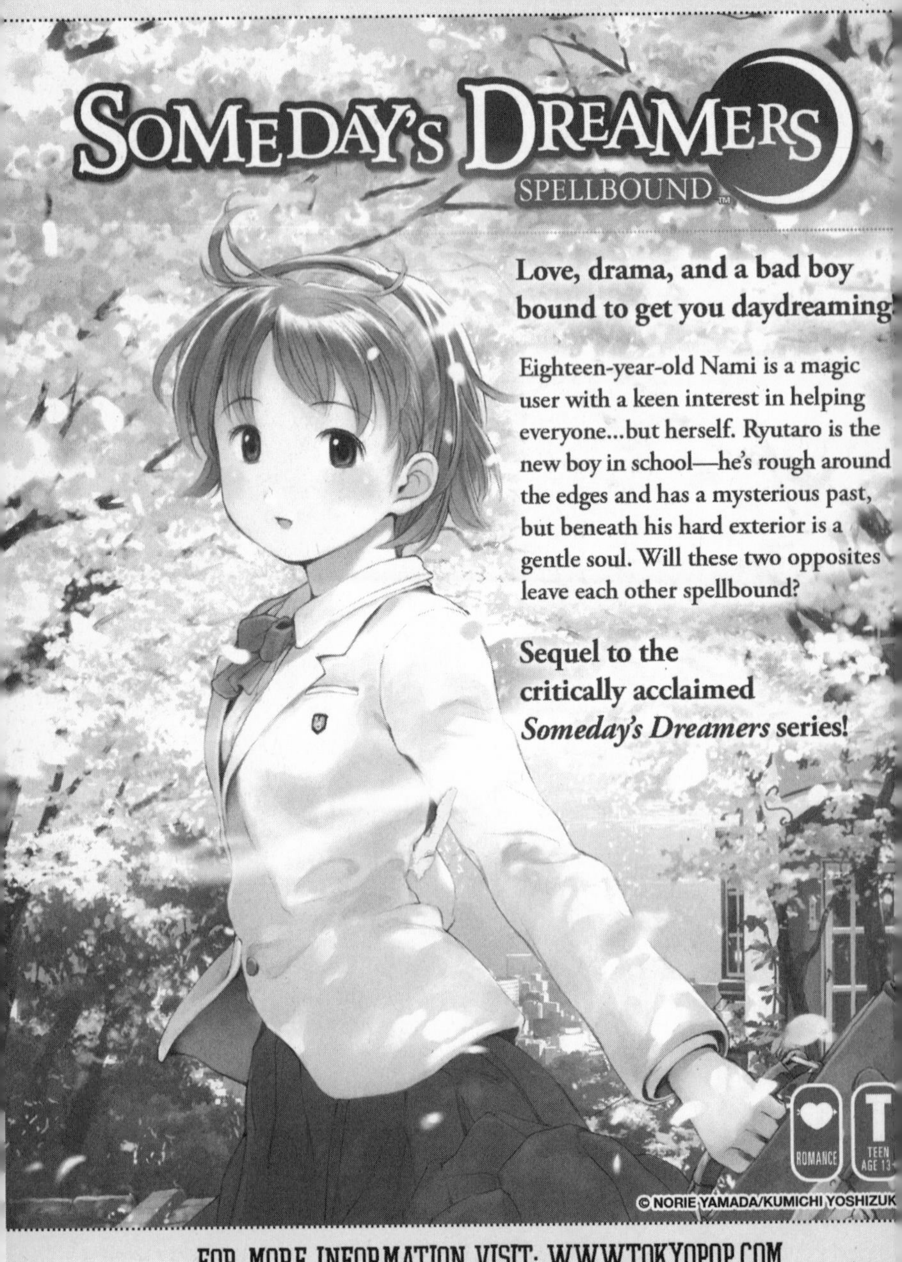
SOMEDAY'S DREAMERS
SPELLBOUND™
Love, drama, and a bad boy bound to get you daydreaming!
Eighteen-year-old Nami is a magic user with a keen interest in helping everyone...but herself. Ryutaro is the new boy in school—he's rough around the edges and has a mysterious past, but beneath his hard exterior is a gentle soul. Will these two opposites leave each other spellbound?
Sequel to the critically acclaimed *Someday's Dreamers* series!
ROMANCE
T
TEEN AGE 13+
© NORIE YAMADA/KUMICHI YOSHIZUK

STOP!

This is the back of the book.
You wouldn't want to spoil a great ending!

This book is printed "manga-style," in the authentic Japanese right-to-left format. Since none of the artwork has been flipped or altered, readers get to experience the story just as the creator intended. You've been asking for it, so TOKYOPOP® delivered: authentic, hot-off-the-press, and far more fun!

DIRECTIONS

If this is your first time reading manga-style, here's a quick guide to help you understand how it works.

It's easy... just start in the top right panel and follow the numbers. Have fun, and look for more 100% authentic manga from TOKYOPOP®!

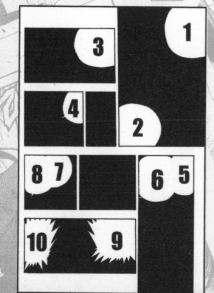

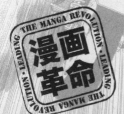